Blackburn
College

Chil<

This volume is designed to be of use to today's teachers and students of children's literature by bringing together a collection of lively and accessible scholarly essays, some reprinted and others newly commissioned, which concentrate on a selection of important classic and contemporary children's books. It is the companion volume to *Children's Literature: Approaches and Territories* (ed. Maybin and Watson, 2009), which provides a complementary set of more generally focused historical, critical and theoretical essays. The two volumes can be used separately or together, as the basis for study of this field.

Both Readers are part of the Open University course Children's Literature (EA300), a level 3 undergraduate course which can count towards many Open University degrees at Bachelor's level, and specifically the BAs in Humanities, Literature (and Humanities with Literature), English Language and Literature and Childhood and Youth Studies. The course is also part of the Diplomas in Literature and in Literature and Creative Writing.

Details of these and other Open University courses can be obtained from the Student Registration and Enquiry Service. The Open University, PO Box 197, Milton Keynes MK7 6BJ, United Kingdom: telephone +44 (0) 845 3006090, e-mail general_enquiries@open.ac.uk.

Alternatively, you may wish to visit the Open University website at www.open.ac.uk, where you can learn more about the wide range of courses and packs offered at all levels by The Open University.

Children's Literature: Classic Texts and Contemporary Trends

Edited by
Heather Montgomery and Nicola J. Watson

First published 2009 by
PALGRAVE MACMILLAN in association with THE OPEN UNIVERSITY.

The Open University, Walton Hall, Milton Keynes, MK7 6AA

Palgrave Macmillan in the UK is an imprint of Macmillan Publishers Limited, registered in England, company number 785998, of Houndmills, Basingstoke, Hampshire RG21 6XS.

Palgrave Macmillan in the US is a division of St Martin's Press LLC, 175 Fifth Avenue, New York, NY 10010.

Palgrave Macmillan is the global academic imprint of the above companies and has companies and representatives throughout the world.

Palgrave® and Macmillan® are registered trademarks in the United States, the United Kingdom, Europe and other countries

ISBN-13: 978–0–230–22714–9   paperback

This book is printed on paper suitable for recycling and made from fully managed and sustained forest sources. Logging, pulping and manufacturing processes are expected to conform to the environmental regulations of the country of origin.

A catalogue record for this book is available from the British Library.

A catalog record for this book is available from the Library of Congress.

10 9 8 7 6 5 4 3 2
18 17 16 15 14 13 12 11 10 09

Printed and bound in Great Britain by
CPI Antony Rowe, Chippenham and Eastbourne

Contents

Figures

Plates

(between pp. 80 and 81)

Acknowledgements

This volume was produced by the team responsible for preparing the Open University course in Children's Literature (EA300) and was a collaboration between the Faculties of Education and Arts. Course team members are credited as the authors of the Introductions for each section. In the preparation of this course we consulted widely, and are grateful for advice provided by Peter Barnes, Peter Hunt, Kim Reynolds, Kay Sambell, Philip Seargeant, Nigel Thomas and other critical readers of the material in draft.

The editors would also like to acknowledge the many people who worked behind the scenes to produce this book. At the Open University, we would like to thank Liz Camp, course manager; and Christine Hardwick, course secretary, for all their help with the preparation of this manuscript and for making sure deadlines were met. Gill Gowans and Gary Nelmes also worked tirelessly to ensure that the book came together on schedule.

At Palgrave we would like to thank Senior Editor Kate Haines, Production Editor Sarah Fry, Administrative Secretary Felicity Noble and Senior Marketing Executive Abigail Coften.

For copyright text

The authors and publishers wish to thank the following for permission to use copyright material:

Allyn and Bacon/Merrill Education for material from Cicely Denean Cobb, 'If You Give A Nigger An Inch, They Will Take An Ell': The Role of Education in Mildred D. Taylor's *Roll of Thunder'* from *Exploring Culturally Diverse Literature For Children And Adolescents: Learning To Listen In New Ways*, eds, Darwin L. Henderson and Jill P. May (2005) pp. 196–204. Copyright © 2005 by Pearson Education;

Continuum Publishing Group for material from Claire Squires, *Philip Pullman, Master Storyteller: A Guide to the Worlds of His Dark Materials* by Claire Squires (2003) pp. 115–33;

Copyright Clearance Center on behalf of Taylor & Francis Group LLC for material from Margaret Mackay, *The Case of Peter Rabbit: Changing Conditions of Literature for Children*, Garland Publishers (1998) pp. 3–13; Naomi Wood, 'Lost and Found: Obedience, Disobedience, and

Storytelling' in C.S. Lewis and Philip Pullman', *Children's Literature in Education*, 32:4 (2001) pp. 237–59; Michael Rosen, 'Robert Louis Stevenson and Children's Play: The Contexts of *A Child's Garden of Verses*', *Children's Literature in Education*, 26:1 (1995) pp. 53–69; Nicholas Tucker, 'Arthur Ransome and Problems of Literary Assessment', *Children's Literature in Education*, 26 (1995) pp. 97–105; Kelly McDowell, '*Roll of Thunder, Hear My Cry*: A Culturally Specific, Subversive Concept of Child Agency', *Children's Literature in Education*, 33:3 (2002) pp. 213–25; Anne-Marie Bird, ' "Without Contraries is no Progression": Dust as an All-Inclusive, Multifunctional Metaphor in Philip Pullman's *His Dark Materials*', *Children's Literature in Education*, 32:2 (2001) pp. 111–23; Melvin Burgess, 'Sympathy for the Devil', *Children's Literature in Education*, 35:4 (2004); Janis Dawson, 'Beneath their cheerful bunny faces, his slippers had steel toe caps': Traction Cities, Postmodernisms, and Coming of Age in Philip Reeve's *Mortal Engines*', *Children's Literature in Education*, 38 (2007) pp. 141–52; Peter Hollindale, 'A Hundred Years of Peter Pan', *Children's Literature in Education*, 36:3 (2005) pp. 197–215; Roni Natov, *The Poetics of Childhood*, Routledge (2003) pp. 95–101; and Jack Zipes, 'The Phenomenon of Harry Potter, or Why All the Talk' from *Sticks and Stones: The Troublesome Success of Children's Literature from Slovenly Peter to Harry Potter*, ed. Jack Zipes, Routledge (2001) pp. 170–89;

Feminist Studies, Inc. for material from Judith Fetterley, '*Little Women*: Alcotts Civil War', *Feminist Studies*, 5:2 (Summer 1979) pp. 369–83;

Four Courts Press for Anne Bogen, 'The Island Come True: *Peter Pan*, Wild Cat Island, and the Lure of the Real' from *Treasure Islands: Studies in Children's Literature*, eds. Mary Shine Thompson and Celia Keenan (2006) pp. 53–61;

Peter Hollindale for his article 'Aesop in the Shadows', *Signal Approaches to Children's Books*, 89 (1999) pp. 115–32, Thimble Press;

The Johns Hopkins University Press for material from Ken Parille, 'Wake Up and Be a Man': *Little Women*, Laurie, and the Ethic of Submission', *Children's Literature*, 29 (2001) pp. 34–51; Sarah A. Wadsworth, 'Louisa May Alcott and the Rise of the Gender-Specific Series Books', *The Lion and the Unicorn*, 25:1 (2001) pp. 17–46; Kay Sambell, 'Carnivalizing the Future: Mortal Engines', *The Lion and the Unicorn*, 28 (2004) pp. 247–67; Christopher Parkes, 'Treasure Island and the Romance of the British Civil Service', *Children's Literature Association Quarterly*, 31:4 (2006) pp. 332–45; and Hamida Bosmajian, 'Mildred Taylor's Story of Cassie Logan: A Search for Law and Justice in a Racist Society', *Children's Literature*, 24 (1996) pp. 141–60;

Methuen Publishing for material from Jackie Wullschläger, *Inventing Wonderland*, Methuen (1995) pp. 177–99;

The Random House Group Ltd for material from Peter Hunt, *Approaching Arthur Ransome*, Jonathan Cape (1992) pp. 84–99;

Scarecrow Press for material from Donna R. White and C. Anita Tarr, 'Peter Pan and the Pantomime Tradition' from *Peter Pan In and Out of Time: A Children's Classic at 100*, eds. Donna R. White and C. Anita Tarr (2006) pp. viii–xix; Maria Nikolajeva, *From Mythic to Linear: Time in Children's Literature* (2000) pp. 103–9; and Carole Scott, 'An Unusual Hero: Perspective and Point of View in *The Tale of Peter Rabbit*' from *Beatrix Potter's Peter Rabbit: A Children's Classic at 100* (2002) pp. 19–30;

Verso for material from Margaret Rustin and Michael Rustin, *Narratives of Love and Loss: Studies in Modern Children's Fiction* (1987) pp. 27–39; and Andrew Blake, *The Irresistible Rise of Harry Potter* (2002) pp. 5–26.

For copyright images

The editors and publishers wish to thank the following for permission to reproduce copyright material:

Alamy Ltd for Plate 2 © Mary Evans Picture Library/Alamy;

Bloomsbury Publishing Plc and Christopher Little Literary Agency for Plate 12, front cover of *Harry Potter and the Philosopher's Stone* by J.K. Rowling, first pub. 1997, Copyright © J.K. Rowling 1997, cover illustrations copyright © Thomas Taylor 1997;

The Bodleian Library, University of Oxford for Plate 1, front cover of *Little Women* by L.M. Alcott, David Boyne, 1880, shelfmark: Bodley 251 a.110; Plate 6, front cover of *The Peter Pan Picture Book* by Daniel S. O'Connor and Alice B. Woodward, George Bell & Sons, 1907, shelfmark (Nuneham): 2527 d.271; Figure 1, from *Treasure Island* by R.L. Stevenson, first illustrated edition 1885, shelfmark (Nuneham): 253 e.38 and Figure 9, illustration from *A Child's Garden of Verses* by R.L. Stevenson, illus. Charles Robinson, Lane & Scribner 1896, shelfmark: 280 e.1641a.

Chatto & Windus for Plate 3, front cover of *A Child's Garden of Verses*, by Robert Louis Stevenson, illus. Millicent Sowerby, Charles Scribner's Sons, 1905;

Curtis Brown Group Ltd for Plate 7 and Figure 10, illustration from *When Were Very Young* by A. A. Milne, illustrated by E. H. Shepard,

23rd edition, Methuen & Co. Ltd, 1932. Copyright © The Estate of E. H. Shepard, reproduced with permission of Curtis Brown Group Ltd, London;

Egmont UK Ltd for Plate 15, front cover of *Coram Boy* by Jamila Gavin © Jamila Gavin 2000, published by Egmont UK Ltd, London and used with permission;

Frederick Warne & Co. for Plate 4 and Figures 4, 5, 7 and 8, illustrations from *The Tale of Peter Rabbit* by Beatrix Potter, Copyright © Frederick Warne & Co., [1902] 2002;

Frederick Warne & Co. for Figures 2 and 3, from *A History of the Writings of Beatrix Potter* by Leslie Linder and Beatrix Potter, pub. Frederick Warne & Co., 1971, courtesy of the Frederick Warne archive;

Frederick Warne & Co. for Figure 6, illustration and text from *The Tale of Peter Rabbit* by Beatrix Potter, Copyright © Frederick Warne & Co., [1902] 2002;

Guildhall Library, City of London, for the John Rocque map of London, 1746 (map and ships) in the front cover design of *Coram Boy* by Jamila Gavin, Plate 15;

Mary Evans Picture Library for Plate 5;

Oxford University Press for Plate 9, cover illustration by Susan Einzig of *Tom's Midnight Garden* by Philippa Pearce (OUP, 1958 and 2008), reproduced by permission of Oxford University Press;

Penguin Books Ltd for Plate 13, front cover of *Junk* by Melvin Burgess (Penguin Books, 1997), Copyright © Melvin Burgess, 1997. Reproduced by permission of Penguin Books Ltd;

Penguin Books Ltd for Plate 14, front cover of *The Other Side of Truth* by Beverley Naidoo (Puffin, 2000), Copyright © Beverley Naidoo, 2000;

Penguin Group (USA) Inc. and Cotsen Children's Library, Princeton University Library for Plate 10, front cover of *Roll of Thunder, Hear My Cry* by Mildred D. Taylor, illustrated by Jerry Pinkney, Dial Press, 1976;

Random House Group Ltd for Plate 8, front cover of *Swallows and Amazons* by Arthur Ransome, illustrated by Arthur Ransome, Jonathan Cape, 2008, first pub. 1930;

Scholastic Ltd for Plate 11, front cover of *Northern Lights* by Philip Pullman. Cover artwork © David Scutt, 1998. Reproduced with the permission of Scholastic Ltd. All Rights Reserved;

Scholastic Ltd. for Plate 16, front cover of *Mortal Engines* by Philip Reeve. Cover artwork © David Frankland, 2001. Reproduced with permission of Scholastic Ltd. All Rights Reserved;

Introduction
Heather Montgomery and Nicola J. Watson

Children's literature is, as Peter Hunt has argued, a 'remarkable area of writing: it is one of the roots of western culture, it is enjoyed passionately by adults as well as children, and it has exercised huge talents over hundreds of years' (1994: 1). Choosing just 14 books to represent such a vast field has inevitably been fraught with problems. What does 'classic' mean? Does it mean those books that have retained their popularity over the years? The ones that are representative of a type? The ones that were seminal in the field or spawned many imitations? The ones that are of the highest literary quality (however we might define that)? And if deciding on what constitutes a classic has proved difficult, how much more so is identifying a contemporary trend, and deciding which books might best exemplify it.

The eleven texts discussed in Part 1 of the Reader, *Classic Texts*, therefore, do not constitute some sort of definitive canon, nor do they endeavour to reflect a received canon, nor are they the only classics that could have been chosen. No doubt another collection, even covering the same themes and historical territory, would present a very different selection of books and remedy some of the necessary glaring omissions. This volume, in short, does *not* aim to be comprehensive in any way. Rather, it is designed as a starting point for study. The books considered here were picked because they all still find a favoured place on the bookshelves of today's children and because they have all attracted a body of critical work. Chronologically organised by date of publication and all originally published in English, they span those designed for the very young, for the 8–12s, and crossover fiction which appeals both to teenagers and adults; they include books first popular in the nineteenth century and books wildly popular in the present day, books originating from both the UK and the USA, books 'for boys' and

1

books 'for girls', books exemplifying the variable mix of the realist and the fantastic that characterises children's books. Included are examples of the family story, historical romance, the holiday adventure, time-slip fantasy, the fantasy epic, science fiction, and teen fiction. In addition to this children's fiction, we have included a picturebook, a play for children, and two classic poetry collections so as to provide a range of genres.

Each section of Part 1 of the Reader serves as a case study of a single book, and is comprised of three or four short critical pieces which, taken together, provide an overview of influential readings of the literary text in question. These essays vary from the seminal to the cutting-edge, from those by authorities in their fields to those by up-and-coming young scholars. They are conspicuously varied, too, in their theoretical and disciplinary orientation, providing a spectrum from the feminist to that which deploys psychoanalytic thinking or multimodal analysis. A short introduction to each section briefly makes the case for the importance of the text within the field of children's literature, situates the text in literary and historical context, lays out the central critical questions around each text, locates the critical material within that general discussion, and supplies additionally as appropriate a sense of the full range of available approaches and interpretations. Each section also comes with a helpful set of suggestions for further reading on the book in question.

The wide variety of contemporary children's fiction allows the critic and reader a dizzying freedom of choice, given that there is no recognised canon of classics on which to draw, no substantial body of literary criticism to consider, and no span of time over which to judge whether such writing has had continuing appeal. Part 2 of the Reader, *Contemporary Trends*, therefore turns to mapping those developments that have emerged in the late twentieth century and are continuing to evolve. Pinpointing such trends is as difficult as identifying the classics. It is hard to know if books being published now will retain their popularity in future years, whether the emerging trends that are apparent in 2009 will come to greater prominence or simply die away, and indeed whether books themselves will be superseded by new technologies as yet unimagined. The essays in this section therefore take an approach that is slightly different to that of Part 1, identifying four types of children's writing selling well in the new millennium, and focusing on one prizewinning text as exemplary of each trend. Included here are three essays by contemporary children's authors, reflecting upon their individual projects and placing them within the literary landscape of the new millennium.

A third noteworthy component of this volume is its reproduction of the colour plates of covers and illustrations to early editions. Perhaps more than any other category of books, children's books have been published to be attractive material objects, and these pictures are designed to convey something of the materiality of the children's book. Taken together with their extensive captions, these plates constitute a vivid and instructive picture-essay on the changing physicality of children's books from the consciously durable hardbacks stamped in gold of the late nineteenth century to the shiny embossed paperbacks designed to fall apart in three readings that dominate today's bookshelves.

Although this volume is designed so that each section is free-standing and may be used without reference to others, it seems useful here briefly to locate each of the texts featured within a general historical overview of the origins and development of children's literature and related changes in the conception of childhood. When and where to locate the origins of children's literature is a matter of scholarly speculation and controversy; Matthew Grenby has claimed that some of the earliest recorded examples of children reading, and being read to, come from ancient Sumeria (Grenby, 2009), so perhaps a history should start here. The case has been made for fairy tales to be considered as the earliest children's literature, but then it has been made, too, for chapbooks (the cut-down versions of books such as Defoe's *Robinson Crusoe* or John Bunyan's *The Pilgrim's Progress*, which were widely circulated in the seventeenth and eighteenth centuries). Yet there is little evidence that any of these books were aimed specifically at children, or viewed as *children's* literature. Children may well have read fairy tales or chapbooks, but such works, with their simple language and woodcut illustrations, were designed for inexperienced rather than specifically young readers and were texts shared between adults and children, according to reading levels rather than age. In general, the origins of a literature designed specifically for children is usually (if not uncontroversially) located in the early to mid-eighteenth century in England with the publication of John Newbery's *A Little Pretty Pocket-Book* (1744) and it is in large part attributed to a new sense of childhood as a special state distinct from adulthood.

Although some eighteenth- and early nineteenth-century writing for children, mostly rhymes for the young, survives as old favourites to this day, the children's fiction that has retained classic status for modern readers mostly dates from the second half of the nineteenth century and the dawn of what has been called the First Golden Age of children's literature. This may be not merely because such literature had reached a new maturity and sophistication fuelled by a rapidly expanding child readership, but because we are still very much living with the legacy of that period's ideas of childhood.

Mid-to-late Victorian Britain and America saw a dramatic shift in ideas about childhood; the idea of childhood as a protected space, characterised by innocence, goodness and purity, derived from as far back as Rousseau's thinking, was reaching its height in the Victorian cult of the child, and especially the cult of the girl-child most famously exemplified in Carroll's 'Alice'. Although many, possibly the majority of children, were still working in the factories or fields with little protection and were still excluded from education, the wider social ideal of childhood emphasised the naturalness of childhood, domesticated in the feminine realm of the house and protected from the male, adult world of work, money and sex. By the end of the nineteenth century there had been a profound change in the way that children were valued. No longer valued only for their economic contribution to the family, it was their social and emotional role that was now emphasised. Viviana Zelizer (1994) has argued that the 1870s onwards saw a change from the child being valued as an economic asset towards becoming a sentimental one, economically 'useless' but emotionally 'priceless', and changing from being viewed as a producer to a consumer. Although this was an ideal which had limited applicability to the reality of many children's lives, this new way of seeing children, and this different way of valuing them, had an important impact on the literature written for them.

These generalisations, though useful, tend to break down when confronted by historical and literary specifics. Of course, childhoods are not homogenous and children experience them differently according to their age, their gender, their ethnicity, or whether or not they are disabled. It is very odd that 'the child', as Judith Ennew points out (quoted in Oakley, 1994: 21), is so frequently referred to as a 'strange, ungendered isolate' when the great variety in the ways that childhood is experienced is so central to children's own lives as well as to adult understandings. Even in literature written for children, childhood is not represented as homogeneous; indeed, one of the effects of children's literature is arguably the production of gender, splitting boys and girls in what they read and promoting different ideals in the literature designed 'for' them. Discussions of gender therefore are central to the first set of essays on Louisa Alcott's *Little Women* (1868), a classic of children's literature in the USA and elsewhere, and one of the most famous and influential books ever written for girls. Its portrayal of a feminised domestic ideal has intrigued, inspired and occasionally appalled critics ever since it appeared, but its importance lies in the ways it genders childhood, both because it was written 'for' girls and in the ways it analyses and challenges the limitations of the expected roles and expectations of girls (and indeed boys). In contrast, Robert Louis Stevenson's *Treasure Island* (1884) has usually been thought of as a boys' story, even *the* boys' story, with its emphasis on adventure and exploration standing in strong contrast to the world of enclosed domestic interiors characteristic of stories suitable for girls. Reading one against the other, it is clear that if *Little Women* idealises a particular form of national femininity, predicated on marriage, so *Treasure Island* promotes a vision of boyhood which can transform into the sort of muscular, Christian masculinity capable of subduing and running the British Empire.

That the histories of children's literature are themselves multiple is suggested by any effort to place Beatrix Potter's *The Tale of Peter Rabbit* (1901). The tradition of talking or anthropomorphised animals can be traced back to sources as diverse as Aesop's fables or Charles Perrault's fairy tales, which, while not written specifically for children, have become, over the years, closely identified with children's literature. *Peter Rabbit* is exemplary here as one of the most famous animal stories of all. Written at the height of the First Golden Age of children's literature, its popularity has remained undiminished ever since. It can be placed in many ways, as part of and as reinvigorating a long-standing tradition of animal stories, but also as part of a tradition of picture books for younger children, in which the images and text work together to create meaning.

Despite its importance in children's lives and literature, from the earliest rhyming picture books to the well-known and well-loved poetic set-pieces in *Alice's Adventures in Wonderland*, and *Through the Looking-glass*, poetry for children has generally been neglected as a category in the study of children's literature. The next section of this reader therefore turns to two important collections of poetry for children as a way of focusing on this genre, Robert Louis Stevenson's *A Child's Garden of Verses* (1885) and A.A. Milne's *When We Were Very Young* (1924), analysing the very different childhoods they invoke and whether or not they still speak to contemporary children. Published fewer than forty years apart, the ideals of childhood they depict and promote are radically different, suggesting a major breach in the notion of childhood itself, occasioned by wider social upheaval. In these books we can see the confident child of empire giving way to the fearful, reclusive, sentimentalised child of the aftermath of the First World War.

Drama, too, can sometimes appear less prominent than fiction in studies of children's literature but J.M. Barrie's stage-play *Peter Pan* (first performed in 1904) is probably one of the most studied and adapted pieces of children's literature; even those who have not seen it as live theatre will know the story about 'the boy who would not grow up'. A seminal work of children's literature, it has played an important, even definitive, role in the history of twentieth-century ideas about childhood. It articulates the dialectic between the safety and innocence of the nursery and the danger and innocence of Neverland in ways that speak powerfully of the separation of childhood from adulthood in the period. Its depiction of the asexual, amoral and anti-adult Peter has attracted much critical work and has both reflected, described and contributed to social anxieties about the child and childhood in the twentieth and twenty-first centuries.

The inter-war period is sometimes seen as the doldrums between the First and Second Golden Ages of children's literature. In 1936, George Orwell wrote rather petulantly that 'Modern books for children are rather horrible things, especially when you see them in the mass. Personally I would sooner give a child a copy of Petrenius Arbiter than Peter Pan, but even Barrie seems manly and wholesome compared with some of his later imitators' (1936: 244). Arthur Ransome's *Swallows and Amazons* (1930) is one notable exception to this blanket condemnation. Its importance lies in the way it builds upon and updates two traditions, the family story, exemplified by books such as Frederick Marryat's *The Children of the New Forest* (1847), and the children's imperial adventure story such as R.M. Ballantyne's *Coral Island* (1858). The children's adventures, conceived by them in terms of a long list of influences from *Robinson Crusoe* to *Treasure Island*, are given a newly middle-class, realist twist by being set in the school holidays. Although on one level a story for boys, it also has strong girl heroines and presents a world where children are liberated from adults and in which they have a freedom that seems unthinkable to modern children.

Tom's Midnight Garden by Philippa Pearce (1958) has been chosen here not only for its enduring appeal to both children and critics, but also because it includes elements and themes which recur in a number of twentieth-century children's novels. It is a classic of time-slip fantasy, for example, deploying an important structuring device in many children's books, where children from different historical eras can meet and make friends across the generations, thus providing a gentle history lesson, suggesting the universality of childhood across time, and idealising children's ability to look beyond superficial difference. It also uses the metaphor of a garden invoking, as other books such as Frances Hodgson Burnett's *The Secret Garden* (1911) have done, both the innocence of Eden before the Fall and the innocence of childhood, in contrast to the corruption of adulthood. It looks back, in that it represents a post-war British sensibility, in which only a child can bridge the destruction and diminution that the successive world wars have wreaked on a house and garden, conceived here as an image for the nation as a whole; but as an achievement, it looks forward to the so-called Second

Golden Age of children's literature, the flourishing of children's books, especially fantasy, in the 1960s and early 1970s.

Children's literature has always been implicitly or explicitly ideological, presenting and promoting particular ideas about childhood and encouraging children to either uphold or challenge particular values. Mildred Taylor's *Roll of Thunder, Hear my Cry* (1976) has been chosen here to serve as an example of an overtly political novel for children. It deals with the oppression of African Americans and tackles the themes of racism and discrimination head-on, although it is worth noting that it does so in a historical rather than a contemporary context, being set in the 1930s. A set text in many American and British classrooms, its importance lies in the fact it challenges the 'whiteness' of many of the recognised classics of children's literature, presenting the voice of the oppressed and exploring the diversities of childhood. As the variety of childhoods are increasingly acknowledged and celebrated, this book points out that childhood can also be a time of multiple subjugations, suggesting that the universal, innocent, protected child, so idealised in the late twentieth and twenty-first centuries, is in fact a socially, economically and culturally constructed ideal which has always been well out of the reach of many, perhaps the majority, of children.

Critics such as Peter Hunt (2009) have recently speculated as to whether the 1990s ushered in a new golden age of children's literature. Certainly in terms of sales and publicity, children's literature became more visible than ever, and the market has grown exponentially. The next two books included, Philip Pullman's *Northern Lights* (1995) and J.K. Rowling's *Harry Potter and the Philosopher's Stone* (1997), can be seen as spearheading this trend and both, in their own ways, broke new ground. The popular phenomenon of Harry Potter has been so extraordinary that it would be impossible not to include the book in any discussion of children's literature in the twenty-first century, if only because it has arguably brought children's literature into greater public prominence than ever before, while the crossover appeal of Pullman, and his intellectual credibility, has appealed to critics and redefined the potential of children's literature. It is perhaps too soon to know whether the impact these books have had on children's literature will be sustained, whether they will still be seen as classics in fifty or a hundred years, and whether they did indeed kick-start a Third Golden Age of children's literature. At the very least, however, both authors (and their publishers) have made considerable sums of money from these books, suggesting that, if nothing else, children's literature in the early years of the century is an expanding market. They have also arguably presented a new, epic vision of childhood. Children in these novels do not simply have magical powers or go on adventures, as in previous works of fiction, but set about saving the world from catastrophe. Adults, in these books, may be morally ambiguous, as in Pullman, or sharply divided into good and bad characters, as in Rowling, but they always lack the powers that children have to protect and save the world from the sins of the past. The child hero or heroine of these stories is not just an adventurer but also a redeemer.

If we are indeed living in a new Golden Age of children's literature, it is worth looking critically at some of the new trends and modes that seem to be emerging: the resurgence of historical fiction, the development of futurist fiction and social realism, and the expansion of Young Adult fiction. Part 2 focuses on these trends in more detail by examining one particular prizewinning book as representative of that trend. Thus new fiction written and marketed to adolescents is considered in relation to Melvin Burgess's ground-breaking and controversial story of child heroin addiction, *Junk* (1996), fiction with a social conscience agenda is dealt with in reference to Beverley Naidoo's account of child asylum-seekers in modern Britain in *The Other Side of Truth* (2000), the resurgence of historical fiction is dealt with in relation to Jamila Gavin's exercise in imagining eighteenth-century London in *Coram Boy* (2000), and the interest in futurist dystopias is illuminated by Philip Reeve's tale of warring cities, *Mortal Engines* (2001). These books clearly exemplify, albeit to different degrees, the long-standing dialectic between stern moral purpose and the need to amuse the child reader, and between social realism and escapist worlds.

All of these books, in different ways, contribute to debates about and visions of turn-of-the-millennium childhoods and the role of literature in their lives. They ask children to engage with issues such as sex, drugs or race-politics, eco-catastrophe, war and people-trafficking, subjects that have no place in an idealised view of childhood as a protected and privileged space, separated from adults and their concerns. The new millennium is a time of great social concern about children and it is not surprising that this is reflected in literature written for them. Whether this is addressed directly, through, for instance, the strong social realism of Naidoo and Burgess, or more obliquely through futurist dystopias or historical fiction, the past, present and future are all presented as dangerous and anxiety-provoking. In these books there is no cosy retreat into safe or protected spaces; children are asked to engage with harsher realities. Yet this is not to posit a strict or absolute dichotomy between classic and contemporary texts; many themes characteristic of the classics can still be traced in these newer works of fiction; there are, for example, strong parallels between time-slip fantasy and historical fiction, and debates as to the didactic function of children's literature are present in discussions of all these texts. Indeed, the classic texts go on coexisting with the contemporary and as they find new readers, go on complicating and qualifying these new accounts of childhood with older versions. Perhaps the most hopeful trend to emerge is the very rude health that children's literature today enjoys. Its profitability for authors and publishers and its growing success in universities as a serious subject of academic study are signs of its continuing vitality. Despite dire warnings that the internet will kill off children's literature, it seems to be thriving, and it is perhaps not too fanciful to look forward to a Fourth Golden Age of children's literature by the end of the century.

References

Grenby, M. 2009. 'Children's Literature: Birth, Infancy and Maturity', in J. Maybin and N.J. Watson (eds) *Children's Literature: Approaches and Territories*. Basingstoke, Palgrave Macmillan

Hunt, P. 1994. *An Introduction to Children's Literature*. Oxford: Oxford University Press.

Hunt, P. 2009. 'Mapping Recurring Themes', in J. Maybin and N.J. Watson (eds) *Children's Literature: Approaches and Territories*. Basingstoke, Palgrave Macmillan.

Oakley, A. 1994. 'Women and Children First and Last: Parallels and Differences between Children's and Women's Studies', in B. Mayall (ed.) *Children's Childhoods: Observed and Experienced*. London, Falmer Press.

Orwell, G. [1936] 2000. 'Bookshop Memories', in S. Orwell and I. Angus (eds) *The Collected Essays, Journalism and Letters of George Orwell: An Age Like This, 1920–1940*. Boston, David R. Godine.

Zelizer, V. 1994. *Pricing the Priceless Child: The Changing Social Value of Children*. Princeton, NJ, Princeton University Press.

Part 1
Classic Texts

1

Louisa May Alcott, *Little Women* (1868–9)

Introduction
Nicola J. Watson

Origins, composition and reception

The publication of *Little Women* in 1868 arguably inaugurated a founding myth of American girlhood, ensured the success of the transatlantic phenomenon of 'fiction for girls', and contributed importantly to the genre of the family story. The story of a family of four girls and how they grow up during the American Civil War and its aftermath, it became an instant classic on both sides of the Atlantic and has never been out of print, successively issued in many different editions after the first which was illustrated rather clumsily by Louisa's sister, May, the model for Amy. It has appeared abridged and in school editions. It has served as the basis for a number of classic stage, musical and film adaptations, most notably those starring Katherine Hepburn (1993) and Winona Ryder (1994) as Jo. It has been translated into almost every world language. At once subversive and sentimental, it describes even in today's America a powerful nostalgia for uncorrupted domesticity; as recently as 2003, the tableau of the March sisters exquisitely rendered into doll-form formed part of the White House's Christmas decorations. In modern Britain, it maintains a different but still high profile: in 2007, it was ranked as eleventh in the list of books people could not live without, in an on-line poll for World Book Day, and this ranking rose to seventh if only women's votes were counted.

Yet *Little Women*'s classic status may have served as much to conceal as to reveal its originality and unusualness in the canon of children's and adult literature alike. As successive covers to illustrated editions have repeatedly asserted in their depiction of the tableau of the girls clustered around their mother, this is, after all, a book about girls together. It is rare in its deeply felt celebration of the bonds between women, whether mothers and daughters or between sisters, and its concomitant treatment of the compulsions of the heterosexual love-plot largely in terms of the threat it poses to the family at its centre. Depicting the struggles of girls to negotiate the conflicting demands of growing up into women, this is teen fiction before there were teens; and despite the whiff of costume drama that clings to it, it has remained relevant and powerful for today's girls.

Origins and composition

Little Women, subtitled *Meg, Jo, Beth, and Amy. A Girls' Book* was groundbreaking both in terms of Alcott's own writing career and in terms of the market for fiction. Alcott had specialised (under a pseudonym) in lurid romances and thrillers, blood-and-thunder adventures and the Gothic sensation story for adult readers, and had under her own name been writing fantasy stories for the child-market, before she turned to producing 'a lively, simple book' 'for girls' (Alcott 1997: 166) at the urging of the publisher Thomas Niles of Roberts Brothers, Boston. Girls' stories at the time, according to Charlotte Yonge, tended to 'high romance or pure pathos' and it may have been Yonge's *The Daisy Chain* (1856), also a heavily autobiographical family chronicle set in modern times and featuring an awkward adolescent girl, that provided Alcott's model (Wadsworth, p. 39, below). In contrast to Alcott's previous output, and to most of what was on the market at the time, *Little Women* was realistic in mode. It relied heavily on Alcott's own memories of childhood games, pastimes and family conflict, depicting herself as Jo, her sisters and mother, drawing a veil over her brilliant father's many incompetencies, and sketching her subsequent home, Orchard House in Concord, Massachusetts as the Marchs' house. As she said herself, it was 'not a bit sensational, but simple and true, for we really lived most of it; and if it succeeds that will be the reason of it' (Alcott 1997: 167).   However new in mode, the aim of *Little Women* was congruent with the ambition of earlier stories for girls, to help them become 'wives and mothers of [a great] race' (Salmon, p. 45, below).   Ideology – Institution

Reviewed well on publication (despite cavils at the play-acting and at the use of slang, toned down for later editions), *Little Women* had an instant success, and there was an immediate call for sequels, supplied over following years with some reluctance by Alcott – *Good Wives* (1869), *Little Men* (1871) and *Jo's Boys* (1886). Confusingly, *Little Women* is often the title under which its immediate sequel, *Good Wives,* also goes. This is because although Alcott published these two volumes simply as *Little Women* and then *Little Women Part 2,* in Britain, where the titles were pirated almost simultaneously, publishers invented new titles to differentiate them, including *Little Women Married, Little Women Wedded, Nice Wives* and *Little Wives.* Eventually *Good Wives* was adopted uniformly (Carpenter and Prichard 1984: 322). As a result, what moderns understand as *Little Women* may be one or both parts; however, American critical tradition has usually read the book in terms of the ending of the second part, so viewing the two volumes as a whole.

Reception/critical terrain

Little Women was to exert considerable influence on the subsequent development of the girls' story in North America; arguably, it is the mother of the *What Katy Did* series, *Rebecca of Sunnybrook Farm,* the *Pollyanna* stories and the *Anne of Green Gables* series, all of which combined domestic detail with tomboyish girls striving to overcome their natural indiscipline to find a place in society and a husband without compromising their own personalities. It has exerted a well-documented hold over women writers' imaginations (and indeed, over some men's), whether they have 'liked' it or not. So the feminist Simone de Beauvoir wrote of her identification with the tomboy Jo: 'I identified myself passionately with Jo . . . . [S]he was much more tomboyish and daring than I was, but I shared her horror of sewing and housekeeping and her love of books' (Alberghene and Clark 1999: xv). Gloria Steinem reflected too upon the possibility of modelling female behaviour according to the novel: 'Where else . . . could we have read about an all-female group who discussed work, art, and all the Great Questions – or found girls who wanted to be women and not vice versa?' (Alberghene and Clark 1999: xvi). Nor is this passionate identification restricted to white women; Ann Petry wrote that 'I felt as though I was part of Jo and she was part of me' (Alberghene and Clark 1999: xvi). This is not to say that many women have not expressed reservations about the book: Brigid Brophy wrote that 'Having re-read it, dried my eyes and blown my nose . . . , I resolved that the only honourable course was to come out into the open and admit that the dreadful books are masterpieces. I do it, however, with some bad temper and hundreds of reservations' (Alberghene and Clark 1999: xv). A more recent feminist, Camille Paglia, wrote fiercely that 'The whole thing is like a horror movie to me' (Alberghene and Clark 1999: xvi). Its critical history has reflected women writers' sense of its import in depicting the struggles of a fledgling authoress: as Ursula K. Le Guin, for example, reflected:

> From the immediacy, the authority, with which Frank Merrill's familiar illustrations of *Little Women* came to mind as soon as I asked myself what a woman writing looks like, I know that Jo March must have had real influence upon me when I was a young scribbler. I am sure she has influenced many girls, for she is not, like most 'real' authors, dead or inaccessibly famous; nor, like so many artists in books, is she set apart by sensitivity or suffering or general superlativity; nor is she, like most authors in novels, male. She is close as a sister and common as grass.
>
> Alberghene and Clark 1999: xvi

The engagement of many women with Jo in her capacity as writer in part accounts for the outburst of critical interest in the novel which coincided with the American flowering of feminism in literary studies from the late 1970s onwards. Much of the best work on *Little Women* dates from this period of the rediscovery and revaluation of women writers, interest in the autobiographical quality of their work, and in the depiction of women, and especially women writers, in fiction and elsewhere. Critical reception of *Little Women* has tended to hinge on what value is accorded to the end of the novel, in which Jo finally marries Professor Bhaer. There is evidence that Alcott, who remained unmarried herself, chafed against the 'happy endings' she provided: 'Girls write to ask who the little women marry, as if that were the only aim and end of a woman's life. I *won't* marry Jo to Laurie to please anyone' (Alcott 1997: 167). She wrote soon after the publication of the second part that 'Jo should have remained a literary spinster but so many enthusiastic young ladies wrote to me clamorously demanding that she should marry Laurie, *or* somebody, that I didn't dare refuse and out of perversity went and made a funny match for her' (Letter to Elizabeth Powell, March 1869, Alcott 1987: 125). Is Jo's marriage, then, merely a convenient fictive resolution, or is it to be viewed as either positive or coercive? Janet Alberghene and Beverley Lyon Clark have usefully summed up the range of positions adopted by critics of the novel:

> Some argue that Jo provides a model of independence, even if she ultimately capitulates to marriage; others, that she embodies a sense of connectedness with a community of women. Some argue that she submits to prevailing cultural norms; others, that she contests them; others still, that she negotiates among competing norms.
>
> Alberghene and Clark 1999: xvii

The essays

Judith Fetterley's seminal feminist essay on the novel, one of a number that appeared in the late 1970s and 1980s, describes the parameters of most subsequent critical arguments over whether or to what extent *Little Women* displays a tendency either to subvert conventional narratives of coming to womanhood, or to contain such subversion. The essay therefore concentrates on the opening of the novel and contrasts it with the outcomes provided for the girls, measuring the rebellions of part 1 by the accommodations of part 2. Ken Parille turns his attention away from the constructions and education of girlhood to the ways this girls' book constructs and controls boyhood in the person of Laurie, reading the book as interested also in the making of American manhood through submission to the disciplines of work. Sarah Wadsworth offers a useful framing account of the genesis, composition, publication and success of *Little Women* within the context of the rise of gender-specific series books, describing the contemporary market for girls' books and for boys' books in the States.

References

Alberghene, J.M. and Clark, B.L. 1999. *Little Women and the Feminist Imagination: Criticism, Controversy, Personal Essays*. New York and London, Garland.

Alcott, L.M. 1987. *The Selected Letters of Louisa May Alcott*, ed. J. Myerson. D. Shealy and M. Stern. Boston, Little, Brown.

Alcott, L.M. 1997. *Journals*, ed. J. Myerson, D. Shealy and M.B. Stern. Athens and London, University of Georgia Press.

Carpenter, H. and Prichard, M. 1984. *The Oxford Companion to Children's Literature*. Oxford, Oxford University Press.

Further reading

Alberghene, J.M. and Clark, B. L. 1999. *Little Women and the Feminist Imagination: Criticism, Controversy, Personal Essays*. New York and London, Garland.

Carpenter, H. 1985. *Secret Gardens*. London, Allen and Unwin.

Estes, A.M. and Lunt, K. M. 1989. 'Dismembering the Text: The Horror of Louisa May Alcott's *Little Women*', *Children's Literature* 17, 98–123.

Showalter, E. 1991. *Sister's Choice: Tradition and Change in American Women's Writing*. Oxford, Clarendon Press.

Little Women: Alcott's Civil War
Judith Fetterley

When, toward the end of *Little Women*, Jo finds her true ' "style at last," ' her father blesses her with the prospect of inner peace and an end to all ambivalence: ' "You have had the bitter, now comes the sweet. Do your best and grow as happy as we are in your success." ' And Alcott adds her bene-diction: 'So, taught by love and sorrow, Jo wrote her little stories and sent them away to make friends for themselves and her, finding it a very charita-ble world to such humble wanderers.'[1] Finding her true style at last was not, however, such a peaceful arrival in safe waters for Alcott herself. She responded with alacrity to the opportunity afforded by the anonymous 'No-Names Series' to write something not in her style, declaring that she was 'tired of providing moral pap for the young' and enjoying the fun of hearing people say, ' "I know *you* didn't write it, for you can't hide your peculiar style." '[2] She prayed more than once for time enough to write a 'good' book and realized that without it she would do what was easiest and succumb to the pressure of the 'dears' who '*will* cling to the "Little Women" style.'[3] And at the end of *Jo's Boys*, the last of her books on the March family, she longs to close with an 'earthquake which should engulf Plumfield and its environs so deeply in the bowels of the earth that no youthful Schliemann could ever find a vestige of it.'

Alcott's commitment to her true style was evidently somewhat less a choice than a necessity, somewhat less generated from within than imposed from without. Her initial resistance to the proposal from Thomas Niles, a partner in Roberts Brothers Publishing Company, that she write a book for girls had its origins perhaps in an instinct for self-preservation; certainly the success of *Little Women* limited her artistic possibilities thereafter. Hard it was to deny the lucrative rewards attendant upon laying such golden eggs; hard to reconcile the authorial image inherent in *Little Women* with the per-sonality capable of the sensational 'Behind a Mask'; harder still to ignore the statement of what was acceptable from a woman writer implicit in the adulation accorded *Little Women*. Indeed, Alcott ceased to write sensation fiction after the publication of *Little Women*. However what these stories, taken as a group, make clear is the amount of rage and intelligence Alcott had to suppress in order to attain her true style and write *Little Women*.

This is an edited version of the article originally published in *Feminist Studies*, 5(2) (Summer 1979), pp. 369–83, and is reproduced by permission of the publisher, *Feminist Studies*, Inc., c/o Women's Studies Program, University of Maryland, College Park, MD 20742.

Alcott's sensation fiction provides an important gloss on the sexual politics involved in Jo's renunciation of the writing of such fiction and on the sexual politics of Jo's relation with Professor Bhaer, under whose influence she gives it up.

Yet clearly both anger and political perception are present in *Little Women*, and, not surprisingly, there is evidence within *Little Women* of Alcott's ambivalence toward her true style. *Little Women* takes place during the Civil War and the first of Jo's many burdens on her pilgrim's progress toward little womanhood is her resentment at not being at the scene of action. Later, however, she reflects that 'keeping her temper at home was a much harder task than facing a rebel or two down South' (12). The Civil War is an obvious metaphor for internal conflict and its invocation as background to *Little Women* suggests the presence in the story of such conflict. There is tension in the book, attributable to the conflict between its overt messages and its covert messages. Set in subliminal counterpoint to the consciously intended messages is a series of alternate messages which provide evidence of Alcott's ambivalence. To a considerable extent, the continuing interest and power of *Little Women* is the result of this internal conflict. As Alcott got farther and farther away from the moment of discovery, as the true style became more and more the only style, this tension was lost and the result was the tedious sentimentality of *Rose in Bloom* or the unrelieved flatness of *Under the Lilacs*. *Little Women* survives by subversion.

The overt messages of *Little Women* are clearly presented in the first two chapters, 'Playing Pilgrims' and 'A Merry Christmas.' The book opens on Christmas eve with the four girls – Meg, Jo, Amy, and Beth – around the fire awaiting the return of 'Marmee.' Remembering the joys of Christmas past when they were rich, they grumble at their present lot: ' "Christmas won't be Christmas without any presents" '; ' "It's so dreadful to be poor!" '; ' "I don't think it's fair for some girls to have plenty of pretty things, and other girls nothing at all" ' (5). Such discontent with what one has inevitably leads to the determination to get something more. They recall their mother's suggestion that they not be self-indulgent when others are suffering, but they rationalize their determination to please themselves by arguing that these 'others' will not be helped by their sacrifice and by protesting that they have worked hard and deserve some fun. In the logic of the true style, such commitment to self can only lead to a querulous debate on the question of who works hardest and who suffers most. Their peevishness and grumbling is luckily averted by the realization that Marmee is about to arrive and as Beth gets out the old slippers to warm by the fire, the girls experience a change of heart and decide to devote their little money to presents for their mother. Such behavior is in imitation of the 'tall, motherly lady, with a "can-I-help-you" look about her,' for unselfish devotion to others is the keynote to Marmee's character (10).

Marmee is the model little woman. Her first words are an implicit reproof to the girl's self-centered, 'poor me' discontent. ' "Well, dearies, how have you got on today? . . . Has anyone called, Beth? How is your cold, Meg? Jo, you look tired to death." ' The little lesson by contrast is followed by a more extended sermon in the reading of a letter from father, away at the war, who urges his girls ' "to conquer themselves so beautifully that when I come back to them I may be fonder and prouder than ever of my little women" ' (12). The paternal exhortation to conquer the self is happily facilitated by Marmee's proposal that they play again their childhood game of 'Pilgrim's Progress,' only this time in earnest. Discussion of this plan for self-improvement enables them to get through an evening of uninteresting sewing without grumbling. At nine, they put away their work and sing, a household custom begun by Marmee, whose voice was 'the first sound in the morning . . . and the last sound at night' (14). It is not enough that little women be content with their condition; they must be positively cheery at the prospect.

The importance and value of renouncing the self and thinking of others is further dramatized in the second chapter. Armed with their presents to Marmee, evidence of their little effort to forget themselves, they arrive at the breakfast table only to find that Marmee has been visiting the Hummels, a poor family in the neighborhood, and wants her girls to give them their breakfast as a Christmas present. After a moment's hesitation before the new level of sacrifice required, the girls enter into the project wholeheartedly, deliver up their breakfast to the poor, and discover that bread and milk and the sense of having helped others make the best breakfast ever.

The rebels that the girls must fight are clearly identified in these first two chapters; discontent, selfishness, quarrelsomeness, bad temper, thinking too much of worldly things (money, appearance, food). The success of their campaign depends on their acquiring one central weapon: self-control. They must learn to control the self so as to ensure that the self does in fact renounce the self. Conquer yourself, says Father, reminding them that their civil war must be fought at home. In the midst of domestic difficulties, Meg remembers 'maternal counsels given long ago': ' "Watch yourself, be the first to ask pardon if you both err, and guard against the little piques, misunderstandings, and hasty words that often pave the way for bitter sorrow and regret" ' (269). To turbulent, restless, quick-tempered Jo, Marmee offers the consolation of her most precious secret: ' "I am angry nearly every day of my life, Jo, but I have learned not to show it; and I still hope to learn not to feel it, though it may take me another forty years to do so" ' (78).

Conquer oneself and live for others are indeed the watchwords of this women's world.

Equal to the concern in *Little Women* for defining the ideal womanly character is the concern for defining woman's proper sphere and proper work. Early in *Little Women* there is a chapter entitled 'Castles in the Air,' in which each girl describes her life's ambition. The final chapter of the book, called 'Harvesttime,' makes reference to this earlier chapter, comparing what each of them dreamed with what each is now doing, clearly to the advantage of the latter. Meg's dream is from the start domestic: ' "I should like a lovely house, full of all sorts of luxurious things – nice food, pretty clothes, handsome furniture, pleasant people, and heaps of money. I am to be mistress of it, and manage it as I like, with plenty of servants, so I never need work a bit" ' (140). All that time and maturity need modify for Meg is her overvaluation of wealth and her desire to have a lot of servants. Meg must learn that love is better than luxury; she must learn to put a man in the center of her picture; and she must learn that without domestic chores to keep them busy, women will be idle, bored, and prone to folly. These are but minor adjustments, however, for Meg's dream, centered on home, is eminently acceptable. Thus she can say at the end, ' "My castle was the most nearly realized of all" ' (472).

In contrast, the lives of Amy and Jo are very different from their castles in the air. Neither Amy's ambition nor Jo's is domestic. Amy wants ' "to be an artist, and go to Rome, and do fine pictures, and be the best artist in the whole world," ' and Jo wants to ' "write books, and get rich and famous" ' (141). In Rome, however, where Amy makes a real bid to realize her ambition, she comes to see that there is a difference between talent and genius, and that she has only the former. In the future, she decides, her relationship to art will be primarily that of patroness, encouraging and supporting the work of others. Through her experience with Laurie, she learns the truth of her mother's dictum that ' "to be loved and chosen by a good man is the best and sweetest thing which can happen to a woman" ' (95), far better than being a famous artist. Although Amy never completely gives up her art, she places it in the service of home and family. In the final chapter she remarks that she has ' "begun to model a figure of baby, and Laurie says it is the best thing I've ever done. I think so myself, and mean to do it in marble, so that, whatever happens, I may at least keep the image of my little angel" ' (472). Amy's motivation has shifted ground. No longer working for frame or fortune, she is inspired by love for her child. Her figure is not intended for public exhibition, for Amy works not to produce great art or to define herself as an artist, but to create a private memorial to her dying child. Her artistic impulses have been harnessed and subordinated to her 'maternal instinct' and thereby sanctioned.

Jo's history is similar to Amy's. In the final chapter she comments on her 'castle in the air' by saying, '"the life I wanted then seems selfish, lonely, and cold to me now. I haven't given up the hope that I may write a good book yet, but I can wait, and I'm sure it will be all the better for such experiences and illustrations as these,"' and she points to her husband, children, and the familial scene around her (472–3). Again, the connection is made between motherhood and 'good' art; when Jo writes her good book, if she ever does, it will be the product of her experiences as a wife and mother. Until then, like Amy, she is content to deploy her talents in the service of the domestic: 'she told no stories except to her flock of enthusiastic believers and admirers' and 'found the applause of her boys more satisfying than any praise of the world' (468).

Earlier treatments of Jo's relation to writing have also served to identify the proper relation of women to art. When Jo at last finds her true style, the impetus to write has been provided by Marmee and the motivation is solace and comfort for the loss of Beth. In contrast is the picture we get when Jo determines to try for the $100 prize offered in the columns of a newspaper for a sensation story: 'She said nothing of her plan at home, but fell to work next day, much to the disquiet of her mother, who always looked a little anxious when "genius took to burning"' (258). As Marmee's anxiety is a barometer for the quality of Jo's writing, there is evidently an inverse relationship between Jo's interest in what she is doing and its accept ability. The more energetic Jo is in pursuing her writing and getting it published, the worse it is and the more anxious Marmee gets. But when Jo is finally brought to the point of saying, '"I've no heart to write, and if I had, nobody cares for my things,"' then Marmee is all encouragement: '"We do. Write something for us, and never mind the rest of the world"' (419). So Jo does what her mother wishes and writes a story which her father sends, 'much against her will,' to a popular magazine and which becomes, 'for a small thing,' a great success. Understandably, Jo is bewildred by this turn of events and when her father explains it to her, she cries, '"If there *is* anything good or true in what I write, it isn't mine; I owe it all to you and Mother and to Beth"' (420). Good writing for women is not the product of ambition or even enthusiasm, nor does it seek worldly recognition. Rather it is the product of a mind seeking solace for private pain, that scarcely knows what it is doing and that seeks only to please others and, more specifically, those few others who constitute the immediate family. Jo has gone from burning genius to a state where what she writes isn't even hers.

At the end of the first volume of *Little Women*, Alcott refers to her book as a 'domestic drama.' Much of the popularity of *Little Women*, then and now, derives from its embodiment of a cultural fantasy of the happy family – the domestic and feminine counterpart to the nostalgia in male American literature captured by Hemingway in the succinct 'long time ago good, now no good.' At the heart of the fantasy family is, of course, the fantasy Mom, the kind of Mom we all at some time or other are made to wish we could have had. The inherent contradictions in the patriarchal mythology of the family are present in *Little Women*, however; it is, after all, a girls' book written from the perspective of the child. Being Marmee's child is one thing; being Marmee herself is another. Resistances to growing up abound in *Little Women* and suggest attitudes in conflict with the overt messages on the joys of little womanhood.

There is a remark of Jo's which reveals an attitude toward 'women's work' in conflict with the doctrinal attempts to ennoble the domestic sphere through the endless endearing diminutives of 'the little mop and the old brush.' When Jo discovers Professor Bhaer darning, she is horrified: 'think of the poor man having to mend his own clothes. The German gentlemen embroider, I know; but darning hose is another thing and not so pretty' (325). But more important than the revelation that women's work is ugly and degrading when done by men is the implication that women's work is not real work. Before their marriage, John says to Meg, ' "You have only to wait, *I* am to do the work" ' (226). This opposition between working and waiting defines the brutal truth about woman's role. After marriage Meg is 'on the Shelf,' still waiting. Only when she gets rid of her servants and *makes work* for herself can she settle down, give up the foolish expenditures which are as much the result of boredom as vanity, and become a good wife. 'Making work' is the implicit subject of the chapter, which deals with Meg's relation to her children. Much of what she does for them is unnecessary; the rest could be done in half the time and could indeed be done better by John: 'Baby respected the man who conquered him, and loved the father whose grave "No, no," was more impressive than all Mamma's love pats'; thus, 'the children throve under the paternal rule, for accurate, steadfast John brought order and obedience into Babydom' (378, 383).

The perception that women's work is made work generates the encounter between Meg and John over her dress and his coat. In protest against the limitations imposed by John's modest salary and desiring to impress a wealthy friend, Meg orders a fifty-dollar silk dress. Meg has been warned by her mother about John and here she discovers one of the sources of this warning. John 'was very kind, forgave her readily, and did not utter one reproach' (273). He simply cancels the order for his overcoat. In response to Meg's inquiry, he comments, ' "I can't afford it, my dear" ' (273). Consumed with guilt, Meg swallows her pride and her desire, prevails upon her friend to buy her dress, and uses the money to get John's coat. 'One can imagine . . .

what a blissful state of things ensued' (273). This blissful state, however, is based on the premise that John needs and deserves a coat because he has to go out in the world and work. Meg, on the contrary, neither needs nor deserves her dress because, with no real work to do in the world, she has no basis for attention to the self.

Implicit in *Little Women* is an understanding of the genesis of the ideal womanly character far different from that overtly stated through the pilgrim's progress metaphor of the first chapter. ' "Women," ' says Amy, ' "should learn to be agreeable" ' (285). With no legitimate function in life, women will not be tolerated unless they are agreeable; only through a life of cheerful service to others can they justify their existence and assuage the guilt that derives from being useless. Women must watch themselves because they are economically dependent on men's income and emotionally dependent on their approval. Marmee's 'maternal counsels' contain an implicit perception of the politics of marriage: ' "John is a good man, but he has his faults, and you must learn to see and bear with them, remembering your own. . . . He has a temper, not like ours – one flash and then all over – but the white, still anger that is seldom stirred, but once kindled is hard to quench. Be careful, very careful, not to wake his anger against yourself, for peace and happiness depend on keeping his respect" ' (269). While Marmee schools Jo in the art of constricting her anger to a tightening of the lips, she admonishes Meg to accommodate herself to John's anger. Indeed, John's anger is ' "not like ours." ' It is male and must be attended to; Meg's Jo's Marmee's anger is female and must be suppressed. Little women must not be angry because they cannot afford it. Marmee's description of John is frightening for the veiled threat it conveys – men's love is contingent; be careful, very careful not to lose it, for then where will you be?

If the cover messages of *Little Women* suggest that the acquisition of the little woman character is less a matter of virtue than of necessity, so do they suggest that women's acceptance of the domestic sphere as the best and happiest place may be less a matter of wise choice than of harsh necessity. ' "To be loved and chosen by a good man is the best and sweetest thing which can happen to a woman," ' says Marmee to her girls; but she might as well have said it is the only thing that can happen. There are no other viable options. When Jo first meets Laurie, she describes herself to him as a ' "businessman – girl, I mean." ' The accuracy of this implicit presumption against her chance for economic independence is clearly supported by her subsequent experience. To earn money for her sick father, Jo can only sell her hair. Selling one's hair is a form of selling one's body and well buried within this minor detail is the perception that women's capital is their flesh and that they had better get the best price for it, which is, of course marriage. Later Jo discovers a source of income in her stories but the economics of her relation to writing are revealing. At first, she gets nothing for her work; she is satisfied simply to have it published. When she finally does get paid, it is because Laurie acts on her behalf. Jo does not assume that she should or will be paid for her work; when payment comes, she treats it as a gift. Thus she is ripe for the exploitation she encounters in the office of the *Weekly Volcano*: 'Mr. Dashwood graciously permitted her to fill his columns at the lowest prices, not thinking it necessary to tell her that the real cause of his hospitality was the fact that one of his hacks, on being offered higher wages, had basely left him in the lurch' (335). Eventually, even this minor source of income is denied because Jo comes to see that writing sensational fiction is a sordid and unwomanly activity and that good writing is not done for money. ' "Men have to work and women to marry for money," ' says Amy; and while her emphasis here is mistakenly on money, nothing in the book contradicts her assessment of what women must do to live.

Little women marry, however, not only because they lack economic options, but because they lack emotional options as well. Old maidhood obliterates little womanhood and the fear of being an old maid is a motivating force in becoming a little woman. Fear is one of several unpleasant emotions simmering just below the sunny surface of Alcott's story and it plays a considerable role in determining the behavior of the 'little women.' Beth, for example, finds it necessary to invoke the fear of death in order to convince Jo of the primacy of loving service over writing 'splendid books.' Fear is always cropping up in Jo's relation to writing – fear of being selfish, fear of losing her womanliness, fear of becoming insensitive, fear of making money, fear of getting attention – requiring that she periodically renounce, in rather violent and self-punitive rituals, her literary ambitions. And fear plays an important role in the larger drama of Jo's conversion from disgruntled rebel to little woman. At the beginning of the book, Jo hates love, dislikes men and women in the romantic context, and has no desire to marry, unless it be to her sister. She finds Amy's flirting incomprehensible and Meg's capitulation to John disgraceful; she insists on viewing boys as equals and the only game she wishes to play with them is cricket. With Meg married, Beth dead, and Amy engaged, Jo begins to change her tune, for what has she to look forward to: ' "An old maid, that's what I'm to be. A literary spinster, with a pen for a spouse, a family of stories for children, and twenty years hence a morsel of fame, perhaps" ' (424). Alcott emphasizes the unpleasantness of this prospect for Jo as much as is possible, given her commitment to the doctrine that every situation in life is full of beautiful opportunities. Jo is surrounded by evidence of Meg's 'happy home' and inundated by glowing letters from Amy about how 'it is so beautiful to be loved as Laurie loves me' (421). On the evening when this happy couple arrives home Jo is stricken with her worst fit of loneliness, for she sees that all the world is paired off but her: 'a sudden sense of loneliness came over her so strongly that she looked about her with dim eyes, as if to find something to lean upon, for even Teddy [Laurie] had deserted her' (433). Just at this moment Professor Bhaer arrives; Jo realizes that she is in love and capitulates to the description of herself as possessing a '"tender, womanly half … like a chestnut burr, prickly outside, but silk-soft within, and a sweet kernel"' (418). Far from being the '"best and sweetest thing which can happen to a women,"' love is the court of last resort into which Jo is finally driven when all else fails and she must grow up.

The overt ideology of *Little Women* on the subject of marriage is undermined from still another direction. The reward for being 'love-worthy,' for acquiring the little womanly character of self-denial, self-control, accommodations, and concern for others, is not simply avoiding the fate of becoming an old maid; it is also getting the good man. As we have seen in the case of John, however, the good man is somewhat mixed blessing. Indeed, while there is a lot of lip service paid in *Little Women* to the superior value of the 'lords of creation,' and to the importance of male reward, the emotional realities of the book move in a rather different direction. The figure of Mr. March is representative. At the beginning of part 2, Alcott assures us that while 'to outsiders, the five energetic women seemed to rule the house,' the truth is that 'the quiet scholar, sitting among his books, was still the head of the family, the household conscience, anchor, and the comforter; for to him the busy, anxious women always turned in troublous times, finding him, in the truest sense of those sacred words, husband and father' (229–30). Yet this reputed center of power makes his first appearance 'muffled up to his eyes,' a broken man leaning on his wife's arm. While Beth's slow death takes place on center stage and occupies several chapters, the illness of Mr. March is consigned to the distant background and is only vaguely referred to. Literally absent during the first half of the book, during the second half he rarely emerges from his library and we are afforded brief glimpses into it to assure us that he is still there. If Marmee, on her departure to Washington, not knowing if her husband is alive or dead, comforts her girls by saying, '"Hope and keep busy; and whatever happens, remember that you never can be fatherless,"' the true object of worship in *Little Women* is revealed in the description of Meg and Jo's vigil with Beth: 'all day Jo and Meg hovered over her, watching, waiting, hoping, and trusting in God and Mother' (161, 181). It is Marmee who does all the things putatively ascribed to her husband; it is Marmee who always has the right word of comfort, love, and advice. Indeed, Beth's miraculous recovery is implicitly attributed to the fact that Marmee is merely on her way home. God may be a father but his agents on earth are women and the only worship we are privy to is that of Marmee and Beth. Similarly, in the question of love, the significance of men is essentially a matter of lip service. Despite Marmee's dictum about being loved by men, what we see and feel in reading *Little Women* is the love that exists between women: Marmee and her daughters; Jo and Beth. Thus while the events of Jo's life are determined by the book's overt message, her wish to resist the imperative to be a little woman and to instead marry her sister and remain forever with her mother is endorsed by the book's covert message.

The imaginative experience of *Little Women* is built on a paradox: the figure who most resists the pressure to become a little woman is the most attractive and the figure who most succumbs to it dies. Jo is the vital center of Alcott's book and she is so because she is least a little woman. Beth, on the other hand, is the least vital and the least interesting. She is also the character who most fully internalizes the overt values of *Little Women*; she is the daughter who comes closest to realizing the ideal of imitating mother. Like Marmee, Beth's devotion to her duty and her kindness toward others are never-failing and, like Marmee, she never expresses needs of her own. Beth is content with the role of housekeeping homebody; her castle in the air is ' "to stay at home safe with Father and Mother, and help take care of the family" ' (140). In her content, her lack of ambition beyond broom and mop and feather duster, Beth is the perfect little woman. Yet she dies. Implicitly, a connection is made between the degree to which she fulfills the prescription for being a little woman and the fact that she dies. The connection is reinforced by the plot since Beth gets the fatal scarlet fever from fulfilling Marmee's charge to the girls to take care of the Hummels while she is gone. Beth registers the costs of being a little woman; of suppressing so completely the expression of one's needs; of controlling so massively all selfishness, self-assertiveness, and anger. In Beth one sees the exhaustion of vitality in the effort to live as a little woman.

One also sees in Beth that negative self-image which is the real burden of the little woman. Such self-image is behind Beth's description of herself as ' "stupid little Beth' trotting about at home, of no use anywhere but there" ' (360); and it is implicit in her identification with those broken dolls, cast off by her sisters, which she absorbs into her 'infirmary' and makes her special care. Yet, if Beth identifies with these broken bits of out-cast 'dollanity' that constitute her imaginary world, her posture toward them expresses the hope that the world may treat her with the same kindness as she adopts toward them; and we are brought again to the connection between a life of loving service to others and the conviction of one's own worthlessness. Behind the paradox that Beth, the object of everyone's adoration, so thoroughly condemns herself that Beth, so apparently content, cannot accept her right to live, rests the ultimate tension of Alcott's story. Beth's history carries out the implication of being a little woman to its logical conclusion: to be a little woman is to be dead.

Yet the drama of *Little Women* is the making of a little woman; and much of the book must be read as a series of lessons designed to teach Jo the value of a more submissive spirit and to reveal to her the wisdom of the doctrines of renunciation and adaptation announced so clearly in the opening pages. Jo is constantly shown the nasty consequences of not following Marmee's model of selflessness and self-control. While Marmee, though angry nearly every day of her life, has learned to control her anger, Jo at the opening of the story is 'wild.' When Amy burns her book, Jo refuses to forgive and forget; she sticks to her anger despite warning signals from Marmee. The results of her contumacy are nearly fatal: she fails to warn her sister of thin ice; Amy falls in and is only rescued by the timely, and manly exertions of Laurie. The moral is clear. Jo's selfishness, followed by her anger, followed by her vindictiveness result in her sister's nearly dying. In the world of 'little women' female anger is so unacceptable that there are no degress to it; all anger leads to 'murder.' The consequence for Jo is horror at herself which in turn results in contrition, repression, and a firm vow to follow in the footsteps of Marmee and never to let anger get beyond a tightening of the lips.

Jo pays for her quick temper and lack of self-control in a more tangible way later in the book. Amy has roped Jo into going with her to pay the family's social calls. Amy thrives on such activity; but Jo finds it intolerable and can only get through the experience by playing elaborate games at each place they stop. The final call is to their Aunt March. Both girls are tired, peevish, and anxious to go home; but when Jo suggests they skip the visit, Amy remonstrates that ' "it's a little thing to do, but it gives her pleasure" ' (285). So Amy devotes herself to being nice to Aunt March and to Aunt Carroll, who is with her, and to making the visit pleasant, while Jo gives vent to her peevishness and irritation in a series of decided remarks on the subject of patronage. Since Aunt March and Aunt Carroll are in the process of deciding which of the two girls should be offered the chance to accompany Aunt Carroll to Europe, Jo's testiness is costly indeed. Amy goes to Europe and Jo is left home to reflect on the fact that she has received a 'timely lesson in the art of holding her tongue' (287) and to draw the inevitable conclusion that in this world it is best to be a little woman like Amy.

An even more traumatic lesson is administered to Jo through her beloved sister Beth. Beth contracts scarlet fever because of the irresponsibility of Meg and Jo, but the burden falls primarily on Jo as she is the one particularly charged with responsibility for Beth. When Beth asks Jo to take over the job of seeing the Hummels, Jo is too busy, Jo is writing; and so Beth, who has never had scarlet fever, is exposed to the disease and catches it. Again there is the pattern of maximum possible consequences for a minimal degree of self-absorption and selfishness. It is a pattern well calculated to teach Jo a more submissive spirit. In fact, one can say that Beth's primary function in *Little Women* is to be a lesson to Jo; Beth's life is a constant reminder to Jo of her own inadequacies and failures and of what she ought to be, and her death is bitter testimony to the consequences of these failures. It is by no means accidental that Jo 'falls in love' shortly after Beth's death. She gets scared, she gets good, she gets Professor Bhaer.

Obviously, one of the major problem Alcott faced in writing *Little Women* was making up someone for Jo to marry since, as we have seen, marry she must. She cannot marry, as she cannot 'love,' Laurie, not, as Marmee claims, because they are too alike in temperament, but because they are too alike in status; they are too equal. If anything, Laurie is Jo's inferior, as her constant reference to him as 'the dear boy' implies. Unfortunately, perhaps, for Jo and Laurie, little women can only love up, not across or down; they must marry their fathers, not their brothers or sons. Thus Laurie gets Amy, who is a fitting child for him, and Jo gets her Papa Bhaer who, as the Germanic and ursine connotations of his name suggest, is the heavy authority figure necessary to offset Jo's own considerable talent and vitality. His age, his foreignness, his status as a professor, his possession of moral and philosophic wisdom all conspire to put him on a different plane from Laurie and John Brooke and to make him an appropriate suitor for Jo, whose relationship to him is clearly that of pupil to teacher, child to parent, little woman to big man. In exchange for German lessons, she will darn his socks; at their school he will do all the teaching and she will do the house-work; he has saved her soul by a timely warning against the effects of sensational literature and later we are told of Jo's future that she 'made queer mistakes; but the wise professor steered her safely into calmer waters' (467). It is clear, however, that such an excessively hierarchical relationship is necessary to indicate Jo's ultimate acceptance of the doctrines of *Little Women*. In marrying Professor Bhaer, Jo's rebellion is neutralized and she proves once and for all that she is a good little woman who wishes for nothing more than the chance to realize herself in the service of some superior male.[4] The process of getting her out of her boots and doublet and her misguided male-identification and into her role as a future Marmee is completed by placing her securely in the arms of Papa Bhaer.

We do not, of course, view this transformations with unqualified rejoicing. It is difficult not to see it as capitulation and difficult not to respond to it with regret. Our attitude, moreover, is not the result of feminist values imposed on Alcott's work but the result of ambivalence within the work on the subject of what it means to be a little woman. Certainly, this ambivalence is itself part of the message of *Little Women*. It accurately reflects the position of the woman writer in nineteenth-century America, confronted on all sides by forces pressuring her to compromise her vision. How conscious Alcott was of the conflict between the overt and covert messages of *Little Women,* how intentional on the hand was her subversion of the book's 'doctrine' and on the other hand her compromise with her culture's norms, it is impossible to say. What one can say, however, is that in failing to give Jo a fate other than that of the little woman, Alcott 'altered her values in deference to the opinions of others' and obliterated her own identity as an economically independent single woman who much preferred to 'paddle her own canoe' than to resign herself to the dependency of marriage.⁵ Clearly, her true style is rather less than true. When Professor Bhaer excoriates sensation fiction in an effort to set Jo on the road to attaining her true style, he exclaims, ' "They haf no right to put poison in the sugar plum, and let the small ones eat it" ' (342). It is to Alcott's credit that at least covertly if not overtly she recognized that the sugar plum was the poison.

Notes

1. Louisa May Alcott, *Little Women* (Oxford: Oxford University Press, 1998), pp. 420. All subsequent references will be to this edition and will be included parenthetically within the text. *Little Women* was originally published in 1869.
2. *Louisa May Alcott: Her Life, Letters, and Journals*, ed. Ednah D. Cheney (Boston: Roberts Brothers, 1890), pp. 296–7.
3. Ibid., p. 303.
4. It is hard for me to comprehend how Elizabeth Janeway can describe Jo as 'the one young woman in nineteenth-century fiction who maintains her individual independence, who gives up no part of her autonomy as payment for being born a woman – and gets away with it. Jo is the tomboy dream come true, the dream of growing up into full humanity with all its potentialities instead of into limited femininity. . . .' Perhaps the answer lies in the fact that her concept of 'full humanity with all its potentialities' reaches no further than the vision of a Jo who 'marries and becomes, please note, not a sweet little wife but a matriarch: mistress of the *professor's* school, mother of healthy *sons* [while Amy and Laurie have only one sickly *daughter*] and a *cheerful*, active manager of events and people' (italics mine). It is doubtful that such a vision would be asserted as 'full' if the character under consideration were male. Auerbach's analysis seems much more sensible and grounded in the facts of the novel. While giving more weight to the realm of matriarchal power which Jo enters on marrying Professor Bhaer than I am willing to do, she nevertheless recognizes that, even when 'stretched to its limit,' this power collides with and falters before 'the history it tries

to subdue. For . . . history remains where we found it at the beginning of *Little Women*: "far away, where the fighting was."' Indeed, Alcott's recognition that she must write not about the external world of male power embodied in the Civil War but about the internal world of Jo's struggle between resistance and capitulation to the doctrines of little womanhood indicates her understanding of Jo's exclusion from the real sources of power. See Elizabeth Janeway, *Between Myth and Morning: Women Awakening* (New York: William Morrow, 1975), pp. 234–7; and Nina Auerbach, *Communities of Women* (Cambridge: Harvard University Press, 1978), pp. 55–73.
5. Alcott, *Life, Letters, and Journals*, p. 122.

'Wake up, and be a man': *Little Women*, Laurie, and the Ethic of Submission
Ken Parille

During the past twenty-five years, *Little Women* has been at the center of the feminist project of reading texts by nineteenth-century American women. A primary reason for the extensive interest in Alcott's novel is its discussion of the cultural spaces women occupied, or were excluded from, during the mid- and late nineteenth century. Although critics have disagreed about whether the novel 'seeks a new vision of women's subjectivity and space' or argues for a 'repressive domesticity,' it nevertheless offers us a complicated and compelling picture of Alcott and her culture's understanding of girls and women (Murphy, 1990: 564). Yet an important story within *Little Women* remains largely untreated in recent criticism, one that will affect our understanding of the novel's exploration of gender: that of the male protagonist, Laurie. Although critics have done important work by drawing our attention to Alcott's exploration of patriarchal structures and their effect on girls and women, they have not looked in any detail at her concurrent examination of their effect on boys and men.

In many ways, Laurie's story is similar to that of many mid- and late nineteenth-century middle-class young men. Like the struggles of the March girls, his struggle and ultimate submission to cultural expectations for young men narrate a typical confrontation with the limitations of gender roles. Throughout *Little Women*, Laurie is subjected to a version of what critics often describe as the 'ethic of submission,' an ethic usually deemed relevant only to girls' and women's lives because only they were expected to submit to patriarchal authority: 'American women,' Jane Tompkins argues, 'simply

This is an edited version of the article originally published in *Children's Literature*, 29 (2001), pp. 34–51.

could not . . . [rebel] against the conditions of their lives for they lacked the material means of escape or opposition. They had to stay put and submit' (1985: 161). For Tompkins and many critics after her, this ethic meant that girls and women were expected to conform to very narrow roles (dutiful daughter, caring mother, obedient wife), in contrast to boys and men, who were free from such limitations.

In Alcott scholarship, the view of submission as a gendered phenomenon goes back to critics such as Nina Auerbach, Judith Fetterley, and Patricia Spacks, who, in her landmark work *The Female Imagination*, takes Jo at her word when she says 'Boys always have a capital time,' forgetting that the narrator and even Jo herself realize that this is often not the case (1975: 100). Although critics have begun to question this gendered understanding of submission as it applies to men's and boys' lives, in Alcott studies it still remains a prevalent assumption; Jo's story is seen as a paradigmatic example of this ethic, while the ways in which Laurie's story parallels hers are neglected. Only Elizabeth Keyser and Anne Dalke have noted that *Little Women* dramatizes Laurie's struggle with patriarchal expectations. Keyser observes that Laurie 'exemplifies . . . the masculine plight,' yet she does not explore at any length what 'the masculine plight' is, how Laurie represents this plight, and what cultural beliefs shape it (1993: 66–7). Dalke mentions that Laurie's narrative parallels the girls', but she does not examine this similarity or discuss its significance (1985: 573). Critics need to see that Laurie's experience, like those of the March girls, is at every point conditioned by the kinds of patriarchal and materialist pressures that affected girls' lives. For boys the pressure to live up to the standards and achievements of other males (especially the pressure to succeed in the market) has, in some sense, always circumscribed their field of possibilities, as it circumscribes Laurie's.

Using studies of masculinity in America during the nineteenth century by Michael Kimmel, Anthony Rotundo, Judy Hilkey, and Joe Dubbert, I will examine Laurie's capitulation to patriarchal and materialist pressures in the form of his grandfather's desire that he become a merchant and the way in which Amy March functions as the grandfather's agent. By repeatedly questioning his masculinity, Amy shames Laurie into acting in accord with his grandfather's wishes. Once we understand Laurie's story in this way – as submission brought about by shame – we can then revise the conventional critical position that the 'feminine quality of self-denial' is 'the novel's . . . message' (Gaard, 1991: 5). In order to understand more fully what Alcott and *Little Women* have to say about gender, we must recover Alcott's narrative of masculine self-denial.

Perhaps critics have not explored the parallels between Laurie's and the March girls' narratives because in letters and journals. Alcott often idealized boyhood and set it in opposition to her life as a girl and a woman, a life filled with disappointments and restrictions. 'Boys are always jolly' she noted in 1860 (1989: 100) . . . Possibly in part because of such idealizations, critics believe that Jo articulates a truth about boyhood when she says that 'boys always have a capital time.' But in *Little Women*, Laurie's story shows us that Alcott's ideas about the lives of boys are much more complex; the text rarely makes any idealizing claims about boyhood. Laurie is definitely not 'always jolly,' and, puzzled that he could be wealthy and sad, Jo exclaims, 'Theodore Laurence, you ought to be the happiest boy in the world' (51). Laurie's unhappiness results from his place in a world of men and the concurrent pressure of proving himself a man to the novel's characters. According to Michael Kimmel, this pressure is a defining feature of American masculinity in the nineteenth century (ix), the era that the historian Joe Dubbert calls 'the masculine century' (13).

Gilded Age success manuals for young men published around the time of *Little Women* often depict a boy's life as fraught with anxiety. They present him as prone to worrying and suffering from 'dissatisfaction with . . . [his] destiny' and 'spells of melancholy' (cited in Hilkey, 1997: 76). Similarly, Alcott introduces us to Laurie as a lonely, frustrated young man. Unlike the nurturing domestic circle of the March girls and their mother, Laurie's world is an isolated male enclave composed of his grandfather and his tutor, John Brooke, both of whom are grooming him for a life he does not want; during a game called 'rigmarole,' Brooke even relates a thinly veiled allegory of Laurie's submission and his role in it. As a knight, Brooke must 'tame and train' Laurie, 'a fine, but unbroken colt' who is a 'pet of the king's,' Laurie's grandfather (125). Although Laurie eventually goes to work for his grandfather, he desperately wants 'to enjoy myself in my own way': 'I'm to be a famous musician myself, and all creation is to rush to hear me; and I'm never to be bothered about money or business, but just enjoy myself, and live for what I like' (31, 140). In spite of these fantasies, Laurie knows that his future involves a different kind of 'capital time' than the one Jo thinks boys always have, namely, one devoted to 'money and business'. As Dubbert observes, men 'were expected to cash in on . . . opportunities to maximize their gains and minimize their losses' and not, as Laurie says, 'live for what [they] like' (15). His grandfather fears that Laurie wants to pursue a materially unproductive and therefore unmasculine career: 'His music isn't bad, but I hope he will do as well in more important things' (55). What is important for his grandfather is that Laurie do well in business, as he had done. . . . . :

I ought to be satisfied to please grandfather, and I do try, but it's working against the grain, you see, and comes hard. He wants me to be an India merchant, as he was, and I'd rather be shot; I hate tea, and silk, and spices . . . Going to college ought to satisfy him, for if I give him four years he ought to let me off from the business; but he's set, and I've got to do just as he did, unless I break away and please myself, as my father did.

141–2

But this dream of breaking away, Alcott says, is difficult for both sexes to realize; pleasing oneself, to use one of her favorite phrases, is an 'air castle' that must be abandoned by little men and women alike. Here, as elsewhere, Alcott dramatizes a central claim of many critics who study masculinity: culture has its designs on male fulfilment (Dubbert, 1979: 1011; Kimmel, 1996: 1–10). So, like many young men, Laurie is not free to pursue the career he wants, for it would be 'working against the grain' of cultural expectations.

Dubbert's and Hilkey's discussions of advice literature for young men shows that manliness was synonymous with success in the market. A boy knew that he would never be viewed as a man unless he was fiscally productive (Dubbert, 1979: 27–8; Hilkey, 1997: 142–6); as success manuals repeatedly announced, 'character was capital' (Hilkey, 1997: 126). That a career as an artist would be counterproductive has already been forecast in the story of Laurie's father, a musician who 'please [d him]self' and ran away, only to end up dead (144). The narrator never tells us how and why he dies, but the implication is that his death results from his career choice; had he become an India merchant – as Laurie's grandfather surely would have wanted – a different outcome is easy to imagine. Though still only a young man, Laurie has been initiated into the male world of negotiation. He trades four years of his life in order to escape becoming an India merchant – a bargain that does not pay off.

Although many men likely fantasized about 'breaking away,' the pressure placed on them to succeed in business meant that most could not and did not. In reaction to pressure and violence directed at him by his grandfather, Laurie tells Jo he wants to run away to Washington. 'What fun you'd have!' Jo replies. 'I wish I could run off, too . . . If I was a boy, we'd run away together, and have a capital time; but as I'm a miserable girl, I must be proper, and stay at home. Don't tempt me, Teddy, it's a crazy plan' (206). In spite of the romance of escape, she believes that Laurie's interests are best served by remaining, so she orchestrates a truce to keep him at home. Critics tend to take Jo's comment as reiterating a cultural truth: boys can run away, but girls must submit. Ann Murphy, for instance, claims that 'as a boy, Jo would be . . . able to . . . "run away [with Laurie] and have a capital time,"' even though the text tells us in no uncertain terms that Laurie cannot (577). . . . . .

In a crucial and often-cited scene in *Little Women*, Mr Bhaer convinces Jo to give up her dream of being a 'sensational' writer. The scene begins with Jo's defense of sensation stories, but after listening to Bhaer's attack on such 'trash,' she feels 'horribly ashamed' (342). The shame Jo feels from seeing herself through, as she calls it, his 'moral spectacles' (342) causes her to throw all her 'lurid' stories into the stove. Though these stories are profitable and give her the opportunity to experience imaginatively a life she is denied, Jo must stop writing them because such a profession is incompatible with the way in which the novel conceives of 'womanhood' (343). Thus Mr Bhaer acts as a kind of enforcer for the text's values, shaming Jo into sacrificing her desires. But rarely referred to are the scenes in which Amy, acting like Mr Bhaer, shames Laurie into giving up his dreams of life as an artist, and the moment in which Laurie, echoing Jo's destruction, destroys his own manuscripts. The striking resemblance between these scenes suggests that Alcott wants to draw our attention to the similar sacrifices that boys and girls must make in order to fit into narrowly defined adult roles.

In order to make Laurie into a man, Amy constantly reminds him of his distance from cultural ideals of masculinity. Elaine Showalter observes that Jo's German husband, Mr Bhaer, is 'unconfined by American codes of masculinity' (1989: xxvii), but she misses the way in which Alcott shows us how Laurie, as an American boy, is all too confined by such codes. Amy sees it as her job to awaken the sleeping 'young knight' from his boyish illusions and bring him into conformity with these norms. She even concludes her sermon by promising, 'I won't lecture any more, for I know you'll wake up, and be a man' (395). As Jo's 'lurid' literary aspirations are in conflict with the way the text imagines her as a woman, so too are Laurie's boyish artistic dreams incompatible with the way it imagines him as a man.

An essential part of Amy's shaming of Laurie involves renaming him; as his friends had called him 'Dora' to emphasize his failure to measure up to their standards of masculinity, Amy calls him 'Lazy Laurence' to feminize him by emphasizing how unindustrious, and therefore unmanly, he seems to her. Laurie's new name comes from Maria Edgeworth's didactic story 'Lazy Lawrence,' published in a popular collection called *The Parent's Assistant*. The tale features two boys, Jem, a model of masculine ambition, and Lawrence, a model of idleness. Like Laurie, Lawrence dreams, dismisses ambition, and enjoys 'amusements,' but eventually he converts to the ways of industry. As Anthony Rotundo observes, one of the key 'deficiencies of character that [was] thought to cause failure . . . was laziness. Again and again we have heard men exhort one another to "industry," "persistence," "hard work." . . . Each of these popular phrases stood not only as an exhortation to positive behavior, but as a warning against negative behavior' (179). Amy's appeal to Laurie to be industrious, then, represents a typical exhortation to be successful, but also a warning to him that if he continues on his present course he will be perceived as a failure. Like a success manual come to life, Amy attempts, as H.A. Lewis attempted with his Hidden Treasures, to 'awaken dormant energies in ONE PERSON who other-wise might have failed' (Cited in Hilkey, 1997: 75).

Though the name 'Lazy Laurence' implicitly feminizes him, Amy tries to make her assault on Laurie's masculinity explicit: 'instead of being the man you might and ought to be, you are only –' (392). . . . . But before she can finish, Laurie interrupts her. He likely believes that she would conclude with 'a girl' or 'a woman,' and in fact she soon says, 'Aren't you ashamed of a hand like that? It's as soft and white as a woman's, and looks as if it never did anything but wear Jouvin's best gloves' (393). . . .

Amy uses her art to further convince Laurie that he has yet to act 'manfully'. She shows Laurie 'a rough sketch of [him] taming a horse; hat and coat were off, and every line of the active figure, resolute face, and commanding attitude, was full of energy and meaning. . . [In] the rider's breezy hair and erect attitude, there was a suggestion of suddenly arrested motion, of strength, courage' (396). The image contains numerous codes of the 'real man' as Amy and the novel conceive of him: active, resolute, in command, and sexually powerful. . . . Even the kind of sketch Amy draws encodes manliness; it is 'rough,' in contrast to Laurie's 'soft' feminine hands. She tells him that this picture represents him 'as you were' and then compares it to a picture that could have been an illustration of Edgeworth's 'Lazy Lawrence.' But it is clear that Laurie never was such a man. Amy makes this claim in order to shame him by calling his virility into question. As she had used Edgeworth's story as a model for Laurie's life, here she uses her drawing to teach him 'a little lesson.'

When Amy says to Laurie, 'instead of being the man you might and ought to be, you are only –,' he concludes for her with 'Saint Laurence on a gridiron' (392). The narrator tells us that this insertion 'blandly finish[es] the sentence,' but Laurie's invocation of one of the most famous Christian martyrs should not be so easily dismissed. That Laurie should see himself as Saint Laurence, a martyr who was burned to death, implies that he recognized the renunciation of his 'boyish passions' as a metaphorical death. The process of converting lazy Laurie into a man, the process that Amy begins, he concludes with a literal act of destruction – he destroys his manuscripts: 'He grew more and more discontent with his desultory life, began to long for some real and earnest work . . . then suddenly he tore up his music-sheets one by one' (406).

Laurie's destruction of his manuscripts and the fiery death of his patron saint both implicitly refer to Jo's similar act of martyrdom: the extinguishing of her writerly self by burning her sensational tales. . . . . But Laurie knows that simply destroying the manuscripts is not enough. The best way to prove to Amy and his grandfather that he is not a 'humbug' is to do what men do: get a job. As critics have shown, male identity in the nineteenth century was intimately connected to work, and Laurie knows that if he fails to work he will be seen as unmasculine, as weak and feminine. He sends Amy a note addressed to 'Mentor' from 'Telemachus' in order to acknowledge the success of her 'little lesson': ' "Lazy Laurence" has gone to his grandpa, like the best of boys' (397). Although Laurie literally goes to see his grandfather, the metaphorical 'going' is most important. He has finally left his boyhood 'air castles' and submitted to his grandfather. Like 'the best of boys' he embraces the values of the patriarchy and abandons idle dreams in favor of 'earnest work.' The boy who earlier said he never wanted to be 'bothered about money or business' now exclaims, 'I'm going into business with a devotion that shall delight grandpa, and prove to him that I'm not spoilt. I need something of the sort to keep me steady. I . . . mean to work like a man' (439). This is perhaps the novel's most compact formulation of the cultural connection between masculinity and material productivity: to be a man is to work. Acting as Mentor, Amy is (to adapt the title of Edgeworth's collection) the 'culture's assistant'; that is, she enforces its codes of masculinity. . . .And given Amy's use of Edgeworth's text in enforcing these codes, a use Laurie acknowledges when he says ' "Lazy Laurence" has gone to his grandpa' – it is difficult to understand Beverly Clark's claims that Laurie can rebel 'against prescribed texts' (81). . . .

Amy thinks she is preparing Laurie to be a man so that he will be a suitable partner for Jo, but the novel has already told us that this pairing is not a possibility (395). Instead, she prepares him to fill the narrowly prescribed categories of middle-class husband, father, and businessman, the roles he ends up playing in her life. . . . . Many critics have suggested that Jo's marriage to Mr Bhaer is a kind of punishment. Rather than marry the erotic young Laurie, she ends up with the asexual older man. Yet Laurie's marriage to Amy – the most traditional of all the March girls – instead of Jo could similarly be seen as a punishment. But, of course, Amy's conventionality is the point. His marriage to her signifies that he has proved his manhood to the novel's characters. He accepts convention by embracing domesticity and business. . . . .

The parallel between Laurie's and Jo's submission makes it clear that he is as crucial to *Little Women*'s exploration of gender as the March girls. As a novel about Laurie's and the March girls' submission, then, *Little Women* remains relevant to us as a story of how both boys and girls confront cultural limitations.

References

[All references to *Little Women* in the text are to the Oxford University Press edition (1998).]

Alcott, L.M. 1987. *The Selected Letters of Louisa May Alcott.* Ed. Joel Myerson and Daniel Shealy. Boston, Little, Brown.

—— 1989. *The Journals of Louisa May Alcott.* Ed. Joel Myerson and Daniel Shealy. Boston Little, Brown.

—— 1998. *Little Women.* Oxford, Oxford University Press.

Auerbach, N. 1978. *Communities of Women: An Idea in Fiction.* Cambridge, MA, Harvard University Press.

Clark, B.L. 1989. 'A Portrait of the Artist as a Little Woman,' *Children's Literature* 17, 81–97.

Dalke, A. 1985. '"The House-Band": The Education of Men in *Little Women*,' *College English* 47: 571–8.

Dubbert, J.L. 1979. *A Man's Place: Masculinity in Transition.* Englewood Cliffs, NJ, Prentice-Hall.

Fetterley, J. 1979. '*Little Women*: Alcott's Civil War,' *Feminist Studies* 5: 369–83.

—— 1978. *The Resisting Reader: A Feminist Approach to American Fiction.* Bloomington, Indiana University Press.

Gaard, G. 1991. '"Self-denial was all the fashion": Repressing Anger in *Little Women*,' *Papers on Language and Literature* 27: 3–19.

Hilkey, J. 1997. *Character Is Capital: Success Manuals and Manhood in Gilded Age America.* Chapel Hill, University of North Carolina Press.

Keyser, E. 1993. *Whispers in the Dark: The Fiction of Louisa May Alcott.* Knoxville, University of Tennessee Press.

Kimmel, M.S. 1996. *Manhood in America: A Cultural History.* New York, Free Press.

Murphy, A. 1990. 'The Borders of Ethical, Erotic, and Artistic Possibilities in Little Women,' *Signs* 15: 562–85.

Rotundo, E.A. 1993. *American Manhood: Transformations in Masculinity from the Revolution to the Modern Era.* New York, Basic Books.

Showalter, E. 1989. Introduction to *Little Women*, by Louisa May Alcott. New York, Penguin, pp. vii–xxviii.

Spacks, P. 1975. *The Female Imagination.* New York, Knopf.

Tompkins, J. 1985. *Sensational Designs: The Cultural Work of American Fiction 1790–1860.* New York, Oxford University Press.

Louisa May Alcott and the Rise of Gender-Specific Series Books
Sarah A. Wadsworth

Few gentlemen, who have occasion to visit news-offices, can have failed to notice the periodical literature for boys, which has been growing up during the last few years. The increase in the number of these papers and magazines, and the appearance, from time to time, of new ones, which, to judge by the pictures, are always worse than the old, seem to indicate that they find a wide market.

William G. Summer, 1878

Girls, like boys, in recent years have been remarkably favoured in the matter of their reading. They cannot complain, with any justice, that they are ignored in the piles of juvenile literature laid annually upon the booksellers' shelves. Boys boast of a literature of their 'very own', as they would call it. So do girls. . . . [T]hat so-called 'girls books' continue to be published in shoals annually is sufficient proof that there is a market for them.

Edward G. Salmon, 1886

Writing in 1878 and 1866 respectively, William G. Sumner and Edward G. Salmon point to a newly emergent trend in British and American juvenile literature: the development of distinct categories of literature written expressly for boys or expressly for girls. To the twentieth-century reader, raised on Nancy Drew or the Hardy Boys, Trixie Belden or Danny Dunn, the Baby-Sitters' Club or Encyclopedia Brown, such a division may seem a natural and obvious one. As Salmon's observation suggests, however, the shift from a more or less homogenous body of literature for 'boys and girls' to a body of juvenile fiction bifurcated by gender was considered an innovation in the latter half of the nineteenth century.[1] In the United States, the transformation began gradually in the 1830s, 1840s, and 1850s with popular authors such as Jacob Abbott, William T. Adams ('Oliver Optic'), and Rebecca Sophia Clarke ('Sophie May'), gaining momentum in the 1860s, 1870s, and 1880s with the contributions of Louisa May Alcott, Horitio Alger, and Mark Twain, and accelerating rapidly toward the close of the nineteenth century as a result of publishers'

Extracted from S. Wadsworth, 'Louisa May Alcott, William T. Adams, and the Rise of Gender-Specific Series Books', in *The Lion and the Unicorn*, 25 (2001), pp. 17–46.

unflagging efforts in the fields of gender-specific periodicals, dime novels, and, especially, series books.

While many critics have noted that 'adolescent or preadolescent boys and girls historically were not encouraged to share reading material' (Vallone 122), few distinguish between books written for either gender but appropriated primarily by one or the other (for example, *Robinson Crusoe*) and books written with a single-sex target audience in mind. An exception is Gillian Avery, who observes, '[f]rom the mid-century onwards, as juvenile publishing became an industry, what had been unisex developed into two sharply differentiated categories. Writing for boys, and writing for girls, became professions in themselves' (190). As Avery suggests, the segmentation of the juvenile fiction market closely parallels the development of children's literature as a specialized branch of publishing.[2]

In this essay, I illustrate the relationship between the segmentation of the juvenile fiction market by gender and the commercialization of children's publishing through an examination of the careers of William T. Adams and Louisa May Alcott. Perhaps more than any other writers in nineteenth-century America, these two authors exemplify how '[w]riting for boys, and writing for girls, became professions in themselves.' As early practitioners of gendered juvenile series, Alcott and Adams together illustrate the separation of boys' and girls' reading in the United States in the mid- to late nineteenth century. A side-by-side study of these two authors and their juvenile series shows that Alcott was both responding to and writing against Oliver Optic's books. At the same time, Alcott's books for girls reveal that she simultaneously resisted and revised traditional models of femininity while mediating her readers' desire for conventional female plots. As a result, Alcott brought about an important development in the history of juvenile literature: in shaping a new kind of fiction aimed specifically at adolescent girls, she ushered in realistic female characters and plots that were as distinct from previous models of femininity and womanhood in fiction, as from the characters and plots of the boys' books against which they were inevitably defined. Ultimately, however, the impact of Adams and Alcott extended beyond the books they wrote to the audience who read them. For, in recognizing the changing roles of boys and girls in American society and their still-tentative presence in the maturing literary marketplace, they (and their publishers) effectively broight these segments of the juvenile fiction market into existence. Just as Adams helped to define not only boys' series but also the audience for boys' books, so Alcott, as the most important contemporary American author to write books specifically for girls, was instrumental in defining, shaping, reinforcing, and revising the qualities, interests, and aspirations of the girls who comprised that market.[3]

In the second volume of *Little Women*, Louisa May Alcott describes Jo March's efforts to produce a type of story that would be both saleable and respectable. After her friend (and future husband) Professor Bhaer persuades her that sensational stories are morally corrupting to young readers, Jo abandons this lucrative genre and attempts a tale in the bland, unobjectionable style of Mary Sherwood, Maria Edgeworth, and Hannah More. The result, Alcott writes, 'might have been more properly called an essay or a sermon, so intensely moral was it.' After failing to find a purchaser for 'this didactic gem' (343), Jo turns her hand to juvenile fiction:

> Then she tried a child's story, which she could easily have disposed of if she had not been mercenary enough to demand filthy lucre for it. The only person who offered enough to make it worth while to try juvenile literature was a worthy gentleman who felt it his mission to convert all the world to his particular belief. But much as she liked to write for children, Jo could not consent to depict all her naughty boys as being eaten by bears or tossed by mad bulls, because they did not go to a particular Sabbath-school, nor all the good infants, who did go, as rewarded by every kind of bliss, from gilded ginger-bread to escorts of angels, when they departed this life with psalms or sermons on their lisping tongues. So nothing came of these trials; and Jo corked up her inkstand. . . .
>
> 343

Unlike her semi-autobiographical protagonist, Alcott refused to cork up her own inkstand but instead went on to write numerous stories for children, beginning with fairy tales in the mid-1850s and continuing largely in the fantasy mode promoted by Hawthorne up until about 1868. Finally, in the spring of that year, she hit upon a combination of style and subject matter that succeeded in earning her the stacks of 'filthy lucre' she dreamed of, in addition to literary fame and respectability as the author of *Little Women*.

Louisa May Alcott did not want to write girls' books, however. In fact, she was rather strongly opposed to the suggestion, offered by Thomas Niles of Roberts Brothers, that she write a novel for girls. In retrospect, her distaste for the project (which she recorded in a journal entry of September 1867) is amusing:

> Niles, partner of Robert, asked me to write a girls book. Said I'd try. Fuller asked me to be the Editor of 'Merry's Museum.' Said I'd try. Began at once on both new jobs, but didn't like either.
>
> Journals 158

As it happened, the task of editing *Merry's Museum* proved to be quite a drain on Alcott's time and energy, and her progress on the 'girls book' was no doubt hindered as much by the demands of reading manuscripts and writing her monthly story and editorial as by her obvious resistance to the project Niles proposed.

While Alcott continued to favor fairy tales, writing for *Merry's Museum* an eight-part serial entitled *Will's Wonder Book* as well as several other fantasy stories, Niles renewed his interest in her 'girls book.' In May 1868, his prompting elicited another tepid response from Alcott:

> Father saw Mr. Niles about a fairy book. Mr. N. wants a *girls' story*, and I begin 'Little Women.' Marmee, Anna, and May all approve my plan. So I plod away, though I don't enjoy this sort of thing. Never liked girls or knew many, except my sisters; but our queer plays and experiences may prove interesting, though I doubt it.
>
> Journals 165–6

The following month, she again voiced her lack of enthusiasm, noting in her journal that she had

> Sent twelve chapters of 'L. W.' to Mr. N. He thought it *dull*; so do I. But work away and mean to try the experiment; for lively, simple books are very much needed for girls, and perhaps I can supply the need.
>
> Journals 166

Thomas Niles's persistence in the face of Alcott's continuing reluctance is perhaps surprising until we consider both the unprecedented success then being enjoyed by authors of 'realistic' juvenile fiction and the talent of this up-and-coming editor for assessing the literary market of the day. Alcott's biography reveals that a powerful incentive to Niles (and, by extension, to Alcott) was provided by the example of 'Oliver Optic' in the arena of boys' books. Niles's obituary in *Publishers Weekly* (9 June 1894) reported that '[t]he success of Oliver Optic's books suggested to Mr. Niles the thought of similar books for girls, and having been much pleased by "Hospital Sketches," by Louisa M. Alcott, published in 1867 by Ticknor & Fields, he sent for Miss Alcott and engaged her for this work' ('T. Niles' 859–60). More recently, Gene Gleasion related that Niles asked Alcott to ' "do something like Oliver Optic," but for girls' (648). Madeleine Stern reconstructs the scenario in her biography of Alcott as follows:

> From his office at number 143 Washington Street he [Niles] had seen vast quantities of books by 'Oliver Optic' leaving the rooms of Lee and Shephard at number 149. There must be a similar market for a full-length novel that would be as popular among girls as 'Oliver Optic's' narratives were among boys.
>
> 168

Who was this paragon of juvenile authorship who reportedly inspired both Thomas Niles and Louisa May Alcott to experiment with realistic fiction aimed specifically at adolescent girls? With approximately 126 books to his credit, 'Oliver Optic' was the enormously prolific Reverend William Taylor Adams (1822–97), whose most popular books sold at a rate of more than 100,000 a year (Gay 16). The indefatigable Adams also wrote approximately 1,000 short stories, used at least eight different pseudonyms, and was editor, at various times, of *Student and Schoolmate, Our Little Ones, and Oliver Optic's Magazine (Our Boys and Girls)* (Gleason 647–8). By the time of his death, an estimated two milliom copies of his books had been sold, making the former principal and Sunday-school teacher one of the best-paid writers of his time as well as (according to at least one source) the most widely read (Jones xvi). Given that Niles evidently hoped that Alcott might provide a female counterpart to Adams's fabulously popular boys' books, a glimpse into the career of the illustrious 'Oliver Optic' provides some insight into the role of the *Little Women Series* in the nineteenth-century literary marketplace.

Just as Niles prompted Alcott with the suggestion that she write a book for girls, so Adams's publisher provided the initial impetus for the young minister to write a book for boys. Although originally published by Brown, Bazin and Co., *The Boat Club: or The Bunkers of Rippleton. A Tale for Boys* (dated 1854), a story about two rival groups of boys and their boating adventures on a New England lake, was picked up by Phillips, Sampson in 1855 and later republished by William Lee, who spurred Adams on to produce sequel after sequel. Lee, as a partner in the newly established firm of Lee & Shephard, capitalized on the popularity of the six-volume *Oliver Optic's Library for young People* (which he helped to create) and managed to keep Adams in his stable of authors for the next forty years.

Lee & Shephard had more authors writing for boys than for girls; . . . but their series for boys achieved a kind of a commercial success that none of their girls' series managed to approach. Fueled by their success in the boys' market and hoping to correct the imbalance, Lee & Shephard decided to enlist their most popular boys' author in a bold attempt to jumpstart their lagging trade in girls' books. 'Adams was summoned to the publishers' office and asked to prepare a new series for girls – which might also be read by boys!' (Kilgour, *Lee & Shephard* 35). Adams agreed to give it a try. The promised volume for girls was *Rich and Humble; or, The Mission of Bertha Grant* (1864), the first volume of the *Woodville Stories*, in which Adams confirms:

> the author presents the following story to his young lady friends, though he confidently expects it will prove as acceptable to the embryo 'lords of creation' as to those for whom it was more especially written.

5

What is perhaps most interesting about *Rich and Humble* is the explicit claim it makes to targeting a female audience. Despite its claims to addressing a female readership, *Rich and Humble* carries the subtitle 'A Story for Young People,' and the series is designated 'A Library for Boys and Girls.' Moreover, in his preface to the volume, Adams addresses male and female readers in turn, directing the attention of the two groups of readers to different aspects of the text:

> The girls will find that Bertha Grant is not only a very good girl, but that her life is animated by a lofty purpose, which all may have, though they fail to achieve the visible triumphs that rewarded the exertions of the heroine of 'Rich and Humble.'
>
> The boys will find that Richard Grant was not always a good boy because his life was not animated by a lofty purpose; but the author hopes, in another volume, to present him in a higher moral aspect, and more worthy the imitation of those who, like him, have wandered from the true path.
>
> 5

Rich and Humble was not an immediate success; still, the long-term sales of this domestic novel eventually outpaced many of Adams's boys' books (Kilgour 39–40), providing persuasive corroboration that a ready market for girls' series books awaited those prepared to meet its demands. In spite of these early beginnings, however, realistic fiction written specifically for the amusement of young girls was still uncommon a full decade after the appearance of Oliver Optic's books for boys. While Lee & Shepard exhibited customary foresight in staking out a corner of the girls' market, most publishers did not yet consider it necessary or sufficiently profitable to publish books for this particular subset of readers.

One reason for the recognition of boys as a separate audience well before girls was that the boys' market was seen as including girls, while the girls' market apparently excluded boys. In fact, it was a common perception that boys *required* a separate body of literature. Girls, however, could enjoy both domestic tales and adventure stories directed at a male audience. The popular British children's author Charlotte M. Yonge (who had been producing novels for teenage girls in England since the mid-1850s and whom Alcott read as a yound woman [Crisler 35]) explained her decision to include a category of 'boys' books' without a complementary listing of 'girls' books' in her compendium of *What Books to Give and What to Lend* (1887):

> The mild tales that girls will read simply to pass away the time are ineffective with [boys]. . . . the works therein [this catalogue] are not merely suited to lads, for though girls will often greatly prefer a book about the other sex, boys almost universally disdain books about girls.
>
> 29–30

Alcott was well aware of this literary fact, for in *Little Women* she has Jo read boys' books, and even delicate Beth finds occasion to feel 'glad that she had read one of the boys' books in which Jo delighted' (152) Given these attitudes toward boys' and girls' reading, it is not difficult to see why entertaining novels conceived specifically for boys emerged earlier than comparable books for girls.

The belated discovery of girls as a separate audience was also influenced by a persistent misapprehension of what girls wanted to (or should) read. Long after the fading of the notion that boys must be spoon-fed didactic and moral tales of the type Alcott satirizes in *Little Women*, stories for girls continued to consist largely of sugar-coated lessons in morality and femininity. Many seemed to agree with Charlotte Yonge's assessment that '[i]f the boy is not to betake himself to "Jack Sheppard" literature, he must be beguiled by wholesome adventure,' while 'If the girl is not to study the "penny dreadful," her notions must be refined by the tale of high romance or pure pathos' (6).

The discrepancy between boys' and girls' literary fare reflects the divergent roles of boys and girls in nineteenth-century society. As Anne Scott MacLeod points out, 'Realistic children's literature nearly always bends toward socializing the young, imparting values, and distinguishing desirable behavior from the deplorable' (*American Childhood* 54). Boys' and girls' novels of the nineteenth century accomplished these tasks through plot as well as characterization: 'Where the boys' books increasingly revolved around a young man's encounter with the outside world – in the army, in the West, in the city – and around active, extroverted adventure, girls' novels focused on character and relationships, as, of course, girls' lives did as they approached womanhood' (MacLeod, *American Childhood* 14) Salmon's 1886 article 'What Girls Read' explicitly prescribed the manner in which juvenile literature should prepare British children for their future roles as grown men and women:

> Boy's literature of a sound kind ought to build up men. Girls' literature ought to help to build up women. If in choosing the books that boys shall read it is necessary to remember that we are choosing mental food for the future chiefs of a great race, it is equally important not to forget in choosing books for girls that we are choosing mental food for the future wives and mothers of that race.
>
> 526

Alcott's entry into the largely untried arena of realistic fiction for girls marked an important advance in the social function of girls' reading. Responding positively to the gradual widening of the female sphere and increasing opportunities for women, *Little Women*, and its sequels acknowledge girls as more than future wives and mothers, advocate education and career opportunities for women, and celebrate the individuality of spirited, intelligent, independent young women. In *Little Women*, which was hailed as '[a] capital story for girls' ('New Publications' 857), two of the three sisters who reach adulthood pursue careers other than (or in addition to) that of homemaker: Jo as a writer and Amy as an artist.

Although Alcott attributed the success of *Little Women* to its realistic portrayal of girls' lives, Jo, the central character, has typically been regarded as an exceptional, rather than a typical, example of nineteenth-century girlhood. Certainly, Alcott's portrayal of Jo flouts the characteristics ascribed by convention to nineteenth-century heroines. Alcott writes, 'Round shoulders had Jo, big hands and feet, a fly-away look to her clothes, and the uncomfortable appearance of a girl who was rapidly shooting up into a woman, and didn't like it' (*Little Women* 6). As MacLeod has recently argued, however, tomboyism, followed by its forced abandonment in the mid- to late teens, was far more widespread among American girls of the nineteenth century than convention has led us to expect. Drawing on diaries, letters, and memoirs, as well as fictional accounts, MacLeod suggests that girls of the later nineteenth century often enjoyed the same kinds of rough-and-tumble activities as their brothers, up until such time (typically between thirteen and fifteen) as society demanded that they beome young ladies. MacLeod's research helps account for the popularity of *Little Women*, and especially of the beloved Jo. Not only did Jo's character exhibit many of the traits of MacLead's tomboys – independence, courage, an adventurous spirit, and a love of the outdoors – but the problem with which Jo contends throughout *Little Women* was evidently a pervasive and enduring one for American girls: the problem of how to bridge the gap between the relative liberty of girlhood and the potentially stifling constraints of womanhood.

The practice of spinning off sequels and series was a marketing innovation that flourished in the nineteenth and early twentieth centuries – an indication that authors and publishers were becoming quite adept at catering to the demands of the marketplace – and, as indicated earlier, William T. Adams and his publisher, Lee & Shepard, were masters of the technique.

If Thomas Niles had indeed persuaded Alcott to follow the example of Oliver Optic and write books directed specifically at a single-sex juvenile audience, it is likely that he also had Adams's success with series in mind when he urged the author of *Little Women* to follow up with subsequent volumes of the 'March Family Chronicles.' Alcott complained in a letter of February 1869, 'I [d]ont like sequels, & dont think No 2 will be as popular as No 1, but publishers are very *perverse* & wont let authors have thier [sic] way so my little women must grow up & be married off in a very stupid style' [Letters 121–2]). But Niles, who '[l]ike most publishers . . . felt that books sold better in series, since a few outstanding titles would carry a mass of trivia' (Kilgour, *Roberts Brothers* 65), had already decided, within a month of the publication of *Little Women*, that the story should have a sequel. Moreover, he encouraged Alcott to keep the ending of *Little Women* open to allow for such a possibility (Shealy 63), and when *Little Women or Meg, Jo, Beth and Amy Part Second* was still in press, he was already urging Alcott to follow it up with a 'new story by Miss Alcott' (Shealy 71).

Alcott readily acknowledged her indebtedness to Niles in establishing her as a famous writer of books for girls, even referring to *Little Women* as a book that was 'very hastily written to order' (*Letters* 118). Her debt to Oliver Optic and the Lee & Shepard mode of mass production and marketing remained largely unacknowledged, however, by both Alcott and her publisher.

As the parallel and intertwining careers of Louisa May Alcott and Oliver Optic show, however, both authors succeeded in the rapidly expanding literary marketplace by staking out segments of the juvenile fiction market defined principally by gender and age. Both authors effectively responded to the literary tastes and interests of thee audiences, and both paid heed to the aspirations of their readers, as well as to the expectations society placed upon them. The books of both authors were created and shaped by the markets they addressed, and, in turn, shaped, defined, and fostered a sense of community among these respective groups of readers.

Notes

1. John Newbery experimented with gender-based marketing gimmicks by packaging *A Little Pretty Pocket Book* (1744) with a ball for boys and a pincushion for girls, but this strategy was designed to make a *single* book equally attractive to both male and female children. Samuel F. Pickering, Jr. traces the first 'significant differentiation made between books for little girls and for little boys' to Mary Ann Kilner's *The Adventures of a Pin Cushion* (1783?) and *Memories of a Peg-Top* (1783) (qtd. in Segal, ' "As the Twig Is Bent" ' 168).
2. Jacob Abbott's *Rollo and Lucy* books (dating from 1835 and 1841, respectively) are the first American juvenile series of note to be clearly differentiated by gender. The series I discuss in this article targeted a slightly older age group than Abbott's series. For a bibliographical overview of series books for girls, see *Girls Series Books: A Checklist of Titles Published, 1840–1991* (Minneapolis: U of Minnesota P, 1992). For discussions of gender differentiation in the British market, see Kimberley Reynolds, *Girls Only? Gender and Popular Children's Literature In Britain, 1880–1910* and J. S. Bratton, *The Impact of Victorian Children's Fiction.*
3. It is significant that Sheryl A. Englund refers to *Little Women* as a 'genre-defining "girl's book" ' (201) and Cary Ryan pronounces it 'a book that redefines what it means to be born a girl' (Alcott, *Girlhood Diary* 36). I argue that her books for girls are both 'genre-defining' and audience-defining and that the two functions are, in fact, interdependent.

References

Adams, William Taylor. *Rich and Humble; or, The Mission of Bertha Grant.* Boston: Lee & Shepard, 1864.

Alcott, Louisa May. *The Journals of Louisa May Alcott.* Ed. Joel Myerson and Daniel Shealy. Boston: Little, Brown, 1989.

———. *Little Women or Meg, Jo, Beth, and Amy.* 1868. Oxford: OUP, 1998.

———. *Louisa May Alcott: Her Girlhood Diary.* Ed. Cary Ryan. Mahwah, NJ: Bridge Water Books, 1993.

———. *The Selected Letters of Louisa May Alcott.* Ed. Joel Myerson, Daniel Shealy, and Madeleine B. Stern. Athens, GA: Univ of Georgia P; 1995.

Avery, Gillian. *Behold the Child: American Children and Their Books, 1621–1922.* London: Bodley Head, 1994.

Bratton, J.S. *The Impact of Victorian Children's Fiction.* London: Croom Helm, 1981.

Crisler, Jesse S. 'Alcott's Reading in *Little Women*: Shaping the Autobiographical Self.' *Resources for American Literary Study* 20 (1994): 27–36.

Englund, Sheryl A. 'Reading the Author in *Little Women*: A Biography of a Book.' *American Transcendental Quarterly (ATQ)* 12 (1998): 199–219.

Gay, Carol, 'William Taylor Adams.' *Dictionary of Literary Biography 42: American Writers for Children Before 1900.* Ed Glenn E. Estes. Detroit: Gale Research – Bruccoli Clark, 1985.

Gleason, Gene, 'What Ever Happened to Oliver Optic?' *Wilson Library Bulletin* 49 (May 1975): 647–50.

Jones, Delores Blythe. *An 'Oliver Optic' Checklist: An Annotated Catalog-Index to the Series, Nonseries Stories, and Magazine Publications of William Taylor Adams.* Westport, CT: Greenwood P, 1985.

Kilgour, Raymond L. *Lee and Shepard: Publishers for the People.* Hamden, CT: Shoe String Press, 1965.

———. *Mssrs. Roberts Brothers, Publishers.* Ann Arbor: U of Michigan P, 1952.

MacLeod, Anne Scott. *American Childhood: Essays on Children's Literature of the Nineteenth and Twentieth Centuries*: Athens, GA: U of Georgia P, 1994.

'New Publications.' Rev. of *Little Women. The Lady's Friend* 5.2 (Dec. 1868): 857.

Reynolds, Kimberley. *Girls Only? Gender and Popular Children's Fiction in Britain: 1880–1910.* New York and London: Harvester Wheatsheaf, 1990.

Salmon, Edward G. 'What Girls Read.' *Nineteenth Century* 20 (October 1886): 515–29.

Segal, Elizabeth. ' "As the Twig Is Bent . . .": Gender and Childhood Reading.' In *Gender and Reading: Essays on Readers, Texts, and Contexts*, ed. Elizabeth A. Flynn and Patrocinio P. Schweickart. Baltimore: Johns Hopkins UP, 1986. 165–86.

Shealy, Daniel. 'The Author–Publisher Relationships of Louisa May Alcott.' *Book Research Quarterly* (Spring 1987): 63–74.

Stern, Madeleine, *Louisa May Alcott: A Biography.* New York: Random House, 1996.

Summer, William G. 'What Our Boys Are Reading.' *Scribner's Monthly* 15 (1878): 681–5.

'T. Niles – In Memoriam.' *Publishers Weekly* 45.23 (June 9, 1894): 859–60.

Vallone, Lynne. *Disciplines of Virtue: Girls' Culture in the Eighteenth and Nineteenth Centuries.* New Haven: Yale UP, 1995.

Yonge, Charlotte. *What Books to Give and What to Lend.* London: National Society's Depository, 1887.

2

Robert Louis Stevenson, *Treasure Island* (1881–2; 1883)

Introduction
Sara Haslam

Treasure Island has been hailed as a 'landmark text' in the history of children's literature (Hunt, 1994: 28). Peter Hunt describes it as such because it both synthesised what had come before, and took the genre forward into new territory. Islands had been features of stories for children since Defoe's *Robinson Crusoe* appeared in 1719. But adventures in which canny-minded boys sought to make their mark on territory far away had a particular resonance and relevance in the age of Empire. It was also enormously popular in its time. Throughout the Victorian years (1819–1901) about one person in three was under the age of 15 (Boone, 2005: 4). A large percentage of the population was therefore likely to want to read books such as *Treasure Island*. George Meredith called it 'The best of boys' books' (Letley, 1998: ix); it offered treasure, travel and adventure, or 'all the old romance', as Stevenson himself put it in his promise 'To the Hesitating Purchaser', which precedes the novel.

Origins, composition and reception

Treasure Island was written specifically for children. In the essay included here, Stevenson gives an account of its genesis. Originally concocted to entertain his family on a wet holiday in Braemar, the story, once written up, was also intended to make its author some necessary money. It first began to appear in print in serialised instalments in the magazine *Young Folks* from October 1881 to January 1882. It was modestly successful. It was only when Stevenson reworked it for publication as a book that its reputation and sales took off. Various theories have been advanced to account for this change in the story's critical fortunes. David Angus (1990) has inventoried the many changes that Stevenson made as he turned the magazine version into the book. He accounts for the book's greater success by arguing that Stevenson's rewrites, which moderated the bombast and introduced a little more piety, widened the book's appeal to an adult audience. But perhaps the muted response to the first version of the story can be attributed to the fact that the original instalments were buried deep in each number of the magazine, in small type. It is possible, too, that it was placed in the wrong kind of magazine: *Young Folks* was considered to be an 'improving magazine': its title in full was *Young Folks: a Boys' and Girls' Paper of Instructive and Entertaining Literature*. One anonymous contemporary reviewer, in *The Dial* of May 1884, certainly doubted that it would provide 'wholesome reading' (Maixner, 1981: 142). Or perhaps the improving magazines were becoming outdated themselves. The comparative popularity of the book version is likely to be a combination of all these factors, as well being promoted by a production schedule that meant it appeared just before Christmas – then, as now, an occasion for giving books as presents. It cannot, however, be attributed to the writer's reputation. Stevenson had published so little by 1881 that the fact his story came out pseudonymously at first – by Captain George North – is unlikely to have affected readers either way.

'The Island . . . is a monstrous success', boomed one reviewer, W.E. Henley, in December 1883, on the publication of the book (Maixner, 1981: 17). Prime Minister Gladstone, according to contemporary rumour, sat up all night reading it. (Stevenson reported this rumour in a letter to his mother – he felt Gladstone should rather have been attending 'to the imperial affairs of England' [Maixner, 1981: 17]). Contemporaries relished the reworking of a familiar tradition, derived from *Robinson Crusoe*, that seemed to be nearing its zenith at this time. 'Buried treasure', as Henley put it, 'is one of the very foundations of romance' (Maixner, 1981: 131). More recently, Troy Boone has attributed its success to its reworking of the type of material published in hugely popular magazines such as *The Boy's Own Paper* from the 1860s onwards, which published 'action-packed imperialist adventure tales' aimed at boys (Boone, 2005: 70).

But this is not the whole story. Stevenson also managed to appeal to those hunting for something new, refreshing and liberating – a marketing combination that could be devastating for the competition. 'In *Treasure Island*', according to the *Graphic* in 1883, 'there is combined with an imagination far stronger than that of [fellow adventure writers Kingston, Ballantyne and Cooper], a power of expression unique in the literature of our day, and an insight into character, and a capacity to depict it, unsurpassed and almost unsurpassable.' 'Under Mr Stevenson's masterly touch', the *Graphic* concluded, 'everything becomes new' (Maixner, 1981: 140–1). The intense attractiveness of Long John Silver, although he was also the 'villain', was a particular case in point. Furthermore, in an important essay on Stevenson, published the year after his death, Henry James focused on his unique passion for youth, and his rare and original illustration of make-believe (Maixner, 1981: 294–5). So far from being an improving or moral writer was Stevenson that in his fiction the 'joys of children are outside our world altogether', or so an earlier reviewer of his work had pointed out (Maixner, 1981: 85). This sense of *Treasure Island* as exceeding dutiful moral commonplaces has endured. In the debate about tradition versus innovation in *Treasure Island*, it is telling that, in a book published in 1981 to evaluate the flood of nineteenth-century fiction for children intended to 'convey moral instruction', there is no single mention of Stevenson's story – despite a fifty-page chapter called 'Books for Boys' (Bratton, 1981). The argument can certainly be made that Stevenson's playful, irreverent attitude outweighed his exploitation of the traditions of the time.

He was rewarded financially (he recorded his delight at the treasure he received for it, a 'hundred jingling, tingling, golden, minted quid' [Maixner, 1981: 16]), and initially with widespread critical acclaim as well. And yet Stevenson's glee at his success was always tainted by a sense of the book's 'lesser' qualities. His wife Fanny didn't want him to publish the 1883 version under his name. In an extraordinary letter to Henley he revealed the tensions in his own relationship to the book that made him famous: 'to those who ask me . . . to do nothing but refined, high-toned . . . masterpieces, I will offer the following bargain: I agree to their proposal if they give me £1000' (Maixner, 1981: 16). Stevenson confessed his embarrassment that he 'should spend a man's energy' upon what he calls dismissively 'this business' and yet still found it impossible at first to earn an independent living at writing.

The tide of critical acclaim began to turn against Stevenson after 1914. This was not solely to do with a notion of his lesser 'calling', or lesser skill, though this certainly featured in what the critics said. Robert Kiely (1964: 7) blames instead a general exhaustion at the cult of personality which had surrounded R.L.S. (itself part of an overwhelming 'critical hysteria') from the 1890s. In 1914 Frank Swinnerton wrote a book (*R.L. Stevenson*) that dragged critical focus back onto the work and found, in the end, that Stevenson was not a great writer – though he accepted that in the genre of the 'boy's book' his work was of 'first-class importance' (Maixner, 1981: 509).

The essays

In his essay 'My First Book' (published in 1894), Stevenson provides an autobiographical perspective on *Treasure Island,* summarising his early writing career, and explaining how he came to write his bestseller. He focuses on the importance of the map as a stimulus to the story, discusses his debts to other writers, and considers the relationship between story and place. The other two essays included here are broadly culturally historical in approach, and relate Stevenson's story to Victorian thinking about masculinity at home and abroad. 'Slaves to Adventure' is extracted from Diana Loxley's book which focuses on a series of nineteenth-century island fictions: Wyss's *The Swiss Family Robinson* (1800), Marryat's *Masterman Ready* (1841), Ballantyne's *Coral Island* (1858), Verne's *The Mysterious Island* (1875) and Stevenson's *Treasure Island* (1883). Loxley argues that these stories of resourceful male heroes who journey to desert islands, struggle successfully against strange environments, beasts and savages and are brought safely home need to be understood within the changing context of expansionist nineteenth-century British imperialism. With regard to *Treasure Island,* she argues that a subtext advocating individualistic colonialist enterprise underpins what has been seen as a 'pure story' of swashbuckling historical romance. The book's message is all the more pedagogically effective, she suggests, because it is implicit. While Loxley reads *Treasure Island* in the context of British imperial activity overseas, Parkes reads it by contrast alongside the rise of the nineteenth-century industrial state at home, and in particular, the 'emergence of the modern civil service and administrative classes of Britain'. He argues that Jim is groomed to become a public servant, signalled through his role at the end of the novel in counting the treasure. Individualistic adventure is subsumed within collective administration and Jim is poised to take his place within the expanding ranks of the English middle classes.

References

Angus, D. 1990. 'Youth on the Prow: the First Publication of *Treasure Island*', *Studies in Scottish Literature*, 25, 83–99.

Boone, T. 2005. *Youth of Darkest England: Working-Class Children at the Heart of Victorian Empire*. London, Routledge.

Bratton, J.S. 1981. *The Impact of Victorian Children's Fiction*. London, Croom Helm.

Hunt, P. 1994. *An Introduction to Children's Literature*. Oxford, Oxford University Press.

Kiely, R. 1964. *Robert Louis Stevenson and the Fiction of Adventure*. Cambridge, MA, Harvard University Press.

Letley, E. 1998. Introduction. *Treasure Island by Robert Louis Stevenson*. Oxford, Oxford University Press.

Maixner, P. (ed.) 1981. *Robert Louis Stevenson: the Critical Heritage*. London, Routledge & Kegan Paul.

Further reading

Calder, J. 1980. *RLS: A Life Study*. London, Hamish Hamilton.
Colley, A. C. 2004. *Robert Louis Stevenson and the Colonial Imagination*. Aldershot, Ashgate.
Eigner, E. 1966. *Robert Louis Stevenson and the Romantic Tradition*. Princeton, NJ, Princeton University Press.
Wood, N. 1998 'Gold Standards and Silver Subversions: *Treasure Island* and the Romance of Money', *Children's Literature*, 26, 61–85.

My First Book: *'Treasure Island'*
Robert Louis Stevenson

It was far indeed from being my first book, for I am not a novelist alone. But I am well aware that my paymaster, the Great Public, regards what else I have written with indifference, if not aversion; if it call upon me at all, it calls on me in the familiar and indelible character; and when I am asked to talk of my first book, no question in the world but what is meant is my first novel.

Sooner or later, somehow, anyhow, I was bound to write a novel. It seems vain to ask why. Men are born with various manias: from my earliest childhood, it was mine to make a plaything of imaginary series of events; and as soon as I was able to write, I became a good friend to the paper-makers. Reams upon reams must have gone to the making of 'Rathillet,' 'The Pentland Rising,'* 'The Kings's Pardon' (otherwise 'Park Whitehead'), 'Edward Daven,' 'A Country Dance,' and 'A Vendetta in the West'; and it is consolatory to remember that these reams are now all ashes, and have been received again into the soil. I have named but a few of my ill-fated efforts, only such indeed as came to a fair bulk ere they were desisted from; and even so they cover a long vista of years. 'Rathillet' was attempted before fifteen, 'The Vendetta' at twenty-nine, and the succession of defeats lasted unbroken till I was thirty-one. By that time, I had written little books and little essays and short stories; and had got patted on the back and paid for them – though not enough to live upon. I had quite a reputation, I was the successful man; I passed my days in toil, the futility of

---

Ne pas confondre. Not the slim green pamphlet with the imprint of Andrew Elliott, for which (as I see with amazement from the book-lists) the gentlemen of England are willing to pay fancy prices; but its predecessor, a bulky historical romance without a spark of merit, and now deleted from the world.

First published in *The Idler*, August 1894.

which would sometimes make my cheek to burn – that I should spend a man's energy upon this business, and yet could not earn a livelihood: and still there shone ahead of me an unattained ideal: although I had attempted the thing with vigour not less than ten or twelve times, I had not yet written a novel. All – all my pretty ones – had gone for a little, and then stopped inexorably like a schoolboy's watch. I might be compared to a cricketer of many years' standing who should never have made a run. Anybody can write a short story – a bad one, I mean – who has industry and paper and time enough; but not every one may hope to write even a bad novel. It is the length that kills. The accepted novelist may take his novel up and put it down, spend days upon it in vain, and write not any more than he makes haste to blot. Not so the beginner. Human nature has certain rights; instinct – the instinct of self-preservation – forbids that any man (cheered and supported by the consciousness of no previous victory) should endure the miseries of unsuccessful literary toil beyond a period to be measured in weeks. There must be something for hope to feed upon. The beginner must have a slant of wind, a lucky vein must be running, he must be in one of those hours when the words come and the phrases balance themselves – *even to begin.* And having begun, what a dread looking forward is that until the book shall be accomplished! For so long a time, the slant is to continue unchanged, the vein to keep running, for so long a time you must keep at command the same quality of style: for so long a time your puppets are to be always vital, always consistent, always vigorous! I remember I used to look, in those days, upon every three-volume novel with a sort of veneration, as a feat – not possibly of literature – but at least of physical and moral endurance and the courage of Ajax.

In the fated year I came to live with my father and mother at Kinnaird, above Pitlochry. Then I walked on the red moors and by the side of the golden burn; the rude, pure air of our mountains inspirited if it did not inspire us, and my wife and I projected a joint volume of logic stories, for which she wrote 'The Shadow on the Bed,' and I turned out 'Thrawn Janet,' and a first draft of 'The Merry Men.' I love my native air, but it does not love me; and the end of this delightful period was a cold, a fly-blister, and a migration by Strathairdle and Glenshee to the Castleton of Braemar. There it blew a good deal and rained in a proportion; my native air was more unkind than man's ingratitude, and I must consent to pass a good deal of my time between four walls in a house lugubriously known as the Late Miss McGregor's Cottage. And now admire the finger of predestination. There was a schoolboy in the Late Miss McGregor's Cottage, home from the holidays, and much in want of 'something craggy to break his mind upon.' He had no thought of literature; it was the art of Raphael that received his fleeting suffrages; and with the aid of pen and ink and a shilling box of water colours, he had soon turned one of the rooms into a picture-gallery. My more immediate duty towards the gallery was to be showman; but I would sometimes unbend a little, join the artist (so to speak) at the easel, and pass the afternoon with him in a generous emulation, making coloured drawings. On one of these occasions, I made the map of an island; it was elaborately and (I thought) beautifully coloured; the shape of it took my fancy beyond expression; it contained harbours that pleased me like sonnets; and with the unconsciousness of the pre-destined, I ticketed my performance 'Treasure Island.' I am told there are people who do not care for maps, and find it hard to believe. The names, the shapes of the wood-lands, the courses of the roads and rivers, the prehistoric footsteps of man still distinctly traceable up hill and down dale, the mills and the ruins, the ponds and the ferries, perhaps the Standing Stone or the Druidic Circle on the heath; here is an inexhaustible fund of interest for any man with eyes to see or twopence-worth of imagination to understand with! No child but must remember laying his head in the grass, staring into the infinitesimal forest and seeing it grow populous with fairy armies. Somewhat in this way, as I paused upon my map of 'Treasure Island', the future character of the book began to appear there visibly among imaginary woods; and their brown faces and bright weapons peeped out upon me from unexpected quarters, as they passed to and fro, fighting and hunting treasure, on these few square inches of a flat projection. The next thing I knew I had some papers before me and was writing out a list of chapters. How often have I done so, and the thing gone no further! But there seemed elements of success about this enterprise. It was to be a story for boys; no need of psychology or fine writing; and I had a boy at hand to be a touchstone. Women were excluded. I was unable to handle a brig (which the *Hispaniola* should have been), but I thought I could make shift to sail her as a schooner without public shame. And then I had an idea for John Silver from which I promised myself funds of entertainment; to take an admired friend of mine (whom the reader very likely knows and admires as much as I do), to deprive him of all his finer qualities and higher graces of temperament, to leave him with nothing but his strength, his courage, his quickness, and his magnificent geniality, and to try to express these in terms of the culture of a raw tarpaulin. Such psychical surgery is, I think, a common way of 'making character'; perhaps it is, indeed, the only way. We can put in the quaint figure that spoke a hundred words with us yesterday by the way-side; but do we know him? Our friend, with his infinite variety and flexibility, we know – but can we put him in? Upon the first, we must engraft secondary and imaginary qualities, possibly all wrong; from the second, knife in hand, we must cut away and deduct the needless arborescence of his nature, but the trunk and the few branches that remain we may at least be fairly sure of.

On a chill September morning, by the cheek of a brisk fire, and the rain drumming on the window, I began *The Sea Cook,* for that was the original title. I have begun (and finished) a number of other books, but cannot remember to have sat down to one of them with more complacency. It is not to be wondered at, for stolen waters are proverbially sweet. I am now upon a painful chapter. No doubt the parrot once belonged to Robinson Crusoe. No doubt the skeleton is conveyed from [Edgar Allan] Poe. I think little of these, they are trifles and details; and no man can hope to have a monopoly of skeletons or make a corner in talking birds. The stockade, I am told, is from [Marryat's] *Masterman Ready.* It may be, I care not a jot. These useful writers had fulfilled the poet's saying: departing, they had left behind them Footprints on the sands of time, Foot-prints which perhaps another – and I was the other! It is my debt to Washington Irving that exercises my conscience, and justly so, for I believe plagiarism was rarely carried farther. I chanced to pick up the *Tales of a Traveller* some years ago with a view to an anthology of prose narrative, and the book flew up and struck me; Billy Bones, his chest, the company in the parlour, the whole inner spirit, and a good deal of the material detail of my first chapters – all were there, all were the property of Washington Irving. But I had no guess of it then as I sat writing by the fireside, in what seemed the spring-tides of a somewhat pedestrian inspiration; nor yet day by day, after lunch, as I read aloud my morning's work to the family. It seemed to me original as sin; it seemed to belong to me like my right eye. I had counted on one boy, I found I had two in my audience. My father caught fire at once with all the romance and childishness of his original nature. His own stories, that every night of his life he put himself to sleep with, dealt perpetually with ships, roadside inns, robbers, old sailors, and commercial travellers before the era of steam. He never finished one of these romances; the lucky man did not require to! But in *Treasure Island* he recognised something kindred to his own imagination; it was *his* kind of picturesque; and he not only heard with delight the daily chapter, but set himself acting to collaborate. When the time came for Billy Bones's chest to be ransacked, he must have passed the better part of a day preparing, on the back of a legal envelope, an inventory of its contents, which I exactly followed; and the name of 'Flint's old ship' – the *Walrus* – was given at his particular request. And now who should come dropping in, *ex machinâ*, but Dr Japp, like the disguised prince who is to bring down the curtain upon peace and happiness in the last act; for he carried in his pocket, not a horn or a talisman, but a publisher – had, in fact, been charged by my old friend, Mr Henderson, to unearth new writers for *Young Folks*. Even the ruthlessness of a united family recoiled before the extreme measure of inflicting on our guest the mutilated members of *The Sea Cook*; at the same time, we would by no means stop our readings; and accordingly the tale was begun again at the beginning, and solemnly re-delivered for the benefit of Dr Japp. From that moment on, I have thought highly of his critical faculty; for when he left us, he carried away the manuscript in his portmanteau.

Here, then, was everything to keep me up, sympathy, help, and now a positive engagement. I had chosen besides a very easy style. Compare it with the almost contemporary 'Merry Men'; one reader may prefer the one style, one the other – 'tis an affair of character, perhaps of mood; but no expert can fail to see that the one is much more difficult, and the other much easier to maintain. It seems as though a full-grown experienced man of letters might engage to turn out *Treasure Island* at so many pages a day, and keep his pipe alight. But alas! this was not my case. Fifteen days I stuck to it, and turned out fifteen chapters; and then, in the early paragraphs of the sixteenth, ignominiously lost hold. My mouth was empty; there was not one word of *Treasure Island* in my bosom; and here were the proofs of the beginning already waiting me at the 'Hand and Spear'! Then I corrected them, living for the most part alone, walking on the heath at Weybridge in dewy autumn mornings, a good deal pleased with what I had done, and more appalled than I can depict to you in words at what remained for me to do. I was thirty-one; I was the head of a family; I had lost my health; I had never yet made £200 a year; my father had quite recently bought back and cancelled a book that was judged a failure: was this to be another and last fiasco? I was indeed very close on despair; but I shut my mouth hard, and during the journey to Davos, where I was to pass the winter, had the resolution to think of other things and bury myself in the novels of M. de Boisgobey. Arrived at my destination, down I sat one morning to the unfinished tale; and behold! it flowed from me like small talk: and in a second tide of delightful industry, and again at the rate of a chapter a day, I finished *Treasure Island*. It had to be transcribed almost exactly; my wife was ill; the school-boy remained alone of the faithful; and John Addington Symonds (to whom I timidly mentioned what I was engaged on) looked on me askance. He was at that time very eager I should write on the Characters of Theophrastus: so far out may be the judgments of the wisest men. But Symonds (to be sure) was scarce the confidant to go to for sympathy on a boy's story. He was large-minded; 'a full man,' if there was one; but the very name of my enterprise would suggest to him only capitulations of sincerity and solecisms of style. Well! he was not far wrong.

Treasure Island – it was Mr Henderson who deleted the first title, *The Sea Cook* – appeared duly in the story paper, where it figured in the ignoble midst, without woodcuts, and attracted not the least attention. I did not care. I liked the tale myself, for much the same reason as my father liked the beginning: it was my kind of picturesque. I was not a little proud of John Silver, also; and to this day rather admire that smooth and formidable adventurer. What was infinitely more exhilarating, I had passed a landmark; I had finished a tale, and written 'The End' upon my manuscript, as I had not done since 'The Pentland Rising,' when I was a boy of sixteen not yet at college. In truth, it was so by a set of lucky accidents; had not Dr Japp come on his visit, had not the tale flowed from me with singular ease, it must have been laid aside like its predecessors, and found a circuitous and unlamented way to the fire. Purists may suggest it would have been better so. I am not of that mind. The tale seems to have given much pleasure, and it brought (or was the means of bringing) fire and food and wine to a deserving family in which I took an interest. I need scarcely say I mean my own.

But the adventures of *Treasure Island* are not yet quite at an end. I had written it up to the map. The map was the chief part of my plot. For instance, I had called an islet 'Skeleton Island,' not knowing what I meant, seeking only for the immediate picturesque, and it was to justify this name that I broke into the gallery of Mr Poe and stole Flint's pointer. And in the same way, it was because I had made two harbours that the *Hispaniola* was sent on her wanderings with Israel Hands. The time came when it was decided to republish, and I sent in my manuscript, and the map along with it, to Messrs Cassell. The proofs came, they were corrected, but I heard nothing of the map. I wrote and asked; was told it had never been received, and sat aghast. It is one thing to draw a map at random, set a scale on one corner of it at a venture, and write up a story to the measurements. It is quite another to have to examine a whole book, make an inventory of all the allusions contained in it, and, with a pair of compasses, pain-fully design a map to suit the data. I did it; and the map was drawn again in my father's office, with embellishments of blowing whales and sailing ships, and my father himself brought into service a knack he had of various writing, and elaborately *forged* the signature of Captain Flint, and the sailing directions of Billy Bones. But somehow it was never *Treasure Island* to me.

I have said the map was the most of the plot. I might almost say it was the whole. A few reminiscences of Poe, Defoe, and Washington Irving, a copy of Johnson's *Buccaneers*, the name of the Dead Man's Chest from Kingsley's *At Last*, some recollections of canoeing on the high seas, and the map itself, with its infinite, eloquent suggestion, made up the whole of my materials. It is, perhaps, not often that a map figures so largely in a tale, yet

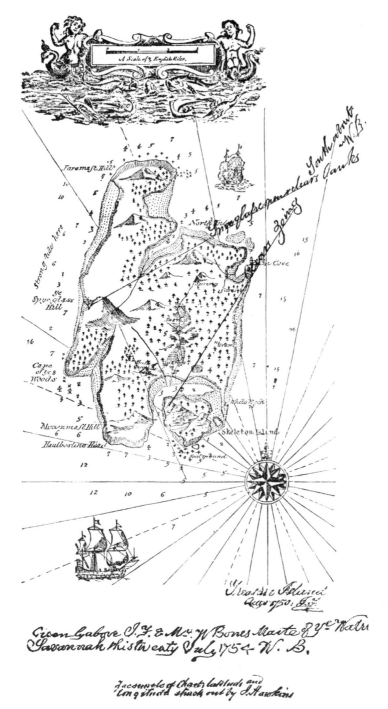

Figure 1 Frontispiece, Robert Louis Stevenson, *Treasure Island*, first illustrated edition, London: Cassell & Co. Ltd, 1885. By kind permission of the Bodleian Library, University of Oxford, shelfmark (Nuneham) 253 e.38.

it is always important. The author must know his countryside, whether real or imaginary, like his hand; the distances, the points of the compass, the place of the sun's rising, the behaviour of the moon, should all be beyond cavil. And how troublesome the moon is! I have come to grief over the moon in *Prince Otto,* and so soon as that was pointed out to me, adopted a precaution which I recommend to other men – I never write now without an almanack. With an almanack, and the map of the country, and the plan of every house, either actually plotted on paper or already and immediately apprehended in the mind, a man may hope to avoid some of the grossest possible blunders. With the map before him, he will scarce allow the sun to set in the east, as it does in *The Antiquary.* With the almanack at hand, he will scarce allow two horsemen, journeying on the most urgent affair, to employ six days, from three of the Monday morning till late in the Saturday night, upon a journey of, say, ninety or a hundred miles, and before the week is out, and still on the same nags, to cover fifty in one day, as may be read at length in the inimitable novel of *Rob Roy.* And it is certainly well, though far from necessary, to avoid such 'croppers.' But it is my contention – my superstition, if you like – that who is faithful to his map, and consults it, and draws from it his inspiration, daily and hourly, gains positive support, and not mere negative immunity from accident. The tale has a root there; it grows in that soil; it has a spine of its own behind the words. Better if the country be real, and he has walked every foot of it and knows every mile-stone. But even, with imaginary places, he will do well in the beginning to provide a map; as he studies it, relations will appear that he had not thought upon; he will discover obvious, though unsuspected, short-cuts and foot-prints for his messengers; and even when a map is not all the plot, as it was in *Treasure Island,* it will be found to be a mine of suggestion.

Slaves to Adventure: The Pure Story of *Treasure Island*
Diana Loxley

[*Treasure Island*] incorporates all the major signifying elements of colonial truth discourse based on the transcription of the reality of lived experience: the narrative 'I', text as journal (although written after the event with the

Extracted from D. Loxley, *Problematic Shores: The Literature of Islands* (London: Macmillan, 1990), pp. 149–68.

wisdom of retrospectivity), the log-book and the map complete with an 'elaborately forged . . . signature of Captain Flint, and the sailing directions of Billy Bones' (Stevenson 1894, p.10). Hawkins, deputised by his fellow adventurers to inscribe the particulars of the island exploits, offers up to the reader a full and sequential narrative from which nothing is omitted except (and crucially as far as the text's impulse as a documentation of truth is concerned) 'the bearings of the island, and that only because there is still treasure not yet lifted'. A supreme strategy for the positing of a material world beyond words and an invocation to reader identification since the yielding of complete information is presented as something that would be a potential threat to the outcome of future events – armed with such knowledge the readers of *Treasure Island* [*TI*] could, of course, take it upon themselves to become adventurers in the real world through participation in a quest for the treasure that 'remains'.

Thus familiarising its readership, the text initiates the classic trajectory of the movement out and back home again, from domesticity and confinement to adventure and freedom. The transition from the enclosed familiar and familial environment of eighteenth-century England (and the early chapters set in the Inn have a distinct flavour of the Gothic in their atmosphere of stifling confinement) to the mythic plane of an exhilarating voyage to an unknown South Sea island, is mediated through the figure of Billy Bones – an envoy of adventure completely misplaced in the context of the oppressiveness of the Inn – who functions to bridge the gap between the two domains. Reinvoking a traditional device, his narratives of adventure provide the preface to the text's reinscription of a particular form of knowledge. As in *Robinson Crusoe, Masterman Ready* and *The Coral Island*, it is his stories which are the authority which speaks the real as it has been experienced:

> His stories were what frightened people worst of all. Dreadful stories they were; about hanging, and walking the plank, and storms at sea, and the Dry Tortugas, and wild deeds and places on the Spanish Main . . . and the language in which he told these stories shocked our plain country people almost as much as the crimes he described . . . but I really believe his presence did us good. People were frightened at the time, but on looking back they rather liked it; it was a fine excitement in a quiet country life . . ..
>
> *TI*, p. 4

Despite the familiar combination of fear, fascination and desire which fixes the apprehension of this alien world, its representation forms the basis of an obsessional fantasy which initiates a compulsion both to repeat and to participate. In this movement *Treasure Island* perfects a significant feature of colonialist discourse whereby an orally, cartographically or transcriptively represented alien world becomes a 'real' or 'actual' world, stranger, more exotic and remote even than its representation:

> I brooded by the hour together over the map, all the details of which I well remembered. Sitting by the fire in the house-keeper's room, I approached that island, in my fancy, from every possible direction; I explored every acre of its surface; I climbed a thousand times to that tall hill they call the Spyglass, and from the top enjoyed the most changing prospects. Sometimes the isle was thick with savages, with whom we fought; sometimes full of dangerous animals that hunted us; but in all my fancies nothing occurred to me so strange and tragic as our actual adventures.
>
> *TI,* p. 36

Yet this fantasy which cannot be constructed without recourse to a prior discursive authority (isles 'thick with savages' and 'dangerous animals') – the pre-text to adventure – turns out in fact to be a misplaced model for this particular fiction's own unfolding. Rather than savages and wild animals, the monsters which will populate *Treasure Island* are, of course, those piratical figures drawn from *within* the ranks of civilisation itself – a threat perhaps all the more 'strange and tragic' for that.

Nevertheless, the recalling of former fictions firmly installs the masculinist colonial dream of discovery and exploration with which the text aligns itself. Initially at least, there exists a clear projection of the hierarchical power structure within which the historic adventure fantasy will be acted out. And, as allocated by the Squire: 'Hawkins shall come as cabin-boy, . . . You, Livesey, are ship's doctor; I am admiral'. The text's impulse, however, is towards a gradual destabilisation of such rigid divisions between subordination and control, rulers and ruled, between those who authorise and those who are authorised. The roles initially designated become finally completely subverted: the Squire (who doubles as a magistrate), displaced from a context in which his title bears meaning, gradually recedes from a central position to the extent that he eventually plays no part whatsoever; the Doctor, the supreme voice of reason throughout, assumes, by contrast, a status and authority disproportionate to his original position; and, of course, the lowly cabin-boy emerges to the fore as the fiction's perfected dream-hero, the initiator, manipulator and controller of the action. This particular blurring of boundaries forms but part of the text's complex patterning designed to subvert not only an image of stasis and predictability at the heart of action, event, character or circumstance but also the possibility that there are any really clearly definable distinctions between such standard polarities as 'good' and 'evil', 'honest' and 'dishonest', 'villainy' and 'legality', 'civilisation' and 'barbarity'. In this confusion of dichotomies is also diffused the historical and political impulses which, it will be argued, in fact form the 'centre' of Stevenson's text, and that all the more pertinently since it resists stabilisation at all.

Power itself is involved in a thematic of circuitry and exchange, continually passing from one group or individual to another, never resting in or reaching a central position and dramatised in the motif of the ship which acts as a symbol of this continuous process of an exchange of control between the pirates and the adventurers. It functions also as the site of mutiny, division, betrayal, conspiracy, the shifting of honour and allegiance amongst each other and between both groups. The problem of treachery is of course central to the text's foregrounding of notions of duality or ambiguity implicit in action, event, motive and 'character' and therefore also to its attempt to fragment the possibility of there being a central, regulating authority at work. This motif is outlined in four major stages: the conspiracy and mutiny of the pirates against the adventurers; internal division between the pirates, and their conspiracy against Silver, their Captain; Silver's duplicity, his shifting of apparent allegiance between both parties ('Silver . . . doubly a traitor . . . He had still a foot in either camp. . . [*TI*, p. 170]); Hawkins' similar ability to bridge both camps, revealed in; (a) his initial role as accomplice to Billy Bones, the pirate, (b) his breaking of vows to Smollett and Trelawney, (c) and by contrast, his unbroken pledge of honour to Silver effecting therefore his temporary desertion from his own group, (d) his decision to act according to his own desires, against the orders of his colleagues ('I was certain I should not be allowed to leave the enclosure, my only plan was to . . . slip out when nobody was looking; and that was so bad a way of doing it as made the thing itself wrong. But I was only a boy, and I had made up my mind' (*TI*, p. 117)).

Two observations need to be made at this stage. First, both Hawkins and Silver become united to the extent that their duplicitous actions set them apart from the groups with which they are primarily aligned: this is part of a process of doubling, a gradual concentration upon the similarities between the two figures which the text increasingly asserts (as Silver himself indicates, Hawkins is 'the picter of my own self when I was young' [*TI*, p. 150; see also p. 155]). Through these actions (and by placing them at odds with either lawful or lawless authority) the text reaffirms the fundamental primacy of the ideology of individualism. In the face of a context in which the traditional mechanisms of law and authority have become superfluous and cannot be asserted efficiently over the evil and lawless, then justice is to depend upon the action of the individual as the champion of order and protector of the community against the threat of anarchy and chaos. This was a basic precept of late-nineteenth-century imperialism in particular, which increased as the fear of subversion, disloyalty and loss of control (not only among its subject peoples but among its subjectors, administrators and out-casts from its system) grew stronger within the context of fierce interna-tional rivalry for power. Second, Silver's continual slippage between the domains of villainy (pirates) and legality (adventurers), so that he mediates between the two without ever really belonging to either, shows how he becomes a marginalised outsider posing a very direct threat (both of identity and potential chaos) to the groups from which he stands apart. Through this ambiguity – of being both representative of an ethos of barbarity and yet also aligned with the preservation of order and control – is power exerted. The pirate is, then, an object of awe and admiration as much as of fear and loathing; a model of both unconstrained masculine individualism and extreme debasement: 'I had taken such a horror of his cruelty, duplicity and power, that I could scarce conceal a shudder when he laid his hand upon my arm' (*TI*, p. 64). To bring together the two main points made above: in figuring an ideology of the individual unconstrained by commu-nity or state, able to act freely in an 'open' environment, the text ends up also having to negotiate – and it does so obsessively – the more unsettling implication of the threat posed by those who are not defined or categori-cally fixed subjects.

Inscribed within the conceptual framework of the text's foregrounding of the child's progression from innocence to maturity, a trajectory towards the values of an ordered adult universe, is the discourse of colonial adventure and exploration. The metaphor of learning (predicated upon seeing, observ-ing and, finally, knowing) is also fundamentally that of encounter and discovery. To this extent *Treasure Island* offers up a far from neutral envi-ronment. A colonial sub-text is interwoven into the very fabric of the fic-tion, providing the ideological boundaries within which the action takes place, giving meaning to the adventure as it unfolds. The primary engage-ment is with a vision of Britain's naval supremacy yet read off against the threat posed by the rivalry of other European powers, notably Spain and France. Given the specific temporal moment with which the text has chosen to align itself (the mid-eighteenth century), this particular context is not historically inaccurate. But neither can this context be severed from the moment of its literary reproduction at the height of Victorian imperialism. Significance must be attached as to why this particular thematic rather than any other should have been brought discursively to the fore. The late Victorian empire was marked by an increasing atmosphere of fear and uncertainty as international colonial rivalry progressively encroached upon the security of its self-image and its achievements. The major ideological

obstacles confronting colonial/imperial stability became less and less associated with the problem of the definition and understanding of subject races
and more with a concern to preserve and protect (both from hostile
European powers and, internally, from the threat of corruption, subversion
and disloyalty of those who existed on the margins of a vast and, in many
respects, fragmented empire) what had already been appropriated, territori-
ally and financially.

In *Treasure Island* the discourse of piracy acts as a double signifier of: (i)
the threat of degeneracy and corruption posed by those who are displaced
from a controlled system of broader signification and discipline (that is,
Empire), and (ii) the inherent superiority of British national assertiveness in
the international struggle for power. The text ceaselessly negotiates the
contradiction of this dual referentiality which demonstrates piracy as being,
on the one hand, a threat to national security and, on the other, a glamorous defender of it. Piracy is justified and justifiable when it provides a vision
which satisfies an heroic image of British colonial identity and when it
perpetuates a timeless narrative which speaks of a glorious national past.
Flint, for example, was 'the bloodthirstiest buccaneer that sailed. . . . The
Spaniards were so prodigiously afraid of him, that . . . I was sometimes
proud he was an Englishman. I've seen his top-sails with these eyes off
Trinidad, and the cowardly son of a rum-puncheon that I was sailing with
put back – put back, sir, into Port of Spain' (*TI*, p. 32). The treasure itself,
amassed over a long period, turns out to be an extravagant symbol of this
fearful national identity, a fine and rich tribute to the unrivalled success of
many a bloody colonial encounter:

> It was a strange collection, like Billy Bones's hoard for the diversity of coin-
> age, but so much larger and so much more varied that I think I never had more
> pleasure than in sorting them. English, French, Spanish, Portuguese, Georges,
> and Louises, doubloons and double guineas and moidores and sequins, the
> pictures of all the kings of Europe for the last hundred years, strange Orien-
> tal pieces stamped with what looked like bits of string or bits of spider's web,
> round pieces and square pieces, and pieces bored through the middle, as if to
> wear them round your neck – nearly every variety of money in the world must,
> I think, have found a place in that collection; and for the number, I am sure they
> were like autumn leaves, so that my back ached with stooping and my fingers
> with sorting them out.
>
> *TI*, p. 187

Traces of the British colonial experience intersect the text at different
points exercising an almost subliminal power. Silver's parrot, for example, –
the most neutral and unlikely bearer of colonial ideology – functions as

witness to perhaps some of the finest moments in almost two centuries of British colonial activity overseas:

> Now that bird . . . is, may be, two hundred years old, Hawkins – they lives for ever mostly; and, if anybody's seen more wickedness, it must be the devil himself. She's been at Madagascar, and at Malabar, and Surinam, and Providence, and Portobello. She was at the fishing up of the wrecked Plate ships. It's there she learned 'Pieces of eight', and little wonder; three hundred and fifty thousand of 'em, Hawkins! She was at the boarding of the *Viceroy of the Indies* out of Goa. . . .
>
> *TI,* p. 54

The construction of the fearfully ambiguous, marginalised other, Silver, is forcefully underpinned by the fact of his having taken a black woman as his wife – although she actually never appears, her absented presence is further legacy to the pirate's hybridity and monstrosity (given, that is, the ideological prohibition surrounding marriage between white colonists and native black women – a far more disturbing contract than the widespread practice of having a negro mistress: the latter could – despite fears of miscegenation – be far more easily assimilated since it was a relationship based so fundamentally on subservience and control, an extension of the expectations and duties implicit in the master/slave relationship).

As forceful an index of the text's engagement with the colonial venture which forms the historic baseline of its literary enterprise is provided in the concluding pages. There is a strongly misplaced episode which interrupts the text's presentation of the homeward voyage. Rather than employing the standard progression whereby the final image is that of reintegration back into the mother country, in *Treasure Island* the adventurers are forced to cast anchor

> in a most beautiful land-locked gulf, and were immediately surrounded by shore boats full of negroes, and Mexican Indians, and half-bloods, selling fruit and vegetables, and offering to dive for bits of money. The sight of so many good-humoured faces (especially the blacks), the taste of the tropical fruits, and above all, the lights that began to shine in the town, made a most charming contrast to our dark and bloody sojourn on the island.
>
> *TI,* p. 190

Not quite able to provide a satisfying ideological closure to the problems of subordination and control posed by those European 'savages' who have threatened the shores of Treasure Island, the text finally reinvokes the old horrors of racial otherness and of the moment of confrontation between the European and the non European in order to exhibit the extent to which they have been historically neutralised, sanitised and contained so that, paradoxically, they now pose no threat whatsoever. The imperialists are brought face to face with those who just thirty years previously (in, for example, *Masterman Ready* and *The Coral Island*) would have been the major actants in their drama, but who are now relegated to a minor role back stage. The good-humoured and charming blacks who once were – like the barbarous, degenerate pirates of the main narrative – the signifiers of fear and revulsion are now made to bear pitiful witness to the efficiency of the maintenance of European power. These, then, are fully interpellated, categorised subjects who act precisely as they are meant to act and who perceive and immediately fulfil their designated roles according to the European system of knowledge and representation through which their oppressors have sought for so long and so hard to identify them. Here is revealed (dialectically, in that progression from *Robinson Crusoe* through to *The Swiss Family Robinson, Masterman Ready* and *The Coral Island* to *Treasure Island*) the extent to which the problems to be confronted and overcome within colonial/imperial ideology become historically restructured and culturally redefined.

It is within this general political context that the fantasy unfolds, and in the form of its narration it is aligned still further with the major signifying elements characteristic of colonial fiction. Although the story is predicated upon a quest for treasure, which renders the island setting as significant only in so far as it functions as the harbour for that treasure, the text nevertheless – prioritising action over description, displaying over telling – provides a vivid portrait of the environment that is moved through; just as in *Masterman Ready* and *The Coral Island* the language of experience and the notion of self-education predicated upon seeing and observing is central to the elaboration of the ideological problematic. It is precisely the *lack* of explicit didacticism which works to remove the sense that the text is being regulated, ordered or controlled: the 'I' which writes of the lived experience thus decentres the fact of the authority with which it writes since it is ostensibly a simple transcription of 'what happened'. Learning the lessons of unrestricted freedom and how to act according to individualistic impulses, part of the boy-hero's function is actually to demonstrate that desire and ability to discover, explore, observe and also hear (Hawkins has a particular flair for this – see *TI*, pp. 56–62) more than his island companions. In this context the fact that he separates himself from his fellows during the course of the adventure is significant in that it is part of this impulse to gather further knowledge:

> I now felt for the first time the joy of exploration. The isle was uninhabited; my shipmates I had left behind, and nothing lived in front of me but dumb brutes

and fowls. I turned hither and thither among the trees. Here and there were flowering plants, unknown to me; here and there I saw snakes. . .

Then I came to a long thicket of these oak-like trees – live, or evergreen, oaks, I heard afterwards they should be called – which grew low along the sand like brambles, the bough curiously twisted, the foliage compact, like thatch. The thicket stretched down from the top of one of the sandy knolls, spreading and growing taller as it went, until it reached the margin of the broad, reedy fen, through which the nearest of the little rivers soaked its way into the anchorage. The marsh was steaming in the strong·sun, and the outline of the Spy-glass trembled through the haze.

TI, p. 73

As at least one commentator has eulogised, it is precisely this accuracy and precision with which the landscape is described that lends to *Treasure Island* its forceful 'realism' (Hammond 1984, pp. 107–8). But the real significance lies in the fact that the text negates its didacticism through this kind of virtually imperceptible slippage from a narrative of adventure into the essentially colonialist discourse of exploration and discovery.

The thirty or so years prior to the outbreak of the First World War witnessed increasing British investment in, and industrialisation of, existing colonies and that as a direct reaction to the forceful challenge being made by other industrial countries. This meant that, as a consequence of British expansionism, colonial territory, rather than being settled, was rapidly carved up in the intoxicated pursuit of new sources of raw material that would yield financial profit. Britain's growing orientation to overseas investment meant that traders, speculators and, indeed, 'adventurers' and 'individualists' were increasingly enticed out to the colonies, constantly on the look-out for new enterprises which would either capture financial backing from London or else would secure the means of immediate personal profit. To this extent, from the early 1880s the 'meaning' of geographical space as beheld by the coloniser/speculator was beginning to be radically redefined since it was no longer so much the signifier of permanent settlement as that of a temporary and often personal wealth. *Treasure Island* cannot succeed in resisting these historical claims upon its ideological unfolding – its non-idyllic, non-familiar landscape is not the object of a desire for containment. It remains at the end of the text just as it was discovered at the beginning, an abandoned outpost of Empire: stark, overgrown, rotting, decaying, 'unhealthy'. A fitting environment for the cargo of gruesome desperadoes – themselves physically deformed, crippled, mutilated, inscribed with otherness – who perpetrate evil, violence and bloodshed in their feverish quest for riches.

In contrast to the forceful images of the smooth-running, tightly-knit, atomised, well-organised, disciplined social organisms displayed in the earlier island fictions, *Treasure Island* presents a society essentially chaotic and orderless, pursuing disparate and individual needs. In this sense *Treasure Island* is more than simply a locus for a literary and temporal nostalgia: the myth of individualism transported some one hundred years on bears the full weight of its ideological alignment with the historic/political/cultural context within which it is reinscribed.

References

Hammond, J.R. 1984. *A Robert Louis Stevenson Companion: A Guide to the Novels, Essays and Short Stories*. London, Palgrave Macmillan.

Stevenson, R.L. [1883]2008. *Treasure Island*. Oxford, Oxford University Press.

Stevenson, R.L. 1894. 'My First Book: Treasure Island', in *My First Book: The Experiences of Walter Besant and Others*. London, Chatto & Windows.

Treasure Island and the Romance of the British Civil Service
Christopher Parkes

Recent scholarship devoted to Robert Louis Stevenson's *Treasure Island* has shown that the novel is constructed around sophisticated arguments about economics, class, and power. Without over-allegorizing the novel, scholars have demonstrated that within the rollicking adventures set in the eighteenth century there is a sophisticated commentary on the emergence, out of Britain's lawless past, of the modern industrial state. In her analysis of imperialism in the novel, Diana Loxley writes, 'the movement from the "reality" of the nineteenth-century world to a mythic plane of eighteenth-century piracy cannot be seen simply as a displacement of reading attention away from the struggles and deprivations of British society in a phase of high capitalism' (139). Similarly, in her analysis of the function of money in the novel, Naomi J. Wood argues that it 'provides an extensive commentary on the mechanisms of capitalist profit' (61). In his analysis of class struggle in the novel, Troy Boone argues that in its depiction of a pirate mutiny, the novel engages Victorian fears about 'a unified agitation to seize power by working-class subjects' (77). In this article I want to continue to uncover the novel's associations with the rise of the nineteenth-century industrial state

This is an edited version of the article originally published in *Children's Literature Association Quarterly* 31(4) (2007), pp. 332–45.

by examining its connections to the emergence of the modern civil service and administrative classes of Britain. In her study of Victorian children's literature, J.S. Bratton argues that there was a burgeoning market in the second half of the century for books that would help make middle-class boys a part of the machinery of the state: 'The greatly expanded ranks of the industrial and administrative middle classes needed all recruits who could be persuaded to make the effort to rise into them' (111).[1] My argument will be that *Treasure Island* grooms its hero, Jim Hawkins, to take his place in this emergent class. Through an analysis of the novel's interest in accurate accounting and the management of resources, I shall argue that in young Jim there emerges an image of heroic civil servant, one with energy and spirit. He comes to embody the myth of a civil service that, in doing the work of state and empire, is a technically proficient, administrative class but one with a taste for romance – a class that can both keep an accurate accounts ledger and fire off a brace of pistols.

In the thirty years before the publication of the novel, the British civil service underwent a period of expansion and reform.[2] By 1870 the reforms of the Northcote-Trevelyan report of 1854 were being implemented.[3] The report called for the end of patronage. It argued for the appointment of men from the universities who could pass an examination. It also argued that university men should no longer begin at the lowest rank and that the civil service should be divided into two classes, clerks and managers, to allow for the rapid advancement of talented individuals. Trevelyan expected the new kind of recruits to be more robust than what he referred to as the 'sickly youths' of aristocratic families: 'It would be natural to expect that so important a profession would attract into its ranks the ablest and most ambitious of the youth of the country' (qtd. in Hennessy 39). The fear that the British civil service would become a dumping ground for sickly youths is one that can be found early on in its history. Peter Hennessy notes in his study of Whitehall that during the reign of Charles II, civil servants were thought to be too meek and mild to do the work of the nation. Charles wanted '"rougher hands," "ill-natured men, not to be moved with civilities"' (qtd. in Hennessy 24). Some had doubts, however, that Trevelyan's men, those who could pass an examination, would fit the ideal of the rugged civil servant. Sir James Stephen, for example, complained that the youths of the Colonial Office 'possessed only in a low degree, and some of them to a degree almost incredibly low, either the talents or the habits of men of business, or the industry, the zeal, or the knowledge required for the efficient performance of their appropriate functions' (qtd. in Campbell 36). He doubted that men of energy and ambition would want to attempt to rise up in the ranks of the civil service given the thankless nature of the job: 'He must listen silently to praises bestowed on others which his pen has earned for them' (qtd. in Campbell 36).[4] The search for robust and literate men to fill the ranks was more successful to an extent after the First World War because large numbers of appointments were held for returning servicemen, but, according to Hennessy, the interwar period was still marked by complacency: 'By the late 1930s the Civil Service was a staid organization at virtually every level' (86–7). He notes that the civil servant H.E. Dale wrote that in this period 'he had only known four officials who displayed "intense energy, great driving force and devouring zeal" ' (qtd. in Hennessy 75). E.J. Hobsbawm writes in *The Age of Empire* that along with the emergence of the modern welfare state, and with the enormous increase in the number of public servants in the late nineteenth century, came a less romantic and more disciplined national landscape: 'the steamroller of collectivism, which had been in motion since 1870, flatten[ed] the landscape of individual liberty into the centralized and levelling tyranny of school meals, health insurance and old age pensions' (103).[5] According to Hobsbawm, the rise of collectivism brought about the death of a romantic age of individualism. In the nineteenth century, however, the civil servant was constructed as the figure that could hold together for society the binary opposites of individualism and collectivism. The civil servant was constructed as a heroic individual working for the safety and security of the state.

The almost impossible balance between a life of office work and a life of romance is one that Stevenson recognized in his own family. As civil engineers, his grandfather and father built Scotland's lighthouses.

Stevenson's family of engineers can be placed in the context of the other great development in the British civil service, the rise of the Victorian expert. While the model of the civil servant envisioned by Trevelyan tended to lean toward a liberal humanist model – his exams involved rather more Greek and Latin than mathematics and chemistry – people of technical ability became increasingly vital to the performance of government. Stevenson's grandfather and father were Victorian experts – men of specialized ability without whom the work of government could not be done; there could hardly be a family that more neatly fits the romantic ideal of the civil service.

Kimberley Reynolds argues in her study of Victorian children's literature that the usual fare for boys, adventure stories by Ballantyne, Kingston, and Hentry, for example, were mostly anti-intellectual: 'Skills such as boxing, shooting and sailing are understood to sharpen the wits more effectively than studying the subjects likely to make up the syllabus for most middle-class boys' (70). Most books for boys from the period give their heroes only physical expertise, and thus they cannot he said to imply directly a future in the administrative classes for their heroes and readers. *Robinson Crusoe*, a book to which Stevenson continually refers in his essays, is a better model for *Treasure Island* than the typical nineteenth-century adventure story for the way it gives its hero administrative expertise. Anyone who has read Defoe's novel knows that the high adventure of the story – stormy seas, shipwrecks, and cannibals – is tempered by long passages in which Crusoe is an accountant figure meticulously tabulating and recording his available resources. As John Bender notes, 'Defoe's pervasive listings – his accountings, inventories, census reports, bills of lading, logs, and diaries – fictionally reinscribe the origins of writing as the medium of power' (58). Crusoe is able to maintain, through writing and accounting, such a control over the island that he rises up through the ranks of the administration that he himself has built. Strange that a shipwrecked man should be able to rise up in rank, but the sea keeps offering up individuals like Friday to become lower than Crusoe in the administrative hierarchy. Crusoe may think of himself as a king but he achieves his power through very modern means – the efficient administration of his resources. He is able to take the liminal space of the island and transform it into an emergent nation-state because he first transforms it into an enclosed jurisdiction with an efficient bureaucracy. In the process, his narrative reconciles individualism and collectivism. Individualism is satisfied as he achieves an upwardly mobile career path – one with virtually no ceiling – and collectivism is satisfied as he establishes a disciplined society.

The idea that Jim Hawkins is destined for a career in the civil service is best supported by the fact that he is mentored by Doctor Livesey, who is the novel's civil servant figure. He is the local doctor and magistrate; he is respectable, educated man whose library is 'lined with book-cases and busts upon the top of them' (30). He is also the only person in the community strong enough to stand up to Bones. Livesey warns Bones that he will be under surveillance; as long as he is in Livesey's jurisdiction he is inside settled society and must act accordingly. As the local magistrate, Livesey's job is to bring lawlessness and liminality under bureaucratic control, and, in doing so, he must himself be heroic and adventurous.

When the treasure map is discovered in Bones's chest, it is turned over to Livesey because he is considered the figure best able to manage it. Supervisor Dance, the local revenue collector who also shows himself to be a rugged civil servant when he saves Jim and his mother from the blind beggar Pew, turns the map over to Livesey on the advice of Jim: 'perfectly right – a gentleman and a magistrate. And, now I come to think of it, I might as well ride round there myself and report to him or squire. Master Pew's dead, when all's done; not that I regret it, but he's dead you see, and people will make it out against an officer of his Majesty's revenue, if make it out they can' (29). Dance will file a report to absolve himself of blame in Pew's death – exciting events will be controlled and disciplined by bureaucracy – and the map will be handed over to a more senior official. There is again the sense of an administrative network keeping the liminal world of romance under control.

Once on the island, Livesey then takes on the role of local health inspector. As the island's medical expert, he works to bring the island under control by mapping its healthy and unhealthy sites. Anne Hardy notes that public health experts were brought into government in the middle of the nineteenth century: 'in the years 1855–1875 they also became administrators and generators of sanitary legislation; by the end of the period, by force of government demand for their services, they had become professionals with specialist qualifications and career patterns' (129). Christopher Hamlin notes that the health of the London water supply was much debated in government in the 1860s; the cholera epidemic of 1866 in particular sparked many reports and inquiries (111).[6] Silver, however, works directly against Livesey's control of the island. At one point, he deliberately fouls the water supply by spitting into the spring near the stockade: 'Growling the foulest imprecations, he crawled along the sand till he got hold of the porch and could hoist himself upon his crutch. Then he spat into the spring' (108). The doctor later informs Silver that the reason many of the mutineers are dying is that they have camped in a swamp. Because the pirates have no public health experts, theirs is an unsafe society. Because the pirate society has no body of knowledge upon which they can draw, to enter into it is to remain an isolated and vulnerable individual. This point is illustrated to Jim when he retakes the Hispaniola and finds that the sickly mutineers have used pages from a medical book to light their pipes.

In the commercial world of Jim's parents, expertise is important, but it does not operate in conjunction with a collective spirit. When Pew's gang attacks the Benbow, Jim's mother remains meticulous in her accounting of the debt that is owed to the tavern by Bones: ' "I'll show these rogues that I'm an honest woman," said my mother, "I'll have my dues and not a farthing over" ' (22). Jim, however, sees her obsession with accuracy as almost pathological because her stubbornness nearly gets them killed: 'But my mother, frightened as she was, would not consent to take a fraction more than was due to her, and was obstinately unwilling to be content with less' (23). Her accurate accounting is what makes her blind to the larger issue of her own escape. As Boone writes, 'Jim represents the upwardly mobile lower-middle-class notions of respectable culture' (73), but respectable culture in this moment comes perilously close to a kind of petty or blinkered individualism. The idea that there is no collective spirit contained within middle-class commercialism is supported by the fact that none of the townspeople will come to the aid of Jim and his mother. She calls them 'big, hulking, chicken-hearted men' (20) because they are too cowardly to stand up to the pirates. The settled world may be respectable but with too much respectability comes a lack of heroism. The local community is a collection of meek and petty individuals who will not, as Livesey does, fight for the greater good. The townspeople in fact come to admire the pirates for their bravery, the kind that 'made England terrible at sea' (4). When Jim first sees the doctor he recognizes how the civil servant figure operated between the two societies: 'I remember observing the contrast the neat, bright doctor, with his powder as white as snow, and his bright, black eyes and pleasant manners, made with the coltish country folk, and above all, with that filthy, heavy bleared scarecrow of a pirate of ours, sitting far gone in rum, with his arms on the table' (5). Livesey has the expertise and respectability of the settled world in combination with the bravery and derring-do of the pirated. The narrative, however, is often aware that the doctor is potentially an unsatisfying compromise between the meek townspeople and the disorderly pirates. Indeed, the narrative acknowledges one of the great dilemmas of children's literature – the stories full of bad characters are almost always more exciting that the stories about good characters. When Bones tells his wild tales to the patrons of the Admiral Benbow, the locals are enthralled: 'People were frightened at the time, but on looking back they rather liked it' (4). With such great excitement, however, comes a short lifespan as Bones soon drops dead from a stroke brought on by the fear of the black spot and his nonstop drinking.

The pirate society may be chaotic and undisciplined but it does have a kind of rudimentary administration. The pirates may not know about health and safety, but they do have a legal system. The may not be literate enough to compose a legal writ, preferring instead the black spot, but, in their alternative society, the same kind of accurate accounting that ensures upward mobility in middle-class society also ensures it in pirate society. In Billy Bones's log book, which is discovered along with the treasure map, romantic and mysterious phrases such as 'Off Palm Key he got it' (32) are found alongside tables of numbers detailing the business affairs of his many voyages. The log book also contains 'a table for reducing French and Spanish moneys to a common value' (33). Bones rose up in rank because of his accounting ability, his attention to detail, and his clear reporting. His managing of accounts formalizes the business of pirating and, as the doctor and squire see it, is the key to his advancement. Ironically, the man who once terrorized the Admiral Benbow comes to be admired for his middle-class frugality; ' "Thrifty man!" cried the doctor. "He wasn't the one to be cheated" ' (62). The business activities of the pirates come to resemble the business activities of Jim's parents. Jim's mother is certainly more scrupulous than the pirates who do not mind taking what is definitely not owned to them, but when the veneer of respectability is stripped away we find that middle-class society is also motivated by profit. The narrative doubles Bones and Jim's mother in order to show that in neither commercial enterprise, legal or illegal, is there a cause greater than the bottom line.

When Squire Trelawney goes to Bristol to outfit a ship, he finds Long John Silver in the guise of a respectable member of settled society, Indeed, the most frightening aspect of Silver's character is his ability, unlike the other pirates, to infiltrate the middle-class world. He is able to contain his violence and criminality within the guise of a respectable publican. As a simple tavern-keeper, his ability to manage the books is taken as evidence of his respectability:

> I forgot to tell you that Silver is a man of substance; I know of my own knowledge that he has a banker's account, which has never been overdrawn.

The bank account is proof enough for Trelawney that Silver is respectable enough to be taken on the voyage. He sees himself in Silver, imagining that both are members of settled society who go to sea in an attempt to escape enclosure and to recapture boyhood romance and adventure.

Jim is not suspicious that Silver is the one-Legged man that Bones has warned him of because he appears to him as a kindly father figure. As Loxley writes, 'The image of nurturing fatherhood is sanctioned . . . not only by Silver's fearsome bravery but by a wealth of internalised knowledge and wisdom' (156). Silver has the same job as Jim's father, and he has the same interest in accurate accounting. He may not be an expert on health, but when Silver takes Jim on a tour of the Bristol docks, he presents himself as both an expert seaman and, as someone who can give a precise account of the work being done on the docks, an expert administrator. Silver's marshalling of resources in his walk with Jim reminds the boy of his own father while his display of technical knowledge gives him an air of middle-class respectability. His apparent balance of romance and expertise makes him a dangerous alternative to Doctor Livesey when it comes to the mentoring of young Jim. The doubling of both Silver and Bones with Jim's parents does not allow us to read the pirates as simply the opposite of respectable middle-class shopkeepers. Rather, the pirate and shopkeeper are two sides of the same coin. Pirates are what happens when the profit motive of the shopkeeper is allowed to operate outside the space of England and beyond notions of reapectability. When the shopkeeper is transported to the colonial world, respectability falls by the wayside as the mercenary pursuit of profit, free of any collective impulse, becomes paramount.

One of the reasons that the pirate society exists in the first place is that the British government does not provide pensions for ex-servicemen. When the blind beggar Pew comes to the Benbow looking for Billy Bones, he is described as a disabled veteran who has not been properly compensated by the government. Similarly, in his letter to Livesey concerning Silver, Trelawney writes that Silver will go on the treasure hunt because he had received no government support after serving his country: 'Long John Silver, he is called, and had lost a leg; but that I regarded as a recommendation, since he lost it in his country's service, under the immortal Hawke. He has no pension, Livesey. Imagine the abominable age we live in!' (69). Clearly, the pirate society does not take care of its members, but, as the squire points out, neither does settled society. The pirates, in turns out, are a product of settled society and its lack of public assistance. In other words, there would be no pirates if ex-servicemen were properly rewarded by a public welfare system.[7] It stands to reason, therefore, that if the pirate identity is created by the state then it can be taken away by the state. This proves to be the case when the mutineers are eventually defeated in battle and laid low by disease. They come to be described as charity cases: 'they had taken [Livesey's] prescriptions, with really laughable humility, more like charity school-children than blood-guilty mutineers and pirates' (275). The pirates are defeated in battle, but, more importantly, they are defeated by Livesey, the civil servant, who brings them under state control. It is as if public assistance has the ability to destroy the pirate identity.

The efficiency with which Livesey's crew wages war would have resonated with readers familiar with Britain's many administrative blunders during the Crimean War. The victory over the mutineers is the result of administrative control working together with military might. Captain Smollett's logbook becomes vital to their success as it allows the good side to keep track of its manpower. When Jim leaves his post to go explore the island, he exists outside the captain's log – outside recordkeeping – and, therefore, outside the settled world. He makes it back just in time, however, to be reckoned in the account. Later on when he deserts his post to capture the Hispaniola he operates outside the logbook, and thus he comes perilously close to being lost to the good side. Even before the mutiny begins, Jim gives an accurate accounting of manpower when he computes the numbers on the good side versus those on the bad: 'In the meantime, talk as we pleased, there were only seven out of the twenty-six on whom we knew we could rely; and out of these seven one was a boy, so that the grown men on our side were six to their nineteen' (67). The ability to keep track of the other side becomes difficult, however, as the war rages. As the account grows imprecise, the good side's victory is threatened: 'There had come many from the north – seven, by the squire's computation; eight or nine according to Gray' (111). The chapter ends, however, with a reestablishment of order through an accurate accounting of manpower: '"five!" cried the captain. "Come, that's better. Five against three leaves us four to nine. That's better odds than we had at starting. We were seven to nineteen then, or thought we were, and that's as bad to bear"' (114). Jim adds a footnote to the captain's words: 'The mutinees were soon only eight in number, for the man shot by Mr. Trelawney on board the schooner died that same evening of his wound. But this was, of course, not known till after by the faithful party' (114). The reader comes to experience the battle not through a wrenching description of blood and valor but through the account ledger. In this way, administrative expertise is shown to be just as important as military strength.

At the end of the novel, when Jim, returns to his post after having deserted it to retake the Hispaniola, he is given the job of counting the treasure, and, in this way, he is absorbed back into the state apparatus. Having proved that like the pirates he has the spirit to 'make England terrible at sea,' he must then prove his administrative hierarchy to assume a position with more responsibility than his original position, cabin boy:

> It was a strange collection, like Billy Bones's board for the diversity of coinage, but so much larger and so much more varied that I think I never had more pleasure than in sorting them. English, French, Spanish, Portuguese, Georges, and Louises, doubloons and double guineas and moidores and sequins, the pictures of all the kings of Europe for the last hundred years, strange Oriental pieces stamped with what looked like wisps of string or bits of spider's web, round pieces and square pieces, and pieces bored through the middle, as if to wear them round your neck – nearly every variety of money in the world must, I think, have found a place in that collection; and for number, I am sure they were like autumn leaves, so that my back ached with stooping and my fingers with sorting them out.

187

The counting is much more like drudgery than fighting to retake control of a ship, but Jim expresses great pleasure at performing the task. He is back inside the settled world of account ledgers and defined ranks. He has become a kind of clerk in the treasury office but he is still connected to the romance of the high seas, which is here embodied in the exotic coins. As Wood writes, the coins 'call up all the romance of fabulous wealth and faraway places, the words suggesting not only buccaneering but also the hoards in the Arabian Nights' (70). By the novel's end, Jim is enclosed inside a hierachical work space, but it is a work space that remains connected to the romance of the global trade network. In the task of counting money, he achieves a kind of romantic drudgery.

The treasure, with its wild and exciting history in the world of romance – 'How many it had cost in the amassing, what blood and sorrow, what good ships scuttled on the deep, what brave men walking the plank blindfold, what shot of cannon, what shame and lies and cruelty, perhaps no man alive could tell' (185) – is, in the end, taken out of the world of the pirates and redistributed within the respectable middle-class world. Rather disappointingly, there are no scenes of characters rolling around on a big pile of money and no conversations about the conspicuous consumption of wealth. As Wood writes, 'Stevenson shows the money gravitating to its "proper" owners, those who will most nurture it in investment, rather than those who would squander it in a grand spree' (71). Each crew member's share of the money becomes a kind of pension. Smollett uses the money as a retirement pension after his years of service, while Gray uses it as a kind of start-up grant to become a ship's mate and owner. He rises in rank because he gains technical knowledge of his profession, but the amount of money is not so great that it frees him from middle-class labor. Jim's accurate accounting of time – not three weeks but nineteen days – indicates that Ben Gunn had lost his money because he could not account for it properly. Unlike the others, he treats the money as if it is still pirate booty. After so many years marooned on a deserted island, he has trouble adopting middle-class respectability. Before he can handle such a large sum of money, he must first adopt the shopkeeper's values, and thus he is, in the end, 'given a lodge to keep, exactly as he had feared upon the island' (191). Ultimately, the reified and fetishized money that Jim counts is transformed into abstract capital; the individual nature of the coins disppears as the money comes to function as a pool of funds for pensions and start-up grants. Just as knowledge is collected in medical books for the advancement of society, so the money is collected in a treasury that can be accessed by the collective.

Jim's final words are calculated to warn others away from the liminal world of romance: 'Oxen and wain-rops would not bring me back again to that accursed island; and the worst dreams that ever I have are when I hear the surf booming about its coasts, or start upright in bed, with the sharp voice of Captain Flint still ringing in my ears: "Pieces of eight! pieces of eight!"' (191). The story concludes with the sense that Jim will remain in the settled world, that he will become a rugged civil servant like his mentor Doctor Livesey. Undoubtedly, *Treasure Island's* great appeal is that it is a wish fulfillment; it allows a young boy to leave home, to run away from both his mother's authority and the drudgery of waiting tables in a tavern; it allows yound Jim to break free of social constraint into the world of romance. When he negotiates his way back into the settled world, however, he does so as a figure that combines the heroism found in the adventure world with the technical expertise found in the settled world. He achieves a respectable career but one that, in working for the good of society, is not involved in crass commercialism. Stevenson's words to a young man choosing a profession – 'if you are in a bank, you cannot be much upon the sea' – indicate that in bringing the liminal world of romance under control, society necessarily dooms itself to a lack of adventure, but in public service Stevenson sees the possibility of reconciling the two. While it is true that government work cannot really compare with the excitement of being a pirate, pirate society offers a very poor pension plan.

Notes

1. Jenifer Hart, in the 'The Genesis of the Northcote-Trevelyan Report,' explores the question of whether middle-class access to the civil service was an influence on civil service reform, the idea that 'middle-class desire for free entry to the public offices was a factor of no little importance in civil service reform; the older professions were overcrowded, and the middle classes were troubled about the future of their sons' (64).
2. Between the 1850s and 1890s the civil service doubled from approximately 40,000 to 80,000 (Hennessy 51). Between 1891 and 1911, it tripled (Hobsbawm 103).
3. Hennessy, Chester, and Chapman and Greenaway provide useful overviews of the report.
4. Hennessy identifies one figure, however, that fit the ideal. Edward Bridges, who went on to become head of the civil service in 1945, was, he notes, 'a war hero and a connoisseur of literature – the incarnation of the romantic ideal' (76). See Bridges for his overview of the civil service. McKechnie's *Romance of the Civil Service* has an intriguing title but does not discuss the romantic ideal of the civil servant.
5. See A.V. Dicey for a contemporary view of the rise of collectivism in the late nineteenth century.
6. See Mary Poovey, *Making a Social Body*, 115–31, for a discussion of sanitary legislation in the 1840s. She writes, 'the sanitary idea constituted one of the crucial links between the regulation of the individual body and the consolidation of those apparatuses we associate with the modern state' (115).
7. The modern welfare state is, of course, a twentieth-century phenomenon, but in the 1880s when Stevenson's novel was published the idea of the public pension was prominent. Friendly Societies, for example, were operating as a precursor to government pensions.

References

Bender, John. *Imagining the Penitentiary: Fiction and the Architecture of Mind in Eighteenth-Century England*. Chicago: U of Chicago P, 1987.

Boone, Troy. *The Youth of Darkest England: Working-Class Children at the Heart of Victorian Empire*. New York: Routledge, 2005.

Bratton, J.S. *The Impact of Victorian Children's Fiction*. London: Croom Helm, 1981.

Bridges, Edward. *Portrait of a Profession: The Civil Service Tradition*. Cambridge: Cambridge UP, 1950.

Campbell, G.A. *The Civil Service in Britain*. Harmondsworth: Penguin, 1955.

Chapman, Richard A., and J.R. Greenaway. *The Dynamics of Administrative Reform*. London: Croom Helm, 1980.

Chester, Sir Norman. *The English Administrative System, 1780–1870*. Oxford: Clarendon, 1981.

Defoe, Daniel, *Robinson Crusoe.* Ed. J. Donald Crowley. London: Oxford UP, 1972.

Dicey, A.V. *Lectures on the Relation Between Law and Public Opinion in England during the Nineteenth Century,* London: Macmillan, 1917.

Hamlin, Christopher. 'Politics and Germ Theories in Victorian Britain: The Metropolitan Water Commission of 1867–9 and 1892–3.' *Government and Expertise: Specialists, Administrators and Professionals, 1860–1919.* Ed. Roy Macleod. Cambridge: Cambridge UP, 1988. 110–27.

Hart, Jenifer. 'The Genesis of the Northcote-Trevelyan Report.' *Studies in the Growth of Nineteenth-Century Government.* Ed. Gillian Sutherland. Lanham, MD: Rowman and Littlefield, 1972. 63–81.

Hennessy, Peter. *Whitehall.* Rev. ed. London: Pimlico, 2001.

Hobsbawm, E.J. *The Age of Empire, 1875–1914.* New York: Pantheon, 1987.

Loxley, Diana. *Problematic Shores: The Literature of Islands.* Basingstoke: Macmillan, 1990.

McKechnie, Samuel. *The Romance of the Civil Service.* London: Sampson Low, Marston, 1930.

Poovey, Mary. *Making a Social Body: British Cultural Formation, 1830–1864.* Chicago: U of Chicago P, 1995.

Reynolds, Kimberley. *Girls Only? Gender and Popular Children's Fiction in Britain, 1880–1910.* Philadelphia: Temple UP, 1990.

Stevenson, Robert Louis. *Treasure Island.* Oxford: OUP, 2008.

Wood, Naomi J. 'Gold Standards and Silver Subversions: *Treasure Island* and the Romance of Money.' *Children's Literature* 26 (1998): 61–85.

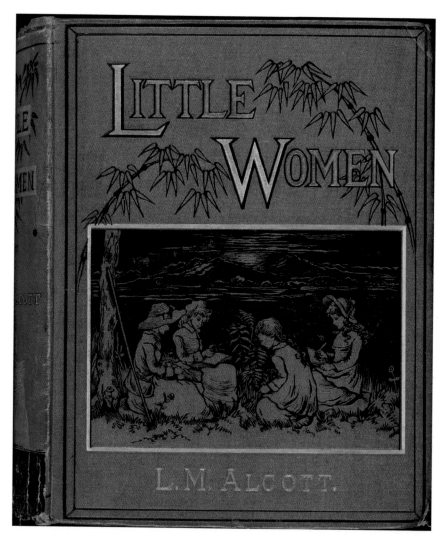

Plate 1 Front cover, Louisa May Alcott, *Little Women* (1868), illus. Frank T. Merrill, London: David Boyne, 1880. By kind permission of the Bodleian Library, University of Oxford, shelf-mark: Bodley 251 a.110. An elaborate gilt pictorial binding on cloth, typical of the closing decades of the nineteenth century, emphasising the genre of *Little Women* as a family story.

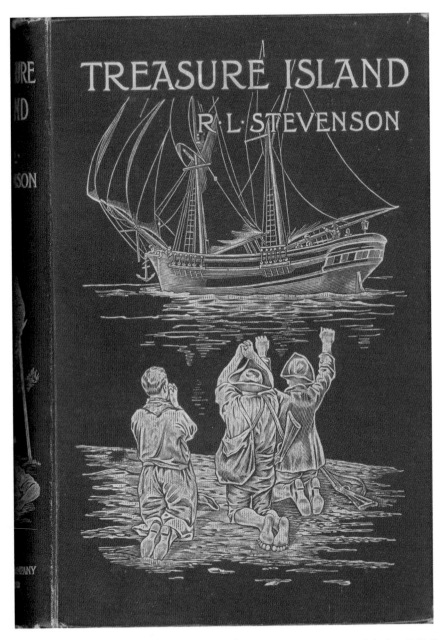

Plate 2   Front cover, Robert Louis Stevenson, *Treasure Island*, London: Cassell & Co., [1881] 1883. By kind permission of Alamy Ltd. © Mary Evans Picture Library/Alamy. An elaborate cloth-binding typical of the period, this time emphasising the story's connections with previous exercises in the Robinsonnade.

Plate 3 Front cover, Robert Louis Stevenson, *A Child's Garden of Verses,* illus. Millicent Sowerby, New York: Charles Scribner's Sons, 1905. By kind permission of the British Library. © British Library Board. All Rights Reserved, shelfmark: 11650.h.36. Early twentieth-century cloth and gilt binding make this edition of *A Child's Garden* a suitable gift-book. Note the slight period flavour given to the children's clothes, denoting the book a 'classic'.

THE TALE OF PETER RABBIT

™

BEATRIX POTTER

THE ORIGINAL AND AUTHORIZED EDITION

New colour reproductions

F. WARNE & Co

Plate 4   Front cover, Beatrix Potter, *The Tale of Peter Rabbit*, London: Frederick Warne & Co. Copyright © Frederick Warne & Co., [1902], 2002. By kind permission of Frederick Warne & Co. Published in the long tradition of small books for children, the *Peter Rabbit* books measure 14.5 cm by 10.5 cm. Their deliberately child-friendly size was not for reasons of economy; in fact, the printers used the most expensive process then available to do justice to Potter's original watercolours. The use of coloured halftone photomechanically produced blocks meant that these books were luxury items. The process required printing on expensive, coated, shiny paper, very different to the rougher paper more usually used for text – the Potter books were printed in their entirety, cover, text and all, on this sort of paper.

Plate 5 Design for a theatre poster by Charles Buchel advertising the original 1904 production of J.M. Barrie's *Peter Pan*. By kind permission of Mary Evans Picture Library. This poster (from a watercolour) shows the original stage costuming of Peter Pan with a red cloak – the green Peter Pan, half Robin Hood, half wood-spirit, was yet to emerge; the Germanic village below and the romantic posture of the flying pair both suggest the play's affinity with Edwardian fairy tales.

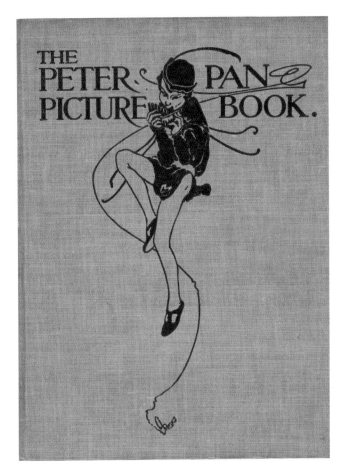

Plate 6 Front cover, Daniel S. O'Connor and Alice B. Woodward, *The Peter Pan Picture Book*, London, George Bell & Sons, 1907. By kind permission of the Bodleian Library, University of Oxford, shelfmark (Nuneham): 2527 d.271. This lavishly illustrated book came to be sold instead of the original souvenir booklet, *The Peter Pan Keepsake*, which was illustrated with production photographs and provided with a continuous prose narrative. The picture book retained the prose narrative, but instead of photographs provided colour illustrations showing children, rather than adults acting as children; the pictures serve both as record of contemporary stage practice (Peter Pan, for example, is still dressed in red) and to suggest the ways in which *Peter Pan* was already becoming independent of theatrical performance.

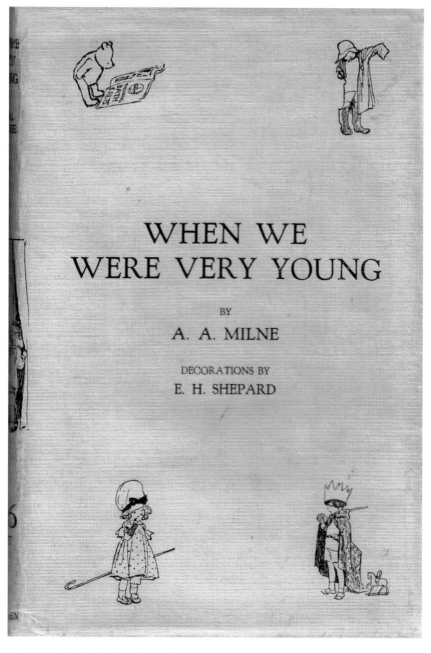

WHEN WE
WERE VERY YOUNG

BY

A. A. MILNE

DECORATIONS BY

E. H. SHEPARD

Plate 7 Dust jacket, A. A. Milne, *When We Were Very Young*, illus. Ernest. H. Shepard, London: Methuen & Co. Ltd, [1924] 1932. Copyright © The Estate of E. H. Shepard, reproduced with permission of Curtis Brown Group Ltd, London. The familiarity of Shepard's black-and-white line drawings (or 'decorations', as they were termed) belies their originality in their time: the pages then appeared very unconventional. In particular, the illustrations seemed airy, unframed and informal in their relation to the text. Shepard drew Christopher Milne and his toys from life.

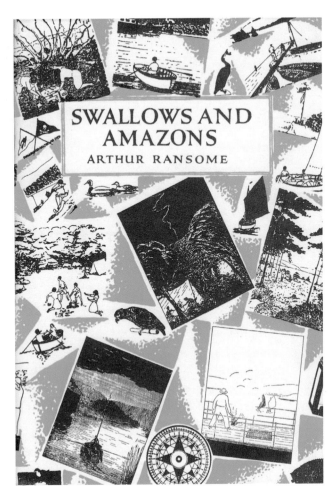

Plate 8 Dust jacket, Arthur Ransome, *Swallows and Amazons*, illus. Arthur Ransome, London: Jonathan Cape, [1930] 2008. By kind permission of Random House Group Ltd. This recent reprint of *Swallows* and *Amazons* reproduces the original dust-jacket design for the 1931 cloth edition. It is a composite of Ransome's own line drawings illustrating the story. Ransome had disliked the original dust jacket by Steven Spurrier, although Spurrier's original map, reminiscent of that accompanying *Treasure Island* was retained in the endpapers. The fact that Ransome's book was reissued in this format in 2008 underscores its current status as a twentieth-century classic, not merely not in need of updating, but enhanced by its period flavour.

Plate 9 Dust jacket, Philippa Pearce, *Tom's Midnight Garden,* illus. Susan Einzig, Oxford: Oxford University Press, [1958] 2008. By kind permission of Oxford University Press. This cover was designed by illustrator Susan Einzig, a *Kindertransport* child and refugee from Nazi Germany. Her own sense of exile and of being a child out of place chimes perfectly with the themes and mood of Pearce's novel.

Plate 10 Dust jacket, Mildred D.Taylor, *Roll of Thunder, Hear My Cry,* illus. Jerry Pinkney, New York: Dial Press, 1976. By kind permission of Penguin Group (USA) Inc. and Cotsen Children's Library, Princeton University Library, Department of Rare Books and Special Collections. Call number: Eng 20 20633. Pinkney's design is consciously social realist in mode.

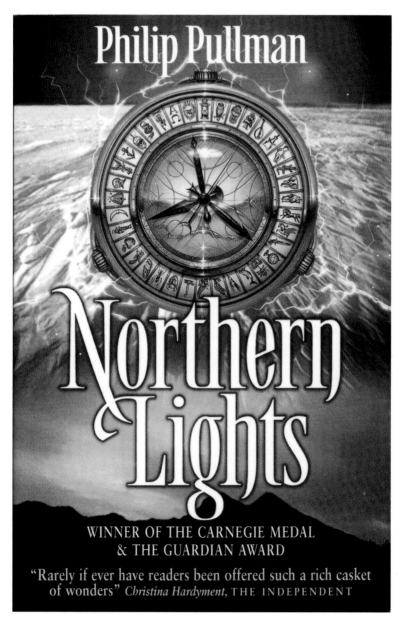

Plate 11 Front cover, Philip Pullman, *Northern Lights*, London: Scholastic Children's Books, 1998. Cover artwork © David Scutt, 1998. Reproduced with the permission of Scholastic Ltd. All Rights Reserved. There are now many different editions of Pullman's novel and many different covers, but this is the original paperback cover. It gives almost nothing away as to the book's contents, but neither does it position the book as aimed at either sex or any particular age group.

HARRY POTTER

and the Philosopher's Stone

J.K.ROWLING

HOGWARTS EXPRESS

Triple Smarties Gold Award Winner

Plate 12 Front cover, J.K. Rowling, *Harry Potter and the Philosopher's Stone*, London: Bloomsbury Publishing Plc, 1997. Cover illustration by Thomas Taylor. By kind permission of Christopher Little Literary Agency and Bloomsbury Publishing Plc. Rowling's Harry Potter series is remarkable in the history of children's publishing for being published almost simultaneously in a variety of covers. In Britain *Harry Potter and the Philosopher's Stone* was originally published as a cheerful-looking fantasy children's book, but it rapidly acquired a new 'adult' cover. Equally remarkably, covers varied from country to country; the German Harry Potter does not look much like the English, nor the English like the Chinese, bar the black hair and round spectacles.

CILIP CARNEGIE MEDAL TOP TEN BOOK

MELVIN BURGESS

junk

winner of the *Guardian Fiction Award* and the *Carnegie Medal*

Plate 13 Front cover, Melvin Burgess, *Junk*, London: Penguin Books, 1997. Copyright © Melvin Burgess, 1997. By kind permission of Penguin Books Ltd. This paperback cover lays claim to photo-realist issue-driven topicality.

CARNEGIE MEDAL WINNER

BEVERLEY NAIDOO

The Other Side of Truth

A lie has seven winding paths, the truth one straight road

Plate 14 Front cover, Beverley Naidoo, *The Other Side of Truth*, London: Puffin, 2000. Copyright © Beverley Naidoo, 2000. By kind permission of Penguin Books Ltd. A cover that advertises social realism and responsible pathos.

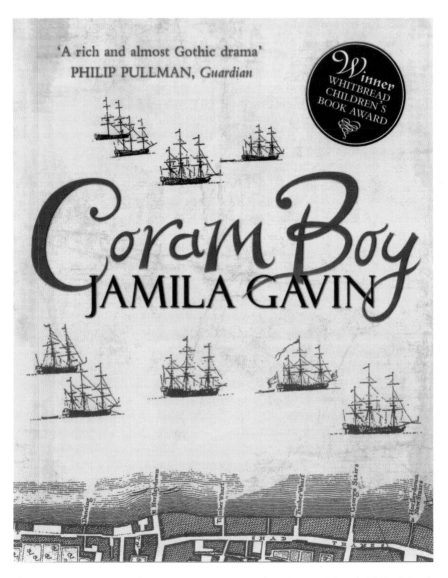

'A rich and almost Gothic drama'
PHILIP PULLMAN, *Guardian*

Winner
WHITBREAD
CHILDREN'S
BOOK AWARD

Coram Boy
JAMILA GAVIN

Plate 15 Front cover, Jamila Gavin, *Coram Boy*, London: Egmont UK Ltd, 2000. © Jamila Gavin 2000. By kind permission of Egmont UK Ltd and Guildhall Library, City of London. A cover that suggests adventure in a historical London.

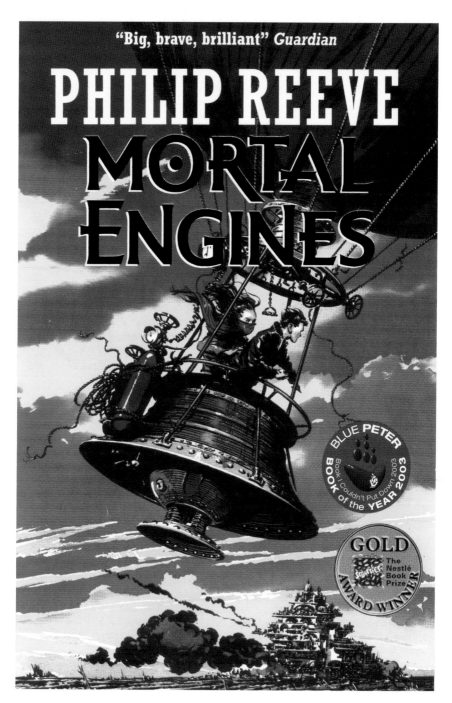

Plate 16 Front cover, Philip Reeve, *Mortal Engines*, London: Scholastic Children's Books, 2001. Cover Artwork © David Frankland, 2001. Reproduced with the permission of Scholastic Ltd. All Rights Reserved. A cover suggesting fantastic excess of subject matter and plot.

3

Beatrix Potter, *The Tale of Peter Rabbit* (1902)

Introduction
Sharon Goodman

The Tale of Peter Rabbit is the first, and the best known, of a series of twenty-three books which came to be known as Beatrix Potter's 'little books' (this series consisted of twenty-one animal stories and two books of nursery rhymes). It was published by Frederick Warne in 1902, and has remained both in print, and phenomenally popular with children, ever since. Part of a long tradition of storytelling involving animals with human (and often child-like) traits – a tradition dating back at least to the fables of Aesop around 600 BC in Ancient Greece – such anthropomorphic tales are often assumed to have as their guiding principle the instruction of the child in important issues of life choices and morality, and to do this in a way perhaps less direct and threatening than straight didacticism might prove. However, Potter's tales, and Peter Rabbit in particular, show some resistance to being read as straightforwardly moral tales.

Beatrix Potter's reputation for the quality of both her writing and water-colour illustrations remains as strong today as ever, and Peter Rabbit is a publishing phenomenon, available in almost any format imaginable, from board and stencil books, to CD-ROMs and dolls. Humphrey Carpenter (1989) points to her influence on other writers, such as Blake Morrison, Graham Greene and Christopher Isherwood; her work continues to be highly valued by academic critics and retains an important place in the canon of children's literature in English.

Origins and composition

The Tale of Peter Rabbit was written initially as a series of 'picture letters' to Noel Moore, the child of Potter's friend and former governess, Annie Carter, in September 1893 is shown below.

Figure 2　Picture letter to Noel Moore by Beatrix Potter from L. Linder, *A History of the Writings of Beatrix Potter,* London: Frederick Warne & Co., 1971, pp. 7–8. Courtesy of the Frederick Warne archive.

'Now my dears', said old Mrs Bunny
'you may go into the field or down
the lane, but don't go into Mr McGregor's
garden.'

Flopsy, Mopsy + Cottontail, who were good
little rabbits went down the lane to gather
black berries, but Peter, who was very naughty

Figure 3 Picture letter to Noel Moore by Beatrix Potter from L. Linder, *A History of the Writings of Beatrix Potter*, London: Frederick Warne & Co., 1971, pp. 7–8. Courtesy of the Frederick Warne archive.

The notion of turning her picture letters into books came to Potter a few years later (she reclaimed her letters from Noel to this end), but although submitted to several publishers, her proposal was at first universally rejected. After much discussion about the size of the book (Potter was adamant that her story should be easily manipulable by little hands, and was keenly interested in all aspects of its production), and after much toing and froing over the number of illustrations to be printed in colour, a private publisher printed 250 copies of the book in 1901; subsequently, Frederick Warne accepted it, and it was an instant success.

Like the artist and author Edward Lear (1812–88) whose work she much admired, Potter thus addressed Peter Rabbit to a real child, and attributed the success of the book, at least in part, to this (Linder, 1971: 110). She also identified the illustrator Randolph Caldecott (1846–86) as a considerable influence on her own style of illustration.

Potter was determined that her drawings should be both anatomically accurate, and complement the nature and character of the creatures she depicted (she studied and sketched animal skeletons in the Natural History Museum in London, so as to understand better the physical characteristics of the animals she wished to draw). Peter may wear a jacket when he leaves his home to 'go out in public', but he remains very much a normal wild rabbit in both appearance and behaviour, and reverts to type once in the vegetable patch. Potter's illustrations often position the reader as sharing the viewpoint of the main protagonist in the story, which, being lower down than the adults depicted, can be seen as a child's perspective also; such is the case in *Peter Rabbit*. A strategy for ensuring empathy with the characters, this goes some way to account for the enduring charm of Potter's illustrations and the longevity of their appeal to children.

Reception/critical terrain

Critics have long been interested in Peter Rabbit because of this enduring popularity and cultural success. In explaining something of the reasons for this, Melissa Gross (2002: 145) notes that certain children's texts come to have an appeal, over and above readers' general expectations of excellence in story, writing and illustration:

> Some characters from children's literature become so strongly associated with childhood itself that exposure to a particular book at the appropriate age is seen by many as a highly desired experience, one not to be missed. Such books have something to say to children that adults and the culture at large feel they need to hear.

Viewed like this, one reason for Peter Rabbit's popularity may well be that some of its central themes relate to the processes of child socialisation and acculturation. Probably the most often discussed of these is the theme of disobedience or transgression. The critical tradition surrounding Peter Rabbit is characterised by disagreement as to whether or not Potter takes a moral stance towards Peter's rule-breaking behaviour – behaviour that so nearly ends in his being killed in the garden by Mr McGregor. Does Potter simply depict the wild rabbit that Peter becomes outside the confines of his safe and comfortable home, once he loses his symbolic human coverings of jacket and shoes while on the run from the gardener? Or is this tale 'about' childish disobedience punished? What is the meaning of the camomile tea that Peter is made to drink at bedtime on his return? It is seen by some as punishment-by-medicine (since Peter's sisters eat the bread, milk and blackberries he is denied) and by others as comfort after his exhausting ordeal.

The camomile tea is only one instance of food in the tale. Other critics have concentrated on the book's emphasis on food; or rather, not food per se, but its meanings – the location of its provision, the distinction between forbidden and permitted food, and the socialising role of family meals. There is already plenty to eat at home, of course:

> By contrast, in the garden – a place outside the civilizing sphere of family and home – the food is, for Peter, hazardous to his health and well-being, because the food is in the garden, a place where Peter is no longer in control of his identity.
>
> Pollard and Keeling, 2002: 119

To critics with a psychoanalytic slant, Peter's desire for – and adventures with – the food available outside the home may also be seen as symbolising a desire to move away from his mother because 'food and the mother are deeply connected':

> The child's relationship with food is entwined with a basic drive to survive, with mother's love, and with comfort, punishment, motivation, and reward. It was food that lured Peter (and his father) to Mr. McGregor's garden.
>
> Gross, 2002: 152

Such themes, then, run through the book; we focus principally here on that of morality, and of the role of text and illustrations in the story.

The essays

The three pieces in this section all deal, in different ways, with the question of the moral tendency of Peter Rabbit. Margaret Mackey traces the adaptation and reversioning of Peter Rabbit into different editions, and different media, focussing on the relationship of text and illustrations. Potter's distinctive language and detached tone receive particular attention, for example her matter-of-fact description of events such as Peter's father having been made into a pie by Mrs McGregor. The integration of text and pictures, and the use of overall design elements in the book are also, Mackey argues, important narrative devices that involve the reader and move the story forward. Peter Hollindale traces the influence of Potter's background, including her early career as a naturalist, on her development as an author/illustrator of children's books, before turning to consider her work in the light of other animal fables, particularly those of Aesop. He argues against the notion that *The Tale of Peter Rabbit* is fundamentally a moral fable in the tradition of Aesop. Carole Scott also tackles the issue of Potter's ambivalent moral perspective in Peter Rabbit. She considers how this ambivalence can be seen to be expressed through word–image interaction, for example via the narrative perspective (point of view) of illustrations and words. She goes on to discuss how, in Peter Rabbit, the separation of words and images differs from techniques used in some more modern picture books.

References

Carpenter, H. 'Excessively Impertinent Bunnies: The Subversive Element in Beatrix Potter', in G. Avery and J. Briggs (eds) *Children and Their Books: A Celebration of the Work of Iona and Peter Opie.* Oxford, Clarendon Press.

Gross, M. 2002. 'Why Children Come Back: The Tale of Peter Rabbit and Where the Wild Things Are', in M. Mackey (ed.) *Beatrix Potter's* Peter Rabbit: *A Children's Classic at 100.* Lanham, MD, Scarecrow.

Linder, L. 1971. *A History of the Writings of Beatrix Potter.* London, Frederick Warne.

Pollard, S. and Keeling, K. 2002. 'In Search of His Father's Garden', in M. Mackey (ed.) *Beatrix Potter's* Peter Rabbit: *A Children's Classic at 100.* Lanham, MD, Scarecrow.

Further reading

Frey, C. 1987. 'Victors and Victims in the Tales of Peter Rabbit and Squirrel Nutkin', *Children's Literature in Education,* 18, 105–11.

Hollindale, P. 'Humans Are So Rabbit', in M. Mackey (ed.) *Beatrix Potter's* Peter Rabbit: *A Children's Classic at 100.* Lanham, MD, Scarecrow.

Linder, L. 1971. *A History of the Writings of Beatrix Potter.* Frederick Warne, London).

Peter Rabbit: Potter's Story
Margaret Mackey

On my table lie 35 books of *The Tale of Peter Rabbit*. Each is different in some important way. There are other versions of the book on the market, but this sample is reasonably representative. All 35 of these books are simply bound sets of words and pictures purporting to tell the story of Peter Rabbit. Some of them are authorized by Frederick Warne; others are not. Some of them include Potter's own words and pictures, although not all of these features Potter's own words and pictures arranged on the page in the form and design she originally dictated. Some of the books include Potter's own words and someone else's pictures; others include Potter's own pictures and someone else's words. Eleven books contain the story both retold and reillustrated. Surely, in such a range of versions, there are discoveries to be made about how we may define and talk about a textual work of art in our time.

The original text

Three of my copies are editions of the little book produced by Potter. To all intents and purposes, this is now a stabilized text. Potter's first telling of the story came in a letter to a friend, followed by a privately published edition and then by the first of many printings produced by Frederick Warne. Early print runs led to some changes, but by the fifth printing the text and pictures were recognizable as we know them today and the text has not changed since 1903 (Linder, 1971, pp. 108–9).

My three copies of this text are very similar but not identical. The quality of production in the artwork varies, but otherwise the most significant differences among them probably lie on the copyright pages. The copy which was bought for my children, probably in 1981, is undated and simply asserts the copyright ('in all countries signatory to the Berne Convention') of Frederick Warne. The 1987 version is more aggressive. It establishes copyright of the text and original illustrations as of the first publication date, 1902, and goes on to declare a separate copyright for the new reproductions, dated 1987. Unusually for a copyright page, it includes a paragraph asserting the virtues of the new edition:

> The reproductions in this book have been made using the most modern electronic scanning methods from entirely new transparencies of Beatrix Potter's original

Originally published as Chapter 1 in M. Mackey, *The Case of Peter Rabbit: Changing Conditions of Literature for Children* (New York and London: Garland, 1998), pp. 3–13.

watercolors. They enable Beatrix Potter's skill as an artist to be appreciated as never before, not even during her own lifetime.

p. 6

I bought the third small-text version in the United States. It is a Dover Edition paperback which purports to be an 'unabridged republication of the work first published in 1903' (p. 2). By 1903, the published text had more or less stabilized into the version familiar today. It is not clear whether Dover's edition is a reproduction of the Warne 1903 copy or of the American pirate edition. There is no mention of Frederick Warne anywhere in the Dover copy.

The colors in the Dover version are very dark and sludgy compared to either of the other two editions. The print is very marginally larger and the arrangement of words on the page is therefore not quite identical, though the differences are extremely slight. The actual ordering of words and pictures is exactly the same.

To my eye, the two Warne editions are identical except for the increased subtlety and detail of the illustrations in the newer production. Brian Alderson, however, suggests that the new reproductions fall short of the standards established in the first editions of the Potter books.

> It has been an honorable, and expensive undertaking and the results compare very favorably with the often wayward reproductions that figured in post-war editions of the books. Many pictures now emerge with a spirited freshness . . . How far the plates measure up to the author's intentions is less easy to assess . . . I have been able to compare all the 23 books with their editions (all of which were supervised by Beatrix Potter) and the new 'authorized' series often falls short of the standards established there. Time and again plates appear to be too lightly tinted so that detail is lost (Lakeland landscapes are a blur; peeping faces fade into the background) or natural appearances alter (blackbirds look like thrushes; bluebells turn mauve). In addition there has been a regular move to enlarge the pictures – which may, in fact, bring them closer to their original size, but which causes them to swamp the books's small pages (nor does poor positioning on the page help here).
>
> 1987, p. 63

It is important to note that every reproduction of a text may carry some costs. For this study, however, I shall not develop any detailed comparisons but simply refer to the 1987 production with the 're-originated' pictures, as representing the original text.

The Tale of Peter Rabbit

There are at least three distinctive elements of the picture book considered as art form: the gutter which divides the two pages of any opening, the demands of the page turn, and the convention that words and pictures will work together in some complementary way. Other aspects of the book (text, pictures, overall design) can be judged by criteria established in other genres.

These six general topics can aid us in reaching judgement on a particular picture book. Potter's work bears investigation under all six headings.

Text

The content of the story of Peter Rabbit is fairly slight. Peter is forbidden by his mother to enter Mr. McGregor's garden, since his father was put in a pie by Mrs. McGregor. He disobeys this injunction and stuffs himself with vegetables to the point of feeling sick. At this point, he encounters the dreaded Mr. McGregor and a terrible chase ensues. Sparrows, a mouse and a cat are all unable to help him. Eventually, Peter escapes and arrives home with a stomach-ache. His mother doses him with camomile tea, but his more obedient sisters have bread and mild and blackberries for their supper.

The telling of the story is considerably more distinctive than the plot outline. Potter's language is spare and ironic. On the surface, she is clearly on the side of law and other; Peter's misdeeds are punished by his terror in the garden and by his stomach-ache and unsympathetic treatment that night. But the detached tone with which Potter describes Peter's disobedience actually functions to raise the question of just whose side she is on.

All the ambiguities of the word 'brisk' may be applied to this story: the pace of the telling is sharp and lively; the author's matter-of-fact attitude suggests that Mrs. Rabbit's strictures about the garden never had a chance with a young rapscallion like Peter. And yet, the wording, while spare and polished, is more than just 'brisk'; it is supple and elegant, without a superfluous syllable. Potter claimed that when in doubt about her style she turned to her Bible which encouraged her to cut and simplify.

> My usual way of writing is to scribble, and cut out, and write it again and again. The shorter and plainer the better. And read the Bible (unrevised version and Old Testament) if I feel my style wants chastening.
>
> quoted in Lane, 1968, p. 135

Much has been written about Potter's refusal to write down to her young readers; the sentence usually quoted as the telling example from *The Tale of Peter Rabbit* is this one:

> Peter gave himself up for lost, and shed big tears; but his sobs were overheard by some friendly sparrows, who flew to him in great excitement, and implored him to exert himself.
>
> p. 36

Similarly, in terms of the content, Potter pulls no punches; Mr. Rabbit's horrible fate is made clear on the second page of the story. Again the word 'brisk' comes to mind, yet the wording is delicate as well as robust. 'Your father had an accident there,' says Mrs. Rabbit; 'he was put in a pie by Mrs. McGregor' (p. 11). The euphemism of the word 'accident' is sharply negated by the subsequent explanation, but even in the final phrase the use of the passive voice and the humor of the incongruity mitigate the appalling facts, if only slightly.

In the original letter to Noel Moore, the reference to Peter's father and the pie does not appear. By contrast, in both the privately published text and in Warne's very first edition, the horror was more graphically conveyed than in the version we have come to know. The remark about Peter's father originally had its own page, complete with a picture of Mrs. McGregor serving a handsome pie (Linder, 1971, Plate 4). These early versions also enlarged on Peter's sensations while lost in the garden. After the mouse fails to help him, the story continued.

> Then he tried to find his way straight across the garden, but he became more and more puzzled. There surely never *was* such a garden for cabbages! Hundreds and hundreds of them; and Peter was not tall enough to see over them, and felt too sick to eat them. It was just like a very bad dream!
>
> Linder, 1971, p. 52

A further section, later deleted, was even more gothic:

> He went towards the tool-shed again, but suddenly there was a most peculiar noise – scr-r-ritch, scratch, scritch. Peter scuttered underneath the bushes. Then someone began to sing. 'There blind mice, three blind mice!' It sounded disagreeable to Peter; it make him feels as though his own tail were going to be cut off: his fur stood on end.
>
> Linder, 1971, p. 53

The text in these early editions also contains further details about Peter's mother, interpolated upon his return to the fir-tree. Most of these eventually appeared in *The Tale of Benjamin Bunny* and emphasize the hardship of her working life.

The deletions were made for reasons which demonstrate that even an original work of art has to work within the constrains of its methods of production. Warne specified that they could afford a total of 30 color illustrations plus the frontispiece, so Potter had to remove 11 pictures from the privately printed edition which included mainly black and white pictures. Sometimes she transferred the corresponding text to another page;

sometimes she deleted the text altogether. Further cuts were made after the fourth edition had been printed in 1903, in order to make room for colored endpapers which, among other functions, advertised other titles in the series of little books.

Insofar as Potter approved all the changes, the text we use today may be considered her final best opinion on *The Tale of Peter Rabbit*. Nevertheless, today's version is really the fourth production of this story, preceded by the letter to Noel Moore, the privately printed book, and the very early editions from Frederick Warne. There were some slight changes made and revoked over subsequent editions, but effectively today's version has been available since 1903. To keep this study readable, that 1903 text, in its 1987 incarnation, is the one I shall refer to as the 'original' *Peter Rabbit*, in order to distinguish it from all its imitators.

In the 1903 text, as in its predecessors, Potter provides an authoritative, though not intrusive, narrative voice. Her editorial comments are direct: 'good little bunnies,' 'very naughty.' The narrative 'I' appears only twice (pp. 35 and 67), but the feeling of a story under the control of the storyteller is always present.

The story of Peter Rabbit raises real questions of great significance for young readers. Peter disobeys his mother without a moment's hesitation, and her powers of punishment appear to be limited to the dose of camomile tea. Her response to the loss of the jacket and shoes is confined to 'wondering' (p. 64). The threat represented by Mr. McGregor, however, is enormous. Peter, running and hiding in the garden, is in a state of very real jeopardy; he and his young readers are entitled to be truly terrified. Potter does not belabor this point, but she does not camouflage it either. Peter, both as a rabbit and as child, lives in a world where some options are closed to him, but all choices have consequences. His dawning awareness of his own mortality is not made explicit anywhere in the book but it does dominate the story.

Contemporary sensibilities have raised questions about gender in this story. The good girls and the bad boy are stereotypes which have a lingering afterlife even in our own enlightened time. The tearaway son of the widowed mother is another highly conventional figure. Mrs. Rabbit's difficulties with Peter are clear to see, but Potter does not take sides. Peter takes foolish risks out in the world, but home is still safe and his mother is there to look after him.

However the details of this story suit us today, it is clear that *The Tale of Peter Rabbit* tells a story and raises issues that are not trivial, and that resonate with small children who must also work out the limits of obedience, assertion and consequences.

Pictures

The small watercolors which also tell the story of Peter Rabbit are as distinctive as the prose. Potter's delicate lines and washes are instantly recognizable. While the stories reflect her acuity about human foibles, her pictures are famous for the care with which she portrays recognizable animal demeanor, despite the clothes and the upright postures.

Overall, the pictures communicate a strongly unified effect. There is no sharp framing of the pictures but none of them floats unanchored in space. If the background does not provide linkage for the figures in the foreground, Potter substitutes a light grey background shading so that no figure is unconnected from the others. Even the picture of Peter slipping into the watering can (p. 41), which is the closest to free-standing, is grounded by a very pale grey shadow.

The little vignettes are irregularly shaped. Many of them are some form of rough rectangle or oval. Often details of the drawing break the boundary of this shape, which is, in any case, rather nebulously established. Mr. McGregor's outline rises above the background on page 26, for example; Peter and Mr. McGregor are both silhouetted against the white page in the next drawing on page 29, although a grey wash connects their feet. Peter and the watering can on page 41 create their own outline. In other cases, smaller details break the frame, such as it is; the rake handle obtrudes past the background wash on page 42, Peter's ears do the same on the next page, as does the mouse's tail on page 50.

The home scenes, with two exceptions, are firmly anchored in a relatively regular shape, some form of rectangle with rounded corners. One exception is the frontispiece which shows Mrs. Rabbit dosing Peter with the camomile tea. The other exception is the second picture within the main body of the story. Mrs. Rabbit is issuing her warning about Mrs. McGregor's garden. Flopsy, Mopsy and Cotton-tail are receiving their baskets and their instruction with equal docility; Peter, with his back turned and his whiskers on the alert, is clearly entertaining rebel thoughts. The picture serves almost as a form of technical foreshadowing; we are not surprised, later on, to find the cosy ovals and rectangles disappearing. This picture makes a similar contribution to the plot; there is nothing in the words to suggest problems to come (except the well-known convention that a character in a book would not issue such a warning for nothing), but the picture makes it plain that Flopsy, Mopsy, Cotton-tail and Peter are not all cut out of the same cloth.

The decision to produce the pictures in color is (as we will often find in this study) one marked by questions of judgement, technology and price. Potter's own privately printed book contained largely black-and-white drawings, partly because of price considerations, partly because of her fears about the technological difficulty of color reproduction and partly because she thought the colors might be repetitive over so many drawings, consisting as they did mainly of 'rabbit brown and green' (Linder, 1971, p. 21). Warne insisted on color but this decision meant that the number of illustrations must be reduced. Potter wanted to use a three-color printing process used by Hentschel and there was much negotiating over costs and royalties as a consequence. Warne's 1987 reorigination of the pictures is simply one more stage in an ongoing process.

Openings and gutters

Potter's use of the gutter is straightforward and conventional; on any double-page opening there is one page of text and one page of picture. In *The Tale of Peter Rabbit*, the pictures alternate without exception between the right page and left page of the opening.

One aspect of the book that sets it apart is the exquisite visual balance between text and picture. The gutter is used almost as an equilibrium-setter. Text and picture are each set slightly towards the top of the page, and the blocks of text contribute much the same weight to the page as the opposing watercolor vignette. The sense of control and regularity thus created is considerable, and may indeed contribute its own weightiness to help answer the question. 'Whose side is Potter really on anyway?' Visually, law and order rule across the gutter. A set of words is associated with a particular picture in an utterly stable way.

Page turns

The page-turning requirement of a picture book contributes a great deal to the overall impact of the text. On a page full of print, it is just about impossible to dictate that the eye must not flick on ahead and spoil the surprise. When the next words and pictures are hidden over the page, the author may be much more definite in announcing surprises. Furthermore, the page turn takes time, builds in obligatory pauses in the reading. Its contribution to the rhythm and pacing of a text is enormous. No amount of punctuating and paragraphing can be as absolute as the built-in break (break?) of a page turn.

Beatrix Potter, working at a relatively early stage in the evolution of the picture book, shows a command of the page turn which has rarely been bettered. The page breaks serve many narrative and poetic purposes. The good behavior of Flopsy, Mopsy and Cotton-tail is established (pp. 16–17); the potential for contrast lingers for the time of the page turn before we see

Peter heading straight for Mr. McGregor's garden (pp. 18–19). Peter's feast on the vegetables (pp. 22–3) lingers for a moment while the page is turned, time enough for the consequence of feeling rather sick to set in on pages 24–5. Mr. McGregor himself, appearing on the very next page (pp. 26–7), comes as a complete surprise to the reader as well as to Peter; the page turn in this case has acted as a shield. When Peter hides in the watering can (pp. 40–1), the delayed mention of the water appears at the end of the page, setting up suspense over the consequences to Peter, and this time the page turn delays resolution. By the end of the book, we are not surprised to find the last two openings (pp. 66–9) returning to the symmetry of contrast between Peter and his sisters. To those who have read the story aloud over and over again, the timing of these pauses becomes an integral part of the story and its performative impact. The story is shaped around the bursts of text and the delays.

And yet, some of these page breaks were based on contingent rather than absolute artistic decisions. When Warne decreed color and also said that 11 drawings would have to go, Potter was obliged to repaginate much of her text. She could play with the limits of convention and form, but some of the limits of technical reproduction were non-negotiable. Such limitations are part and parcel of almost any form of art which is publicly distributed.

Design

Size, shape, arrangement of words and pictures on the page, choice of typeface and arrangement of lines of print, all these design details contribute to the overall impact of a picture book. The element from this list which is most immediately associated with Potter's books, of course, is size. The little books, which Potter insisted should be the right size for small hands, are as distinctive for their dimensions as for many other ingredients. Libraries and bookshops often locate them separately and very early on in the book's publishing history, special bookshelves were marketed for the Peter Rabbit stories.

Other design elements also contribute to the overall effect, and another distinctive element in *The Tale of Peter Rabbit* is the use of white space. Margins are generous, especially at top and bottom. The amount of text varies from page to page, a fact which provides yet more reassurance that the page turns were chosen for esthetic impact rather than because the author ran out of room. The effect is one of spaciousness and stability. A particular set of words and a particular picture are juxtaposed on purpose. The words end at a given point because the next words belong to the next picture. No matter how contingently the original decision was made, more than 90 years of fixity have made their mark. The effect is subtle but psychologically real: each opening is *under control*.

Integration of pictures and text

One of the conventional distinctions between a picture book and a story with illustrations is that, in the picture book, both words and pictures are essential to the telling of the story. The pictures are not simply an additional embellishment; they share with the words the task of conveying the import of the story.

On this level, *The Tale of Peter Rabbit* is s triumphant success. The illustration of Peter and his sisters on page 11 conveys far more about character and potential plot of development than any word in the text. At the opposite end of the spectrum, words and picture on pages 42–3 work quite differently. The rabbit in the illustration could be merely disconsolate; from the text we know that Peter was in a state of extreme terror and confusion. On pages 52–3, where Peter sees the cat, text and picture combine to create a *tour de force* of reticence; neither is explicit about the sinister potential of the cat, but the sense of menace is clearly conveyed.

All the elements of this little book combine to create a commentary on a issue of vital importance to small children: the importance and limits of order and stability versus the importance and risks of disobedience and self-assertion. The overwhelming achievement of the book is its ultimate ambiguity on this topic. The reticences of the text (Peter had a stomach-ache, but he also had the feast and Potter never makes any explicit judgement on his behavior), the potential for anarchy in the frame-breaking pictures versus the containing stability of the surrounding white space and page boundaries, the security of the rhythms of words and page turns, all combine to support a bounded and limited consideration of the important idea that risks have consequences.

References

Alderson, Brian. 'Peter's New Colors.' *Times Educational Supplement*, June 5, 1987: 63.

Lane, Margaret. *The Tale of Beatrix Potter: A Biography*, 1946. Revised edn. London: Frederick Warne, 1968.

Linder, Leslie. *A History of the Writings of Beatrix Potter, Including Unpublished Work*. London: Frederick Warne, 1971.

Potter, Beatrix. *The Tale of Benjamin Bunny*. London: Frederick Warne, 1904.

———. *The Tale of Peter Rabbit*. New reproduction. London: Frederick Warne, [1902] 2002.

Aesop in the Shadows
Peter Hollindale

The name of Leslie Linder is rightly an honoured one for students of Beatrix Potter. It can be an intimidating one too. How can we match the dedication and the scholarship that he brought to the task he set himself? To Leslie Linder we owe the breaking of the code in which Potter wrote her journals, and hence the publication of a text which has permanently altered the way we think and write about her. For Linder it was a labour of love. All literature – and especially children's literature – ought to be the province of the amateur as well as the professional, but Linder was the most formidable kind of amateur, who can beat the professionals at their own game without even being aware of a spirit of competition. For Linder there were no rivalries; just love of a chosen author, and unstinting industrious pleasure in the work. He is a salutary model for professional academics, and for me it is a great pleasure to contribute to the lecture series founded in his memory.

Leslie Linder the code-breaker is the special model I have in mind. His work reminds us that Beatrix Potter was a specialist in concealment, a person not habitually disposed to show her hand. Literary critics love writers who offer them the challenge of codes. Like Benedick in *Much Ado About Nothing*, we delight in saying 'Ha! There's a double meaning in that!' But the ingenuity can often be the critic's rather than the author's. So I shall proceed with caution, and try to show the importance of a much simpler and more obvious code than the one that Linder unlocked: the partially coded presence of Beatrix Potter the naturalist in the work of Beatrix Potter the artist and storyteller.

Alison Lurie, in her essay on Potter called 'Animal Liberation', makes a key point: 'If Beatrix Potter had been born in this century, or if she had been born a man, there is little doubt that she would have become a famous painter, a well-known naturalist, or both' (90).

It seems there's quite a tendency to claim Beatrix Potter for some other potential role in life – something else that she did or might have done rather than make books for little children. After all, she staked her own claim to different ways of life and achievement – as a mycologist before she wrote the books, and after them as a farmer and sheep-breeder. Other people have not been slow to follow, and still aren't. In April 1997 Professor Roy Watling saluted her work as a biologist in a commemorative talk at the

---

This is an edited version of the article originally published in *Signal*, 89 (1999), pp. 115–32.

Linnean Society, and in an article luridly headed 'Beatrix Potter boiled squirrels', the *Sunday Times* reported him as saying:

> I have to confess I hate those books. It is incongruous that anyone could treat animals so scientifically and then make them into stories like those. If only the Linnean Society had behaved better it need never have happened.

God bless the Linnean Society for not behaving better. However, Professor Watling inadvertently points us in the right critical direction. What he regards as incongruity is actually the centre of Potter's originality and the source of her pervasive influence on the modern animal story.

So much for the might-have-beens. As for the things she did do, here is the National Trust Handbook (1996): 'Beatrix Potter's most important achievement [was] her saving of 2429 hectares of the Lake District, and her careful and sensitive conservation of this magnificent area on behalf of the nation.' Her achievement as a conservationist is very important, certainly, just as the mycology is very important – but *most* important? Surely not if we read the little books properly. Remarks like these are evidence of the continuing tendency to belittle children's literature – with some complicity in this case from the author herself, it must be admitted. But Margaret Lane in *The Magic Years* admires the very incongruity that Watling so deplored, referring to 'the fascination which her mice held for her as subjects both of study and fantasy . . . which remained with her to the end of her life.' This is a better clue to a reading of the books, and it is that ruthless combination of study and fantasy in the little books themselves that I want to examine: the dialogue between anthropomorphic human comedy and biological truth.

Although we might all feel that the books matter most, we must nevertheless recognize with Margaret Lane that always – from the early childhood dissections, carried out upstairs at Bolton Gardens, via the South Kensington Museum (now the Victoria and Albert Museum), the Natural History Museum, and Kew, to later life as a Lakeland farmer – Potter was a meticulous student of natural history and natural science. Unless we follow her example, we may fail to decode her stories.

The interest in natural history expressed itself in two equally important ways. On the one hand there is the fondness for real, individualized animals, for animals as a kind of *people* – the childhood pets, and those of adult life, with names and characters immortalized: Peter Rabbit; Mrs Tiggy-winkle; later on the black Berkshire pig who didn't meet pedigree requirements and inspired Pig-wig; in due course the individual stock on the farms. And simultaneous with that, the scientific, detached observation, the dissections, the forensic skill, the ruthlessly practical farming. There is here a consistent double perspective which can make the brown rat, Samuel Whiskers, both a person and a pest.

Although an original, Beatrix Potter was not an eccentric or a one-off. She belongs to an artistic and – as a naturalist – an intellectual tradition. She moves with ease, as [Konrad] Lorenz does, between the biological reality of the animal and the social behaviour of the human. By taking her seriously as both a naturalist and a satirist, and reading the books as conversations through the medium of fantasy between these two selves, these two Beatrix Potters, we can appreciate the originality of her achievement.

An obstacle to understanding her in this way can be that it is all too easy to see her as a moralist – to make her a fabulist like Aesop rather than the post-fabulist artist of the modern age which I think she is. 'Post-fabulist' can be a helpful term for Potter. She recognizes Aesop, and a debt to Aesop: he's an ancestor. But he is truly 'in the shadows', while she is an imaginative artist in the daylight of a scientific age.

This means that Potter the moralist is a slippery customer. It is easy to decode the books and find a satisfying moral in them: treacheroulsy easy. We can see the pitfalls in a comment by the novelist Susan Hill. Hill, a poor naturalist whose books are littered with ornithological solecisms, is also un-Pottersque where morals are concerned:

> Beatrix Potter was a realist, as she was also a moralist. Naughtiness may be understood. It is never condoned. Flopsy, Mopsy and Cotton-tail, who were good little rabbits, ate bread and milk, and blackberries for supper, but Peter was dosed with camomile tea. This is the world of the Victorian nursery.

This is pure nonsense. Alison Lurie comments more shrewdly on the same incident:

> Another new and very important feature of Beatrix Potter's books was that they broke completely with the traditional pattern of the animal tale or fable, which had always been used to point an improving moral. Usually the unconventinal message is concealed behind a screen of conventional morality, which might have fooled adults, but not their juniors and betters. In *Peter Rabbit*, for instance, Potter at first seems to be recommending restraint and obedience. At the end, Peter is sent to bed in disgrace after his exciting adventures in Mr McGregor's garden, while good little Flopsy, Mopsy and Cotton-tail 'had bread and milk and blackberries for supper'. But when I asked a class of students which character in the book they would have preferred to be, they voted unanimously for Peter, recognizing the concealed moral of the story: that disobedience and exploration are more fun than good behavior, and not really all that dangerous, whatever Mother may say.

This is much nearer to the moral centre of Potter. Of course she·is morally aware. She is also subversive, as Alison Lurie and Humphrey Carpenter, among others, have suggested. But that is not the most important thing.

Natural history, I would suggest, governs both moralism and sedition in Potter's little books. Morals, in Potter stories, are not so much rules of conduct as facts of life – which is what you might expect of a scientific naturalist, pathologist and field observer. It *is natural* for young animals to explore their surroundings, to leave the nest and their mother's protection, to play away from home. (Who had better cause to know that than Beatrix Potter, with her childhood and early adulthood of close familial confinement?)

When young animals explore, they often come to grief. Every naturalist knows that. So the little books show a spectrum of such adventures, and they do not fall into a simplistic moral pattern. In *The Tale of Samuel Whiskers* Tom Kitten is, so to speak, 'strung up' for *his* adventurings. In *The Tale of Benjamin Bunny* the cat is a serious danger, but pain and retribution really come from old Mr Bunny's switch. (And the disciplinary parent gets his own comeuppance in *The Tale of Mr. Tod.*) But Peter Rabbit is *not* sent to bed in disgrace. He is sent to bed because he caught a cold by hiding in the watering can. This is not a moral at all, but a fact of life for juvenile explorers: a case of bed by misadventure.

There is not a common moral pattern in these stories, only a common pattern of natural animal and child behaviour, with the haphazard consequences that life itself provides.

Everywhere in Potter's work we find both the artist and the natural scientist – the double self which draws on storytelling traditions but used the skills of a biological observer to remake them in the image of a new century.

References

Susan Hill, *The Lighting of the Lamps*, Hamish Hamilton, 1987.

Margaret Lane, *The Magic Years of Beatrix Potter*, Warne, 1978.

Alison Lurie, 'Animal Liberation', in *Don't Tell the Grown-ups: Subversive Children's Literature*, Bloomsbury, 1990.

Beatrix Potter, *The Journal of Beatrix Potter from 1881 to 1897*, transcribed from her code writing by Leslie Linder, Frederick Warne, 1966.

Beatrix Potter, *The Tale of Peter Rabbit*, Frederick Warne, [1902] 2000.

Roy Watling, 'Beatrix Potter boiled squirrels', *Sunday Times*, 16 February 1997, News Section, p. 3.

Perspective and Point of View in *The Tale of Peter Rabbit*
Carole Scott

Like the Victorian-Edwardian period itself, the apparently straightforward *The Tale of Peter Rabbit* – the archetypical naughty-boy story with appropriate moral ending – readily reveals its intricate nature as soon as its surface is penetrated. While the story itself may be relatively simple, the complexity of the narrative perspective and point of view epitomizes the multiple levels of apparent and covert ideologies, values, attitudes, biases, and hypocrisies that the era sustained and toward which Potter's own ambivalences are apparent. Margaret Mackey, in *The Case of Peter Rabbit*, states that 'On the surface, she is clearly on the side of law and order . . . . But the detached tone with which Potter describes Peter's disobedience actually functions to raise the question of just whose side she is on' (Mackey, 1998: 5–6). This important question deserves careful attention, and not only raises issues that involve the techniques and forms of communication that Potter employs to convey her ambivalent perspectives, but also leads us to examine the nature and role of her protagonist.

It is true that somewhat moralistic overtones pervade the book's verbal narrative and that only adults' words are recorded as spoken (we never hear directly from Peter or his sisters). However, I am not alone in my judgment that the sympathies of Potter, and thus the reader, are with Peter, despite, or perhaps even because of, his naughtiness, his flouting of the adults' received wisdom. The inherent discord or disharmony between moral stance and affect gives energetic life to the plot. Although Peter disobeys his mother and causes her anxiety and grief, commits trespass and theft, and evades paternalistic authority symbolized by Mr. McGregor (who also represents the landed sector of society defending its borders from propertyless rabble), nonetheless he escapes all punishment for his misdeeds, except for a temporary stomachache resulting from his greediness. We cannot even applaud Peter's actions as revenge for his father's death, for it is his delight in breaking rules that motivates him.

While Potter as a young woman was a comfortable supporter of the class system and expresses in her diary her lack of sympathy with unemployed rioters to whose antisocial actions she was a witness (Potter, transcribed by

Originally published as 'An Unusual Hero: Perspective and Point of View in *The Tale of Peter Rabbit*', in M. Mackey (ed.) *Beatrix Potter's* Peter Rabbit: *A Children's Classic at 100* (Lanham, MD and London: Children's Literature Association and Scarecrow, 2002), pp. 19–30.

Linder, 1966: 172–6), there is little doubt that Peter, who stands for rebellion on all fronts, is the hero of the story. The techniques Potter uses to manipulate her reader to identify with Peter, and the characteristics of this unlikely hero will form the focus of this discussion.

The role of word-image interaction in establishing perspective and point of view

Narratologists have made many attempts to grapple with the viewpoints from which a story is told, categorizing the relationship between the author and his or her narrative voice or voices, and the techniques involved in description, dialogue, and analysis that persuade the reader to see the characters and events as the author intends. We are all familiar with the range stretching from the omniscient third person to the single character's filtered analysis, with the variety of explicit and implicit values and world views of author and narrative voice(s), and with the tone and use of words that convince us with their honesty or, by means of delicate irony, subtly undermine the apparent statement.

The complexity of narrative perspective is multiplied in picture-books, for pictures present characters and events in different ways and with different techniques from verbal texts, providing additional or alternative perspectives that add dimension to the reader's experience. The dynamic and sometimes unrecognized interaction between verbal and visual perspective and point of view deepens the reader's involvement in and comprehension of the story. In Potter's books, because she is both author and illustrator, the interplay between the two forms of communication is of special interest, since the two together express the creator's intention.

In many of Beatrix Potter's books, *Peter Rabbit* included, the boundary between verbal text and illustration is absolute, in one sense at least, for words and pictures are on separate pages, divided by the gutter between them. In *Peter Rabbit*, except for the title page, cover and endpapers, no word of any kind appears in the pictures, and no hint of illustration creeps into the words. This format is totally consistent, with text and picture facing each other and printed with text back-to-back with text and picture back-to-back with picture, providing a sequence of doublespreads that read picture/text, text/picture, picture/text, etc.

This absolute division is softened, though, by the absence of a frame or border around the illustration, and by the irregular shape of the picture, which gives it a sense of freedom on the page rather than a feeling of being fixed in one place or form. This effect is reinforced by the variability in the illustrations' shape and the degree of contextual detail they provide. While the picture of Peter looking from the wheelbarrow toward the gate (57) is in rough rectangle form with detailed foreground, middle, and distant views in perspective, the picture of Peter jumping into the watering can is completely without background or contextual setting (41). Between these two extremes is the picture of Mr. McGregor chasing Peter and waving a rake (29) in

Figure 4   From Beatrix Potter, *The Tale of Peter Rabbit*, London: Frederick Warne & Co., p. 48. Copyright © Frederick Warne & Co., [1902] 2002. By kind permission of Frederick Warne & Co.

which the patch of ground on which Peter stands and the strip between them is featured, thus depicting the relationship between the two figures in spatial terms, but providing no further detail in the way of context.

This continual shift in perspective, scope of vision, and setting creates a fluctuating rather than a fixed viewpoint. The variability of shape, detail, and degree of perspective finds echoes in the verbal text that involves changes in extent – from a few words to a full page – as well as in voice, diction, and approach. Thus the mutability of the two forms, especially the visual inconsistency, tends to subvert the formal separation between the picture page and the word page, as does the rhythmic reversal of picture-text order. We are alerted to the restless interaction that occurs between the facing pages with their different modes of expression, rather than to the gutter that divides them.

The narrative voice sometimes takes an adult judgmental tone: 'Flopsy, Mopsy and Cotton-tail . . . were good little bunnies.' 'But Peter . . . was very naughty' (16–19). And certainly Mother Rabbit's perspective is focalized through her instructions and warnings to her children, and in her concern about Peter's irresponsibility: 'It was the second little jacket and pair of shoes that Peter had lost in a fortnight!' (64). More often, the narrative voice is objective, even distanced in its presentation, and contrasts with the closeness and immediacy of the pictures. The full justification of the text adds to the formality of the tone. As we examine the interaction between the two more closely, the skillfully crafted dynamic becomes increasingly apparent. While the narrative voice of the verbal text may be ambiguous, the illustrations are clear.

The story opens with a picture of wild rabbits at the root of a tree, but the narrative voice of the accompanying text immediately challenges the veracity of the woodland scene, since the rabbits, though pictured as wild, are named and humanized. This naming is a foreshadowing of the next double-spread, where both image and words transform the rabbits into clothed creatures capable of human speech. This initial picture, though, establishes the perspective of the illustrations, for the rabbits are looking directly at the reader, at their own level, not upward to a large human being. This sense of closeness and immediacy is reinforced by the limits of the illustration, for the picture is all foreground, and the line of sight includes just a few feet of the tree trunk. While a hazy background of other trees provides an impressionistic context, the scene itself is quite limited, rather like looking through a peephole. This low-to-the-ground and close-up, limited view is repeated in most of the illustrations. Almost every picture features Peter close up and within touching distance, focusing on the small rabbit and helping us to identify with him. When Mr. McGregor appears, he is always on the far side of Peter, it is Peter's line of sight that we share. The illustrations rarely give us a long view or range of perspective: when they do, the reader takes Peter's point of view, or one close to it. Examples may be found in two consecutive pictures that feature Peter and the gate to freedom: the first shows Mr. McGregor interposed between Peter and the gate (57); the second features Mr. McGregor running toward it and us, but too far away to catch Peter (58).

Setting the viewpoint of the illustrations so low to the ground and with such a constricted vision continually reinforces the sense of peril and the reader's identification with Peter and his plight. This identification dramatically instills fear and tension in the reader, and interacts with the frequently distanced voice of the verbal narrative. An excellent example is the scene where Mr. McGregor attempts to trap Peter under a garden sieve (38–9). The voice of the verbal narrative is matter of fact, and the use of words cleverly chosen for their inappropriate affect: 'Mr. McGregor came up with a sieve, which he

Figure 5   From Beatrix Potter, *The Tale of Peter Rabbit,* London: Frederick Warne & Co., p. 51. Copyright © Frederick Warne & Co., [1902] 2002. By kind permission of Frederick Warne & Co.

Figure 6   From Beatrix Potter, *The Tale of Peter Rabbit,* London: Frederick Warne & Co., pp. 34–5. Copyright © Frederick Warne & Co., [1902] 2002. By kind permission of Frederick Warne & Co.

intended to pop upon the top of Peter; but Peter wriggled out just in time, leaving his jacket behind him.' The word 'came up with' are inadequate to express Mr. McGregor's motivation to hunt and trap the plaguey rabbit, whereas 'pop upon the top of' is tea-party language, a casual and bland expression that masks and trivializes Mr. McGregor's murderous intention to capture, kill, and eat Peter. The choice of the third verb in the series, 'wriggle out,' is once again a gentle, restrained term to describe a fight for one's life.

While the narrative voice passes politely and distantly over the scene, the illustration offers a very different interpretation. Although the reader is not directly under the sieve with Peter, watching it descend, the reader's eye is extremely close, and the movement of the sieve is reinforced by the image of the three birds that fly away to left and right. Peter's crouching stance, with forepaws low and head and ears down and thrown back, his eyes black and all energy centered in the hind legs that propel him forward, transmits the sense of desperate escape, while the very large hands that hold the sieve accentuate the sense of disparate power. At the same time, the phrase 'leaving his jacket behind him' takes shape in the picture's image of Peter's nakedness, his transformation back into a simple nameless animal. And the jacket on the ground behind him still snared in the netting communicates his hairsbreadth deliverance.

These two pages not only express very different affective messages but also involve diverse and contradictory attitudes. While the verbal narrative, in its objective way, focalizes first Mr. McGregor and then Peter as it describes their actions, the choice of words for the narrative voice, which reduces the drama and intensity to an everyday occurrence, is clearly that of the powerful class and paternalistic authority of which Mr. McGregor is representative. The major conflict takes place between Mr. McGregor and Peter, between the fixed order of society and the forces that seek to undermine it, between those who have and those who want, between human civilization and animal nature. Mr. McGregor is clear about the rules, crying 'Stop thief!' as he chases the intruder. Rabbits reduce the output of Mr. McGregor's business, availing themselves of food, which is owned by another, and which, although there is plenty, is not for them. The land has been claimed, fenced, and gated, and they must stay outside. Although the forces of nature produce the food, the rabbits may not enter the garden, which belongs to human beings. Entering the garden leads to the loss of the clothes that mitigate the boundary between animals and human beings, and to possible loss of life. Eat and you will be eaten is the warning.

Meanwhile the pictures, which involve the reader in Peter's plight, are operating in a very different realm, one in which the have-nots see no reason why they should not help themselves to nature's bounty, and where gates and fences are boundaries to be challenged. Peter, it is true, does not enter the garden because he is hungry, for his mother feeds him well, but because he will not accept restraints to his freedom. For this he is willing to risk danger, and the loss of the clothes that may make him more human but that hamper his liberty of movement. This restriction is expressed not only in his narrow escape from the sieve but also in the early picture in which Mrs. Rabbit buttons a tight collar around his neck, while telling him, 'don't get into mischief' (12). Thus the socio-political message of the verbal text is countered repeatedly by the individualistic stance of the pictures.

A comparable interaction between verbal and pictorial presentation may be found when Peter is first caught in the gooseberry net. 'I think he might have got away altogether,' says the narrator, using one of the 'I's that make her presence felt, 'if he had not unfortunately run into a gooseberry net, and got caught by the large buttons on his jacket' (35). Once again the diction sets the action at a distance: 'unfortunately' and 'got caught' are unemotional, reserved words that accentuate the observer's remoteness and render the action low in drama and energy. And the tangential comment that follows, 'It was a blue jacket with brass buttons, quite new,' further detaches the narrator from the scene with its present danger. In contrast, the illustration shows Peter upside down, pinioned into immobility, enmeshed in the netting, with his feet poking through. The reader's viewpoint is right at ground level, the level of Peter's eye, a technique that thrusts the reader directly into the net. And because the netting forms the edge of the narrowly focused scene on all sides, with just a corner free, the sense of entrapment is accentuated.

Potter's balance of text and picture involves a variety of alternative functions, for example, disharmony in focalization between words and picture. The doublespread on pages 44–5 focalizes Mr. McGregor in the verbal text, but Peter in the illustration: '[Mr. McGregor] tried to put his foot upon Peter, who jumped out of a window, upsetting three plants. The window was too small for Mr. McGregor, and he was tired of running after Peter. He went back to his work' (44). The illustration, featuring Peter in mid-jump, once again puts us at Peter's eye-level, while Mr. McGregor's presence is represented by only a hob-nailed boot. But the identification with Peter is less intense than in some of the earlier pictures, for Peter is drawn as a veritable rabbit, with no hint of human posture or movement.

An interesting variant of this technique is found in a later doublespread where the verbal text describes Mr. McGregor's thought process and action: 'Mr. McGregor hung up the little jacket and the shoes for a scare-crow to frighten the blackbirds' (60–1). The picture is one of the few that offer a longer perspective, and the angle of view is set quite high, so that the observer looks down on the scene from a raised position. While the words are simply descriptive, the illustration makes a clear comment. First of all, even though Peter himself isn't present, it is Peter's coat and shoes, placed upon a wooden cross, that dominate the picture, while Mr. McGregor is a faint figure in the background. Secondly, Mr. McGregor's action is humorously depicted as completely ineffective, for the robin perches on one of the scarecrow's arms, while three birds, at least two of them crows, stand at the base of the pole, looking inquisitively up. Two more large birds are sketched in a little further back. None is in the least afraid of the scarecrow, nor does Mr. McGregor's presence nearby cause any distress.

One rather different but very interesting technique shows a reversal of the more common picture–text combination in which the illustration carries the drama of the action in contrast to the verbal text's diffident or tangential discourse. In this case the words carry the action and the affect, while the illustration provides the diversion. 'Peter was most dreadfully frightened,' the text relates. 'He rushed all over the garden, for he had forgotten the way back to the gate. He lost one of his shoes among the cabbages, and the other

Figure 7   From Beatrix Potter, *The Tale of Peter Rabbit*, London: Frederick Warne & Co., p. 52. Copyright © Frederick Warne & Co., [1902] 2002. By kind permission of Frederick Warne & Co.

shoe amongst the potatoes' (31–2). The accompanying illustration focuses not on Peter's plight, his actions, or his feelings, but upon a robin peering curiously at one of his lost shoes. While the verbal text certainly gives the access to the picture, the illustration itself distracts from the action. Placed midway between the illustrations of Peter fleeing Mr. McGregor and Peter caught in the gooseberry net, this detailed, static image has an after-the-fact effect and distances the reader from the story. The little vignette features a small corner of the garden, and the perspective is not as close up nor as low to the ground as so many others. The large, almost square picture has a stillness and self-sufficiency about it, separate from the parallel action of Peter's desperate flight. This particular combination provides an anomaly to the more common pattern we have analyzed, and the verbal focus upon

Peter's feelings permits the authorial voice to express in words the identification with Peter that had been repressed by the didactic voice but expressed through the images.

Potter does not always use contradictory effects in her word–picture interaction. The doublespread that features Peter standing by the locked door offers a harmony of the techniques and assumptions that guide the point of view (48–51). The verbal text is once again descriptive in a relatively objective manner, but, unlike the earlier passage cited, it states the facts without flippancy. Here the theme of disempowerment and inability to overcome obstacles is reinforced in both words and pictures: the door 'was locked,

Figure 8   From Beatrix Potter, *The Tale of Peter Rabbit*, London: Frederick Warne & Co., p. 44. Copyright © Frederick Warne & Co., [1902] 2002. By kind permission of Frederick Warne & Co.

and there was not room . . . to squeeze underneath'; the mouse 'had such a large pea in her mouth that she could not answer. She only shook her head at him.' The statement 'Peter began to cry' is simply a reporting of fact, but the words are true and clear without irony or attitude, and set less distance between Peter's emotions and the reader.

The picture of Peter is a masterpiece. He is without clothes but, unlike his presentation in the earlier unclothed pictures, Peter is not just an animal, for his body, though anatomically accurate, as are all Potter's drawings, is posed in a human stance. He stands upright, one foot resting on the other as he leans against the door, and his left paw rests upon the door above his head, while his right is held against his face. A large tear runs from his eye. At least one critic has likened the illustration to Anna Lea Merritt's *Love Locked Out* (1889), with which Potter would have been familiar and which represents a spiritual union denied by death (Hobbs, 1989: 22–3). Whether or not the reader carries this somewhat spiritual reference into the illustration, the sense of identification with Peter is intense and the mood of entrapment and disillusion emphatic in both the picture and in the events described: the locked door, the too narrow space beneath, the only other living creature unable to speak to him. When Peter begins to cry, his human childlikeness speaks strongly to the reader because the illustration and the verbal text work in harmony to present his hopelessness and fearful exhaustion. The earlier vision of the garden as wealth and Peter as invader has given way to the sense of the garden as a place of fear and captivity and of Peter as its prisoner.

This analysis of the ways in which perspective and point of view operate in the interplay of verbal text and illustration reveals Potter's mastery of the picturebook form. Her manipulation of the reader's perception of and sympathy for her protagonist and his challenge of the sociopolitical boundaries she appears to defend is subtle and subversive, for the unmistakable perspective of the illustrations patently and intentionally undermines the studied ambiguous stance of her verbal message.

Peter as unlikely hero

Potter's ambivalence, which raised Mackey's question of 'just whose side she is on,' is not simply a manifestation of Potter's own feelings about individual freedom and her experience of the constraints of the accepted paternalistic Victorian society that many of her works express (Scott, 1994). It is also strongly tied to the accepted concept of an appropriate hero, and interrogates my earlier affirmation that 'there is little doubt that Peter, who stands for rebellion on all fronts, is the hero of the story.'

In considering the significance of Potter's perspective and her fore-grounding of her protagonist, I have been repeatedly reminded of another rebellious figure challenging authority and established order, Milton's Lucifer in *Paradise Lost*. A number of readers, especially those with Romantic tendencies, have seen Lucifer-Satan rather than Christ as the 'real' hero of the epic, for Satan displays any number of heroic traits with which readers may sympathize and identify: courage, leadership, intelligence, fortitude and resolve in the face of adversity, and a longing for freedom and self-determination. Thus, like Potter, Milton has provoked similar charges of ambivalence in his relationship to the established order, his choice of hero, and his covert heresies (though in Milton's case these were religious rather than sociopolitical).

While the supporter of Satan points to the heroism of the rebel who defies the power of the established order and sacrifices everything for individual autonomy, a study of the perspectives established by Milton reveals a different picture. Although *Paradise Lost* is a purely verbal text, Milton's verse is vivid in visual description and in image and, like Potter's work, displays a similarly fluctuating perspective. In Book I, Lucifer-Satan is foregrounded and presented through epic similes as larger than life, as he frees himself from the chains on the burning lake and presides over the construction of a great hall, where in Book II he addresses his followers in stately rhetoric from a lofty throne.

But this up-close viewpoint is juxtaposed to the longer view: first Milton's simile compares the massing hordes of hell to a swarm of bees, and is accompanied by a switch in perspective, in which 'they who now seem'd / In bigness to surpass Earth's Giant Sons / Now less than smallest Dwarfs' (I, 777–9). And, shortly thereafter, when Satan's voyage from hell is described, the perspective of the piece is transformed when seen from God's panoramic viewpoint, and Satan is revealed as a small force in the magnitude of the universe, and compared to a vulture, a wolf, and a cormorant. Thereafter, when the reader is brought close to Satan's side, any sense of magnitude is lost, and Satan's manifestations as toad and snake further distance the reader.

In the case of *Paradise Lost*, the didactic approach of the author is reinforced by the perspective and by the images presented, in complete contrast to the situation in *Peter Rabbit*. Although faced with a degree of ambiguity in his challenge to 'justify the ways of God to man,' a highly complex task in view of the conflicting values of the time with regard to freedom and authority, the subtle distinctions of church theology and dangers of heresy, and the conventions of the epic genre, Milton manipulates his readers both rationally and emotionally to the conclusion he determines.

Margery Hourihan, in her work *Deconstructing the Hero*, adds an interesting dimension to this discussion of unlikely heroes in her analysis of the adventure story and her inclusion of *Peter Rabbit* as an example. She states that '*The Tale of Peter Rabbit* recognizes the division in our culture between the domestic sphere and the public world where power is situated, just as it recognizes the perceived division between humans and animals but, unlike most hero tales, it values the private world above the public and denies the imagined boundary between humanity and nature' (1997: 218). While I am in full agreement with her sense that this book undermines some of the dualities upon which the adventure story is set, I believe that Potter goes much further than Hourihan suggests.

In many ways Peter is the exact antithesis of the qualities that Hourihan identifies as necessary for the traditional hero, a difference that allows Potter to subvert rather than endorse the usual pattern of adventure. According to Hourihan's analysis, the traditional hero of the time is a young, white male; he leaves the civilized order of home to venture into the wilderness; he meets difficulties and dangerous opponents; he overcomes them because he is strong, brave, resourceful, rational, and determined to succeed; he achieves his goal; he returns home and is gratefully welcomed and rewarded. Further-more, if we examine the good/evil dualism pairs that Hourihan selects from Val Plumwood's list – reason/emotion; civilization/wilderness; reason/nature; male/female; order/chaos; mind-soul/body; human/nonhuman and master/slave – Peter embodies few of the positive aspects and most of the negative ones.

Potter is completely breaking the mold of the hero in this story, for Peter is a small, easily frightened, emotionally driven, and certainly not very rational animal. Although he is male – the one boundary Potter was unable to fracture – he is no heroic representative of the 'innate superiority of civilized, rational, male order as against wild, emotional, female chaos' (Hourihan, 17). *The Tale of Peter Rabbit* is thus subversive not only of the period's premises and expecta-tions of what it takes to be a good child – obedient, dutiful; respectful of authority, social mores, and conventions – but of the hero genre itself, together with its implicit values, whereby 'the reader is required to admire courage, action, skill and determination, while qualities like creativity, sensitivity and self-questioning have no presence in the hero's world' (Hourihan, 41). Potter's polite, socially correct narrative voice is revealed as a façade, shielding the author from self-revelation.

In her seemingly gentle and her subtle way, Beatrix Potter has, like many other great children's literature authors, laid a depth charge beneath the calm surface of an innocent children's story. Her tale has been providing an explosive force for many generations of children, encouraging them to self-indulgence, disobedience, transgression of social boundaries and ethics, and assertion of their wild, unpredictable nature against the constrictions of civilized living. Potter also implies that this battle will be a constant, cyclical one, for there is no closure to the story, just a temporary hiatus. Mr. McGregor's spoils of victory – Peter's clothes – are hollow, and transient; they do not empower McGregor, as the scarecrow picture reveals, and, as we see in the Benjamin Bunny sequel, Peter has already outgrown them like a snake shedding its skin. The struggle for personal independence will include moments of panic and terror, and real danger. But the subliminal message is that this struggle is what life is all about, and that the price one must pay – a stomachache and no supper – is well worth the exhilaration and self-realization that results from the confrontation.

References

Hobbs, Anne Stevenson. *Beatrix Potter's Art*. New York: Viking Penguin, Inc., 1989.

Hourihan, Margery. *Deconstructing the Hero*. London and New York: Routledge, 1997.

Mackey, Margaret. *The Case of Peter Rabbit: Changing Conditions of Literature for Children*. New York: Garland Press, 1998.

Plumwood, Val. *Feminism and the Mastery of Nature*. London and New York: Routledge, 1993.

Potter, Beatrix. *The Journal of Beatrix Potter*, transcribed by Leslie Linder. London: F. Warne, 1966.

———. *The Tale of Peter Rabbit*. London: F. Warne, 2002.

Scott, Carole. 'Clothed in Nature or Nature Clothed.' *Children's Literature* 22 (1994): 70–89.

4

Two Classic Poetry Collections: Robert Louis Stevenson, *A Child's Garden of Verses* (1885) and A.A. Milne, *When We Were Very Young* (1924)

Introduction
Nicola J. Watson

This section pays homage to the neglected area of poetry for children by pairing two classic poetry collections, Robert Louis Stevenson's *A Child's Garden of Verses* (1885) and A.A. Milne's *When We Were Very Young* (1924). Although separated by forty years, these collections do have things in common. Neither has ever been out of print. They have, unusually, by and large retained their integrity and identity *as* collections. This may be attributed in the case of *A Child's Garden of Verses* to the way the text is built up of poems almost entirely couched in the same child's voice. In the case of *When We Were Very Young* it may be attributed to copyright restrictions which stabilised the text in a fixed relation to Ernest Shepard's famous illustrations, and to the focus on the figure of a single child, Christopher Robin. The books also share an interest in representing the voice of the child as it articulates a child's view of the world, and in describing child-space, respectively rural and urban. Standing as bookends to the First Golden Age of children's literature, both envisage Arcadian child-space in which make-believe transforms home into the wider world, and then brings the virtual adventurer back again; but the proto-imperial vigour and conviction of Stevenson's boy sits in strong contrast with Milne's slightly mocking evocation of Christopher Robin's cosy nursery adventures after the First World War. With historical distance both collections may be seen as essays on contemporary boyhood and its destinations; given intervening world events, it is not surprising that Milne's volume, though traversed by the same

114

familiar figures of pirates, Red Indians and images of far-flung lands, feels more concerned than Stevenson's with making it home safely in time for tea.

Origins and composition

A Child's Garden of Verses was composed by Stevenson while he was bed-ridden with suspected tuvberculosis and incapacitated from more extended work. Comprising sixty-four poems organised into unequal sections ('A Child's Garden'; 'The Child Alone'; 'Garden Days'; 'Envoys'), it is in large part an exercise in recapturing his own childhood experience and sensations, framed with some material describing this childhood as seen by an adult self. It was nonetheless intended for a child readership: Stevenson was writing in conscious and mercenary imitation of Sale Barker's and Kate Greenaway's best-selling *Birthday Book for Children* (1880). Individually, the poems are often teasingly slight (one, 'A Thought', runs in its entirety, 'The world is so full of a number of things/I'm sure we all should be as happy as kings'), but taken together, as Carpenter and Prichard have argued (1999: 114), it was the most notable collection of serious poems to be written for children since the Taylor sisters' *Original Poems for Infant Minds* (1804–5). It was originally published without illustration, and it was only after Stevenson's death in 1896 that the fourth edition appeared with drawings, hand-lettered titles and head and tail pieces for the poems by Charles Robinson, then virtually unknown. Subsequently, it has been regularly reillustrated, abridged and anthologised, often for use in formal education. In 1902, for example, an abridged version (leaving out the sub-sections 'The Child Alone', 'Garden Days' and 'Envoys' as too 'philosophical' for younger children) was reillustrated by E. Mars and M.H. Squire for use in primary grades in America. In 1922, it appeared in parallel Latin translation, again for use in schools (Stevenson 1922).

When We Were Very Young was also composed in a desultory fashion, the bulk of it at a wet house-party in Wales. It is organised around an evocation of Milne's 4-year old son, and fuelled by Milne's own recollections of earliest childhood. Milne's child is rather younger than Stevenson's, and part of the enterprise of the volume is the new representation of this very young child's voice. Milne commissioned a young Ernest Shepard who had illustrated 'The King's Breakfast' when it was originally published in *Punch* to provide 'decorations'. Instantly successful, the book was reprinted six times between its first appearance in November 1924 and Christmas 1924. Within six months the verse had been set to music, and the sheet-music was flying out of the shops. By 1963 it had been reprinted 65 times, making it probably the most popular book of children's verse ever.

Reception/critical terrain

For all their longevity, these collections have been the subject of remarkably little recent critical attention. In part, this has simply been because studies in children's literature have historically been more interested in fiction than in other genres. In part, it has been because Stevenson, when considered as a children's author, has usually been dealt with as the author of *Treasure Island* and *Kidnapped*. Similarly, attention has tended to slide away from Milne's collections of verse towards his other stories featuring Christopher Robin and Pooh, *Winnie the Pooh* (1926) and *The House at Pooh Corner* (1928).

Such modern criticism as there has been hails Stevenson as something of a radical, the first writer to systematically explore voicing the child (Styles 1998). In this, it has revalued a long tradition of seeing Stevenson's verse as inaugurating a special vision of childhood accessed through the 'childlikeness' of the verse, whether conceived as authentic voice, simplicity of form, 'unaffectedness' of sentiment, or fancifulness. This has long been regarded as a guarantee of its appeal to the child-reader. The introduction to the 1902 edition, for example, remarks:

> In these 'Verses' he writes as a child rather than about children, and in this lies much of the charm which they possess for little readers. There is in them the surprise of reality, the beauty of a simple rhythm, and the mysterious flavour of magic that grips a boy's heart and will not let him go until the book has become a part of him
>
> Stevenson 1902: 5

The writer also notes firmly that the book will 'start' such a boy 'on the straight path of culture' (Stevenson 1902: 7). This valuation of the child voice is a constant in criticism of the volume; consequently, critics have regularly been rendered uneasy by the many and variously ironised lapses in the book into grown-upness, citing especially those poems that rethink moral verse by posing it within child or adult voices that occupy the instructional position rather tenuously – as in 'A Thought', quoted above. In the Introduction to the 1927 edition, for example, Laurence Alma Tadema writes perceptively of the multiple stances required of the adult reader. He values the lyric and playful over the quasi-moral and instructional, and he values especially the possibility of indulging in childlikeness, counterpointed with the parental sense of listening in to a child's psycho-drama:

> As we read . . . the poet's persistent childlikeness speaks to the undying child within ourselves – we respond, we are small again and his playmates; yet, as we read on . . . it is not with a child's heart that we turn back to the first page and

read each verse anew. We find ourselves leaning tenderly, with all the motherhood or fatherhood that may be in us, over one solitary child.

1927: 12

Tadema concludes that the classic status of the collection, or rather, of the boy evoked by the collection, is assured because of its/his appeal to adult readers:

> Live he will, beyond ten generations of children; not, perhaps, to be the playmate of other little ones; rather to fill with delight the empty nurseries of those whose children have grown up and gone away or else have never been.

1927: 25

Tadema's strong note of mourning and nostalgia is characteristic of the post-First World War years; the same sense of a lost Arcadian childhood animated *When We Were Very Young*, published three years previously, and accounted for its enormous success. But critics have always been less enthusiastic about Milne than Stevenson. Ever since first publication, as Jackie Wullschläger documents below, Milne's version of childhood has been perceived as embarrassingly middle-class, suffocatingly cosy, and toxically nostalgic in exact proportion to its evident and continuing popularity. This accounts for the acrid note in the popular parody: 'Hush, hush / Nobody cares / Christopher Robin / Has fallen downstairs.'

The essays

The essays included here are modern takes on the history of this differential valuation of Stevenson and Milne. Michael Rosen is celebrated for transforming the tone of children's verse with the publication of his first collection of verse *Mind Your Own Business* in 1974, sidelining the lyrical and cautionary traditions in favour of voicing an anarchically playful child. Rosen argues for *A Child's Garden of Verses* as innovatory: 'the first time a writer published a sequence of poems expressed in the first person as if the writer were a child, addressed directly to a children's audience with the clear intention of expressing scenes and feelings of their own childhood'. He sets this innovation within the context of late Victorian theorisation of children's play and then surveys the volume in detail. Unsurprisingly in view of his own poetic agenda, he argues for the greater freshness and integrity of the poems about imaginative play over those that seem to foreground adult sentiment or adult instruction, 'rescuing' the poems that seem to him truly to speak from the child perspective.

Jackie Wullschläger's essay is extracted from her book-length study of fantasy from Carroll to Milne, and reads *When We Were Very Young* within the continuum of the Pooh stories, within Milne's life-story, and within the cultural context of post-war England. She argues against reading Milne as the supposedly uncomplicated sentimentalist of 'Vespers' and urges attention to Milne's strain of self-mockery and ironic diminution, and to his portrayal of childish egotism. Like Rosen, she evaluates the poetry on truth to 'childness', identifying Milne's 'genius' as fixing 'the character of the archetypal child, in the context of a child's vision, and within the limits of children's language, as no one before or since has ever done'. The unanimity of these two essays on this point should perhaps prompt examination of the underlying assumption that such truth to childness has anything to do with child-readers at all; and might perhaps, too, open up the question of why modernity has been and still is so invested in preserving the child-voice.

References

Carpenter, H. and Prichard, M. 1999. *The Oxford Companion to Children's Literature*. Oxford, Oxford University Press.

Stevenson, R.L. [1885] 1902. *A Child's Garden of Verses*, illus. E. Mars and M.H. Squire. Chicago, New York and London, Rand McNally.

Stevenson, R.L. 1922. *A Child's Garden of Verses/De Ludis et Hortis Virginibus Puerisque: English and Latin*. Cambridge, Heffer & Sons.

Styles, M. 1998. *From the Garden to the Street: An Introduction to 300 Years of Poetry for Children*. London, Cassell.

Tadema, L.A. 1927. 'Introduction', in R.L. Stevenson, *A Child's Garden of Verses*, illus. Kate Elizabeth Olver. London and Glasgow, Collins.

Further reading

Colley, A.C. 1997. '"Writing towards home": The Landscape of A Child's Garden of Verses', *Victorian Poetry*, 35, 303–18.

Colley, A.C. 2004. *Robert Louis Stevenson and the Colonial Imagination*, Aldershot, Ashgate, chapter 6.

Lewis, L. 1989. '"How far from Babylon?" The Voices of Stevenson's Garden', in C.F. Otten and G. Schmidt (eds.) *The Voice of the Narrator in Children's Literature*. New York, Greenwood.

Lukens, R. 1980–1. 'Stevenson's Garden: Verse is Verse', *The Lion and the Unicorn*, 4, 49–55.

Webb, J. 2002. 'Conceptualising Childhood: Robert Louis Stevenson's *A Child's Garden of Verses*', *Cambridge Journal of Education*, 32, 359–65.

Wilson, A. 1987. 'A.A. Milne's *When We Were Very Young* and *Now We Are Six*: A Small World of Everyday Pleasures', in P. Nodelman (ed.) *Touchstones: Reflections on the Best in Children's Literature*. West Lafayette, IN, Children's Literature Association.

The Contexts of *A Child's Garden of Verses*
Michael Rosen

When Robert Louis Stevenson began work on the poems that were to be published as *A Child's Garden of Verses* (1885; hereafter referred to as *Child's Garden*), he had already put on paper some thoughts about his own childhood and the nature of childhood itself. In 1874 he wrote an essay called 'Notes on the Movements of Young Children' ('Notes'); in September 1878, he published in *Cornhill Magazine* an essay on childhood called 'Child's Play'; and in 1880 he wrote 'Memoirs of Himself.' The work on *Child's Garden* began in 1881. In these three pieces of prose he developed some of the ideas that were to appear later in the poetry.

'Notes' is a rather whimsical piece in which Stevenson observes children in two situations, the first at an 'impromptu dancing-school in the drawing-room of an hotel in France,' where he expresses the conventional, idealized view of childhood and girls in particular as being 'natural' and 'pure':[1]

> Two little girls, about eight years old, were the pupils; that is an age of great interest in girls, when grace comes to its consummation of justice and purity, with little admixture of that other grace of forethought and discipline that will shortly supersede it altogether.[2]

It was he says, 'grace in the making.' This then develops into an admiration of one of the girls for the way in which she appears to be able to dance with 'verve,' 'gusto,' and 'passion' in spite of the 'inefficacy of the dull, half-informed body.'[3] The child, then, is not admired for something she is achieving now, but for what she might become, with all the suberotic baggage that notion carries.

The second scene that Stevenson observes takes place with 'quite common children' in Hampstead, London. 'A little congregation' of girls, including two sisters, are skipping in the lane beneath his window. While one skips, another looks after a baby. As before, Stevenson admires the skill of the older girls ('spontaneous agile flexure,' 'harmonious,' 'infinite variety'), but this time his attention is caught by a younger girl who cannot really skip: 'The clumsiness of the child seemed to have a significance and a sort of beauty of its own, quite above this grace of the others in power to affect the heart.'[4]

Extracted from 'Robert Louis Stevenson and Children's Play: The Context of *A Child's Garden of Verses*', in *Children's Literature in Education* 26:1 (1995), pp. 53–72.

Why should this have pleased Stevenson more? He says it is because it expresses a battle between a will to perform a task and an 'unwilling body' that prevents the achievement. So we sympathize with a struggle, he says. But he also admires the 'sincerity' of the children: 'a directness, an impulsive truth, about their free gestures that shows throughout all imperfection, and it is to us as a reminiscence of primitive festivals and the Golden Age.'[5] Once again this is the conventional and idealized view of the time, that children are like the precursors of 'civilized' humans because they are 'free' and 'impulsive.' The use of the word *savage* (though not used by Stevenson here) to describe both children and aboriginal peoples was common at this time.[6]

At this stage, Stevenson's thinking is only of interest here in that he is spending time thinking about childhood, rather than for any new or unconventional insights. In 'Memoirs of Himself,' written some five or six years later, we meet a much less idealized view of childhood:

> I have three powerful impressions of my childhood: my sufferings when I was sick, my delights in convalescence at my grandfather's manse of Colinton, near Edinburgh, and the unnatural activity of my mind after I was in bed at night.[7]

He describes 'the sorrow and burden of the night,' the 'undecipherable blackness,' and 'hideous nightmares.' These are quite different from the times at the manse, with its 'sense of sunshine,' 'the singing of birds,' 'the laurel thickets,' and 'the sharp contrast between this place and the city where I spent the other portion of my time, all these took hold of me, and still remain upon my memory, with a peculiar sparkle and sensuous excitement.'[8] It is not fanciful to see here one aspect of the origins of the *Child's Garden* as an Arcadian relief from the pain of his illnesses.

More interestingly, he goes on to describe a piece of imaginative play: 'Once as I lay, playing hunter, hid in a thick laurel, and with a toy gun upon my arm, I worked myself so hotly into the spirit of my play, that I think I can still see the herd of antelope come sweeping down the lawn and round the deodar: it was almost a vision.'[9] This kind of play figures in the poems, and Stevenson thought such play was part of the creative and re-creative spirit that animates the writing and reading of poetry and fiction in general. He was to write two years later, 'Fiction is to the grown man what play is to the child.'[10]

But it is in the third of these essays, 'Child's Play,' that Stevenson fully develops the idea of imaginative play. He sees play as a way of transforming reality:

> When my cousin and I took our porridge of a morning, we had a device to enliven the course of the meal. He ate his with sugar, and explained it to be a country continually buried under snow. I took mine with milk, and explained it to be a country

suffering gradual inundation. You can imagine us exchanging bulletins; how here was an island still un-submerged, here a valley not yet covered with snow; what inventions were made; how his population lived in cabins on perches and travelled on stilts, and how mine was always in boats; how the interest grew furious, as the last corner of safe ground was cut off on all sides and grew smaller every moment; and how in fine, the food was of altogether secondary importance, and might even have been nauseous, so long as we seasoned it with these dreams.[11]

Because children are like this, Stevenson says, we should not expect of children 'peddling exactitude about matters of fact . . . it's less than decent':

You do not consider how little the child sees or how swift he is to weave what he has seen into bewildering fiction; and that he cares no more for what you call truth, than you for a gingerbread dragoon.[12]

This time of childhood he sees as a time of innocence, before the onset of unpleasant adulthood:

It would be easy to leave them in their native cloud-land, where they figure so prettily – pretty like flowers and innocent like dogs. They will come out of their gardens soon enough, and have to go into offices and the witness-box. Spare then yet a while, O conscientious parent! Let them doze among their playthings yet a while! for who knows what a rough wayfaring existence lies before them in the future?[13]

However, this view stands in contradiction to what he has said earlier in the essay, namely, when we think of our childhood:

we are apt to stir up uncomfortable and sorrowful memories and remind ourselves of old wounds. Our day-dreams can no longer lie all in the air like a story in the 'Arabian Nights'; they read to us rather like the history of a period in which we ourselves had taken part, where we come across many unfortunate passages and find our own conduct smartly reprimanded.[14]

These 'unfortunate passages' seem to have something to do with the 'dread irrationality' of parental punishment:

What can [children] make of these bearded or petticoated giants who look down upon their games? . . . who profess the tenderest solicitude for children, and yet every now and again reach down out of their altitude and terribly vindicate the prerogatives of age? Off goes the child corporally smarting, but morally rebellious. Were there ever such unthinkable deities as parents?[15]

And there is another unpleasant side to childhood: 'a sense of terror for the untried residue of mankind.'[16]

In summary, childhood is a time of play, imagination, innocence, and dread; adults should not expect rationality of children, but children can expect the irrational of adults, too. Imaginative play is a glorious escape but also a way of making the humdrum and the unpleasant palatable. Childhood is, in some ways, preferable to adulthood. None of these ideas are unfamiliar to us today, but how would they have seemed in 1879?

The essay appeared just as a new movement, the empirical study of childhood, was developing. Pioneered by a German, Dietrich Tiedemann, in 1787, the movement did not really get underway until the late 1870s with observations of specific children in the journal *Mind*. Hippolyte Taine published there 'On the Acquisition of Language by Children' in April 1877. This was followed up by Charles Darwin in the same journal in July of that year with 'A Biographical Sketch of an Infant.' One of the first scientific specialists in childhood, J. Sully, published an article, 'Babies and Science,' in 1881 in *Cornhill Magazine* (No. 43), the same publication in which Stevenson had published 'Child's Play' three years earlier. The scientific interest at this stage was concerned with how children develop adult faculties, and it was not until the end of the century that play was brought under the microscope, too. Karl Groos, professor of philosophy at the University of Basle, is generally credited with the first scientific analysis of play in *The Play of Animals*, published in 1896, and *The Play of Man*, in 1900.

The new empiricists drew on the observations of people like Schiller, the German playwright, and above all, Froebel. Herbert Spencer had 'made popular' Schiller's observation that 'aesthetic sentiments originate from the play-impulse.'[17] We know that Stevenson read Spencer because he draws on Spencer in his easy on Walt Whitman published in 1878, and Archibald Bisset described an argument between Stevenson and his father over Spencer's ideas in 1872.[18] Peter Coveney casts doubt on the impact of Froebel in England in the first half of the nineteenth century.[19] However, the Froebel Society was founded in England in 1874, and according to Carolyn Steedman, 'Extensive discussion of his educational theory in family magazines and childcare manuals all ensured his ideas a substantial middle-class audience.'[20] Froebel had said, 'Play . . . is the highest expression of human development in childhood, for it alone is the free expression of what is in the child's soul.'[21] 'But what is this play of the little-ones? It is the great drama of life itself, only in its small beginnings. Therefore its high seriousness, which penetrates joy and pleasure and often becomes dominant.'[22]

So, Stevenson's essay and poems on childhood were produced at precisely the moment the issue of play was being formally discussed in Britain for the first time. More specifically, in relation to children's books, Alexander Hay Japp, in an essay published in 1869, wrote of 'the childlike law of association,' where the imagination can hop between the real and the fantastic: 'Out of the fluent unceasing play that comes spontaneously from this element of magic and grotesque mystery, flows that peculiar verbal antithesis . . . which is the flowery zigzag, of fancy-maze, by which the young mind is led ever upward to fresh realities, and to new ideas of the world. And in poetry we may legitimately expect more of this buoyant antithetic verbal play than in prose.'[23] (As we shall see later, Japp is a crucial figure in the origination of the *Child's Garden*.) [Thus] by the time Stevenson was writing, children's play had been legitimized as a suitable topic in literary circles.

[In an excised section, Rosen discusses Stevenson's championing of the interconnected ideas of childhood innocence and imaginative play against Calvinist concepts of education, duty, discipline and punishment associated with adults, noting that in his essay 'A Penny Plain and Twopence Coloured', published just as he was finished writing *A Child's Garden* in 1884], we get a glimpse of precisely how, at a personal level, the struggle between 'fancy' and Puritanism was enacted. One night, the young Stevenson rushed home with the *Arabian Entertainments* 'in the fat, old, double-columned volume with the prints. I was just well into the story of the Hunchback, I remember, when my clergyman-grandfather (a man we counted pretty stiff) came in behind me. I grew blind with terror. But instead of ordering the book away, he said he envied me. Ah, well he might!'[24]

So, *A Child's Garden of Verses* cannot be seen as a piece of naive writing. It is born out of a clear sense of purpose about a view of childhood, play, imagination, and the forces that oppose such views. The immediate stimulus for the writing came from a chance happening. On holiday in Braemar in 1881, his mother had a copy of a new book, Kate Greenaway and Mrs. Sale Barker's *Birthday Book for Children* (1880). This is a smallish, Beatrix-Potter-size book, where each double spread consists of a left-hand side with three verses and three illustrations, each to go with a day of the year. Opposite each of these three verses are blank lined sections for the reader to write in a diary entry or a verse of his or her own. Duty, useful work, propriety, and sensible behavior are the sentiments that prevail:

January 1st
What are the bells about? what do they say?
Ringing so sweetly for glad New Years Day:
Telling us all that Time will never wait,
Bidding us use it well, ere it's too late.[25]

May 8th
This girl is dressed all spick and span,
And neatly as can be;

Her sash well tied, her mitten straight,
She's going out to tea.[26]

Humor appears occasionally with the odd limerick or conventional racism:

December 20th
And where do you come from, with shillalagh in your hand?
'Shure, and plase yer honor, I come from Paddyland,
Auld Ireland, the island of praties and milk;
And shure, blarney, too – ain't our tongues as soft as silk?'[27]

Stevenson's recorded response to these was 'These are rather nice rhymes and I don't think such verses would be difficult to do.' And he went off and composed fourteen poems.[28] Over the next three years, while taking up residence in Nice and Hyères in France, he wrote the rest. 'Many were composed,' says Adam-Smith, 'during his illnesses, when he could not work on prose; several were written in the dark, with the lefthand, at Hyères in 1884, when he was laid up with a haemorrhage, sciatica, and Egyptian ophthalamia.'[29] He played with various combinations of poems for the volume and various titles, including *Nursery Verses, Penny Whistles for Small Whistlers*, and, significantly, *New Songs of Innocence* or *Rimes of Innocence*.

These titles and the eventual one show a vacillation between trying to depict children *doing* something (that is, whistling) and *being* something symbolic (that is, innocent). The choice of *garden* was a conscious link with Arcadia. Stevenson spent many holidays with his grandfather and cousins at Colinton Manse. 'That was my golden age,' he wrote, '*et ego in Arcadia vixi.*'[30] Nicholas Rankin recounts how Stevenson played with his cousins in the garden and how, in later years he was to describe this as a 'fury of play.'[31] Several of the poems, like 'Keepsake Mill,' can be taken to be about specific local landmarks. The collection, when first published in 1885, was divided up into different sections: 'A Child's Garden of Verses' (ACGOV), 'The Child Alone' (TCA), 'Garden Days' (GD), and 'Envoys' (E).

What makes the *Child's Garden* unique is that, to my knowledge, it is the first time a writer published a sequence of poems expressed in the first person as if the writer were a child, addressed directly to a children's audience with the clear intention of expressing scenes and feelings of their own childhood. There had been poetry for children expressed in the voice of the child. In 1809 Charles Lamb had published a poem, 'Choosing a Name':

I have got a new-born sister:
I was nigh the first that kiss'd her . . .[32]

Juliana Horatia Ewing's 'The Doll's Wash' (1874)[33] is a miniepic of children's experience told in the first person, but there is little to indicate that Mrs. Ewing was attempting to convey a sense of her own childhood in the poem. Of course, there had been countless poems about children and childhood that must have drawn on poets' own experiences, but Stevenson's innovation was to have made the link between the poems, his own life, and a children's audience. When he writes *I*, he means *I*, and when he writes *you*, he means the child reader.

The reasons why it was Stevenson who made this creative leap must derive in part from the combination of (1) his active engagement in the debate about childhood; (2) his willingness to incorporate his own experience into this debate rather than pretending scientific objectivity; (3) the sudden arrival of a stepson, Lloyd Osborne (aged 13 in 1881), into his life, which we know helped generate *Treasure Island*; (4) the arrival at Braemar of Alexander Hay Japp.[34] It is Japp whom I cited earlier with strong views on play and children's books. In reconstructing how the *Child's Garden* came to be written, it does not seem fanciful to imagine that Japp and Stevenson engaged in conversations about play, childhood, and children's books; and the presence in Scotland of a tradition of verse either for or about children. *The Children of the Poets: An Anthology* was published in 1886,[35] and a volume for children called *Little Ben Bute* by one Matthew Browne was published in Edinburgh two years before the *Child's Garden*.[36] If Stevenson needed to find a poetic voice to match the thoughts and speech of his childhood, then there were patterns of writing already in circulation, and, we might assume, some he heard as a child.

The question we can ask of the poems themselves is to what extent we can match Stevenson's views with the poems. Some twenty-two (see 'Appendix') of the sixty-seven published deal directly with imaginative play, or what Stevenson calls 'play-business' in 'To Any Reader' (E VI). The personal voice in this group of poems is clear and confident: In a poem like 'Pirate Story' (ACGOV VII), 'three of us' playing in a meadow is a cue to imagine that 'we' are sailing to Africa, 'a-steering of the boat':

> Hi! but here's a squadron a-rowing on the sea—
>   Cattle on the meadow a-charging with a roar!
> Quick, and we'll escape them, they're as mad as they can be,
>   The wicket is the harbour and the garden is the shore.

Note that the wicket 'is' the harbor, not 'seems as if it is.' Casting the narrative into the voice of a child in the first person seems to have given Stevenson a way of expressing the experience of imaginative play without apology, without explicit reference to how adults might perceive it. Some of Stevenson's best poems belong with this group, like 'The Land of Counterpane' (ACGOV XVI). As he lies sick in bed, the narrator says, 'I . . . sometimes sent my ships in fleets, / all up and down among the sheets. . . . I was the giant great and skill / That sits upon the pillow-hill.' Or in 'Block City' (TCA VI), the blocks make a palace, then, 'Now I have done with it, down let it go! / All in a moment the town is laid low. / Block upon block lying scattered and free, / What is there left of my town by the sea?' And in 'The Land of Story-Books' (TCA VII), ' . . . I crawl / All in the dark along the wall, / And follow round the forest track / Away behind the sofa back.' These are all acutely observed activities and feelings belonging to a view of childhood that is making no claims for its 'innocence' or requiring it to be obedient or dutiful or less sinful. There is a clear attempt here to make a connection between Stevenson's own pleasurable memories of playing and the child reader's similar experiences. It is this attempt that makes the verses unique. In contrast to the ideas in his essay on childhood, Stevenson made a decision to share his views of the value, power, and pleasure of imaginative play *with children*.

Another group of the poems looks at the child's activities, not necessarily imaginative. These correspond more closely to poems for children that had already been in circulation before Stevenson wrote these. 'The Swing' (ACGOV XXXIII) celebrates swinging but seems to lack the power of the 'imaginative play' poems: 'Oh, I do think it the pleasantest thing / Ever a child can do!' The adult presence and sensibility are more obvious here with the reference to 'a child,' and the lines feel as if there are some redundant words making up the scansion (use of *do* and *ever* here), though perhaps this was a way of imitating childlike diction. Again, in 'Farewell to the Farm' (ACGOV XI.), we have 'the eager children' rather than 'we.' In 'North-West Passage' (ACGOV XII), the child-narrator adopts the mock-heroic voice to see his way to bed: 'Let us arise and go like men, / And face with an undaunted tread / The long black passage up to bed.' This leans toward adult humor and the rhetorical device that diminishes through hyperbole. 'Picture Books in Winter' (TCA IV) fares rather badly in comparison to the vigor of 'The Land of the Story-Books' with the weakly adult line, 'How am I to sing your praise . . .'

More consistent with the 'imaginative play' group of poems that I have described is a group where the facts of the world are seen through a child's eyes. The intellectual game being played here is that the adult remembers what the features of the world around him felt like when he was a child and uses his skills as an adult writer to convey these feelings in verse, but does so with a language and rhetoric that children can enjoy. This process is slightly different from the total-immersion method of the imaginative play group in that these 'facts-of-the-world' poems often contain a small philosophical point of a significance that, we can sense as adults, derives more directly from an adult consciousness. In 'Bed in Summer' (ACGOV I), the narrator muses on the absurdity of going to bed in the day-time in summer. The narrator's voice wobbles from child ('In winter I get up at night') to ear-adult ('And does it not seem hard to you . . .') and back to child (I should like so much to play . . .'). This group of poems is full of rhetorical questions and observations of little ironies; 'what can be the use of him is more than I can see' ('My Shadow,' ACGOV XVIII); there are 'millions of stars' ('Escape at Bedtime' ACGOV XXI); but 'There n'er were such thousands of leaves on a tree.' A cow wanders, 'and yet she cannot stray' ('The Cow,' ACGOV XXIII). In 'The Flowers' (GD III), he looks at the 'tiny woods' of the flower beds, 'where if I were not so tall, / I should live for good and all.'

The least successful group of poems in the collection are those with an adult speaker. At times we can hear the voice that Hugh Cunningham identifies as 'the search for order'.[37] 'A Thought' (ACGOV II) says:

It is very nice to think
The world is full of meat and drink,
With little children saying grace
In every Christian kind of place.

I am unable to find any irony or satire here or in 'Good and Bad Children' (ACGOV XXVII): 'You must be bright and quiet, / And content with simple diet; / And remain, through all bewild'ring, / innocent and honest children.' Yet, elsewhere, as in 'System' (ACGOV XIX), using the child's voice, Stevenson is able to undermine such precepts:

The child that is not clean and neat,
With lots of toys and things to eat,
He is a naughty child, I'm sure –
Or else his dear papa is poor.

Another tone adopted by the adult voice in the collection is the teacher showing the child the beauties of nature: 'Patience, children, just a minute – / See the spreading circles die' (from 'Looking-Glass River,' ACGOV XXXV). Much less ponderous is the celebrated, 'From a Railway Carriage' (ACGOV XXXVII), where the voice is clearly adult but sufficiently excited to carry us along with the rhythm of the train and the montage of sights. The last line, however, is that note of wistfulness that seems an inevitable part of the adult talking about his or her own childhood: 'Each a glimpse and gone for ever!' This becomes more explicit in the 'Envoys': 'But ah! we children never more / Shall watch it from the water-door! . . . Our phantom voices haunt the air / As we were still at play' ('To Minnie,' E IV).

Cunningham wants to place Stevenson's work as 'middle-class sentimentalizing of childhood,' typical of the period.[38] And it is certainly true that the *Child's Garden* was being widely quoted and referred to very soon after publication: Eric Robertson's collection, *The Children of the Poets*, already mentioned, anthologized Stevenson in 1886, one year after publication of a *Child's Garden*. Kate Douglas Wiggin, in a polemic for kindergarten education, *Children's Rights: A Book of Nursery Logic* (1892), described 'Bed in Summer' (ACGOV I) as 'deliciously real.'[39] The seminal scientific analysis, J. Sully's *Studies of Childhood*, was, in 1895 in New York, using 'The Land of Counterpane' (ACGOV XVI) as an example of imaginative 'transformations' in childhood.[40]

Yet Stevenson's verse did not meet with unmixed appreciation. The *Saturday Review* of 21 March 1885 complained that, though some of the 'lyrics would undoubtedly delight any child old enough to take delight in such things at all,' there was not enough in the collection to appeal to the adult sense of humor, which 'can enjoy the undercurrent of thought or meaning with a relish proportioned to the completeness of its concealment from the younger reader.'[41] *The Spectator* of 21 March 1885 said that children's poetry 'must embody the child's feeling, but it must embody it in a form far beyond the child's power of expression.'[42] This *Child's Garden* failed to do, with its 'verse which children might be supposed to write.' The reviewer added, with his foot in his mouth, 'Mr. Stevenson may be sure that those of his rhymes, . . . which a lively boy might have made, will never seize hold of children.'[43]

William Archer, in the *Pall Mall Gazette* of 24 March 1885, made a more severe criticism: 'Mr. Stevenson knows nothing of the fierce rebellions, the agonised doubts as to the existence of justice, human or divine which mar the music of childhood for so many; or if he realises their existence, he relegates them to that other life, the life of pain, and terror, and weariness into which it is part of his philosophy to look as seldom as possible.'[44] Stevenson was stung into replying on 29 March:

You are very right about my voluntary aversion from the painful sides of life. My childhood was in reality a very mixed experience, full of fever, nightmare, insomnia, painful days and interminable nights; and I can speak with less authority of gardens than of that other 'land of counterpane.' But to what end should we renew these sorrows? The sufferings of life may be handled by the very greatest in their hours of insight, it is of its pleasures that our common poems should be formed, these are the experiences that we should seek to recall or to provoke; and say with Thoreau, 'what right have I to complain, who have not ceased to wonder?' and, to add a rider of my own, who have no remedy to offer.[45]

Here, then, we have a writer admitting to the crime of reconstructing and idealizing his childhood, if only for the reason that he is unable to offer a 'remedy.' Should we take Stevenson at face value here? It is true the book is free of the pain that he himself admits to. But in 'Child's Play,' he located some of the pain of childhood in how adults treat children, and in a child's fear of what adulthood might turn out to be. Does *Child's Garden* touch on any of this?

I take 'Whole Duty of Children' (ACGOV V) as a child trying to repeat what an adult has told him, but because of the way he expresses the adult precepts, he reveals them in the last line to be faintly absurd:

A child should always say what's true
And speak when he is spoken to,
And behave mannerly at table;
At least as far as he is able.

'Farewell to the Farm' (ACGOV XL) touches on the helplessness of children when faced with adult orders to move on. Here it feels like the end of a holiday and the end of pleasure. In 'North-West Passage' (ACGOV XLI), an adult is implied with 'Must we to bed indeed?' and on the way there are 'All the wicked shadows coming, tramp, tramp, tramp, / With the black night overhead.' In 'My Treasures' (TCA V), we have the uncomprehending adult: the narrator has found a stone, but 'though father denies it, I'm sure it is gold.' These references and allusions are the nearest we come in the collection to a disparaging or pained view of adults.

Child's Garden does not encompass all the aspects of childhood that Stevenson himself identified, nor did he want it to do so. However, in particular in the poems that deal with imaginative play, he was both innovative and insightful. These do not fit neatly into concepts of innocence or sentimentality (whereas some of the other poems do) as they celebrate the pleasure derived from the transforming power of creativity. The collection is not a simple monotonal composition and expresses various contradictory positions which can be located in Stevenson's own theorizing.

Figure 9   From Robert Louis Stevenson, *A Child's Garden of Verses,* illus. Charles Robinson, London: Charles Robinson, Lane & Scribner, 1896. By kind permission of the Bodleian Library, University of Oxford, Shelfmark 280 e. 1641a.

Note on Abbreviations

References to specific poems are abbreviated according to the four sections of the book. The edition of *A Child's Garden of Verses* used is Janet Adam-Smith, *Robert Louis Stevenson: Collected Poems* (London, 1950): the Roman numerals adjacent to the abbreviated references follow the numbering in Adam-Smith.

Notes

I am indebted to Nicholas Rankin for help and advice, in particular for pointing out that Alexander Hay Japp visited Braemar at the time of Stevenson's writing of the *Child's Garden*.

1. Robert Louis Stevenson, 'Notes on the Movement of Young Children' (1874) from *The Works of Robert Louis Stevenson*, Vol. 22 (London, 1912), p. 98.
2. Ibid., p. 98.
3. Ibid., p. 99.
4. Ibid., p. 101.
5. Ibid., p. 102.
6. Hugh Cunningham, *The Children of the Poor: Representations of Childhood Since the Seventeenth Century* (Oxford, 1991), pp. 97–132.
7. Robert Louis Stevenson, 'Memoirs of Himself,' written in 1880, first published in 1923, pages cited here are from Vol. 25 (Edinburgh, 1925), p. 220.
8. Ibid., p. 221.
9. Ibid., p. 222.
10. Robert Louis Stevenson, 'A Gossip on Romance,' first published in *Longman's Magazine*, November 1882, and then as an essay in *Memories and Portraits* (London, 1887); page cited here is from *Memories and Portraits* (Glasgow, 1990), p. 187.
11. 'Child's Play' originally in *Cornhill Magazine*, September 1878, then *Virginibus Puerisque* (London, 1881); pages cited here are from *Virginibus Puerisque* (London, 1918), pp. 161–2.
12. Ibid., p. 164.
13. Ibid., p. 165.
14. Ibid., p. 160.
15. Ibid., p. 163.
16. Ibid., p. 163.
17. Alexander Francis Chamberlain, *The Child: A Study in the Evolution of Man* (London, 1900), p. 10, citing Herbert Spencer, *Principles of Psychology*.
18. Retold in Nicholas Rankin, *Dead Man's Chest: Travels After Robert Louis Stevenson* (London, 1987), p. 60.
19. Peter Coveney, *The Image of Childhood, the Individual and Society: A Study of the Theme in English Literature*, first published as *Poor Monkey* in 1957, thereafter, as above (London, 1967), p. 280.
20. Carolyn Steedman, *Childhood, Culture and Class in Britain: Margaret McMillan, 1860–1931* (London, 1990), p. 82.
21. Cited in Margaret Lowenfeld, *Play in Childhood* (London, 1935), p. 30, from Friedrich Froebel, *Chief Writings on Education*, translated by S. S. F. Fletcher and J. Welton (London, 1912).
22. Cited in Joachim Liebschner, *A Child's Work Freedom and Guidance in Froebel's Educational Theory and Practice* (Cambridge, 1992), p. 21, from A.B. Hanschmann, *Friedrich Froebel: Die Entwicklung seiner Erziehungsidee in seinen Leben* (Eiscnach, 1875), p. 225.
23. Alexander Hay Japp, 'Children and Children's Books,' *The Contemporary Review*, 11 May 1869; reprinted in Lance Salway, *A Peculiar Gift, Nineteenth Century Writings on Books for Children* (London, 1976), p. 198.
24. Robert Louis Stevenson, 'A Penny Plain and Twopence Coloured' (1884), reprinted in *Memories and Portraits* (London, 1887, Glasgow 1990), p. 152.
25. Mrs. Sale Barker and Kate Greenaway, *Birthday Book for Children* (London, 1880), pages unnumbered.
26. Ibid.
27. Ibid.
28. Quoted in Robert Louis Stevenson, *Collected Poems*, edited by Janet Adam-Smith (London, 1950), p. 549.

29. Ibid., p. 552.
30. Graham Balfour, *The Life of Robert Louis Stevenson*, Vol. 1 (London, 1901), p. 40. (The comment is dated as Swanston, 18 May 1873).
31. Rankin, p. 30.
32. Charles and Mary Lamb, *Poetry for Children, Entirely Original* (London, 1809), cited by Iona and Peter Opie, *The Oxford Book of Children's Verse* (Oxford, 1973), p. 141.
33. Juliana Horatia Ewing, originally printed in *Aunt Judy's Magazine*, September 1874; reprinted in Iona and Peter Opie, *The Oxford Book of Children's Verse* (Oxford, 1973), p. 257.
34. Robert Louis Stevenson, 'My First Book, *Treasure Island*,' first published in *The Idler*, August 1894, page cited here from Vol. 2 (Edinburgh 1925), p. 196.
35. Eric S. Robertson (Ed.). *The Children of the Poets: An Anthology from English and American Writers of Three Centuries* (London, 1886).
36. Matthew Browne, *Little Ben Bute Children's Poems* (Edinburgh, 1883).
37. Cunningham, p. 45.
38. Ibid., p. 154.
39. Kate Douglas Wiggin, *Children's Rights: A Book of Nursery Logic* (London, 1892), p. 17.
40. J. Sully, *Studies of Childhood* (New York, 1895), p. 36.
41. Paul Maixner (Ed.), *Robert Louis Stevenson: The Critical Heritage*, (London, 1981), p. 148.
42. Ibid., p. 152.
43. Ibid., p. 154.
44. Ibid., p. 157.
45. Ibid., p. 158.

A.A. Milne: *When We Were Very Young*
Jackie Wullschläger

A.A. Milne's misfortune was that in a casual moment one holiday, he wrote a few poems and then stories for children which made him rich and famous and which became so popular that he was never allowed to forget them. Eventually they came between him and everything else he wanted to do, and caused his estrangement from his beloved son. The Pooh stories sprang from his own happiness just as Carroll's or Barrie's fantasies grew out of their disappointments. In a horrible way, they then destroyed the very idyll they celebrated.

Milne and his son were the last victims of the literary obsession with childhood, and their story is tied to the development of British cultural life in the first part of this century. It is entirely appropriate that by the 1920s, when Pooh was created, the great new fantasy writer was neither an eccentric, nonliterary outsider like Lear or Carroll nor an unusual literary personality like Barrie or Grahame, but a conventional member of the English establishment

Condensed from J. Wullschläger, 'A.A. Milne: The Fantasy Tamed', in *Inventing Wonderland* (London: Methuen, 1995), pp. 177–99.

whose work and life reflected the widespread desire for lightheadedness, escape and post-war fun. For by the time Milne was writing after the First World War, the cult of the child, which had been a matter of passionate belief for the Victorians and of earnest idealism for the Edwardians, had turned into pure escapist whimsy: mawkishness based not on a Wordsworthian faith in the purity of children and nature but on a desperation to be flippant, unchallenged, intellectually and emotionally cosy. The 1920s saw the last twinkle of the romance of childlike innocence become decadent before it flickered out altogether in the depressed 1930s. Milne represents the fantasy tamed. Instead of Grahame's or Potter's real animals, his models are toys bought at Harrods; instead of Barrie's and Grahame's Pan, wild god of nature and spiritual core of the Edwardian classics of childhood, his god-like figure is a six-year-old who has just started school and cannot spell.

It is tempting to dismiss Pooh as the epitome of romantic innocence turned degenerate. And yet, Milne created in the Hundred Acre Wood a fantasy world as strong and definitive as Wonderland or Neverland, with characters more popular than any in children's literature. A century after Wordsworth, his was an original vision of the golden age of childhood that had obsessed generations of writers. No one who did not believe at some level in the idyll could have written it. But Pooh's forest is also shot through with irony. Milne knows the bathos, the unreality, of his stuffed toys as well as their nostalgic power. His fantasy survives its sweetness and sentimentality just because he does not wholly believe it, because he suffuses it with self-mockery which even very young readers enjoy.

In 1922, Milne wrote the sentimental verse 'Vespers', about his son saying his prayers, as a gift for his wife, and in 1923, at a dull house party in Wales, he retired to the summer house to dash off a children's poem he had promised for an anthology. It was the nonsense rhyme 'The Dormouse and the Doctor'; when it was finished Milne hung about the garden looking for an excuse to avoid the other guests. He scribbled out a few more poems, and by the time he fled the holiday, a quarter of *When We Were Very Young* had been written. He then, like Barrie twenty years earlier, took his doubting American publisher to lunch at the Garrick and persuaded him into what seemed a doomed venture. E.H. Shepard, a *Punch* artist of whom Milne had despaired during his days on the magazine, was commissioned as illustrator, and Methuen, who had gambled on *The Wind in the Willows*, risked an edition of 5,000 in November 1924. Six weeks later, over 40,000 copies were in print in England, the American market was flourishing, reviewers were ecstatic, and Milne was a marked man: the bestselling children's author of the decade.

The following Christmas, the *Evening News* pressed him for a children's piece and he adapted a story he had told Christopher Robin about his teddy bear. The first Winnie-the-Pooh episode appeared on Christmas Eve 1925 under a front-page headline and was broadcast on Christmas Day from all radio stations. *Winnie-the-Pooh*, with more stories, was published in 1926, its successor *The House at Pooh Corner* in 1928, and another volume of poems, *Now We Are Six*, in 1927. All were instant bestsellers and have been ever since.

Figure 10 'Halfway Down', from A.A. Milne, *When We Were Very Young*, illus. Ernest H. Shepard, London: Methuen & Co. Ltd, 1932, p. 80. Copyright © The Estate of E.H. Shepard, reproduced with permission of Curtis Brown Group Ltd, London

The Pooh books, with their backcloth of nannies and nurseries, owe much to Barrie's Edwardian world; even the title of the first, *When We Were Very Young*, suggests parental nostalgia, and this powerful nostalgic quality already in the 1920s was put of their appeal. In the poems, the Twinkletoe fairies, the Lake King's daughter floating on a water lily, the

Brownies behind the curtain, recall Barrie but also reflect the craze for fairies which was a feature of 1920s escapism. Milne was writing two years after Arthur Conan Doyle, creator of the super-sleuth Sherlock Holmes, published in *Strand* magazine the sensational 'photographs' of the Cottingley fairies, which he was convinced some Yorkshire children had actually seen and photographed, and which experts 'confirmed' as authentic. Other poems, like 'Hoppity' ('Christopher Robin goes/Hoppity hoppity', said to send adult dinner parties hopping round tables in Kensington and Chelsea), or 'Halfway Down', with its arch pictures of Christopher Robin as an updated Little Lord Fauntleroy perched on the staircase, caught the mood of playful distraction then in demand.

Yet Milne's tone is worlds away from Barrie's dream of never growing up. The Edwardian work is morally earnest; Milne is a 1920s humorist – ironic, cynical/sentimental, an escapist who knows he escaping. Barrie, in *Peter Pan and Wendy* in 1911, calls children heartless, but he recalls Wordsworth in the ideal of childhood imagination and innocence expressed in the book:

> On these magic shores children at play are for ever beaching their coracles. We too have been there; we can still hear the sound of the surf, though we shall land no more.

Ten years on, the popular children's writer is a realist. Milne wrote of a child's natural lack of moral quality, which expresses itself . . . in an egotism entirely ruthless'. His genius was to fix the character of the archetypal child, in the context of a child's vision, and within the limits of children's language, as no one before or since has ever done. Earlier fantasies are as much about adult longings as childhood pleasures, and adult readers return to find new depths in them. The Pooh stories are primarily children's books; they offer adults only the nostalgia of a child's eye view. Unlike earlier fantasy writers, Milne is a devastatingly accurate child psychologist. The witty conviction with which he presents his child-centred universe has kept young readers hooked for seventy years. But it also marked the end of an idealism which had provided the climate for the fantasy genre to develop. With Milne, the cult of the innocent child was over.

Instead, here is a world of games, songs and rhymes, food and easy affection, which any child can recognise instantly. The dramas of *When We Were Very Young* are entirely childish – stepping between the lines and squares on the pavement, putting on wellington boots, eating up your supper, washing your hands before tea. The best poems, the ones children recite and adults remember, are all humorous revelations about the workings of a child's mind. There is the child's awestruck diffidence combined with the belief that he is the centre of the world in 'Buckingham Palace':

> They're changing guard at Buckingham Palace –
> Christopher Robin went down with Alice.
>> 'Do you think the king knows all about *me*?'
>> 'Sure to, dear, but it's time for tea,'
>>> Says Alice

There is the fear of desertion and the confusion at adult ways, mockingly reversed in 'Disobedience' when a mother strays out of bounds:

> James James
> Morrison Morrison
> Weatherby George Dupree
> Took great
> Care of his Mother,
> Though he was only three.
> James James
> Said to his Mother,
> 'Mother,' he said, said he;
> 'You must never go down to the end of the town,
>> if you don't go down with me'.

There is the teddy bear, who muses in the ottoman about a King of France pictured as fat as himself, and assumes this is the first person he meets on falling out of the window into the adult world: a perfect pastiche of a child's ability to refer all things to himself and to mix fantasy and reality:

> Our bear could only look and look:
> The stout man in the picture-book!
> That 'handsome' King – could this be he,
> This man of adiposity? . . .

> 'Are you,' he said, 'by any chance
> His Majesty the King of France?'
> The other answered, 'I am that,'
> Bowed stiffly, and removed his hat;
> Then said, 'Excuse me,' with an air,
> 'But is it Mr Edward Bear?'
> And Teddy, bending very low,
> Replied politely, 'Even so!'

After the conversation, the bear is handed in at the door – 'Your bear, I think – and deflated to toy-size: a perspective shift as clever as Grahame's with Toad, and one which gives a sense of how fleetingly a child can feel himself first grand and then insignificant.

Milne uses the simplest language of any children's author, but he is also the greatest nonsense writer since Carroll and Lear. Language and rhythm; the mad repetition of poems like 'The King's Breakfast' and 'Disobedience', whose distorted perspectives come out best, as in Lear's 'The Akond of Swat', when chanted aloud; nursery-rhyme archetypes like Little Bo Beep, on which Milne elaborates as Carroll had done; nonsense rhymes, chosen as in Lear and Carroll for sound before meaning – dormouse/e-nor-mouse, foxes and sockses, shopses and copses and wopses: all have a timeless appeal for children. But this is also nonsense tamed, domesticated: the teddy bear sleeping in the ottoman, tin soldiers feeding on cream buns, Nurse and Percy in his slippers. Milne retains just a hint of the anarchy of mid-Victorian nonsense – the bears who lurk in wait in 'Lines and Squares', the satire on the self-satisfied doctor and the hapless dormouse, the escaping mamma, and of course the oddball types, from Tigger to Eeyore, whom we have come to expect from a children's classic. But where Carroll invented a wild, unrecognisable wonderland, Milne, the realist, paints children as they are, and brings nonsense into the world of everyday: his characters are middle-class household commodities that seems to emerge out of Harrods, the Chelsea nursery, the Sussex garden.

In 1929, Milne wrote confidently that 'all I have got from Christopher Robin is a name which he never uses, an introduction to his friends . . . and a gleam which I have tried to follow. However . . . I do not want C.R. Milne ever to wish that his names were Charles Robert.'[1] His worries were well-founded, for Christopher Robin's fame would not die. Pictures of father and son had adorned newspapers and the frontispieces of the books, and in 1933 *Parents Magazine* celebrated Christopher Robin, along with Yehudi Menuhin, Princess Elizabeth, Crown Prince Michael of Romania and child film star Jakie Coogan, as one of the most famous children in the world.

Unlike them, Christopher Robin had neither the background nor the talent to cope with such pressure. As he grew up, the shadow of Pooh was embarrassing and constraining. At Stowe, his schoolmates mockingly played an old gramophone of 'Vespers', which he had recorded as a child; when eventually they handed it to him, he broke it into hundreds of fragments and scattered them across a field. He was familiarly greeted with lines like 'Hello, Christopher Robin! Still saying your prayers?' He trembled, stammered and was cripplingly shy. Yet he could mould himself only on his father, and could not break away. He was, he wrote later, 'very close indeed to my father, adoring him, admiring him, accepting his ideas'.[2] The two played cricket together, chattered, solved simultaneous equations together on the sofa in the evenings, had childish holidays together in Dorset while Daphne, Milne's wife, flitted off to the Mediterranean. 'He needed me to escape from being fifty', said Christopher.[3]

Milne's problem in the 1930s, like Christopher's was that he was ineradicably associated with the Pooh books, and, haunted by their fame, he blamed them for every misfortune:

> It is easier in England to make a reputation than to lose one. I wrote four 'Children's books', containing altogether. I suppose, 70,000 words – the number of words in the average-length novel. Having said goodbye to all that in 70,000 words, knowing that as far as I was concerned the mode was outmoded, I gave up writing children's books. I wanted to escape from them as I had once wanted to escape from *Punch*; as I have always wanted to escape. In vain.[4]

In fact, his brand of escapist whimsy, which fitted so well with the simple themes of childhood in *Winnie-the-Pooh*, was anyway going out of fashion in the depressed and cynical 1930s. His adult plays, previously successful, began to flop. By the end of the decade he was regarded as a spent force.

For the rest of his life he continued to watch his adult works fall from fashion while Pooh remained a bestseller. In the Second World War, sales of the Pooh books rose so steeply that Methuen could not get enough paper to keep them in print; even in Sweden translations of *Winnie-the-Pooh* were selling 5,000 copies a year by 1946.

For Milne, fame had turned sour with dazzling speed. The Pooh books rested on an appeal to nostalgia, so that in a sense Milne was old-fashioned even when he was the height of fashion, a fact which proved to make Pooh enduringly popular white Milne was soon seen as hopelessly out of date. Here he differed crucially from the other fantasy writers, who all reflect the themes of their times. Carroll's concerns, his highly wrought tone, his vision of chaos, his girl-fixation, were typically mid-Victorian, and strong parallels in language, ideas, images, mark him as a contemporary of, for example, Dickens. The same common ground links Grahame and his vision of Arcadian England to his Edwardian contemporaries, Forster, Saki, Edward Thomas. But Milne was a throwback who had nothing in common with 1920s modernism, and it is incredible that Pooh appeared after *Ulysses* and *The Waste Land*. There was something inauthentic about the Pooh books from the start, which crities very soon picked up.

The 1930s modernists made mincemeat of Milne. Cyril Connolly, reviewing his autobiography, criticised Milne's 'gentlemanly good taste which veils both a shrewd eye on the main chance and perhaps a fear of life', and wrote:

> He reminds me of Noel Coward, a pre-war Noel Coward springing from the same unexpectedly lower middle class stock, but moving with pre-war acceleration into a smooth heaven of light verse, cricketing weekends, good society, whimsical taste and money, money, money.[5]

Parodies also began at once: a pastiche of 'Vespers' – 'Hush, hush, nobody cares/Christopher Robin's fallen downstairs' – was followed as early as 1926 by a collection of parodies, *When We Were Rather Older*, updating the nursery world to the Jazz Age:

> James James
> Morrison's Mother's
> Had her hair shingled off.
> She's late
> Home for her dinner,
> Being out shooting golf.
> Jim says
> Somebody told her
> That was the modern view,
> And since it's the rage not to be your age, well,
> what can any son do?

Pastiches and variations on Pooh have thrived ever since, most famously in *Winnie ille Pu* (1960), the Latin translation which became the first foreign-language bestseller in America, and in *The Pooh Perplex* (1963), Frederick Crews's skit on different schools of literary criticism as a 'student casebook' on Pooh. Crews's mockery, which as a bonus included much perceptive criticism of the Pooh books and their times, silenced almost all work on Milne for decades, and it is still difficult to write a line about Pooh without hearing Crews's satiric laughter over one's shoulder. Despite the pastiche, it is of course the very familiarity and cosiness of Pooh that makes the joke study so popular and accessible.

> This Sir Edward Bear, Sir Pooh de Bear, is the very image of a fat old Tory who passes all his time pampering his depraved tastes and reminiscing about his imaginary exploits. Substitute port and brandy for condensed milk and honey, and you will recognise the likeness at once. He is a *flabby* bear, and flabbiness in literature is a thing I detest above all else.

Everyone can laugh at Pooh because everyone knows him, and the very security and middle-class complacency and parochial Englishness of the

Pooh world, which has led critics to savage it, are precisely the qualities which continue to endear the books to children and adults more than half a century after they were written.

Notes

1. A.A. Milne, *By Way of Introduction*, London, 1929, pp. 205–6.
2. Christopher Milne, *The Enchanted Places*, London, 1974, p. 141.
3. Ibid, p. 159.
4. Ann Thwaite, *A.A. Milne: His Life*, London, 1990, p. 362.
5. *The New Statesman*, 11 September 1939.

References

Milne, A.A., *When We Were Very Young*, London, 1924.
Milne, A.A., *Now We Are Six*, London, 1927.
Milne, A.A., *By Way of Introduction*, London, 1929.
Milne, Christopher, *The Enchanted Places*, London, 1974.
Thwaite, Ann, *A.A. Milne: His Life*, London, 1990.

5
J.M. Barrie, *Peter Pan* (1904)

Introduction
Nicola J. Watson

Arguably the most famous and influential of all stage-plays for children, since its first performance in 1904, *Peter Pan* has occupied an unassailable position for more than a hundred years in both children's mythology and the mythology of childhood. It remains an unavoidable reference-point for all those interested in children's literature and culture and in the history of the construction of childhood.

Located at the epicentre of the so-called First Golden Age of children's literature, *Peter Pan* recapitulated, exploited, and contained much of the nineteenth century's stock of entertainment for children, whether print or theatre. Never Land, for instance, is compounded of the century's adventure stories for boys. The island's domesticity is pure *Robinson Crusoe* mixed up with bits of Captain Marryat's *The Children of the New Forest*. The Red Indians have escaped from Fenimore Cooper's Leatherstocking series of novels and Longfellow's *Song of Hiawatha*. The pirates are clearly reworkings of the villains of *Treasure Island* and the related pleasures of penny dreadfuls. The mermaids are related to the sisters of Hans Christian Andersen's *Little Mermaid*. The excitement of imperial adventure has seeped in from Charles Kingsley's *Westward Ho!* The central story – the stealing away of children by the fairies – although older still – resonates with other Victorian and Edwardian rethinkings of the fairy-tale, Charles Kingsley's *The Water Babies*, Christina Rossetti's *Goblin Market*, or George Macdonald's *The Princess and the Goblin*.

If Never Land is compounded of classic boys' fiction, the play itself is heavily indebted to the stage tradition of Victorian pantomime and to the emergent Edwardian 'fairy play', borrowing pantomime's use of children, the ambiguous sexuality of the Principal Boy, the frightening unreliability of Harlequin, the ubiquity of fairies and fairy tales, the transformation scene to a 'magic' landscape, the animal characters, and its use of audience participation from pantomime, and the sense of refined prettiness, charm, whimsy, and nostalgia from fairy plays, such as Seymour Hicks's *Bluebell in Fairyland* (1901).

Both the imaginative child-spaces of Never Land and the popular stage-practices of pantomime are framed (however tongue-in-cheek) within the authoritative social realism of the Nursery; and this framing points to the play's simultaneous indulgence of, and investigation into, adult fantasies of childhood. Accordingly, in the post-Freudian twentieth and twenty-first centuries, the figure of Peter Pan has haunted thinking about childhood as a privileged space of fantasy, make-believe and escape from the rigours and disappointments of growing up, becoming particularly powerful at moments where growing-up to be a man is visibly liable to have a dubious outcome – as in the First World War. It has also haunted thinking about male sexuality, and about paedophilia, as the persistent and ever-growing body of criticism narrating Barrie's life in terms of the fantasies of Peter Pan (such as in the 2004 film *Finding Neverland*) demonstrates.

Origins, composition, and first stage production

The story of the composition of *Peter Pan* is complicated, and further complicated by Barrie's own accounts of the process. A version of the plot first appears in an episode in a novel for adults, *The Little White Bird* (1902), which was subsequently extracted and published as *Peter Pan in Kensington Gardens* (1906). Another source for the play is the early, privately printed book he wrote and supplied the photographs for as an account of his summer holiday adventures with the Llewellyn Davies family of boys, entitled *The Boy Castaways of Black Lake Island* (1901). The first draft of the play was written between November 1903 and March 1904, and staged in the West End of London in the season of 1904–5.

Barrie was then at the height of his fame as a playwright and The Duke of York Theatre billed it as a theatrical extravaganza. The play required a large number of complicated special effects: the most famous of these is the flying in and out of Peter Pan and the children, but this was, if dangerous, child's play to a theatre accustomed to flying fairies in and out by the dozen for *A Midsummer Night's Dream*. Barrie also called variously for great birds to swoop down and carry off actors by the seats of their trousers, the crocodile to eat a wooden boat, Peter to sail off stage in a gigantic bird's nest, and a pirate ship to sail onto the stage. Perhaps unsurprisingly, technical difficulties postponed the opening night by five days, and even on the opening night the machinery to raise the Wendy house to the top of the Never Land trees at the end of Act 5 was not operable. The first production experimented with a number of scenes excised from later versions; in particular, the ending seems to have given trouble, and Barrie supplied a number of alternative accounts of the return to London: a harlequinade to round off the piece, in which Hook played a schoolmaster, and Peter and Wendy elude him by transforming into Harlequin and Columbine, the arrival of '20 Beautiful Mothers' in the final nursery scene to undergo tests of motherhood to fit them to claim the Lost Boys (played in the first season and dropped because it proved excruciatingly embarrassing), and, most startling evidence of all, the scene played just once in Barrie's life (22 February 1908) entitled 'An Afterthought'. Not published until 1957, it has become since the 1980s the standard ending to the play. Other changes to the play were driven by actors: the extension of Hook's part, especially his soliloquy on death, seems in part to have developed from improvisation on the part of Gerald du Maurier (who was also doubling as Mr Darling); the introduction of Peter's untouchableness followed from the replacement of Nina Boucicault, the original Peter Pan, by Pauline Chase.

One of the consequences of this persistent evolution is that the play-text that we have, published in 1928, is not and never has been an entirely accurate record of how *Peter Pan* has been performed; this is not merely that the play-text includes a great deal of material interpolated from his novelisation of the play *Peter Pan and Wendy* (1911), but because it departed from the acting script as we can reconstruct it from manuscripts by leaving out a number of scenes that have traditionally been played. One example of this is the largely improvised 'front of cloth scene' (a scene played in front of a backcloth that conceals much of the stage while a major scene-change is being carried out) featuring the pirate Starkey dismally playing an accordion and lamenting his fate with the refrain 'miserable Starkey'. The play-text as we have it is the play as Barrie wished us to see it in print, a reading version of the theatrical experience shorn of the technical limitations of the theatre.

Reception, publication, and afterlives

Audience reception of the play was generally enthusiastic. Reviews were generally favourable if a little cautious and puzzled. Closing briefly on 1 April 1905, the play was subsequently revived, complete with an entire new act, 'The Mermaids' Lagoon', and became thereafter a London institution, performed every Christmas except in 1940. The play also had a hit in the States, opening in New York and running for seven months, before touring for some years. It was revived in 1912, 1915 and 1924.

Subsequent stage versions have included musicals (including one with music by Leonard Bernstein in 1950), but on the whole productions throughout the twentieth century were highly traditionalist, aiming to reproduce the original to every last detail, until Christmas 1982, when the Royal Shakespeare Company staged a Peter Pan directed by Trevor Nunn and John Caird, casting a male adult, Miles Anderson, as Peter, and introducing material from other variant texts, much of it spoken by an actor-narrator dressed and made up to look like Barrie. In 1924, it was first made into a film; Walt Disney's animated version came out in 1953; more recently it has appeared in a Hollywood version of 2003.

The essays

White and Tarr's essay amplifies the introductory remarks above, usefully placing *Peter Pan* as a play within the tradition of pantomime and the Edwardian fairy-play, both associated with Christmas. Rose's essay is extracted from her book *The Case of Peter Pan: or, The Impossibility of Children's Fiction* (1984) which has not only, as its provocative subtitle might suggest, exerted a profound though by no means uncontested influence upon the theorisation of the field of children's literature, but has also dictated the terms in which much critical discussion of *Peter Pan* has been conducted since. The book as a whole is structured as an enquiry into the cultural import of *Peter Pan*, via a set of close readings of the many texts that have gone to make up the mythos: *The Little White Bird, The Boy Castaways of Black Island, Peter Pan in Kensington Gardens*, the play itself, and *Peter Pan and Wendy*. In the very broadest terms, Rose deploys the language of psychoanalytic criticism to consider the way that the history of *Peter Pan* has dramatised and exemplified the adult production of childhood in modern culture. In this extract she concentrates on the play, exploring the problem of 'setting the child up as a spectacle' through staging it, enquiring to what extent *Peter Pan* is a 'spectacle of childhood for *us*, or [a] play for children', and reading it symptomatically as a drama that thematises the refusal of 'normal' adult heterosexuality. Hollindale's essay describes the current status of *Peter Pan* in modern culture, noting that this is dependent upon 'two co-existent' stories, 'each with the capacity to distort or confuse our understanding of the other', one the play/fiction (most recently incarnated in the 2003 film *Peter Pan*) and the other the story of its biographical genesis and aftermath (redacted in 2004 in the film *Finding Neverland*). Hollindale's essay is here provided as a thoughtful meditation upon the way in which biographical criticism is especially likely to encroach on criticism of children's literature.

Further reading

Green, R.L. 1954. *Fifty Years of Peter Pan*. London, P. Davies.

Jack, R.D.S. 1990. 'The Manuscript of Peter Pan', *Children's Literature*, 18, 101–13.

Rose, J. 1984. *The Case of Peter Pan: or, The Impossibility of Children's Fiction*. London, Macmillan.

White, D.R. and Tarr, C.A. 2006. *J.M. Barrie's* Peter Pan *In and Out of Time: A Children's Classic at 100*. Lanham, MD, Scarecrow.

Peter Pan and the Spectacle of the Child
Jacqueline Rose

Setting the child up as a spectacle, shining a light on it and giving it up to our gaze – there is something in this which needs to be questioned. It links up with a history of the visual image in relation to the child, in which *Peter Pan* has its part. Barrie, like Lewis Carroll, took photographs of children. Barrie's collection, *The Boy Castaways of Black Lake Island* (Llewellyn Davies, 1901),[1] consists of thirty-six photographs of the Llewellyn Davies boys, and the rudiments of an adventure narrative. Together with *The Little White Bird*, it almost constitutes a second source book for *Peter Pan*. Only two copies of it were ever produced, one of which Arthur Llewellyn Davies, the boys' father, promptly mislaid on a train.

A photograph offers itself as something innocent and authentic which speaks for itself – merely capturing the moment it records. Its immediacy belies the technique, the framing, the pose, all of which make the photograph possible (terms of artifice and calculation which are cancelled out by the natural and effortless feel of the best pictures). The innocence of the photograph as a record or document seems to vouch for the innocence of our pleasure in looking, and no more so perhaps than when what we are looking at is a child.

Extracted from 'Peter Pan and Freud', in J. Rose, *The Case of Peter Pan: Or, The Impossibility of Children's Fiction* (London: Macmillan, [1984] 1992), pp. 28–39.

The Boy Castaways of Black Lake Island is made up almost exclusively of photographs of little boys. The book comprises thirty-six captioned photographs, a preface and a series of chapter headings with no text. The preface is the only extended piece of writing in the book: the voice of it is unmistakably the voice of an adult who offers the document as instruction for the boy, Michael, as well as a record of his childhood (proof, indeed, that he once was a child). But this question of voice is not restricted to the preface – it is evoked by the photographs themselves. For, in exactly the same way as the adult reveals himself in the preface, the innocence of the photographs (the idyllic romping, the adventure) calls up the question of who – that is, which adult – is taking them? Where, we ask, is the creator of these pictures, the very transparency of the image (boys presented to us so unequivocally at play, that is, *their* play and *their* story) uneasily evoking the necessary presence of the one who is watching (in this case, as we know, Barrie himself). Capturing a moment has, therefore, two meanings – the record of a past history which is lost, and the seizing of the child by an image which, as the very condition of its effectivity, leaves outside its frame the look of the adult who creates it.

What are we doing, therefore, when we put the child on the stage? This is not as uncalled for a question as it might seem. Barrie was a highly successful playwright when *Peter Pan* was first performed as a play in 1904, and it had been billed as his new theatrical extravaganza. The audience was made up of London's theatre-going élite, and there was hardly a child among them (Mackail, 1941, p. 366; Green, 1954, p. 85; Birkin, 1979, p. 116). Calling *Peter Pan* a play for children, we have to ask not only what we think we are doing when we put the child on the stage, but also what we are doing when we assume, as we have for more than three-quarters of a century, that the child belongs in the audience.

The 1904–5 production script of *Peter Pan* (Beinecke, 1904–5B) and the 1905 script for Act I are prefaced with 'A Note. On the Acting of a Fairy Play'. This note emphatically places the child on the stage, but it never once refers to any children in the audience. What distinguishes a fairy play from a realistic drama is the fact that all its characters are children: 'this applies to the so-called adults of the story as well as to the young people' (Beinecke, 1904–5B, p. i). I think that this has to mean by implication that children are not real. But they are the authors of the play which was 'written by a child in *deadly* earnestness' (my italics), and they are also behind the scenes: 'The scenic artist is another child in league with them' (Beinecke, 1904–5B, p. i). The whole performance and its staging is, therefore, given up to the child; but what about the child in the audience?

Barrie's note in fact indicates that stage space, in and of itself, redistributes in another form the divisions which lie behind any act of representation. There is an off-stage to the play, where Barrie's note puts the child as 'scenic artist', but where the child in the audience cannot go, and which it is not allowed to see without risking the collapse of the whole stage illusion. And there is a barrier in the theatre between the stage and the audience, which the audience, for much the same reason, is not allowed to cross. The child is there precisely to watch what is happening, to query only up to the point of the limits on either side of the stage, and to recognise itself in the scenario which unfolds before its eyes. But that recognition also has its limits. The actors are mostly adults, and, as likely as not, there will be an adult with the child in the audience, watching the child at least as much as what is going on on stage. If we want to call *Peter Pan* a play for children, therefore, we should start by recognising our place in its history and performance, and the complexity of the relations which once again lie behind the transparency of the term.

Spectacle of childhood for *us*, or play for *children*? The question goes beyond the issue of trying to determine how many children might have seen *Peter Pan* (millions by now), or whether or not they said they liked it (for that you will find evidence either way).

When *Peter Pan* becomes a play, the first thing to notice is the way that this question of how a space of representation is being constituted for the child has been forced to the outer limits of its performance. *Peter Pan* takes the difficulties of *The Little White Bird* – of the adult-child relationship, and of how and why a story is told to the child – and either cuts them out completely, or reduces them to mere child's-play. From this point on in *Peter Pan*'s history we will see all these difficulties surfacing constantly in different forms, and just as constantly being suppressed. It is, however, the very definition of suppression – according to Freud at least – that it never really works, especially perhaps when what is being got rid of are all the queries, at the level of sexuality and language, which Freudian psychoanalysis was uncovering at exactly the same time that *Peter Pan* was being promoted and reproduced. As Freud himself puts it in another context: 'the distortion of a text resembles a murder: the difficulty is not in perpetrating the deed, but in getting rid of its traces' (Freud, SE, XXIII (1934–8) 1939, p. 43).

Roger Lancelyn Green has pointed out that *Peter Pan* is the perfect adventure story (Green, 1954, p. 31). A little boy breaks into a nursery and takes the children away to an island of redskins and pirates, where they act out the adventures which they normally read in books, before safely returning home. In *Peter Pan*, these adventures, with all their risk and danger, come true, but their threat is contained, first by Peter Pan himself who comes from the island to which he takes the children, and who has already been through the whole thing several times before, and secondly by the nursery which is the start and the finishing point of the whole story. This structure – of an exploration which is finally held in place by the world which we recognise and know as real – is one which is frequently used in children's fiction to this day.

Bringing the children home is one of the most striking things which happens in *Peter Pan* as a play. The child is put back in the nursery, and the act of telling stories is given to the little girl, Wendy. It is because of the stories which Wendy knows that she is invited to the island to tell stories to the lost boys. Mothers tell stories to their children, and nothing could be safer than that. As a play, therefore, *Peter Pan* assigns the act of telling stories to its socially recognisable context. The difficult relationship between the narrator and the boy child of *The Little White Bird* is turned into a relationship between a mother and her child. Hook is the male villain, but he so recognisably belongs to literary and theatrical convention that the sexual problem is dissolved. The success of *Peter Pan*, then, would stem from the way in which it brings together adventure fantasy and the recognisable domestic scene.

None of this, however, really works. Staging always carries with it something of the question of how things are done, as well as for whom, and by whom, they are produced, the question which the child first asks when confronted with the family drama. No nursery is ever *just* safe. The play opens with the Darling children (the name of the family) playing at mothers and fathers, acting out the history of their own birth and stopping the game when there is one of them whom they do not wish to be born: 'Michael. Am I not to be born at all?' (Beinecke, 1904–5B, Act I, p. 5). Peter Pan, like the child in the audience, watches from outside. This is the one performance in which he cannot play a part. The play therefore opens with the question of the child's place in the most familiar, and primary, of family scenes. It is a question which is repeatedly posed in the play, and it shows up in the most unlikely of places. On the island, Wendy tells the story of growing up and of life back in the nursery (this is unheard of in the adventure stories of Marryat, Kingston and Henry, and in any case she had been invited to tell *Cinderella*). It is when Peter Pan challenges her story as untrue, and tells her that, like him, she will not be able to go home, that the whole island sequence breaks up and the children rush to depart. This leads to the final confrontation between Peter Pan and Hook, and then between Peter and Wendy after he has taken her back to the nursery. Barrie did not know how to end the play and the difficulty appears to have revolved around the two relationships – between Peter and Hook and between Peter and Wendy – in which the sexual difficulty had only seemingly been neutered.

There are in fact two conflicts in *Peter Pan*, that between the nursery and the Never Land (originally the Never Never Never Land), and that waged by Peter Pan against both. Thus Peter Pan attacks the family scene in the home underground and precipitates it break-up, but this is in turn attacked by Hook and the pirates who are waging war on Peter. Peter Pan, having differentiated himself from the children, is left behind and it is the children who are captured. Putting it crudely, we can say that this was not what Hook was after since his object was Peter himself. This produces a series of structural confusions and panics which spread across the different arenas of the spectacle – thus Hook tries to get at Peter and fails, Tinkerbell swallows the poison in order to save Peter, Peter comes *off* stage in order to get the children in the audience to save Tinkerbell (the famous episode), and then goes off to save the children which leads to the battle with Hook. The fight between Peter and Hook has a clear logic in relation to the family drama – part of a retaliation fantasy, the completion of the Oedipal circuit for John and Michael with Peter Pan exactly the 'avenger' (Mr Darling and Hook almost invariably double in performance) – but it has the secondary effect of bringing Peter, who had been left behind, back up against the maternal nursery. Peter's battle with Hook, therefore, leads to his accidentally siding with the nursery, and the difficulties of the final act can then be read in terms of the need to re-differentiate him.

In point of fact it is too easy to give an Oedipal reading of *Peter Pan*. The father, Mr Darling, is humiliated – he plays a joke on Nana the nurse (the Newfoundland dog) which falls flat and then challenges the family: 'Am I master in this house or is she?' (Beinecke, 1904–5B, Act I, p. 13). The children fly off and he crawls into the kennel out of shame. On the island, the children meet their father in another form, symbolically murder him through Peter Pan and return home. Whereupon Mr Darling crawls out of the kennel and the children can grow up.

It is equally easy to describe the difficulties which Barrie had in writing, and especially in ending *Peter Pan*, in terms of the magic elusiveness of the play and the mystery of the eternal boy child: 'no real beginning and no real end . . . obviously a little piece of immortality' (Noyes, *The Bookman*, December 1911, p. 132); 'there was behind this willingness to change a feeling that [this finale] was rather out of keeping with the character of Peter himself who, as is the case with creations of genius, was beginning to develop an independent personality of his own' (Green, 1954, p. 65). The drama of the performance – the fact that the actors were all sworn to secrecy and that no one knew how the play was going to end (Green, 1954, p. 72) – can then be seen as appropriate to something which defies description, understanding and even representation, an intangible factor which can only add to the essential mystique of the play.

I see these responses as related, because of their shared resistance to the idea of any trouble or disturbance in the play: whether that of the difficulty which always persists from any Oedipal 'resolution',[2] or whether that of Barrie's own confusion which seems to have manifested itself in an almost physical inability to write the play down. The problem of the ending can easily be exaggerated (for instance, revisions and major editing, right up to and even after the first performance, were a regular feature of pantomime production). On the other hand, looking through the different production scripts, programmes, reviews and the various endings which they offer of the play, it is clear that the particular forms of hesitancy, at the level of writing and performance, belong in different ways to those questions about origins, sexuality and death which the play tries, unsuccessfully, to bring to a resolution.

The main problem is Peter Pan himself. How can he be got rid of or 'resolved' given that it is the very definition of the child who does not grow up that he will always remain and constantly returns to the same place? Peter Pan is *stuck*, and the play with him. In all versions, Peter fails to answer the sexual query which Wendy puts to him when he invites her back to the island: 'But what as, Peter, what as?', she asks, to which he replies 'Your son' (not the reply she wanted); and his failure merely underlines the fact that the play cannot assimilate him to the 'normality' which it has constructed all around him. But in the earliest versions of *Peter Pan*, this sexuality is far more explicit. There is a seduction attempt on the part of Tiger-Lily which is subsequently cut out. Furthermore, Peter recognises that Tinkerbell, Wendy and Tiger-Lily all want the same thing which he cannot understand:

> *Peter.*   Now then, what is it you *want*?
> *Tiger-Lily.*   Want to be your squaw.
> *Peter.*   Is that what you want, Wendy?
> *Wendy.*   I suppose it is, Peter.
> *Peter.*   Is that what you want, Tink?
> Bells answer.
> *Peter.*   You all three want that. Very well – that's really wishing to be my mother.
>
> Beinecke, 1904–5B, Act ii, scene iii, p. 26

There is also the other side of this sexual refusal, Hook's desire for Peter, which in the earliest versions brings him hot on Peter Pan's tail and right into Kensington Gardens (Beinecke, 1904, Typescript i, Act iii, scene vi).

The effect of all of this is that *Peter Pan* constantly slides into moments of excess (disavowal always has something of the overstatement about it), as the insistence on motherhood (Wendy as a mother to Peter as opposed to anything else) starts to go over the top. The best example is 'The Beautiful Mothers Scene' (Beinecke, 1904, Act III, scene ii) which was performed for part of the first run of the play, in which the assorted mothers of London rush onto the stage to lay claim to the lost boys and are subjected to various tests of true maternity (the scene was mercifully cut during the first run). But the same insistence can be seen in scenes which are still performed today, such as the front-scene of the final act in which the pirate, Starkey, has been taken prisoner by the Redskins and is left to watch over their babies (an unlikely combination, but one which has its logic here).

As was the case with *The Little White Bird*, there is an anxiety about sexuality and birth which goes hand in hand with this all-too-cloying innocence, sweetness and light (the last act is called 'Home Sweet Home'). In one of the earliest versions of the play's ending, Peter reacts with distress when Wendy claims as her own a baby who appears under a pile of leaves in Kensington Gardens where they are living together (Beinecke, 1904, Typescript I, Act III, scene vi). That distress is most obvious in Barrie's *Afterthought*, the ending of the play which was only performed once on 1908 (Beinecke, 1908B–D and Barrie, 1957). Peter Pan returns to the nursery after many years and finds Wendy a grown woman with a child. Faced with the 'living proof' of the irreducible difference between them (the fact of growing up and of passing time), Peter goes to Wendy's daughter, Jane, with a dagger (the resistance is already there in the title of the piece – conception as something which can only be *thought* of, if indeed it *can* be thought of, *after*). This version copes with the crisis by having the child wake up and address Peter Pan with exactly the same words that Wendy had used in the opening scene of the play which then sets off the whole cycle again. This in ieself shows how repetition, in the sense of doing the same thing over and over again, serves above all to ward off something with which it is impossible to deal.

Between the lines of *Peter Pan*, we can see not only the question of origins (mothers and fathers), and of sexuality (boys and girls), but also the reference to death which is latent to the other two. An autographed addition to the second draft of the 1908 ending gives us the term around which *Peter Pan* endlessly circulates:

Don't be anxious, Nana. This is how I planned it; if he ever came back. (You see – I think now – that Peter is only a sort of dead baby – he is the baby of all the people who never had one.) (Beinecke, 1908C, words in parenthesis are an autograph addition in Barrie's hand facing page 21)

There is no way of talking about sexuality and origins without raising death as an issue; but in a play for children it can, finally, have no place. The end of *Peter Pan*, as it is best known, removes most of this. Peter Pan takes the children home and then returns to the island, where Wendy visits him once a year to do the annual spring-clean. The island is domesticated, Wendy will grow up, and Peter Pan is sent back to where he came from (the ultimate clean-up job we could say).

Peter Pan has, therefore, come into its own by the successive repudiation of those questions which every child has the right to ask despite the fact – or perhaps precisely because – they are virtually impossible to answer; questions out of which *Peter Pan* was itself produced and without which Peter Pan's innocence becomes not only lost as we know it, but also without meaning. They are there, however, in the various trouble spots which remain in the play, but perhaps even more in the demand that we continue to make on the child that it should recognise itself in that scenario – both in the place of the child spectator (which is also that of Peter Pan at the window), and in the happy family scene which is so miraculously reconstituted before its eyes. *Peter Pan* plays itself out with all the innocence of the symptom – which speaks what it intends, and exactly the opposite, at one and the same time.

Notes

1. References to Beinecke and date refer to the J.M. Barrie collection at the Beinecke Rare Book and Manuscript Library, Yale University; full details are given in the bibliography.
2. Both John Skinner (Skinner, 1957) and Martin Grotjahn (Grotjahn, 1957) comment on the failure of the Oedipal resolution in *Peter Pan* (Grotjahn criticises Skinner for not making this explicit enough), but make this the basis of an aesthetic (and moral) condemnation of Barrie himself.

References

Barrie, J.M. *The Little White Bird* (London: Hodder & Stoughton, 1902).

Barrie, J.M. *Anon*, Two typescripts, with autograph manuscript revisions, of Act III of the three-act version of the play, 1904; varies from other texts of Act III in the Barrie Collection and from the text published in *The Plays of J.M. Barrie* (Barrie, 1928) (Beinecke P45, 1904).

Barrie, J.M. *Anon*, typescript of the three-act version of the play (with manuscript revisions in an unidentified hand and interleaved with lighting-plots, stage business and prompt cues in several unidentified hands) used in the 1904 production (Act III is incomplete); accompanied by one leaf labelled Scene v of a version of Act III. Produced in London 27 December 1904 at the Duke of York's Theatre; varies from the text published in *The Plays of J.M. Barrie* (Barrie, 1928) (Beinecke P45, 1904–5B).

Barrie, J.M. *An Afterthought*, autograph manuscript, with revisions, of an epilogue to the play *Peter Pan*, with a signed note dated March 1908 ('To Hilda Trevelyan, My incomparable Wendy'); produced in London, 22 February 1908 at the Duke of York's Theatre; published in *When Wendy Grew Up* (Barrie, 1957) accompanied by a signed manuscript in the hand of Hilda Trevelyan explaining how the play came to be written and produced and how the manuscript came to be given to her (Beinecke P45, 1908B).

Barrie, J.M. *An Afterthought*, typescript of an epilogue to the play *Peter Pan*, with autograph manuscript revisions and manuscript revisions in Hilda Trevelyan's hand, 1908; produced in London, 22 February 1908 at the Duke of York's Theatre; published in *When Wendy Grew Up* (Barrie 1957) accompanied by a TLS from the Assistant Comptroller in the Lord Chamberlain's Office to Sidney Blow, concerning *An Afterthough*, 22 May 1956 (Beinecke P45, 1908C).

'*When Wendy Grew Up*, An Afterthought on *Peter Pan* by Sir James Barrie', *John Bull*, 1957 (*Enthoven*).

Birkin, A. *J.M. Barrie and the Lost Boys* (London: Constable, 1979).

Freud, S. *Moses and Monotheism* (SE, xxiii (1934–8) 1939), pp. 3–137.

Green, R.L., *Fifty Years of Peter Pan* (London: Peter Davies, 1954).

Grotjahn, M. 'The Defenses Against Creative Anxiety in the Life and Work of James Barrie', *American Imago*, 14 (1957), pp. 143–8.

Llewellyn Davies, P. *The Boy Castaways of Black Lake Island* (London: published by J.M. Barrie in the Gloucester Road, 1901) (Beinecke B276, 1901).

Mackail, D. *The Story of J.M.B.* (London: Peter Davies, 1941).

Noyes, A. 'Peter and Wendy', *The Bookman*, 41, 243 (December 1911).

Skinner, J. 'James M. Barrie or the Boy Who Wouldn't Grow Up', *American Imago*, 14 (1957), pp. 111–41.

A Hundred Years of *Peter Pan*
Peter Hollindale

December 27th 2004 was the centenary of the first performance of *Peter Pan*. Events and productions to mark the centenary were everywhere. The BBC produced a series of radio programmes about the work, including an important one presented by the psychologist Oliver James about the play's and its chief character's continuing psychological appeal. On BBC television over Christmas a more light-hearted documentary. 'Happy Birthday, Peter Pan', traced the play's century of fame, and managed to present both its exuberant stage life and its often darker contextual history. Productions were mounted in many towns and cities throughout Britain, occupying the Christmas pantomime slot that the play claimed for itself from the beginning.

Many of them were musical adaptations for a children's holiday audience, but this is nothing new: Barrie's text has lent itself to revision and adaptation

This is an edited version of the article originally published in *Children's Literature in Education*, 36:3 (2005), pp. 197–215.

from the start, with the author's blessing; he himself was a compulsive reviser. Since *Peter Pan* is full of dance-like movement and spectacle, it responded with ease to reinterpretation as a ballet, admirably produced by Northern Ballet Theatre in Leeds. And above all, the centenary had been marked by two major feature films, one of the story itself, P.J. Hogan's *Peter Pan* (2003) and one a fictionalised 'biopic' of the tragic personal story that engendered and succeeded it, Marc Forster's *Finding Neverland* (2004).

It would be quite wrong to suppose that this was merely a short-term flourishing of anniversary interest in an otherwise dormant play. *Peter Pan* has never been dormant in its hundred years of life. By its own hyperactive standards it perhaps snoozed a little in the first few decades after the Second World War, though this period still included not only regular productions but Disney's famous 1953 animated film. But for the last quarter-century, and certainly since the Royal Shakespeare company's ground-breaking 1982 production by John Caird, the play has been a vigorous presence in the theatrical repertoire. In London in 1997 the National Theatre staged a major production, with Ian McKellen as Mr Darling and Captain Hook. In December 1995 the West Yorkshire Playhouse, probably the most enterprising of present-day English provincial theatres, presented a Christmas production so successful that it was revived the following year. The film industry was far from inattentive also. Steven Spielberg's *Hook* (1991) was not the director's finest hour (although Dustin Hoffman's Hook must rank with the very greatest interpretations of the role) but it did attest the continuing seductive energies of the story.

Clearly the centenary celebrations were not a brief revivalist sentiment, but an intensification of ongoing life. There are in fact two co-existent stories, each with the capacity to distort or confuse our understanding of the other. One is the play *Peter Pan* (1904), with its protean and elastic theatrical history, which still draws audiences of both adults and children, in spite of massive changes in society, culture and child development, into complicity, assent and pleasure. The other is the biographical story of its genesis and aftermath, which has diverse elements of tragedy. I shall suggest where we now stand in relation to each of these parallel, intertwining, narratives. This essay marks the 'state of play' of *Peter Pan* at its centenary in 2004.

Man and boy

In 2004, the origins of *Peter Pan* have become a narrative in their own right, affecting the reception of the play itself. Biography and text can be mixed together in a speculative psycho-sexual cocktail, as they were for example in a centenary newspaper article by Richard Morrison, sensationally titled

'Peter Panic: is it a paedophile nightmare, or an innocent tale?' Morrison's article somehow contrives both to convict and acquit Barrie of paedophilia, and both to impugn and celebrate the play. He states that 'there is much that is odd, disturbing and dark about the play – not least the irony that the family which inspired this tale of childhood infinitely prolonged was later to be so horribly hit by multiple tragedy', and he refers to 'what, for modern sensibilities, is the play's most jarring aspect: the fact that its creation was triggered by Barrie's attraction to five beautiful boys.' Barrie's relationship with this family, interpreted far more discreetly and generously, is the theme of the film *Finding Neverland*.

The play has been intimately associated from the outset with the five children of Sylvia and Arthur Llewellyn Davies, and rightly so. Without them there would be no *Peter Pan*. But that is a provocative occurrence in a period when justified terror of paedophile assault has been seen to mutate into witch-hunts aimed at the innocent and proscription of harmless contacts between male adults and children. Hence, as Morrison says with his other voice, 'if Barrie's friendship with the boys disturbs our sensibilities so much today, when it seems to have been acceptable both to the boys' mother and Edwardian society generally, doesn't that say something about our own age's paedophile phobia – a collective obsession that makes it near impossible for a male adult to develop *any* friendship with children?' It is clear that modern western societies are both anxious and confused about this problem, and at an opposite pole from the attitudes of Edwardian Society, to such a degree that in the case of *Peter Pan* it encroaches messily on our understanding of the play and almost rivals it in popular interest.

It was Barrie himself who first advertised the link between the Llewellyn Davies family and Peter Pan, in his curious novel *The Little White Bird* (1902). This work is two books in one, and strangely anticipates the subsequent double history which the release of *Peter Pan* and *Finding Neverland* has kept alive in the centenary year. Most of *The Little White Bird* is a fictionalised version of Barrie's relationship with the Davies family. The narrator, a bachelor ex-soldier, having helped to contrive a successful romantic marriage between a nursery governess and a painter whose precarious courtship he has happened to observe, later conducts a benign and permitted abduction of their small son David, with whom he can briefly practise a surrogate fatherhood. All the essential features of Barrie's own actions are present here: the primary role of the interfering observer, the half-comic, half-serious predation of parental rights, the desperate need for a borrowed parenthood. In the middle of this wish-fulfilling personal narrative Barrie suddenly introduces the first story of Peter Pan, composed in Kensington

Gardens for the delectation of George Llewellyn Davies and his brothers. These chapters were abstracted 4 years later to become the free-standing story of *Peter Plan in Kensington Gardens*, thus cutting the umbilical cord which tied them to the fantasised autobiography. *The Little White Bird* was the shape of things to come. Henceforward the two stories were to live both intimately linked and fully independent lives.

Some crucial events, together with Barrie's physical nature, were fixed and finished long before Barrie met the Llewellyn Davies family. They belong to his own childhood. Barrie was the second youngest of a large family, among whom his mother's favourite was the second son, David, a gifted, handsome and athletic boy who was destined for the Ministry. In January 1867, when Barrie was six, David was killed in a skating accident on the eve of his 14th birthday. This was a massively traumatic loss for Barrie's mother, and in consequence for Barrie himself. He attempted without success to fill the lost boy's place (quite literally, by imitating him) and developed his own intense relationship with his mother, always in the knowledge that he could not compensate for the bereavement. As time passed for Barrie, it remained fixed for David, so that as Barrie famously wrote in his biography of his mother, *Margaret Ogilvy*, 'When I became a man . . . he was still a boy of thirteen'.

Barrie did not in all respects 'become a man'. Physically his own growth and development were stunted. He was only 5 feet tall, and did not begin shaving till he was well into his twenties. It seems certain that he never matured sexually either, that his later disastrous marriage to the actress Mary Ansell was never consummated, that he was in effect sexless, and that as Andrew Birkin has remarked, 'the reality of sex was something he preferred not to think about'.

Yet it would be quite wrong to think that Barrie's childhood was unhappy. For his future personality, his happiness was just as arbitrary and fatal as his grief. Whatever his physical shortcomings, manifestly they did not extend to his intelligence and imagination. He loved stories, enjoyed 'Penny Dreadfuls', and borrowed from the library the famous adventure stories of the day to read with his mother. As a boy he was well-versed in tales of Red Indians, pirates and mermaids. From his mother he learned the story of her own very different childhood. 'She was eight when her mother's death made her mistress of the house and mother to her little brother' [*Margaret Ogilvy*]. His mother's childhood would later provide him with a model for Wendy. Moreover, the future dramatist was quickly active, as a child Barrie staged amateur theatricals in the family washhouse. A childhood rich in stories and imaginative play reached its apotheosis when at thirteen he went to school at Dumfries Academy for what he later said were the happiest 5 years of his life. Certainly they gave him an extended lease on boyhood, where fortunate friendships allowed his imagination to flourish in a happily asexual paradise. Much later he recorded its effects:

> when the shades of night began to fall, certain young mathematicians shed their triangles, crept up walls and down trees, and become pirates in a sort of Odyssey that was long afterwards to become the play of *Peter Pan*. For our escapades in a certain Dumfries garden, which is enchanted land to me, were certainly the genesis of that nefarious work.
>
> *From a speech on being awarded the Freedom of the City of Dumfries,*
> *11th December, 1924*

When Barrie met the Llewellyn Davies family many years later – first the older children, on his afternoon walks in Kensington Gardens, then by chance their mother at a dinner party – he certainly seized quite ruthlessly the chance to infiltrate the household and obtain the surrogate family of boys that he could not engender himself. Being physically stuck in childhood, he found in the Davies children readymade confederates in whose company he could repossess the adventurous and asexual happiness that he had once enjoyed. Far from being paedophilic activity, Barrie's raid on the Llewellyn Davies family was driven by the very absence of sex and sexuality. When the boys were very young, they were Barrie's collaborative audience in inventing the Peter Pan of *Peter Pan in Kensington Gardens*. As they grew older, the stories and games (especially during the idyllic summer of 1901, sharing a holiday at the Barries' cottage in Surrey and making use of the ideal piratical playground, Black Lake Island) ignited *Peter Pan*: Dumfries and Surrey came together to create the Never Land. More seriously, Barrie's takeover of the family was a species of abduction, blatantly declared in the dedication of *Peter Pan in Kensington Gardens*: 'To Sylvia and Arthur Llewellyn Davies and their boys (my boys)'.

The story of the Edwardian decade during which first Arthur and then Sylvia Llewellyn Davies died of cancer and their boys did indeed become Barrie's boys is now a famous one. It is in almost all respects a tragic story, some elements of which intersect sombrely with the light-hearted terrors of the play itself. What is perhaps less obvious (though Barrie's writings make it clear) is the ironic consequence for Barrie himself. He got what he wanted, the family of boys who were a passport to his lost childhood, but of course he also, as they grew older, lost the thing that made them magical, the world of boyhood games. Barrie's ruthless although sexually innocent appropriation of boys who could reactivate his childhood turned into a real family, steadily growing older, for whom he was responsible and cared deeply, and never stopped caring – long after they were grown up, and as further tragedy overtook them.

Peter Pan and the First World War

Peter Pan opened in December 1904, and returned in 1905 when it also opened for the first time in America. A success in both countries, it amply rewarded the theatrical judgement and financial bravery of its first producer, the American Charles Frohman. Thereafter the play enjoyed an almost unbroken trajectory for 100 years. But after its first decade of success, the play picked up a darker personal history linked to the fate of the Davies boys, and a darker shading of public history. The play was born of innocence, and it survived the ruin of that innocence, but not without acquiring some bleak fortuitous ironies.

True to its curious immunity to the effects of historical change, *Peter Pan* continued to play annually throughout the First World War. (It only failed to do so during the Second World War because theatres were closed by the London Blitz.) One important change was made to the text, however. At the end of Act 3, as Peter stands alone on Marooners' Rock with the waters of Mermaids' Lagoon rising round him, he says: 'To die will be an awfully big adventure'. This line was omitted for the duration of the war, in deference to the many troops on leave who came to the play. The fate of this famous line is one of several ways in which the darker comedy of *Peter Pan* was suddenly touched by a far greater darkness.

The Home Under the Ground had its ugly counterpart in the squalid, fragile shelter of the trenches. Above waited not the evil Captain Hook and his pirates but no man's land and the German guns. In 1915 George Llewellyn Davies was killed in the trenches by a sniper. Also in 1915, the liner *Lusitania* was torpedoed off Ireland, and quickly sank. On board was Charles Frohman, but for whose risk and insight *Peter Pan* might never have been staged. Frohman refused a place in a lifeboat, and was reported to have said, 'Why fear death? It is the greatest adventure in life'. It is quite possible, of course, that he was misreported, and had quoted the play even more accurately.

These were Barrie's own bereavements. They were part of a multitude. Like George (and his brothers Jack and Peter, who survived the war, though Peter suffered irreparable nervous damage), many hundreds of boys who formed the play's first audiences also fought and died. In Act 5 of *Peter Pan*, when Hook has captured the children and the boys are to walk the plank, Wendy addresses them with 'a mother's last words to her children': 'Dear boys, I feel that I have a message for you from your real mothers, and it is this, "We hope our sons will die like English gentlemen".' This is Barrie's skit on the heroic jingoism of Victorian adventure novels, but it turned into dreadful reality with the emotional propaganda of the war, which led to such practices as women giving white feathers for cowardice to young men not in uniform.

For Barrie, *Peter Pan* had one more terrible irony to play. In May 1921 Michael Llewellyn Davies, the fourth and Barrie's favourite of the Davies boys, was drowned with a fellow Oxford undergraduate in a pool near Oxford. He was not quite twenty-one (just young enough to have escaped the war). A homosexual suicide pact was suspected, but the inquest verdict was accidental death. So it may have been. Michael could not swim, but had never stopped trying to learn. He may well have been having a secret lesson, and panicked, dragging his amateur teacher down. Barrie had photographed him many years earlier in the water at Black Lake Cottage. And then there had been Peter, with the lagoon water rising and the mermaids threatening, bravely saying 'To die will be an awfully big adventure'. *Peter Pan* played strange tricks, and for Barrie this was the worst. In his Dedication 'To the Five' of the first published edition of the play in 1928 he wrote, in a bitter sentence deftly hidden in a lighter context, 'There is Peter still, but to me he lies sunk in the gay Black Lake'.

Yet there was Peter still, and he proved necessary and popular both during and after the war. In the 2004 radio discussion of the play's psychology, 'Never Netherland', Ann Yeoman observed: 'Right after the First World War, when everything was looking exceptionally bleak, that's what we needed to know, that we could leave the nursery window open and make contact again with that creative spirit, and it is that, I think, the whole notion of futurity that is around that image of the special divine child, that helps us meet the future'.

The Lost Boys and *Finding Neverland*

Eighty years on this clearly remains true. There is Peter still: the play retains its magical elasticity and its ongoing modernity. After a decade or two of treading water in mid-century, both narratives, the biographical and the artistic, received a crucial reinvigoration at almost the same time, the first in 1978 with Andrew Birkin's television drama *The Lost Boys*, followed a year later by his biographical study, and the second in 1982 with the Royal Shakespeare Company production of the play in London. Birkin enriched the biographical story with immaculate research and fresh psychological insight conveyed though powerful dramatic narrative. John Caird and the Royal Shakespeare Company at long last cast a male actor as Peter, thereby cutting the play free from the pantomime tradition. Many actresses had played Peter with great distinction, but they inevitably tied the play to conventions which nowadays do not suit it. This production also found a place for *When Wendy Grew Up: An Afterthought* which, while not diminishing the fun, has the effect of exposing the play as the serious drama which at root it is. Without *The Lost Boys* there would not be *Finding Neverland*, and without the RSC production there probably could not be Hogan's *Peter Pan*, in which Peter is played as when practicable he really should be, not by a woman, or even a young man, but a boy.

The real-life narrative reached its dramatic apotheosis with *The Lost Boys*. This long three-part drama is one of television drama's finest achievements. Although dramas based on real lives do not have to be factually accurate, this one is so. It is a work of scholarship as well as imagination. And it is beautifully acted. An eerily convincing Ian Holm as Barrie is matched by a fine cast, with a great and heartbreaking performance by Maureen O'Brien as the dignified, frustrated and neglected Mrs Barrie, the victim of Barrie's sexlessness and cold indifference. This painfully detailed psychological drama never suggests sexual impropriety on Barrie's part. but it does show with pitiless candour the extended act of social and emotional trespass by which he took possession of the Davies boys, and through them his own lost childhood. Humour and wit and the gift of storytelling were his weapons in enticing the boys (and indeed their mother) to crew his own fantastic pirate ship. And out of all that came *Peter Pan*. It is a strange irony that as things turned out the Davies family in its tragedy of illness was saved from disaster by Barrie's generous attentions, and a stranger irony still that the only harm he did them lay in writing *Peter Pan*, and, in consequence, afflicting them with fame.

To compare *The Lost Boys* with *Finding Neverland* is not to compare like with like. *Finding Neverland* is a commercial feature film for family audiences, much shorter than Birkin's play. It does not pretend to factual accuracy. For example, it kills off Arthur Llewellyn Davies in advance of the action, it singles out Peter because of his name as the most important of the Davies boys, it invents the mother of Sylvia Llewellyn Davies as an obstructive harridan figure, and it shows Barrie smuggling children into the first performance of *Peter Pan* to act as cheerleaders for the dying Tinker Bell, when far more remarkably that first almost wholly adult audience clapped spontaneously, not even needing to be prompted by the orchestra, which has been primed to start the clapping if a terrible silence fell. The film had also caused a totally mistaken belief that Barrie's dramatic career was in decline until *Peter Pan* arrived to rescue it.

All the same, it treats Barrie kindly – much more kindly than *The Lost Boys* does. Johnny Depp is a delightful Barrie, but being tall, handsome, confident and not to all appearances emotionally stunted, he bears little resemblance to the true one. Like Ian Holm, however, he beautifully conveys the deadpan, fantasising jokiness that ingratiates Barrie with the boys while preserving his ongoing watchful detachment. But when Depp plays with the children, he does so deliberately, and without true need, not with the obsessive and spontaneous reinvention of boyhood that Holm caught so wonderfully. And the casual injuries that Barrie caused to adults are either omitted (Arthur being tidily dead), or discreetly hinted at in such details as the Barrie household arrangements, where the couple have separate rooms. In short, as a dramatisation of Barrie's personal story the film is both inaccurate and bland.

Peter Pan for a modern audience

From all these strands it is now perhaps possible to 'place' *Peter Pan* as a dramatic work, and account for its lasting appeal. This is a play about the boundaries between childhood and adulthood. These boundaries are ever-changing, They differ radically between one society and another, and in the same society across time. Because they are nearly always being tested and stretched, they are nearly always contentious. Is there a clear line of demarcation between them, like a national frontier, with no chance of return once crossed? This is very much what Barrie thought, and what the play says. Peter is a 'tragic boy' because he believes exactly this (or wilfully pretends to) and hence refuses maturity. But what the play enacts is different from what it technically says, and is far more optimistic and reassuring for both child and adult in the audience. The line between childhood and adult life has certain crucial crossing-points, most importantly the passage to active sexuality, but in other respects it is fluid and shifting, and can be crossed and re-crossed in imagination, games and play. Children make experimental incursions into adult roles, secure in the possibility of retreat. Going to *Peter Pan* is one such incursion. On the other hand, adults are often nostalgic for a forfeited playfulness, so the play provides a shared arena for children and grown-ups, playfully living forward and living back.

Peter Pan himself, the eternal boy, appears either sexless or latently sexual and when played by an adult actress seems almost to inhabit a mysterious third gender. This is what promoted Barrie's biographer, Denis Mackail, to write as he did about Nina Boucicault, the first actress to play Peter.

> Other [would] be more boyish, or more principal-boyish, or gayer and prettier or more sinister and inhuman, or more ingeniously and painstakingly elfin. After all, the part can never really be played except by one form of convention or another. But Miss Boucicault was the Peter of all Peters who made you forget this. She was unearthly but she was real. She obtruded neither sex nor sexlessness.

In fact the surviving clips of Jean Forbes-Robertson's famous performance suggest that she accomplished the same feat. Roger Lancelyn Green speaks of the 'eeriness and mystery' of both.

Even so, some element of unconscious or refused male sexuality must always be present in the role, not only to account for Peter's otherwise masculine activities but also Wendy's female interest in him. The balance here is delicate. It depends on the age and sex of the actors, and on changing norms of childhood. P.J. Hogan's 2003 feature film, I believe, gets this balances exactly right for the present age.

The play has moved since 1982 towards using a male actor for Peter, but legal constraints on the permissible number of performances by child actors mean that in professional theatre it is usually impracticable for the part to be played by a boy. Hogan's film is therefore an exceptional opportunity to see the play case in ideal conditions.

P.J. Hogan's 2003 film (the third, following a 1924 silent version and the Disney 1953 cartoon; Barrie himself wrote a film scenario which was never used) is a wonderfully imaginative re-creation of the story for the medium and the times. Some of Barrie's dialogue is retained, but most is new. The domestic scenes in the Darling house (the only part of the play to seem dated) are completely re-drawn, and Mr Darling's childishness removed, Never Land scenes are revised and restructured. This is not a film for the textual purist. But it retains the spirit and essence of the play unerringly, making use of the modern director's armoury of resources and special effects to do things that Barrie would certainly have done if he had had the means. Although the film was successful and warmly praised, its achievement had not been fully recognized.

The thing I wish to single our is the film's casting of the two child roles, Peter and Wendy, played by a 14-year-old American boy, Jeremy Sumpter, and a 12-year-old English girl, Rachel Hurd-Wood. It is, as I have said, unusual for these parts to be playable by children. However deviant the scripting, in one sense this was the first authentic performance of the story – the first, that is, where it was possible to align the conventions and artifice of the two stage roles with a recognizable boy and girl of the present day. Something of the 'eeriness and mystery', not least the mystery of gender, is inevitably lost when Peter and Wendy are played by 'peer-ground' contemporaries of children in the cinema audience. But that same audience is no longer easily reachable through the old conventions. Children now, both in the audience and as actors, are not the children of 1904. They mature earlier in a world transformed. In Barrie's playscript there are hinted intuitions about childhood closer to the norms of 2004 than those of his own period. Merely by being children, but especially by being 21st century children, the excellent Sumpter and Hurd-Wood are both revising and revealing Barrie's characters. The combination of their own revising presence and Hogan's modified script is, if I can put it so, in some respects nearer to Barrie than Barrie's own play.

The film stripped Wendy of most of the trappings of precocious mothering that dominate the original. These conceal her obvious attraction to Peter by linking it to surrogate shared parenthood in the family of Lost Boys. As Rachel Hurd-Wood plays Wendy, she was chiefly attracted to Peter. The crucial difference between them was that the word 'love' was active in her life and vocabulary and neither felt not understood in his. In the course of the film she visibly grew from a playful girl in the nursery, keen on stories, to a sexually aware young woman. It is unimaginable that a 12-year-old actress could have conveyed this in 1904, but if we look at Barrie's script it is exactly what happens to Wendy. In 2003, 100 years on, it is entirely normal and acceptable, When Wendy's kiss revives Peter, after he had been drained of morale and energy in the pirate ship duel by Hook's sneering accusation that he is 'incomplete', she kisses him, in Barrie's phrase, as 'a very woman'. Hogan's modern Wendy, by the way, also takes part in the fighting. Rachel Hurd-Wood's performance is admirable, in my view, and woefully underpraised.

The same is true of Jeremy Sumpter's Peter. He is not, and could not nowadays be, 'sexless' in the role. It is questionable whether he is even sexually latent', or whether he is (like Barrie's Peter, after all) *refusing* sexuality, as the boy who, in the play's original subtitle, '*would* not grow up' (as opposed to Barrie himself, who sexually *could* not). Sumpter's performance is subtle and exact in close-up. He conveys moments of unwary unrecognised and perplexing sexuality which he wilfully controls and harnesses as *play*, only to recoil when they impinge upon unwanted emotional reality. His Peter is on the verge of adolescence, a fact perceived by others, especially Wendy, but repressed and unidentified by himself. The word 'love' frightens and repels him. So Wendy's kiss in the duel, a lover's kiss on her part revives him with ambivalent meaning, lost somewhere between motherhood and sexuality – both of which he outwardly rejects. Once again this is entirely plausible psychology for Barrie's Peter, the *puer aeternus* who is actually *puer* still, but it has been unplayable till now. These two outstanding child performances mean in my judgement that Hogan's free adaptation of Barrie's plot both brings to life the discreetly suggested truth of Barrie's original pair of children, and allows them to 'grow up' sufficiently to live convincingly for 21st century audiences.

Peter's line, 'I want always to be a little boy and to have fun', is spoken twice in the play, and as Peter's 'greatest pretend', is the key to it.

What Barrie's great dramatic story shows incomparably is that the tragic and impossible wish to halt, reverse or subdue time may arise in anyone, adult or child, concurrently with realisation of its futility. Peter is no more 'unsuspecting' than Wendy is: hence his defiance. As Hogan's film so ably shows, the essential truth of Barrie's tragi-comedy is alive and well in 2004.

References

Barrie, J.M., *Margaret Ogilvy*. London: Hodder and Stoughton, 1896.

Barrie, J.M., *The Little White Bird*. London: Hodder and Stoughton, 1902.

Barrie, J.M., *Peter Pan*, Theatre Production, 1904.

Barrie, J.M., *When Wendy Grew Up*, Theatre Production, 1908.

Barrie, J.M., *Peter Pan*. London: Hodder and Stoughton, 1928.

Birkin, Andrew, J.M. *Barrie and the Lost Boys*. London: Constable, 1979.

Finding Neverland, directed by Marc Forster, 2004.

Green, Roger Lancelyn, *Fifty Years of 'Peter Pan'*. London: Peter Davies, 1954.

Hook, directed by Steven Spielberg, 1991.

Mackail, Denis, *The Story of J.M.B.* London: Peter Davis, 1941.

Morrison, Richard, 'Peter Panic: is it a paedophile nightmare or an innocent tale?', in *The Times*, 29 December 2004.

Peter Pan, directed by P.J. Hogan. 2003.

Yeoman, Ann, in 'Never Netherland'. BBC Radio 4. 2004.

Peter Pan and the Pantomime Tradition
Donna R. White and C. Anita Tarr

Peter Pan is a pantomime. The *Peter Pan* we are referring to at this point is the play produced in 1904 and every year thereafter. However, we are not the first to call it a patomime. Barrie himself said he was writing a pantomime. Contemporary audiences and theater critics knew it was a pantomime. As late as 1937, George Bernard Shaw referred to it as a pantomime (qtd. in Mander and Mitchenson 44).

Pantomime is a peculiar British phenomenon, with the accent on peculiar. It is a form of popular entertainment produced at Christmas time, featuring

Extracted from 'Introduction', in D.R. White and C.A. Tarr (eds), *J.M. Barrie's* Peter Pan *In and Out of Time* (Lanham, MD: Scarecrow, 2006), pp. vii–xix.

stock characters, standard plots, and extravagant sets and stage effects. To quote from one history of pantomime,

> It takes its name from classical times and changes the meaning, its characters from Italian comedy and changes their names, its stories from continental fairy tales and mixes historical figures, then adds every conceivable trick and resource of the theatre, opera, ballet, music hall and musical comedy. It has moulded all these elements together over the past three hundred years into something which no-one but the English understand, or even want!
>
> Mander and Mitchenson 1

By Barrie's time, pantomime had become a Christmas extravaganza for children, but it certainly did not start out that way. During the first decade of the eighteenth century, the traditional Italian *Commedia dell' Arte* characters were introduced to English audiences by acting troupes from France that performed in English theaters and at fairs. In 1716 an enterprising London theater manager, John Rich, who was also an actor and a gifted mime, started adding a silent pantomime based on the Italian characters to the end of an evening's double bill. On the English stage, the most popular of these characters became known as Harlequin and Columbine, the lovers; Pierrot, the clown; and Pantaloon, the old skinflint. Rich's pantomimes were so successful that other theaters began to copy him. Eventually a standard form developed for these entertainments. First there was an Opening, which told a familiar story or classical legend in verse and song – sometimes burlesquing the latest Italian opera playing at the Queen's Theatre in Haymarket but usually serious in tone. Then, by means of a magician or other benevolent agency that thwarted the powers of evil, the characters were transformed into Harlequin, Columbine, Pantaloon, Pierrot, and other Italian types, who went through a series of usually comic and acrobatic adventures mimed to music, known as a Harlequinade. The Harlequinade featured elaborate sets and costumes, and much stage machinery was employed to create impressive effects, such as characters flying or ascending into heaven (or, in one production, ascending into hell).

Audiences loved it.

They came to pantomimes in droves. In fact, pantomime's popularity brought in so much revenue for the London theaters that it was virtually underwriting the productions of more purely literary plays. As the form developed during the eighteenth century, the Harlequinade characters began to speak and sing. In the nineteenth century, pantomime became more closely associated with the Christmas season, and the plots were drawn from popular stories and fairy tales rather than from classical myth and legend. The shows became longer, stand-alone productions, and pantomime became more and more a family entertainment. Even the literary elite began to enjoy the shows. Charles Dickens was a fan; he even edited the memoirs of the great Grimaldi, the most famous of the pantomime clowns.

The Victorian Era was the heyday of pantomime. By the mid 1800s it had become a lavish children's entertainment produced only at Christmas. In the 1850s elements of burlesque theater were introduced into pantomime, adding popular songs and new stock characters like the comic Dame played by a man in drag. The special effects grew more and more elaborate, as did the casts, which needed lots of extras to portray fairy troupes or comic armies. Every theater in London as well as regional theaters throughout the country produced a pantomime for Christmas, and much of the rest of the year went into planning and preparing for these productions.

At the beginning of the twentieth century, when Barrie began to escort the Llewelyn Davies boys to annual Christmas pantomimes, 'panto,' as it is often called, was a long-standing English tradition. The Harlequinade itself had shrunk to a short final scene at the end of an extravagantly produced fairy tale or other popular story. Aladdin and Cinderella were favorite pantomime subjects, and so was Robinson Crusoe, although it was not a Crusoe Defoe would have recognized. Children sat entranced by amazing transformation scenes that created magical fairy lands using every imaginable trick of lighting and stagecraft.

In 1901 Barrie took his young friends to a new Christmas pantomime called *Bluebell in Fairy Land*, written by its male star, Seymour Hicks. Unlike most pantos, which remounted the same popular stories again and again, *Bluebell* boasted an original plot not based on any traditional fairy tale. Several biographers suggest that this may have given Barrie the idea of writing his own original pantomime, although they also mention a private pantomime called 'The Greedy Dwarf,' which Barrie wrote, produced, and performed in his home on January 7, 1901. In any case, Barrie cannot be credited with being the first writer to conceive of an original story for a pantomime. Nor could Hicks. In pantomime's then two-hundred-year history, original stories had been introduced now and again, after which they soon became 'traditional' stories, as indeed *Peter Pan* was to become the 'traditional' Christmas entertainment for English children for over a century.

In 1904, the original audience would have easily recognized *Peter Pan* as a pantomime. First of all, it was produced as one, scheduled for a short run during the Christmas season. The only unusual aspect of this panto, besides the original story, was the fact that it was written by a famous playwright of the legitimate stage. Despite (and maybe because of) its immense popularity, pantomime was still viewed as Pope had seen it: vulgar entertainment for the uneducated masses. Becoming a children's entertainment had actually improved pantomime's reputation among the intelligentsia. Even though children, like the masses, have not developed any discernment in theatrical matters, the late Victorians and the Edwardians had an idealized view of childhood and valued it highly. Most newspapers reviewed the pantomimes just as they would a new production of *Hamlet*, only with a difference in tone: arch or whimsical or patronizing. Nevertheless, one seldom found a well-known playwright contributing to the pantomime tradition. The mass appeal of pantomime is also why it has often been overlooked in literary history, just as early histories of children's literature ignored such widely popular forms as dime novels and penny dreadfuls and comic books.

Barrie's first audience also would have recognized and accepted numerous elements in *Peter Pan* as part of the pantomime. For example, the matter of casting provides important evidence. Peter Pan has almost always been played by a woman. This cross-gendered casting has puzzled some critics and Barrie biographers. They have come up with interesting and sometimes convoluted reasons to explain it. The favorite theory is that Barrie was working around a British law that made it illegal to have children under fourteen on stage after 9:00 at night. Casting a grown woman as Peter meant that the other children's roles could be scaled according to her height rather than a boy's, allowing older children to play younger parts (Birkin 105). Other scholars suggest that the part of Peter Pan was so demanding that a child could not have handled it. However, the most logical reason for the cross-gendered casting is that the male lead of a pantomime was always played by a woman. One of the burlesque elements introduced into pantomime in the 1850s was the practice of cross-gendered roles, usually for comic effect. Thus, Cinderella's ugly stepsisters were usually played by men, preferably big, hairy men. Similarly, the young male lead was a role called Principal Boy, always played by a woman. There was a Principal Girl too, also played by a woman. In *Peter Pan*, Wendy is the Principal Girl. There was never any question that Peter Pan would be played by an actress. All but one of the Lost Boys were also portrayed by women, as was one of Wendy's younger brothers. The other brother, John, and the sixth Lost Boy were tall young male actors, and their size in comparison to the others was used for comic effect.

Ever since John Rich first introduced pantomime to an English audience, the serious Opening had ended with a benevolent agent transforming the classical characters into the humorous stock characters of the Harlequinade. The actors thus performed double roles in every pantomime. By Barrie's day, the Opening had itself been transformed into a humorous fairy play and the Harlequinade had all but disappeared, but the tradition of double casting is reflected in the dual role of Mr. Darling/Captain Hook.

This hybrid character is a king of Pantaloon figure: the enraged father chasing the trickster Harlequin, who has eloped with daughter Columbine. Why does Hook hate Peter Pan and constantly seek to kill him? Because Peter is Harlequin, and Pantaloon always goes after Harlequin.

Peter is clearly a Harlequin figure. According to Peter Holland, the role of Principal Boy originated as Harlequin (198). Harlequin was the star of the Harlequinade; he was adept at disguise and mimicry and was a gifted acrobat, musician, and dancer. Mostly, though, he was an inveterate trickster and magician. Peter Pan's antics and actions retain much of Harlequin's personality. His self-identification as 'a little bird that has broken out of the egg' may actually be a tribute to John Rich, the original English Harlequin, who always portrayed Harlequin hatching from an egg – a famous bit of stage business (Wilson 22).

In a similar fashion, Columbine became Principal Girl, or Wendy in *Peter Pan*. The focus of Harlequin's affections, Columbine willingly ran off with him (though usually not with two younger brothers in tow) and participated in his various tricks and transformations. The Principal Girl, states Holland, is 'a fantasy of girlhood. . . . Pretty but not beautiful, wholesome and innocent, the Principal Girl is the fantasy of the girl-next-door. . . . The figure is de-eroticized: a focus not for sexual desire but for sentimentalized, non-sexual, romantic love' (199). In Wendy's case, of course, her Harlequin, Peter Pan, seeks maternal love rather than romantic love.

Another type of pantomime character used in *Peter Pan* was the animal character. Actors call such roles 'skin parts.' Wendy and her brothers have a large Newfoundland dog as their nursemaid. Nana, the dog, was usually played by a man, but never by an actual dog, although Barrie claims he allowed his pet Newfoundland to do a walk-on one night. In more minor roles, *Peter Pan* features several wolves and a very large crocodile. Individual actors were in the wolf costumes, but the crocodile had two actors – a front half and a back half. This was typical of traditional pantomimes, which often featured actors in animal costume. After all, most of the plots came from fairy tales. What would *Puss in Boots* be without Puss? Dick Whittington was also a favorite subject for pantomime, and his cat played an important part. *Mother Goose* always included a large goose, and *Robinson Crusoe* featured a dog. Animal characters were so popular that they were often introduced into stories that did not originally include animals, for example, a dog in *Aladdin*. Pantomimes were populated by comic cows, chickens, monkeys, storks, and other livestock.

The diminutive fairy Tinker Bell was also derived from the pantomime tradition. The Victorians had popularized fairylands in their pantomimes.

Bluebell in Fairy Land, the panto some think inspired Barrie, had lots of fairies. The closing scene of *Peter Pan* also contained hundreds of fairies. Representing fairies by means of bells and stage lights was the normal practice, but seldom were they used as effectively as in the portrayal of Tinker Bell. Variations of the tinkling bell and the flickering light created the illusion of a real person with a complex personality. In this, as in many other ways, Barrie improved on usual pantomime practice.

Besides characters, much of the stage business in *Peter Pan* comes from the pantomime tradition. As Michael Booth explains in *Victorian Spectacular Theatre*,

> In a real sense melodrama and pantomime were creations of technology. The very existence of new materials, new stage machinery, and new methods of lighting impelled them into a dramatic structure which in part existed to display the ingenuity of machinist, gasman, head carpenter, costume designer, and stage manager.
>
> 64

Pantomime was thus ostentatious, extravagant, and elaborate, and it provided a grand display of technical virtuosity. All of Barrie's biographers have commented on the difficulties of producing *Peter Pan* because of these very elements. They focus particularly on the problem of flying across the stage. Although Barrie is often credited with inventing stage flight for *Peter Pan*, characters had been flying on stage in pantomime since the early 1700s. Barrie improved on the practice by hiring a professional aerialist to invent a new kind of harness. To protect himself and the theater, he required his actors to take out insurance policies before they learned to use the harness.

Elaborate sets and stage effects such as those in *Peter Pan* were standard in pantomime. Towards the end of every panto there was a transformation scene that was expected to outdo all the previous sets and effects. A character would cross the stage and wave a magic wand, then cue the music and the curtain. When the curtain rose on the transformation scene, the audience should gasp in wonder and coninue to do so as the transformation unfolded. Booth describes the process:

> The effects of a transformation, which might take twenty minutes to unfold, were dependent upon a combination of machinery, lighting, changing scenic pieces and gauzes, and the display of a large number of beautifully costumed women, some floating high above the stage. More then half the machinery for a transformation scene was worked from beneath the stage, and basically what happened was that a large platform suspended by ropes and counterweights rose through an opening in the stage created by removing that section of the stage floor during the preceding

scene. On this, platform were about twenty fairies, mermaids, water-nymphs, angels, or the like . . . . While this was going on the lighting intensified, gauzes were raised, scenery changed, the orchestra played, other performers appeared on stage, and the transformation moved in a leisurely way toward a climax.

80

In the orginial production of *Peter Pan*, the transformation scene began when the minor character Liza, a housemaid (who was also in Barrie's whimsy listed on the program as author of the play), walked across the stage with the magic wand, which in the stage directions was referred to as Harlequin's wand, and initiated the transformation. The curtain opened on a scene of Peter's little house in the treetops, where Wendy is saying good-bye after her annual visit to do his spring cleaning. She leaves, and dusk settles as Peter plays his pipes and thousands of fairy homes start to twinkle around him. Music, lights, and set combined to create stage magic. This one scene is proof enough that *Peter Pan* is a pantomime because its only reason for existence is the pantomime tradition. The scene contributes nothing to the story of Peter Pan; the previous scene in the children's nursery was the natural end of the play.

Song and dance were also required elements in pantomime. However, pantomimes were not musicals the way *My Fair Lady* or *Oklaboma* is a musical; in panto the songs did not help to develop character and plot or set the mood. Years later there would be a musical version of *Peter Pan* on Broadway, not to mention the Disney musical cartoon, but the first production used music in a different way. It was musical like a variety show. There were set pieces so that various actors and actresses could show off their singing and dancing talents. In the opening scene, Mrs. Darling sang an old lullaby to her children and Peter performed a shadow dance. Later the pirates sang pirate songs, the Indians performed a tribal dance, and one of the Lost Boys did a well-received pillow dance. The songs and dances often changed from one production of *Peter Pan* to the next, according to the talents of the cast. For example, the pillow dance was the specialty of Americal actress Pauline Chase. After she was promoted to the role of Peter in later productions, the Lost Boys no longer did a pillow dance. This kind of change is a common feature of pantomime, as are elaborately staged mock battles like those between the Lost Boys and the pirates and between the Indians and the pirates.

One of the most famous moments in *Peter Pan* occurs when Tinker Bell has drunk from a poisoned cup to save Peter's life. Peter turns to the audience to save Tinker Bell, asking them to clap if they believe in fairies. And, of course, the audience claps resoundingly and Tinker Bell revives. According to most of Barrie's biographers, this was seen as a bit of risky stage business. What if the audience did not clap? However, it was not as risky as some people think. Audience participation was a standard part of pantomime, rather like melodrama, in which the audience is expected to boo and hiss when the villain enters and cheer the hero. In pantomime, ritual dialogues developed between characters and audience, and shouting back at the actors at set times was part of the entertainment. Although *Peter Pan* does not offer that level of audience involvement, Barrie could count on the fact that the audience was trained to respond to an actor's appeal, so they were bound to clap to save Tinker Bell.

Other common features of pantomime included panoramic tableaux and formal processions. As the play has come down to us, *Peter Pan* no longer contains either of those elements, but the first production featured both. When Wendy persuaded the Lost Boys to return with her to England, there was a procession of beautiful mothers who came to claim their lost sons. In fact, there were far more mothers than there were Lost Boys to be claimed. And after Peter vanquished Captain Hook, the curtain opened on a Napoleonic tableau – Peter as a victorious Napoleon on the ship, with the other characters posed appropriately around him wearing French officers' uniforms. The scene was presented without motion or dialogue.

The main feature of the early pantomime – the Harlequinade – had shrunk almost out of existence by Barrie's day, but it was still the final scene of many pantomimes. The original manuscript for *Peter Pan* ends with a Harlequinade set in Kensington Gardens. Captain Hook appears as a schoolmaster; there are six schoolgirls accompanied by a governess, a couple of Lost Boys, Peter, and Tinker Bell (called in the manuscript Tippytoe). In this scene Peter and the boys are transformed into clowns (as Pierrot became known), the schoolgirls into Columbines, and the governess into Harlequin (Jack 105). By this point in panto's development, Clown had replaced Harlequin as the trickster, with Harlequin relegated to a dancing role; thus Barrie transforms Peter into a clown rather than a harlequin. The clowns vanquish the schoolmaster, who then is finished off by a crocodile. According to Denis Mackail, Barrie's first biographer, 'a harlequin and coulmbine flitted across the stage in the first acted version – who take part in a kind of ballet with a corps of assistant-[school]masters' (352). This scene was dropped amost immediately, but it provides more evidence that Barrie was writing a pantomime. The governess was clearly meant to be a comic Dame and would have been played by a man in drag. The only sign of the Harlequinade that remained in the early productions of *Peter Pan* was the stage direction for the transformation scene, which specifically states that Liza carries a Harlequin wand. From its earliest days, pantomime included this object, often called Harlequin's bat and viewed as a phallic symbol. Harlequin used it as a magic wand to transform characters and scenery into new and unusual people and things. Liza and the Harlequin wand did not make it into any of the published texts of *Peter Pan*, so all traces of the Harlequinade have disappeared.

Peter Pan would not exist if not for the pantomime tradition.

References

Birkin, Andrew. *J.M. Barrie & the Lost Boys: The Love Story that Gave Birth to Peter Pan.* New York: Clarkson N. Potter, 1979.

Booth, Michael R. *Victorian Spectacular Theatre 1850–1910.* Theatre Production Studies. Boston: Routledge & Kegan Paul, 1981.

Holland, Peter. 'The Play of Eros: Paradoxes of Gender in English Pantomime.' *New Theatre Quarterly* 13 (1997): 195–204.

Jack, R.D.S. 'The Manuscript of *Peter Pan.*' *Children's Literature* 18 (1990): 101–13.

Mackail, Denis. *Barrie: The Story of J.M.B.* New York: Charles Scribner's Sons, 1941.

Mander, Raymond, and Joe Mitchenson. *Pantomime: A Story in Pictures.* New York: Taplinger, 1973.

Wilson, A.E. *The Story of Pantomime.* 1949. Totowa, NJ: Rowman & Littlefield, 1974.

6

Arthur Ransome, *Swallows and Amazons* (1930)

Introduction
Sara Haslam

Swallows and Amazons was Arthur Ransome's twenty-first book, but it was the first in the now famous series of twelve titles that he wrote for children. Though the first two in the series, *Swallows and Amazons* and *Swallowdale*, were well received and reviewed, by the time the third one, *Peter Duck*, came out, it was clear that the books were properly a hit. Further titles in the series are, like *Swallows and Amazons*, also set in the Lake District, and feature the Walkers and their companions the Blackett sisters (or Amazons), but others add new characters, and take place in the Norfolk Broads, in East Anglia and Scotland, and even in the South China Sea. Ransome was awarded the first British Library Association Carnegie Medal in 1936, for *Pigeon Post*, the sixth book in the series.

The success of these books might be unkindly attributed, if only in part, to the quality of the competition. Published in 1930, *Swallows and Amazons* finds itself, in Peter Hunt's overview of children's literature, placed squarely in the Age of Brass (which Hunt dates from 1920 to 1939) between the First and Second Golden Ages (Hunt 1994: 14–15). However, Ransome is also credited by critics with doing important things in these texts: challenging what came before, and developing the scope of modern children's literature. The books have remained in print and very popular throughout the twentieth and twenty-first centuries, suggesting intrinsic rather than comparative quality. 'A brilliant story', says the *Daily Mail* on the back of a current edition of *Swallows and Amazons*. *Swallows and Amazons* was cited in January 2008 as one of only ten classic books for children, and featured as one of the '100 Books Every Child Should Read' in the introduction to the *Daily Telegraph*'s guide to the best children's books in the same month (*Daily Telegraph*, 2008).

Origins, composition, and reception

Like Lewis Carroll's *Alice's Adventures in Wonderland* (1865), Robert Louis Stevenson's *Treasure Island* (1883) and J.M. Barrie's *Peter Pan* (1904), *Swallows and Amazons* was inspired by, written for, and dedicated to particular children. The Swallows (or the Walker children, as they are also known in the book) were originally based on the children of Ransome's friends, Dora and Ernest Altounyan. In 1928 this family returned from abroad to live in the Lake District, where Ransome and his wife were then based. The author helped to teach the children to sail, and also began the series thanks to their catalytic presence – though as he began to write, he felt he had to redress nature by transforming the eldest Altounyan child, Taqui, who was a girl, into a boy.

Ransome had only returned to live in the Lake District, an area made important to him during childhood holidays, in 1925. A journalist by profession, he had been reporting on the Russian revolution for the *Daily News* and the *Observer* from 1917 onwards. Later in his life, he described this life change:

> The Russian revolution had failed utterly in altering me personally, and I vowed that once I had a little peace and quiet and had got my sketch of the development of the revolution written, I would write 'finis' and fetch politics a good boost with the boot in the latter parts and return with no regrets whatever to pen, tobacco, fishing, and the lake country.
>
> Hunt, 1992: 54–5

And so he did. After the Altounyans arrived he resigned his then post at the *Manchester Guardian* and set to work, remembering and representing one version of an ideal (and increasingly lost) world.

If *Swallows and Amazons* has roots in real-life people and places, it also has a literary lineage. *Treasure Island* has long been recognised as a 'parent text' of *Swallows and Amazons*. This readily suggests that we should think in turn about *Robinson Crusoe* as a 'grandparent' text. *Swallows and Amazons* establishes itself firmly within the tradition of island fiction, so these intertextual relationships function at a formal level; Ransome also makes specific allusions via the repetition of Stevenson's map and explicit references to both books. Peter Hunt deduces an additional generic influence at work in Ransome's text, that of the folk-tale. In such tales, Hunt writes, 'the first third of the story is given over to preparation; the children acquire skills that they will use later, just as the heroes and heroines of folk-tales acquire gifts or magic devices that they later use' (Hunt, 1994: 123). The originality of *Swallows and Amazons*' texture derives from the juxtaposition of realistic descriptions of ordinary middle-class children camping out in the school holidays, with their imaginative games derived from Defoe and Stevenson, amongst others. Manual-level instructions in practical life-skills – from sailing to making tents at home – jostle with their imaginative construction of their skirmishes with other children, or 'pirates' as they are more properly known.

The book was published by Jonathan Cape in August 1930 (in the holidays, of course), and is still issued in a hardback edition by this London firm. It first appeared without illustrations, but as Eleanor Graham, a contemporary bookseller who discussed the issue with Ransome knew, a children's book without attractive illustrations was unlikely to do well (Hunt, 1992: 62). Clifford Webb was brought in to provide some drawings for a subsequent edition and for the sequel, *Swallowdale*. Ransome wasn't happy with Webb's efforts, and from *Peter Duck* onwards, he did the drawings himself. Further examples of his own drawings quickly replaced Webb's in *Swallows and Amazons* and *Swallowdale* as well, and are an integral, though idiosyncratic, element of the books (Hunt equates them with Tenniel's drawings for the *Alice* books and Shepard's for *The Wind in the Willows*): all subsequent editions have incorporated Ransome's drawings, and have attempted as far as possible to place them in the same positions relative to the text that they held in the earliest editions.

Having found producing *Swallows and Amazons* such an enjoyable and liberating experience, Ransome awaited publication with the 'utmost eagerness'. 'I feel quite childish about it', he wrote to his mother on 4 July, 'bursting to see the brute and feel it' (Brogan, 1984: 315). *Swallows and Amazons* was the first of Ransome's many books to be well received. Despite some good notices in the papers, it didn't sell as well as he might have hoped. In fact, it took two years to recoup the advance Ransome was paid. Sales picked up over the next couple of years, slowly and then much more quickly, however, and even from the outset Hunt writes that it elicited 'devotion and addiction' from its readers (Hunt, 1985: 222). The publishers at least were eager for a sequel, and it wasn't long until news spread, and the series began to work its magic. By the mid-1930s, according to Hugh Brogan, the tales were 'universally accepted as classics of children's literature' (1984: 312).

Critical opinion as to the reasons for the success of the book, and for its status as a key text in almost all accounts of British children's literature, varies. Most critics note the attractiveness of Ransome's innovatory use of holidays as a focus; the freedom of the children he represents; the security of family that underpins their freedom; the relationship between imagination and reality he traces; and the book's powerful sense of place. Eyre (1971) writes well of the way that Ransome, in addition, introduced a more realistic and natural approach, and used true-to-life dialogue, allowing children to see themselves and a world that they could recognise, as well as get excited about, in his books. Tucker and Bogen, as outlined below, each provide powerful readings of the appeal of Swallows and Amazons, one noting the power of nostalgia and make-believe over its adult readership, the other noting, by contrast, that the children's empowerment is not entirely a matter of fantasy (thus making a calculated appeal to child readers). The 'genetic' relationship with other island texts has also been an important thread in Ransome studies, and there is a related debate about its microcosmic representation of late imperialism. Absent protecting the Empire's interests in the South China Sea, the children's father leaves behind a brood of small sailors who ape naval language and behaviour, assume the privilege of mapping and naming their environs, and regard others (benignly) as 'natives', all as part of their games. The nature of the books as series fiction has also received some critical attention. Swallows and Amazons ends as the summer holidays draw to a close, although that ending, and its cleansing, dramatic storm, also contain the promise of many more holidays – and therefore books – to come. 'But perhaps you'll be coming again next year', says farmer's wife Mrs Dixon. 'Every year. For ever and ever', replies a Swallow earnestly. Though our focus here is on the first of what became twelve linked books, it is significant that it forms part of a series (defined as a sequence of related stories about the same groups of characters). Victor Watson has argued that series fiction 'has played an enormous and largely unacknowledged part in children's reading throughout most of the twentieth century' (2000: 8–9). In the case of Ransome, who contributed enormously to the growth of series fiction, critics have noted that the texts become progressively less 'closed', or circular – where a circular text means coming more or less back to the beginning, a real or metaphorical place of safety – appropriate to the fact the subjects are themselves growing up. Their readers are, of course, busy doing so too.

The essays

The first essay is extracted from Peter Hunt's book, which remains a key resource for studying Ransome. It combines biographical with textual analysis, examining *Swallows and Amazons* primarily as an exercise in the family adventure story. Tucker's essay concentrates on Ransome's balancing of fantasy and realism, relating this to changing concepts of childhood and to the author's dual audience of adult and child readers. Anna Bogen also discusses the blend of the real and imaginary in *Swallows and Amazons*, and traces how the narrative control shifts between the primary adult narrator and the voices of the child characters. While Bogen acknowledges the influences of *Robinson Crusoe* and *Treasure Island*, she traces the links between Ransome's book and *Peter Pan* throughout this essay, suggesting that Wild Cat Island contrasts with Never Land because it brings the imaginary and the real together in the same space at the end of the narrative, thus imbuing the child characters with agency to effect real change.

References

Brogan, H. 1984. *The Life of Arthur Ransome*. London, Jonathan Cape.

Daily Telegraph 2008. 100 books every child should read. http://www.telegraph.co.uk/culture/books/3670596/100-books-every-child-should-read---Pt-2.html, accessed 18 December 2008. Originally published 31 January 2008.

Eyre, F. 1971. *British Children's Books in the Twentieth Century*. London, Longman.

Hunt, P. 1985. 'Arthur Ransome's *Swallows and Amazons*: Escape to a Lost Paradise', in P. Nodelman (ed.) *Touchstones: Reflections on the Best in Children's Literature*, vol. 1, West Lafayette, IN, Children's Literature Association.

Hunt, P. 1992. *Approaching Arthur Ransome*. London, Jonathan Cape.

Hunt, P. 1994. *An Introduction to Children's Literature*. Oxford, Oxford University Press.

Watson, V. 2000. *Reading Series Fiction: From Arthur Ransome to Gene Kemp*. London, Routledge.

Further reading

Hardyment, C. 1984. *Arthur Ransome and Captain Flint's Trunk*. London, Jonathan Cape.

Hart-Davies, R. (ed.) 1976. *Arthur Ransome: The Autobiography of Arthur Ransome*. London, Jonathan Cape.

See also the Arthur Ransome Society at http://arthur-ransome.org/ar/

The Lake District Novels
Peter Hunt

Swallows and Amazons

Structure and family

Ransome seems to have approached writing as he did sailing or fishing; certain things would work for logical reasons, provided they were done well. Consequently, the structural patterns that can be clearly seen in his novels may not have been deliberate, but they certainly reflect an unconsciously highly skilled narrator, and they are entirely appropriate to the narrative content.

As the novels progress – and the Lake District novels form an interesting unit in this respect – they form for their readers, even more than for their characters, a *Bildungsroman*. As we shall see, the closure that is so characteristic of books for younger children is strong in *Swallows and Amazons* [*SA*] and progressively weakens. *Swallows and Amazons* is notably circular: it begins and ends with the same character in the same place. Although *Swallowdale* [*S*] ends with Susan's remark, 'Isn't it a blessing to get home?' (*S*. 453), they are not at home, but on their own island. *Winter Holiday* and *Pigeon Post* both end away from home, but in the comforting presence of adults, after great danger. *The Picts and the Martyrs* is a book most concerned with displacement and disruption, and it ends without the restitution of normality. These structural patterns are integral with the freedom that Ransome gives his children and the limits that he imposes.

From the beginning, the Walkers' mother establishes the limits of freedom. She stipulates not only where they shall be, but also orders small details. ' "No medicines. . . . Anyone who wants doctoring is invalided home." "If it's really serious," said Titty, "but we can have a plague or a fever or two by ourselves" ' (*SA*, 32–3). (This concern for their safety does not, as Tucker points out, extend to being careful with bows and arrows or wearing lifejackets, but Ransome was a man of his time, a time when such things were not considered.[1]

Suitably provided for, the children sail to the island; Mother comes to check on them before they go to sleep and brings more food. The next morning, after only a single uneventful night, John and Roger sail back to Holly Howe to report (and find it an oddly alien place).

Extracted from 'The Lake District Novels', in P. Hunt, *Approaching Arthur Ransome* (London: Jonathan Cape, 1992), pp. 84–99.

Whenever there is a problem, or a difficulty, psychological closure is applied by a compensation. When John is accused by Captain Flint of lying – which is, of course, to be accused of breaking a fundamental code – he first applies a suitably ruralistic philosophy ('But the big hills far up the lake helped to make him feel that the houseboat man did not matter. The hills had been there before Captain Flint. They would be there for ever' [*SA*, 178]), and then physical therapy (he swims around the island). But the real healing comes when Mother appears once again for Vicky's birthday party.

Mother is therefore a great link with the rest of the world. She knows all about the children's troubles with the houseboat and reacts very calmly to John's distress, in a somewhat Victorian way: ' "It doesn't matter what people think or say if they don't know you. They may think anything" ' (*SA*, 85). Similarly, whenever the children are in danger, or there is some real displacement, she is there.

After the big climactic storm, when a tent collapses and the children fantasize in the best literary manner about the loss of their ship, they receive a massive reinforcement of security: 'And then came the natives.' First the local farmer's wife, Mrs Dixon, with her bucket of porridge (' "This really is eating out of the common dish," said Titty' [*SA, 361*]), and then both mothers. The reaction of the children mixes an appreciation of reality with a demonstration of family loyalty:

After they were gone the Swallows and Amazons looked at each other. . . .
'It's the natives,' said Nancy. 'Too many of them. They turn everything into a picnic.'
'Mother doesn't,' said Titty.
'Nor does ours when she's alone,' said Nancy. . . . 'It's when they all get together. . . . They can't help themselves, poor things.'

SA, 367

The strength of this relationship between adults and children and its structural effect are both so clear that it is curious that many critics have overlooked it. John Rowe Townsend, in what is in many ways the British standard work on children's literature, *Written for Children*, says, 'We may wish we could see [the children] in a living relationship with their parents, instead of having the parents mainly as understanding figures in the background.'[2] Juliet Dusinberre, in her study of children's books and radical experiments in art, *Alice to the Lighthouse*, notes in passing, 'The child unhampered by parents has become a commonplace of twentieth-century children's books since Arthur Ransome.'[3] Crouch in *The Nesbit Tradition* suggests that 'one might feel a theoretical regret that Ransome did not choose to show children and adults in partnership.'[4] (In an extreme misreading, Crouch goes on to suggest that most of the adults are 'hostile and barbarous.')

All of this is quite untrue, for throughout the book the adults are very much there, providing security. Fred Inglis, possibly the most authoritative of contemporary politically orientated British critics, notes, however, that 'Arthur Ransome . . . wrote of the absolute safety of a Lake District (and Norfolk Broads) bounded by the absolute justice of the parental writ.'[5]

Ransome's young children, then, are in the ideal circumstance; they have an idyllic playground and a sense of place: in the hills, in the family, and in the moral order of things. The hills that ring the lake, with their heather-covered slopes above the woods, are a secure boundary, rather like the hills that enclose the Thames valley in *The Wind in the Willows*. Consequently, the children can play and grow within known limits.

Family codes and characters

Probably the most common accusation by those who feel that children's lit-erature is a contradiction in terms is that child characters are necessarily limited. Do the Swallows and Amazons themselves escape from this stric-ture, or are they submerged by the twin restraints of public and family role?

John Walker is initially the rather priggish, solemn, bland boy, very much under his father's shadow – a boy who, when rowing 'navy stroke', made it 'a point of honour that the oars should not splash when they went into the water' (*SA*, 173). One of the recurrent motifs is his references to his father; he carries his books as totems, and he quotes him in moments of need. For example, when they are, unwisely, sailing at night, he says, 'Even Daddy used to say, "Never be ashamed to reef a small boat in the dark"' (*SA*, 255).

In a sense, John's part is necessarily ambivalent to the adult, but under-standable to the child. His relationship to adults is possibly the most real-istic of all characters. He does not expect them to be nice; they are in a different, authoritative world.

Susan, the domestic, occupies a place similar to her mother in the family hierarchy. (It is worth noting – although it may jar for the modern reader – that mother 'without leave from daddy, could [not] let them go alone' [*SA*, 18].) She provides a firm undercurrent of responsibility that unfortunately makes her character rather intractable. In *Swallowdale* and *Pigeon Post*, her motherly role becomes a cliché for both the reader and the other characters. She is not, however, above a mild criticism of the Captain: ' "Lucky we brought a sailmaker's needle." "Luckier if you knew how to use it," said the mate a moment or two later, when she looked up and saw the captain sucking his thumb' (*SA*, 278). Susan's domestic efforts are never actually ridiculed by author or characters; they are taken quite seriously by the other children.

So is Titty. She is the romantic, who reads *Robinson Crusoe* when she is alone on the island, and stands looking out over the storm-swept lake and getting soaked to the skin. But like her siblings, she comes to life most subtly in her interactins with other members of the family.

Roger, similarly, is most convincing at moments such as that on Octopus lagoon, in the dark, when the oars are tangled in water-lilies: ' "Perhaps they are octopuses," said Roger. "Titty read to me about how they put their arms out long, and grab people even out of a boat." In Roger's voice there were clear signs of panic in the forecastle. Captain John took command at once' (*SA*, 231–2).

On the whole, the children's fears and loyalties are straightforward, because they understand the underlying value of skills and honour. Like E. Nesbit before him and William Mayne in our own day, Ransome implies the complexity of relationships by small touches. This is especially the case when the Walker family is contrasted with the Blacketts. Increasingly, as the series progresses, their codes conflict.

The Amazons, in this book, are perhaps the most crudely stereotyped characters; they develop only as the landscape and people-scapes to which they belong also develop. (By *The Picts and the Martyrs*, Nancy and Peggy can be understood in a complex context.) In *Swallows and Amazons*, it is family, and family differences, that provides their identity.

For example, John and Nancy have different views of the future: Nancy, the child's child, proposes to live on the island all the year round; John, the adult's child, quietly puts down such nonsense: 'I shall be going to sea some day . . . and so will Roger. But we'll always come back here on leave' (*SA*, 368). Similarly, John takes a quiet pleasure in the fact that the Amazons (despite their local knowledge) cannot translate the naval 'four bells of the middle watch' (*SA*, 349).

Susan takes some time to realize that the interaction with adults is rather different in the Blackett-Turner household from that in the Walkers'. Mrs Blackett, 'a very little woman, not really much bigger than Nancy' (*SA*, 363) is not the calm mother that Mrs Walker is; nor, as we see in the rare glimpse of adult life in *Swallowdale*, is her domestic life as smooth. Thus, when Captain Flint chases Nancy back to the island to apologize, Susan does not immediately understand what is going on.

'I say, Susan,' [John] shouted, 'Captain Flint is coming after her.'

'You're as bad as Titty with her treasure,' said Susan. 'Natives don't do things like that.'

'But he is,' said John.

SA, 291

More seriously, Nancy and Peggy's standard of honesty is perhaps not quite as rigid as that of the Swallows, which possibly makes them more alive for today's reader. Nancy at one point says, 'And there's lots to eat. We brought a plum pudding to cut up in pieces, and fry. Most luscious. Cook gave it to us. And then afterwards we found a cold tongue. It had hardly been touched, so we brought it too. But we came away rather privately because we thought we might be stopped' (*SA*, 298).

Nancy's simple character suffers slightly from her involvement in the uncharacteristically melodramatic plot of *Swallows and Amazons*. She is rude, or at least spoiled and superior, to Sammy the policeman. Ransome makes the excuse that she has known him all her life (*SA*, 280), but his dismissal and subsequent apology smack very much of a lesser kind of children's book. This relationship has none of the mutual respect shown elsewhere.

Ransome has a good eye for the minutiae of behaviour – perhaps especially of small children. For example, when Vicky has her second birthday, on the island, she brings her lamb and her elephant with her. 'Vicky had her elephant with her. She forgot her lamb in the boat, and it had to be fetched later. Vicky liked the elephant better than the lamb because it was smaller. The lamb was so large that it was always being put down and forgotten' (*SA*, 182).

Outdoor skills

The family codes and standards of behaviour are also expressed practically and pragmatically: the skills of sailing and camping and fishing are skills of craft and love. To understand and to achieve them is to be initiated into a very select club. Some of the appeal of *Swallows and Amazons* may well lie precisely in the vicarious pleasure that the audience can take in being admitted into these circles. In a very important sense, the family unit is like the skilled group.

Of course, the sailing elements will exclude as many children as they will attract. Although Ransome's prose is consistently simple and uncluttered, his approach to describing boats can easily leave readers out of their depths. When the small sailing dinghy, *Swallow*, is first described, one might be forgiven for abandoning all hope, especially when Ransome does supply *some* explanation, clearly implying that the rest of what he is talking about is obvious:

'She doesn't seem to have a forestay,' said John. 'And there isn't a place to lead the halyard to in the bows to make it do instead.'

'Let me have a look,' said Queen Elizabeth [their mother is temporarily in this role]. . . . 'Is there a clear under the thwart where the mast is stepped?'

'Two,' said John, feeling. The mast fitted in a hole in the forward thwart, the seat near the bows of the boat. It had a square foot, which rested in a slot cut to fit it in the kelson.

SA, 29

But when they are setting the sail for the first time, Ransome is, some-what awkwardly, forced to insert a gloss into a line of dialogue: 'Is that what those blocks (pulleys) are for hooked to a ring in the kelson . . . ?' (*SA*, 29).

Perhaps the detail that most adults remember most vividly from childhood reading is the ability of Susan and Peggy to light fires with only sticks and moss and leaves. (For a meticulous description, see *SA*, 160–1).

People and places

Swallows and Amazons was, as Margery Fisher writes, 'by no means the first English holiday-adventure, but it brought to a tired, bland genre a new exuberance in narrative and circumstance, an emphasis on practical techniques . . . and a positive affirmation of the way children could absorb and adapt to new places and events.'[6]

Integral with the sense of detail is the sense of the people. Bob Dixon, in his book on sexism and racism, *Catching them Young*, places Ransome in the 'exclusively middle-class' tradition of Nesbit: 'if members of the lower classes appear at all, it's decidedly on the fringe.'[7] There is some truth in this but, as we have seen, Ransome was studiously democratic. *Everyone*, in one sense, is peripheral to the children's viewpoint.

None the less, this is a 'middle-class' book, and the characters use the middle-class dialect of the period: 'I say' and 'Look here' are endemic. But it is not always easy to distinguish among period, class, and family dialect – as when Peggy speaks of using the water breaker (or barrel) 'as a puncheon for feastable drinks' (*SA*, 124). Also, the Amazons have a cook, the Swallows have a nurse; the farmers and farmers' wives form a kind of retinue. Yet they are far from being caricatures; they are people in their own right, and the children have to respect this individuality.

The nurse, for example, when John and Roger report back on the first morning, 'somehow did not seem to feel that she was talking with sea-men from other lands' (*SA*, 74). Mr Jackson, the 'powerful native' from Holly Howe, stands silently (and very expressive the silence is, too, in class terms), while Mrs Walker talks gobbledegook with her children (*SA*, 64–5). Mr Dixon, who provides continuity with *Swallowdale* and has quite a large part to play in *Winter Holiday*, is even more taciturn: 'Mr Dixon, who was waiting down by the boat, had said "Good morning," when he came, and now he said "Good day to you," as he rowed Mrs Dixon away. He was always a very silent native' (*SA*, 364).

The children are treated well, but not indulged, either by parents or 'natives'. After the storm, 'Nancy wanted to take the hay out of the haybags to make a last blaze on the camp fire. "Nay," said Mr Jackson, "it's good hay that." So it was spared to be eaten by cows' (*SA*, 366).

The charcoal-burners – Ransome's own clay-pipe-bakers – are the same. The Swallows visit them on a day of calm, leaving blazes and pattens in the wood in the best literary exploring fashion. Ransome describes the process of charcoal-burning (to be used, initially, for keeping the camp-fire alight overnight, and, more spectaculary, for helping in the smelting in *Pigeon Post*) and the two ancient men (Old Billy and Young Billy), with their adder (or viper) that they keep for luck. On Ransome's principle that everything should be relevant, this incident becomes structural. The Billies have a message for Captain Flint, and their approach to the children is quite unsentimental:

> 'Shall you be seeing those lasses again? . . . Well, you can tell them to tell their Uncle Jim . . .'
>   'They can't,' Titty broke in, 'they're at war with him.'
>   'They 'll tell him right enough.'
>
> SA, 155

The people are set in, and form part of, the landscape. As Inglis points out, 'Ransome mattered fundamentally because I saw him also as a celebrant of the great world of home. The splendour and detail of his stories, taking place . . . in an unending and paradisal holiday, were woven from a love of the landscape.'[8]

Ransome never makes the common error of cutting the landscape down to child-size. The view may be myopic (it is not so much adults who are cut out of Ransome's books, but other children), but it is real. The evocations of the area never intrude; they are sketched only, forming a subtle background to the details of food and stores and activity. But they can also act as Ransome's most effective atmospheric passages when they are functional. For example, there is the children's first glimpse of the charcoal-burners, from the lake, at the night (*SA*, 138).

The literary tradition

It is important to see *Swallows and Amazons* as being part of, and deriving some of its density from, a literary tradition. The book begins with a literary reference, the epigraph to the first chapter:

> Or like stout Cortez, when with eagle eyes,
> He stared at the Pacific – and all his men
> Looked at each other with a wild surmise –
> Silent, upon a peak in Darien.

These lines from Keats's 'On First Looking into Chapman's Horner' (the source is not given) are perhaps another unconscious link with that other major formative children's book, Richard Jefferies's *Bevis*.

Part of that *epic* of boyhood involves Bevis and his friend Mark in building a hut and living on an island on a lake for over a week. They construct a gun that works (Jefferies gives meticulous instructions), and kill a disconcertingly large number of birds with it; they catch fish; they cook; they learn (at immense length) to sail. It is a book that, on the surface, celebrates the amorality of childhood as well as freedom and self-reliance. Yet it is underpinned by a sense of responsibility and tradition.

To say that Ransome owes something to Jefferies is not to suggest imitation, although it is true that in both books there is a lake, an island, sailing, fishing, and a resolutely practical air. Rather it is that Ransome and Jefferies shared a romantic and practical love of nature and of country skills, and a very similar literary heritage.

A comparison of the books that Bevis, and the Swallows, take to their respective islands is fascinating. Bevis's collection is perhaps a little more intellectual than the Walkers': 'The "Odyssey", Don Quixote, the grey and battered volume of ballads [Percy's *Reliques*], a tiny little book of Shakespeare's poems . . . and Filmore's rhymed translation of Faust. He found two manuscript books for the journal; these and the pens and ink-bottle could all go together in the final cargo.'[9] The ship's library of the *Swallow* includes Titty's *Robinson Crusoe* ('It tells you just what to do on an island'); likewise, 'John took *The Seaman's Handybook*, and Part Three of *The Baltic Pilot*. Both books had belonged to his father, but John took them with him even on holidays. Mate Susan took *Simple Cooking for Small Households*' (SA, 33).

Quite apart from confirming the typecasting, it is significant that Defoe should strike the keynote for *Swallows and Amazons*, as contrasted with the more fantastic Homer for *Bevis*. Yet, as we have seen, Ransome quotes Homer in *Swallowdale*, while his ballad-epigraphs to the second and third chapters of *Swallows and Amazons* are matched by Jefferies's quotations from 'King Estmere' and Longfellow's 'Secret of the Sea'.

Other, more important parallels exist between *Bevis* and *Swallows and Amazons* (and the first few chapters of *Swallowdale*). The children live in a dual world of fiction and reality; the fiction is of the late nineteenth-century kind, of wild adventure, often maritime and in an empire-building context. Titty makes most conscious use of it, but the mood, or technique, is initially announced by Roger.

Ransome's use of the device of crossing over between the real and the imaginary is helped by his range of characters. John is most orientated to the 'real' world. On the day after they catch sight of the Amazon pirates and Captain Flint's houseboat is attacked, John 'woke in ordinary life. Well, he thought, one could hardly expect that sort of thing to last, and it was almost a pity it had begun. After all, even if there were no pirates, the island was real enough and so was *Swallow*. He could do without the pirates. It was time to fetch the milk' (*SA*, 104).

Narrative technique

The most consistent and consistently striking and original feature of Ransome's books is his control of pace. With *Swallowdale* as perhaps the supreme example, what is important in his books is not so much what happens as what does not happen. He is not afraid of the 'dull' day, and this may have been surprising to the contemporary audience – as it probably is to many young readers today. It takes, for example, 113 pages of *Swallows and Amazons* before Nancy Blackett makes her appearance in the flesh. Until then, the book has been concerned with provisioning, exploring, setting up camp, fishing, cooking and swimming. Two chapters have what might now be regarded as suicidally downbeat titles – 'Island Life' and 'More Island Life'. But Ransome has sufficient faith in the *intrinsic* interest of his material not to have to rely continually on the narrative urge. Finding out is excitement enought.

The burglary of Captain Flint's houseboat, then, stands out as an anomaly. It involves one of the standard devices of children's books – the child who is right, and the adults or siblings who disbelieve in the face of what they would otherwise know to be likely. By Ransome's own standard, Titty's capture of the *Amazon* is incident enough, without loud-voiced and loquacious burglars having revealing conversations conveniently in the dark – let alone the caricatured things that they actually say: 'Told you, you blamed fool. You've blooming well smashed the blighted boat' (*SA*, 229).

Similarly, at the end of the book, Captain Flint give Titty and Roger a monkey and a parrot, the kind of exotic gifts so often found in wish-fulfilling (and impractical) children's stories. But the fact that monkey and parrot only reappear together in the fantasy novel *Missee Lee* suggests that Ransome knew their place in the literary scheme of things.

Many incidental delights may also contribute to the way in which the books have been handed down through families. *Swallows and Amazons* is set precisely in August 1929 (*SA*, 121), and progressively, the books celebrate a lost world. (*The Picts and the Martyrs*, for example, published in 1943, is set in 1932). It could be argued that, in fact, Ransome pictures a world even earlier than that. As the background is progressively filled in with farmers, the policeman, the doctor, the postman, local boys, the cook, shopkeepers, fire-fighters, and so on, another dimension of interest is added. From the beginning, critics recognized the appeal to adults; the *Saturday Review of Literature* described *Swallows and Amazons* as having 'both silvery present and golden retrospect'.[10] Cars and telephones and crowds of people are very rare.

Similarly, the monetary values occasionally bring one up short. John and Susan go shopping in the village by the lake and buy four bottles of ginger beer and *twenty yards* of rope for less than five shillings (*SA*, 99–100).

These, then, are some of the elements that made *Swallows and Amazons* and its successors such influential and radical texts *for children*. In looking at the later novels set in the Lake District, there are, to some extent, variations played on established themes, a steady refining of Ransome's art. Ransome, as Trease observes, 'deflected the stream of fiction into new channels',[11] and by using the Lake District as a backbone and exploiting the cumulative virtues of the series, he moved toward greater realism and, indeed, greater originality. In comparison with the later books, *Swallows and Amazons* is apprentice work, but its flaws are relatively minor. [Elsewhere Hunt suggests these are to do with his handling of the burglary sub-plot, and also the amount of technical detail.] Ransome was doing something quite new, and at least in its major characteristics, his art is remarkably mature.

Notes

1. Nicholas Tucker, *The Child and the Book* (Cambridge University Press, 1981), 215.
2. John Rowe Townsend, *Written for Children* (Harmondsworth: Penguin [Pelican], 2nd rev. ed., 1983), 185.
3. Juliet Dusinberre, *Alice to the Lighthouse* (London: Macmillan Press, 1987), 90.
4. Marcus Crouch, *The Nesbit Tradition: The Children's Novel, 1945–1970* (London: Ernest Benn, 1972), 18.
5. Fred Inglis, *The Promise of Happiness: Value and Meaning in Children's Fiction* (Cambridge University Press, 1981), 66.
6. Margery Fisher, *Classics for Children and Young People* (Stroud: Thimble Press), 61–2.
7. Bob Dixon, *Catching Them Young 1: Sex, Race and Class in Children's Fiction* (London: Pluto Press, 1977), 58.
8. Inglis, *Promise of Happiness*, 66–7.
9. Richard Jefferies, *Bevis*, ed. Peter Hunt, The World's Classics Series (London: Oxford University Press, 1989), 236.
10. T.M. Longstreth, review of *Swallows and Amazons*, *Saturday Review of Literature*, 9th May 1931.
11. Trease, *Tales Out of School: A Survey of Children's Fiction* (London: Heinemann, 1949), 139.

Arthur Ransome and Problems of Literary Assessment
Nicholas Tucker

Children's literature has always encompassed masterpieces which have never been confined to child readers alone, such as *Alice's Adventures in Wonderland, Treasure Island,* and in our own day *Tom's Midnight Garden* and *Carrie's War.* There are moments in Ransome's books which also offer something to readers of all ages. His descriptions of nature and of a working rustic world, now disappeared, are accurate and charming. He is a brilliant storyteller, expert in creating minicrises toward the end of a chapter. He always makes each word tell, avoiding false emotion in favor of lean, spare dialogue.

Yet elsewhere there are serious barriers in Ransome to all but the most nostalgic adult reader. His frequent overinsistence on detail in his stories is always likely to be of more interest to children than to grown-ups. The various 'How to' sections of a Ransome novel (read a chart, skin a rabbit, sail a dinghy) convey a powerful image of self-reliance more meaningful to a child than to most adults, for children are still experimenting in their imaginations with the possibilities of their own growing competence once they are freed from adult interference. Adult readers do not generally have the same constant need to suggest to themselves in fantasy that they, too, now have the capacity to bring off small technical achievements (although there may still be satisfaction in imagining their own *super* competence, by identifying with heroes like James Bond).

An atmosphere of only partial truth is also typical of Ransome's books. Young children do not easily form themselves into the cohesive social groups found in his novels, capable of surviving for long periods of time without adult supervision even when faced by major difficulties. In real life, quarrels are apt to flare up, and accidents will happen (the only Ransome character who ever ends up in hospital is the highly capable eighteen-year-old Jim Brading in *We Didn't Mean to Go to Sea*). The parents in Ransome's books are also subject to the workings of a consistently benign imagination. Any mother or father who did allow a group of children to set off for days on a dinghy with no lifejackets would in reality be seen as culpably negligent. The famous telegram from Daddy, 'BETTER DROWNED THAN DUFFERS IF NOT DUFFERS WON'T DROWN' (*Swallows and*

This is an edited version of the article originally published in *Children's Literature in Education,* 26:2 (1995), pp. 97–105.

Amazons, p. 5), would get short shrift were it to be read out by a coroner at an inquest to investigate a fatal boating accident involving small children. Yet such an accident could so easily have occurred during the night sailing in *Swallows and Amazons*.

Parents would be at risk as well as children if they were ever to take advice like this seriously in their own dealings within the family. But no reader goes to Ransome books for such literal messages. These are holiday stories, to be read for their adventures, not for their veracity. Taking them as an absolute model for real life would certainly lead to some disappointments. When, in William Golding's *Lord of the Flies* (p. 38), child characters refer optimistically to their own island in terms of *Swallows and Amazons*, the irony is justified.

Other omissions in Ransome stories can also be easily spotted by adults, who now know there is more to going on camping holidays in the wild than problems with putting up a tent or lighting a fire. At the most basic level, who digs the latrines? More important, do healthy young adolescents of both sexes always sleep alongside each other without incident? And if they do, should they? The development of sexual feeling is a closed book to Ransome and his child characters. By adopting and then following a rigid naval command structure, the young Swallows and Amazons avoid any trace of emotional attachment to each other above and beyond the call of duty. The sexless world of a Ransome story fitted well into what was required by children's publishers between the wars. But it was often remote from the real thing.

Child readers themselves do not generally mind this. Particular or pre-existing emotional ties in favorite characters often pose a threat to adventure stories based on the idea of a loyal band of comrades. From *Beowulf* to *The Hobbit*, bachelor adventurers have regularly departed on their travels unencumbered by any lingering emotions for those they leave behind. Nor do such heroes generally develop any extra partial feelings for one of the opposite sex once on their travels. Adults know that untoward or occasionally uncontrollable emotions are sometimes strong enough to bring down even the court of King Arthur. Denying their existence may help a story along, but often at the expense of having to make a fairly strong suspension of disbelief. This is easier to achieve when one is a comparatively inexperienced child reader than it is for any adult with a good memory of their own past.

Naval discipline also puts a stop to any expression of sibling rivalry within Ransome's two main fictional families. Brothers and sisters may be devoted to each other, but some occasional disruption is also inevitable. This is not simply the opinion of family therapists; the Bible and fairy stories suggest the same thing. Family quarrels do not usually make for elevating listening, whether conducted in public, in private, or in a story. Unlike some children's authors, Ransome ignores this problem. Once Captain John gives an order and it is relayed by Mate Susan, there is no further argument. It is harder for a novelist to make occasionally whingeing child characters seem as attractive as Ransome's stoical counterparts. Younger readers like the flattering picture that emerges here of children their own age. Adult readers, often more critical of themselves as children, may look more closely for a realism that encompasses childish faults as well as virtues.

[Tucker proceeds to discuss in detail one book he feels 'falls outside these criticisms' – Ransome's *We Didn't Mean to Go to Sea* (Vol. 7 in the series).]

[Tucker then moves to praise novels which paint 'a truthful picture'.]

Yet it is at this point that I start wondering whether we critics may not be putting our own needs as readers too much to the fore when we sing the particular praises of a story like *We Didn't Mean to Go to Sea*. As adults, we naturally prefer fiction that remains credible because it treats its characters and events realistically. But do children themselves always most need writing that addresses the mature side of themselves as readers? And if they do not always want such stories, should critics still routinely urge them in that direction? As it is, the insistent quality of reality in *We Didn't Mean to Go to Sea* also makes this story rather tense and, for some, not to be compared in terms of total, relaxed pleasure with the reassuringly gentle adventures found in other Ransome tales.

There is of course an alternative point of view about children's literature, more common with noncritics looking back nostalgically to their own youthful reading. This holds that some of the most effective writing for children may be that which reflects a child's basic immaturity. The best books, in this reasoning, often contain fictional worlds that, while internally consistent, remain different from the real one in a number of ways acceptable to a child's still limited experience and understanding. Creating and sustaining a fictional world that remains believable, however unlikely, demands a great deal of imaginative commitment from writers. If they are going to pull off such a demanding task satisfactorily, it may sometimes be because they are particularly able to call on deep sources of childlike fantasy still surviving within their own imagination.

Which type of broadly reality-based or fantasy-based writer is thought best for young readers depends, therefore, on our particular understanding of what childhood is properly about. Those who see this period of development primarily as a transitional stage leading to adulthood will generally welcome novels that describe life more or less as it is. Giving readers the truth is seen as providing them with an important aid to their own eventual better understanding of themselves and others. Those who see childhood more as an end in itself may prefer literature that is more clearly fantasy-based.

Far from believing that children's books should try to build bridges toward a more adult understanding, this school of thought prefers stories that celebrate childhood in terms that are themselves childlike. Adult understanding is seen here as the enemy of childhood: an unwelcome intrusion into a magical period of life when fantasy for a short time reigns supreme over reality, particularly when it comes to indulging in imaginary games and favorite stories.

Ransome himself usually took this softer line in his stories. While he preferred to write truthfully about day-to-day practicalities, he left most bigger personal or social questions largely untouched. In all his long life, he made only one fictional use of his extensive firsthand knowledge of what took place during the Russian Revolution. In his various stories written just before or during the last war, there is no discussion of any dangerous, uncertain world beyond the Lake District or the Norfolk Broads. References to Daddy's work as a naval officer are never followed up, even when – in *We Didn't Mean to Go to Sea*, published in 1937 – he returns to his family having just paid a visit to Berlin. For some, this type of omission in otherwise realistic contemporary fiction smacks of willful obfuscation: a desire to keep children in the dark just when they could and should become better informed about what sort of world they are shortly going to inherit.

But there is also much to be said for books that enable readers to escape so comprehensively into a settled, uncontentious imaginary world, even if only for a few hours. Is there any critic who would really begrudge a young reader an imaginary glimpse of an idealized Lake District? I remember reading these books in wartime Britain as a welcome relief from the much grimmer realities around me. Even in more normal circumstances, imagination can always thrive and possibilities extend in a fantasy world all the more enticing for having little to do with any recognizable reality. The end result need not be mere escapism, given that the ideals we form for ourselves in our imagination when young sometimes become reality in adulthood. In [Dingle, 1992] *Distilled Enthusiasms*, numerous adults testify to Ransome's influence on them. For some, this has specifically to do with their own later choice of sailing as a lifetime hobby. For others, the claim is that his books influenced their whole approach to life in general.

That is why it does not matter if child readers of Ransome have their own boats or not. As Malcolm Muggeridge once wrote in a review of *Swallows and Amazons*:

> The book is the very stuff of play. It is make-believe such as all children have indulged in: even children who have not been so fortunate as to have a lake and a boat and an island but only a backyard among the semis of Suburbia.
>
> quoted in Brogan, 1984, p. 315

Assessing children's books by the quality of creative play they give rise to afterward would be an impossible task. But it is surely one important consideration to bear in mind, and my guess is that, judged by this criterion, Ransome's books would come out very high.

Arriving at a stable critical assessment of Ransome satisfying to all parties is therefore impossible, given the legitimacy of two quite different ways of looking at children's literature and what it should be doing. For some, his concentration mainly on activities in which many young readers are most interested, in settings which transmit a powerful illusion of reality mixed with pleasurable fantasy, make him one of the great children's authors. For others, the omissions in his writing rule him out as someone who is usually enjoyed for long by a discerning adult reader for reasons other than nostalgia. And while children's books are properly written for children, there is still often a feeling that the very best of older children's fiction should have much to offer adult readers, too. Authors who talk successfully to the adult in child readers often manage to get through to adult readers as well.

'I will make, if possible, a book that a child shall understand, yet a man will feel some temptation to peruse should he chance to take it up' (quoted in Brogan, 1984, p. 298.) This quotation from Walter Scott's diary was noted by Ransome in an undated memorandum. He then went on to add, 'I have always thought this a perfect description of the books I should like to have written.' In this aim, I believe he failed, but only just. Other bestselling children's authors have often written really badly, turning in stereotyped plots and characters which barely nod in the direction of likelihood. Ransome always wrote well and took pains to provide children with adventures that could very nearly have happened. Occasionally he wrote well enough for adults, too, though seldom in my experience over a whole book.

But if Ransome is measured on a different scale of values, where strict realism in children's fiction is seen as less important than the provision of convincing, consistently child-centered imaginative escape, he must be accounted a total success. In his books, different types of fantasy are integrated into some beguilingly realistic settings so expertly that only a very experienced reader generally sees where the joins occur. This is not the only way to write for older children, but it is one acknowledged approach with a long provenance and an excellent record in satisfying young audiences. Such fiction does not show up consistently well when judged by the canons of adult literary criticism and preferences. But as a children's writer working in one particular literary tradition, Ransome has nothing to apologize for, and it is as a children's writer of this type that he should always be judged.

References

Bawden, Nina, *Carrie's War*, 1973.
Brogan, Hugh, *The Life of Arthur Ransome*, Cape, 1984.
Dingle, Rodney, *Distilled Enthusiasms*. Amazon Publications, 1992.
Golding, William, *Lord of the Flies*. Faber, 1954.
Pearce, Philippa, *Tom's Midnight Garden*, 1958.
Ransome, Arthur, *Swallows and Amazons*. Random House, [1931] 2001.
Ransome, Arthur, *We Didn't Mean to Go to Sea*. Cape, 1937.
Tolkien, J.R.R., *The Hobbit*, 1937.

Peter Pan, Wild Cat Island, and the Lure of the Real
Anna Bogen

Arthur Ransome's 1930 novel *Swallows and Amazons* famously opens with a scene in which 'Roger, age seven', runs across the lawn pretending to be a sailing ship:

> He could not run straight against the wind because he was a sailing vessel, a tea-chipper, the *Cutty Sark*. His elder brother John had said only that morning that steamships were just engines in tin boxes. Sail was the thing, and so, though it took rather longer, Roger made his way up the field in broad tacks.[1]

The perspectival shifts between child and adult consciousness that occur in this scene, as well as its conviction that 'sail is the thing,' provide an appropriate opening to Ransome's twelve-book *Swallows and Amazons* saga, which is characterized above all by a blend of the real and the imaginary so subtle that the texts themselves seldom betray a dividing line. Starting with Roger's ship, each book of the series contains both lived and imagined adventures that structurally complement one other. Even in *We Didn't Mean to Go to Sea*, often cited as the most 'grown-up' book of the series, when the children set sail on the very real waters of the English channel, a parallel world of the imagination continues to possess both the minds of the characters and the text's narrative voice.

The *Swallows* saga is therefore characterized by a persistent flexibility in which narrative control shifts almost imperceptibly between the adult voice

Originally published as 'The Island Come True: Peter Pan, Wild Cat Island and the Lure of the Real', in M.S. Thompson and C. Keenan (eds), *Treasure Islands: Studies in Children's Literature* (Dublin: Four Courts Press, 2006), pp. 53–61.

of the primary narrator and the secondary 'voices' of various juvenile characters, made accessible to the audience through a strategic use of free indirect discourse. This is combined with a level of almost scientific realism, so much so that, as Eric Linklater has said, Ransome 'makes a tale of adventure a handbook to adventure'.[2] It is this level of realism that has attracted the most critical attention; indeed, critics seem drawn to what Hugh Shelley has categorized as the 'incidental delights' of the book,[3] namely the supplementary instruction offered by Ransome in things maritime, while the more fantastic elements of his writing have been largely ignored. While Phillips and Wojcik-Andrews do pay attention to the children's imagination in their post-colonial study of *Swallows and Amazons,*[4] their otherwise compelling analysis fails to look at the intersection of the imaginary with the real. Rather, in Ransome, it is the *combination* of textual fantasy and textual reality that demands attention. Ransome elevates children's imaginary games to a level that parallels that of their real adventures; and as children's games come to make up an integral part of textual structure, they also become an integral part of textual politics. By examining the interaction of fictional reality and fictional imagination in a Ransome text, we can see the extent to which Ransome stretched the boundaries of the children's fiction that he inherited from his Edwardian predecessors.

The influence of these earlier texts is most visible in the first book of the series, *Swallows and Amazons* itself. Within the twelve books of the saga, *Swallows and Amazons* serves as a microcosm of Ransome's project, just as Roger's tack across the field summarizes his narrative style, establishing a founding myth that provides a referential framework within which all future adventures take place. The book takes the form of a traditional island adventure story, drawing on an inheritance of eighteenth- and nineteenth-century island fiction, from *Robinson Crusoe* through *Treasure Island,* which Juliet Dusinberre has persuasively read as a 'parent text' of *Swallows and Amazons.*[5] By the early twentieth century, the island had established its privileged position within novels written for and read by children. Criticism of island fiction follows that of children's fiction as a whole, which often casts the children's novel as a special form of *Bildungsroman* in which growth to maturity provides, in disguised or overt form, an organizing structural principle. In island fiction, an exotic location often becomes an educative impetus, with discovery of place leading to discovery of self.[6] This tradition was significantly embellished when in 1904 J.M. Barrie's play *Peter Pan* began its famously long run, and in 1911, just nineteen years before *Swallows and Amazons* was published in novel form with the title *Peter and Wendy.* The strange history of this play-turned-novel has been well documented by critics, as well as its problematic status as a very adult book positioned in a canon of books written for children.[7] Nevertheless the play, and later the novel, took a hold on the popular consciousness in a way seldom seen since. Through the uneasy Edwardian compromises that make up *Peter and Wendy's* Neverland, the island adventure took a significant leap into the realm of the social world, ensuring that sophisticated children's adventure stories would be forever haunted by the need for real-world resolutions. Despite Peter Pan's iconic status as a fantasy hero, *Peter and Wendy* is a book that clings more to its ties in the real world than most. In this book, the *Bildungsroman* pattern that had attached itself to island adventure reached an apex of sorts, but one which tended to sacrifice island adventure for the sake of island *bildung*. With *Peter and Wendy*, the island ceased to be an identifiable physical location, symbolizing instead what Phillips and Wojcik-Andrews call the 'metaphorical topography' of play,[8] a mere narrative agent within a bildungsroman of place.

The ultimate metaphorical topography is of course the Neverland, whose very name seeks to deny its own actuality. Within *Peter and Wendy*, the Neverland functions as a training ground for the young, characterized less by the dangers and pleasures of the desert island than by a haunting resemblance to real life, in which adventures remain consistently imitative of domestic realities. The Neverland is overrun less by pirates and Indians than by domesticity gone wild, featuring houses both above and below the ground, a washing line, a mending-basket, and a strict bedtime of 6.30. Play literally becomes social practice in *Peter and Wendy*; Peter refers to himself as 'father', Wendy spends most of her time darning, and even the Lost Boys' battles with pirates or Indians take on the form of a ritualized, playful combat in which 'the biggest adventure of all was that they were several hours late for bed.'[9] The Darling children, and particularly Wendy, use the Neverland in order to try out the adult roles that they will inevitably be called upon to fill, while Peter's own inability to learn its lesson and grow up keeps him caught in a reductive holding pattern of childishness that Barrie effectively dismisses as innocent but 'heartless'.[10] It is possible, therefore, to see Barrie's Neverland as nothing more than a static backdrop for the politics of play, two-dimensional scenery literally transplanted from the theatre in order to serve as a thin screen for the inculcation of Edwardian family values. Within the cocoon of Barrie's novel, the fantastic possibilities of island life are all carefully softened, so that the children's first sight of this abode of savages and crocodiles is 'not as something long dreamt of and seen at last, but as a familiar friend to whom they were returning home for the holidays'.[11]

For Ransome, hailed by Hugh Shelley as 'the Holidays' champion and chronicler',[12] this presentation of island life as an exotic form of playing house would have been impossible to overlook. *Swallows and Amazons* clearly shows the influence of the *Peter Pan* tradition – particular in its treatment of Susan's domestic trials – but from the beginning the text rejects *Peter and Wendy's* limited conception of play. Like Barrie's book, Ransome's opens with departure for the island, as the four Walker children, crew of the sailboat *Swallow*, set off for a week's camping. Unlike Wendy, John and Michael, whose adventures are dependent upon the agency of the extra-familial Peter, Roger and his siblings are endowed with power to create and sustain narrative, albeit at the author's discretion. The early part of the text sees the children's imaginary plots frequently controlling the distribution of language, as Ransome's skilful use of free indirect discourse signals a shift from the 'real' narrative to the children's imaginary one. Their mother becomes Queen Elizabeth, a female native, or Man Friday in turn, and they themselves are transformed from the Walkers to the Swallows, made up not of two brothers and two sisters but of a captain, mate, and crew. The text's adoption of the children's own formalized rhetoric acts as a linguistic cue to signal a shift in perspective that grants them temporary narrative control, resulting in the neat illusion that the children have stepped forward to direct the story themselves. And while the agency granted to the children *is* fundamentally illusory – Ransome's children are very much creations of an adult authorial voice – this king of narration still takes significant steps away from the didactic tone of *Peter and Wendy* by making room for seemingly independent fantasies within the scope of the larger adventure.

After they arrive on the island, the children's adventures continue within this doubled perspective, which gradually takes on distinctive structural attributes. A sequential, linear storyline unfolded by the adult narrator charts the children's growing abilities to deal with their real environment. Roger's struggle to learn to swim is a process that typifies the narrative's pattern of discovery, practice and mastery. Such demonstrations of competence in the 'real world' or outdoor activity are a key part of the *Swallows and Amazons* ethos and serve both to bolster the children's self-confidence and to reassure the adult reader, like the Walker's own father, that his children are not drownable duffers. This narrative of progress, however, is periodically undercut by a series of as yet unconnected fantasy episodes of the children's own devising. While Roger hones his newfound swimming skills, for example, his sister Titty narrates an alternative adventure in which she imagines herself to be diving for pearls. Unlike the linear progress of learning to swim, Titty's pearl-diving is characterized by a persistent circularity:

> Able-seamen Titty swam about on the bottom with her eyes open, looking for the whitest stones [. . .] as soon as the stones were dry – and they dried quickly in the sun – they stopped shining, and could not be counted as pearls any more.

81

Since the pearls cease to be pearls after drying and must therefore be dived for again, pearl-diving represents an imaginary activity unbounded by narrative sequentiality and, as such, is infinitely repeatable. Fantasy tends to occur in this episodic form, which when combined with the linear narrative of the real, results in a dynamic and shifting notion of time that characterizes this early part of the text. Such a pattern has been frequently noted as an aspect of the adult bildungsroman. Indeed, the bildungsroman as a genre has been virtually defined in criticism by the clash between its linear and circular elements, typically a teleological, linear form and a spatially focused, or circular content.[13] Within *Swallows and Amazons*, the division occurs not over form and content, but over two aspects of form that seem to vie for control, creating a tension that is complicated by the book's own self-consciousness as a work of children's fiction intimately concerned with questions of agency. This differentiation serves both to underscore the children's agency (since they appear to control both the language and the pacing of the narrative) but also, paradoxically, to separate further their fantasies from the reality that goes on around them.

The limitations imposed by these temporally indicated boundaries are made particularly clear when the children are asked to deliver a grown-up message to the hostile houseboat owner that they have privately re-christened 'Captain Flint'. The honour code of the 'real world' compels a reluctant John to deliver the message:

> You see, 'he went on, 'it's all business. It's got nothing to do with us, even if he is a beast, and thinks we've been touching his houseboat [. . .] but all the same, about this native business, it wouldn't do not to tell him'.
>
> 180

The children use the visit for a dual purpose: to deliver the real message and to declare an imaginary war. Captain Flint's response to John's visit, however, makes such a declaration impossible. The moment is transformed from one of imaginary power to one of real shame:

> 'Did you declare war on him?' asked Titty.
> 'No,' said John. He pulled *Swallow* up on the beach.
> 'He called me a liar,' he said, and went off by himself to the look-out place.
>
> 187

The word 'liar' functions as an important double signifier, suggesting first of all a significant failure in the 'real' realm of social relations – a 'real' injustice – and, on the imaginary level, a symbolic negation of the children's creative powers.

'Captain Flint' becomes merely an angry adult, and 'Captain John' a dishonest little boy. The episode thus suggests a lack of affinity between the imaginary and real worlds, and more importantly, the punishment attached to mixing the two. Here the forces of the imagination, seen within the context of the real, appear not only powerless but also self-defeating and dangerous.

Despite their narrative, therefore, early episodes in *Swallows and Amazons* do suggest some affinity with the *Peter and Wendy* version of the island, as the children learn how to be good sailors and swimmers while their more fantastic adventures, although allowing for a limited narrative agency, remain firmly within the realm of the unreal. The didacticism of *Peter and Wendy* can even be glimpsed in Captain John's shameful defeat, which could be construed as a particularly cynical version of *bildung* intent on teaching children not to trust an empowering fantasy. As the book continues, however, Ransome begins to empower his characters through plot rather than language, a move that ultimately results in a firmer rejection of the Neverland pattern. While the island in *Peter and Wendy* becomes increasingly domesticated – by the end even the pirates want Wendy to be their mother – in the second half of *Swallows and Amazons* it is the imaginary, rather than the real, that is foregrounded. The temporal demarcations within the text also begin to break down, as the imaginary world of the children comes into sustained contact with the real world that surrounds them. Only through this proximity can the text legitimately begin to question, rather than underscore, the conventions of adult behaviour.

Appropriately enough, it is through a change in language that Ransome first signals a shift away from a broadly *Peter and Wendy*-style island adventure. When the Walker children meet Nancy and Peggy, the local girls who call themselves the Amazon pirates, the linguistic markets that serve to separate 'imaginary' from 'real' language in previous chapters become by necessity less formalized. Suddenly the literary language that signalled the onset of an imaginative episode is forced into the realm of the spontaneous as the children must negotiate a conversation that simultaneously covers both real and imagined relations. The alliance between the Swallows and the Amazons, sealed by a 'treaty of offence and defence', brings the real and the imaginary into a new proximity, allowing Nancy and Peggy to function as both real friends and imaginary enemies. The Island, as the site of the meeting, acts through a metonymic shorthand as a symbol of these newfound relations, its importance acknowledged by the words of the treaty, which for the first time reveals the island's name: 'signed and sealed at this place of Wild Cat Island' (123) Wild Cat Island, as the location that underpins both the real and the imaginary, as campground and war-zone, is symbolically christened by the official merging of its two roles.

The tentative synthesis suggested by the treaty of offence and defence is played out through the book's climax, which describes the night-time war between the Swallows and the Amazons. This section sees the flagrant breaking of rules, both parental and textual. From the beginning, the real and the imaginary are connected, as the children, through their imaginary war for control of the island, run the very real risk of drowning. More significantly, because of their game, they are able to overhear local burglars who have stolen Captain Flint's trunk. In a deliberate shift from the conventions of earlier chapters, fantasy and reality here exist in a causal relationship, centering on the contested space of the island, under cover of whose darkness the temporal boundaries that mark the divisions between the real and the imaginary become increasingly intertwined. The causal acts as a deliberate connector of the previously separate forms of linear and circular time. Through the carefully delineated chain of events – the imaginary war that requires night sailing, the overhearing of the burglars on the darkened lake, the retrieval of the stolen property – what were previously isolated fantasy episodes are drawn into a liner progression, and, moreover, act as the primary forces behind that progression.

Wild Cat Island, therefore, acts as both symbolic and literal centre of the night's events, its position represented by the lights that indicate its harbour in the dark. Unlike the nightlights of *Peter and Wendy*, these leading lights provide no illumination of the border between fantasy and reality. Rather, they serve to connect the two worlds. As 'fantasy' props they guide the Amazon pirates into the Swallows' camp in order to capture their ship; as 'real' lights they serve to guide the criminals to a nearby island on which to bury their stolen goods: When the children put up the leading lights in preparation for their games, they are putting in motion a chain of events that will allow them, for the first time, to make a difference not only in the imaginary register but in the only hitherto unexplored part of the their map: the unmarked settlements of real life.

The Swallows and the Amazons thus escape the grim choice of joyless maturity or powerless permanent childhood that faces the children at the end of *Peter and Wendy*. Wild Cat Island, rather than serving as the site of social practice, has, through playing its part in the children's two worlds, served to bring them together, becoming 'the island come true' in a way that the Neverland cannot. The island come true has consequences in the children's fantasies, their reality, and the meta-narrative of the text itself, as is evidenced by the long denouement that occupies the last third of the book. Within the world of the text, the children are able to effect real change, most notably through the conversion of the angry houseboat man into grateful Captain Flint, who, when his stolen property is restored, enters into an imaginative relationship with the children, making peace and declaring war in a way reminiscent of the treaty of offence and defence. More significantly, through acknowledging the children's heroism, Captain Flint accords Captain John and the rest of the Swallows a new respect that retro-actively invalidates their previous relations as angry adult and lying children. The island has not taught the children to conform to their environment but to change it. The remaining moments of fantasy within the text are similarly imbued with a latent potential for action, one that remains throughout the entire saga. At the end of the book the children make what appear to be unrealistic plans for 'next year' – climbing mountains, prospecting for gold, sailing in the North Sea – all of which eventually feature in further instalments of the series. The sequence as a whole thus acts to validate the place of the imagination, so much so that the imaginative power of the children eventually transcends the narrative confines of the single text.

The children's past fantasies thus empower their future realities, and as they fill in the map of the island with names derived from their adventures, they are also transforming the island adventure story that Ransome inherited from Barrie. The island is no longer a static background for *bildung* but a space embodying the potential for creative action. On Ransome's island, *bildung* itself reaches a level of complexity seldom seen in children's fiction. One could perhaps argue that, despite the differences between *Peter and Wendy* and *Swallows and Amazons,* they are both essentially *Bildungsromane* and hence both promote, on a structural level, a curtailing of the childish spirit to fit mould of maturity. But this would be a serious misreading of both the letter and the spirit of the *Swallows* books. However much the children manage to grow up on the island (and Roger does learn to swim) it is ultimately Captain Flint, the adult, who goes through the moral change that is an essential aspect of *bildung*. In a very basic way, *Swallows* and *Amazons* turns the bildungsroman on its head to suggest that true moral insight is based on retention, rather than rejection, of the childish imagination. While both sets of children learn from their islands in *Peter and Wendy* and *Swallows and Amazons,* only in *Swallows* do adults also feel the effect of 'the island come true'.

Within children's fiction, such an island presupposes a different kind of child inhabitant. Unsurprisingly, Ransome's children represent a version of the modern child that is both more imaginative and more capable than J.M. Barrie's Edwardian nursery-dwellers. Like *Peter and Wendy, Swallows and Amazons* ends with a return to the mainland, but it is not a return, like Wendy's that presupposes the exchange of childish imagination for adult responsibility. Instead, *Swallows and Amazons* deconstructs this dichotomy to suggest a connection between the children imagination and an ability to effect the world hitherto reserved for grown-ups. Jacqueline Rose has suggested that *Peter Pan* represents what she calls the 'impossibity' of children's fiction[14] – that any imagined child, whether reader or character, is impossibly constrained within an adult point of view – but Ransome's book turns this point of view on its head by advocating a child character, and by implication a child reader, whose child status acts to erase the very category that defines it. Unlike Peter Pan, whose anarchic childishness acts as an impediment to the linear development of maturity, Ransome's children, by enacting childhood, paradoxically put an end to its imprisonment.

Perhaps the best proof of this change comes in the vexed question of readership. Ransome famously claimed that he wrote not to please an idealized 'child reader', but to please himself,[15] and this respect for the reader is evident in the sort of child character that his books feature. Moreover, in his actual child readers Ransome did more than instruct and amuse. *Swallows and Amazons* is one of the few children's books to inspire what might be called a 'fan fiction' – the novel *The Far-Distant Oxus*, written by two adolescents who, after reading Ransome, decided that they wanted to write their own adventure story. The existence of *The Far-Distant Oxus* shows a connection between Ransome's textually empowered children and an empowered child reader; despite the book's derivative origins, it stands as a text in its own right, but this time written by the children that it describes. Ransome's manipulation of island adventure did bear fruit in reality, albeit in an unexpected way, and the opening pages of *The Far-Distant Oxus* pay homage to the empowered fantasy of *Swallows and Amazons*: 'Now she was actually here, now her imaginings were happening at this very moment'.[16] Without Ransome's *Swallows*, the book's own reality as imagining literally come true, would be unthinkable. Surely Ransome's readers owe some-thing to Ransome's characters, whose island fantasies refused to be mere rehearsals for the real.

Notes

1. Arthur Ransome, *Swallows and Amazons* (London: Random House 2001). All other references are to this edition.
2. Quoted in Marcus Crouch, *Treasure seekers and borrowers: children's books in Britain, 1900–1960* (London: Library Association 1962), p. 23.
3. Hugh Shelley, *Arthur Ransome* (London: Bodley Head 1960), p. 58.
4. Jerry Phillips and Ian Wojcik-Andrews, 'History and the politics of play in T.S. Eliot's "The burial of the dead" and Arthur Ransome's *Swallows and Amazons*' in *The Lion and the Unicorn* 14 (1990), pp 53–69.
5. Juliet Dusinberre, *Alice to the lighthouse: children's books and radical experiments in art* (London: Macmillan 1987), p. 90.

6. For an analysis of this pattern in detail, see Diane Gustra, 'The island pattern', in *Children's Literature Association Quarterly* 10 (1985).

7. See Jacqueline Rose, *The case of Peter Pan: or, The impossibility of children's fiction* (London: Macmillan, 1984) and Andrew Birkin, *J.M. Barrie and the lost boys* (London: Constable, 1979).

8. Phillips, 'History', p.55.

9. J.M. Barrie, *Peter Pan* (originally entitled *Peter and Wendy*, London: Penguin 1994), p. 130.

10. Barrie, *Peter Pan*, p. 185.

11. Barrie, *Peter Pan*, p. 43.

12. Shelley, *Ransome*. p. 10.

13. For theories of the *Bildungsroman* that treat this topic, see M.M. Bakhtin, 'The bildungsroman and its significance in the history of literary realism' in *Speech genres and other late essays*, tr. Vern MCGee (Austin: U. Texas P. 1986), and Martin Swales, *The German bildungsroman from Wieland to Hesse* (Princeton: P.U.P. 1978).

14. Rose, *The case of Peter Pan.*

15. You write not *for* children but for yourself, and if, by good fortune, children enjoy what you enjoy, why then you are a writer of children's books.' Quoted in Aidan Chambers, *Booktalk: occasional writing on literature and children* (London: Bodley Head 1985), p. 41.

16. Katharine Hull and Pamela Whitlock, *The Far-Distant Oxus* (London: Cape 1937), p. 10.

7

Philippa Pearce, *Tom's Midnight Garden* (1958)

Introduction
Heather Montgomery

Origins and composition

Tom's Midnight Garden was published in 1958 and is regarded as one of the classics of British post-war children's fiction, famous, in particular, for its time-slip narrative. It was Philippa Pearce's second novel, following on from *Minnow on the Say* (1955). It is infused with a sense of place and her childhood memories of growing up in Mill House on the banks of the Cam near Great Shelford. She claimed that she was inspired to write *Tom's Midnight Garden* when, in her early thirties, 'My father had to retire and they sold the Mill House. Suddenly my childhood was chopped off from me. As they were in the process of selling, I began thinking of writing a story based on the house and the garden and this feeling of things slipping away' (Penguin Books, 2008).

Reception

The novel was initially well received, winning a Carnegie Medal in 1958, and its reputation has remained high over the years. Since its publication, *Tom's Midnight Garden* has 'received probably more critical praise than any other post-war book' (Hunt, 1994: 137) and has been called 'one of the finest pieces of writing for children produced since World War II, a classic in the front rank of children's literature' (Carpenter and Walsh 1989: 766).

John Rowe Townsend has written: '"Masterpiece" is not a word to be used lightly, but in my view *Tom's Midnight Garden* is one of the tiny handful of masterpieces of English children's literature' (Townsend, 1990: 240). The book has been filmed and adapted several times for stage and television and remains a much-loved book by both children and adults. Despite its popularity with both critics and the public, however, *Tom's Midnight Garden* has not been without its detractors and it has been criticised as nostalgic and conservative, extolling the virtues of the past over those of the present and over-romanticising the rites, rituals and hierarchies of Victorian England which it positions as a lost golden age (Krips, 2000; Cosslett, 2002).

Critical terrain

Scholarly interest in *Tom's Midnight Garden* has centred on the themes of loss and the sense of 'things slipping away', and critics have analysed the ways in which the ravages of time are central to the book and give it its elegiac tone. The book is imbued with a feeling of loss and longing for the past; it confronts the inevitable losses of growing up and growing old and recognises that childhood is a transient phase of life that can never be revisited. Death also haunts the novel; the reader eventually learns that not only is young Hatty an orphan at the start of the book, but that by the end she is a widow who lost two sons in the First World War. Despite the melancholy tone of much of the novel, however, it is not tragic, and ends in harmony and resolution. As David Rees comments:

> Many people reading the book for the first time, who have not noticed that Mrs Bartholomew and Hatty are one and the same person, speak of the almost unbearable tension as the book proceeds into what looks like an inescapable tragedy, their sense of relief when this is averted, and their delight that the ending is so credible.
>
> Rees, 1980: 43

Humphrey Carpenter draws an interesting parallel between *Tom's Midnight Garden* and *Peter Pan*, arguing that 'the story's conclusion describes Tom's acceptance of what Peter Pan can never accept: that Time must be allowed to pass, and growth and even old age must be accepted as necessary and even desirable facets of human existence' (Carpenter, 1985: 220).

In order to emphasise the importance of time, and the sense of it slipping away, Pearce uses a time-shift narrative. This device is a recognisable and repeated device in children's literature, found in novels such as Alison Uttley's *A Traveller In Time* (1939) or Susan Cooper's *King of Shadows*

(1999). In her article on the subject, Tess Cosslett describes the pattern of such novels:

> [A] deracinated child comes to stay in a new locality; a special place, often in conjunction with a special object, provides access to the past; an empathetic bond is formed with a child in the past; a connection is made between the past experience and the memory of someone still living; names, inscriptions and their decoding are important; the history that is accessed is the everyday life of an ordinary child; the subjectivity of the present-day child is an important element in the story; this child does some form of archival research to establish the truth of his or her experience of the past; the experience of the past becomes part of a theme of moving on, growing, accepting change, death and loss.
>
> Cosslett, 2002: 44

Tom's Midnight Garden was published four years after Lucy Boston's *The Children of Green Knowe* and in the same year as that book's sequel, *The Chimneys of Green Knowe*, both books which feature a time-shift device and deal with similar relationships between children now and in the past, and between childhood and place. In Boston's work, a child called Tolly goes to stay in an ancient family manor house called Green Knowe. His great-grandmother tells him stories of Toby, Linnet and Alexander, children who lived in the house in the seventeenth century. He gradually becomes aware of their presence and, although they live in a different century to him, they too inhabit the house alongside him and he is able to make friends with them. He is thrilled to have playmates and to realise that these children, along with the house itself, are part of his family.

While Boston is particularly concerned with the relationship between the house and the child, Pearce is more concerned with the garden, placing her work within a pastoral tradition of writing which positions the garden as physically and morally redemptive. In this respect, *Tom's Midnight Garden* can also be usefully be compared with Frances Hodgson Burnett's *The Secret Garden* (1909). This book tells the story of Mary, a spoilt and sickly orphan who is sent to live with her uncle in Yorkshire. Here she stumbles across the secret garden of her dead aunt and, with her maidservant's brother, Dickon, she restores the garden and finds redemption in doing so. Meanwhile Mary discovers that there is another child living in the house, her bedridden and hysterical cousin Colin. Through challenging his disability and by bringing him into the garden he is restored to health. There are strong parallels between *The Secret Garden* and *Tom's Midnight Garden* and, while the former does not contain a time-shift narrative, the two books are linked through the restorative magic of the respective gardens. One, of course, is a lost garden that is restored for real; the other only through the strong workings of memory, but in both novels the authors emphasise the importance of the garden in restoring and regenerating not only health and family, but also national identity. Furthermore, the metaphorical association between the Edenic garden and childhood innocence, the hope and optimism of childhood and the possibilities of regeneration, are obvious themes in both books.

The essays

The first essay, by Margaret and Michael Rustin, is strongly informed by psychological theory and suggests that the novel is an exercise in psychological realism, dealing with the difficulties of sexual awakenings and emotional development, as well as presenting child-readers with a way of coping with loneliness and loss. The second, by Maria Nikolajeva, explores, as do many critical articles on *Tom's Midnight Garden*, Pearce's concept of time. Nikolajeva differentiates between two types of time: eternal, mythic time (the 'Once upon a time' of fairy tales), which she calls *kairos*, and measurable, linear time, which she calls *chronos*. The interplay between these two types of time is central to her interpretations of the novel, and her understandings of the relationship between the two children, and to the book's conclusion. Roni Natov's theme is how children's experiences are represented, what these representations can tell us about how modern childhood is constructed, and how the inevitable loss and sadness of growing up and leaving childhood behind can be resolved through fiction.

References

Carpenter, H. 1985. *Secret Gardens: A Study of the Golden Age of Children's Literature.* London, Allen & Unwin.

Carpenter, H. and Walsh, G. 1989. 'Philippa Pearce', in T. Chevalier (ed.) *Twentieth-Century Children's Writers*, 3rd edn. Chicago, St. James Press.

Cosslett, T. 2002. '"History from Below": Time-Slip Narratives and National Identity', *The Lion and the Unicorn*, 26: 243–53.

Hunt, P. 1994. *An Introduction to Children's Literature.* Oxford, Oxford University Press.

Krips, V. 2000. *The Presence of the Past: Memory, Heritage and Childhood in Postwar Britain.* New York, Garland.

Penguin Books. 2008. *Philippa Pearce* http://www.penguin.co.uk/nf/Author/AuthorPage/0,,1000024801,00.html, accessed 27 November 2008.

Rees, D. 1980. *The Marble in the Water: Essays on Contemporary Writers of Fiction for Children and Young Adults.* Boston, Horn Books.

Townsend, J.R. 1990. *Written for Children: An Outline of English-language Children's Literature*, 6th edn. London, Bodley Head.

Further reading

Aers, L. 1970. 'The Treatment of Time in Four Children's Books', *Children's Literature in Education*, 2: 69–81.

Hall, L. 2003. '"House and Garden": The Time-Slip Story in the Aftermath of the Second World War', in A. Lawson Lucas (ed.) *The Presence of the Past in Children's Literature*. Westport, CT and London, Praeger.

Jackson, B. 1994. 'Philippa Pearce', in M. Meek, A. Warlow and G. Barton (eds.) *The Cool Web: The Pattern of Children's Reading*. London, Bodley Head.

Philip, N. 1982. '*Tom's Midnight Garden* and the Vision of Eden', *Signal*, 37: 21–5.

Loneliness, Dreaming and Discovery: *Tom's Midnight Garden*
Margaret Rustin and Michael Rustin

Philippa Pearce's *Tom's Midnight Garden* is one of the finest stories for children to be published in Britain since the war. The story describes the way in which a child of modern times comes to enter imaginatively into the lives of a period two generations ago. The story explores in quite complex ways the balance of gain and loss involved in this process of change. The story achieves its effect in part through its intense power of metaphor. The story involves its readers in understanding that loving communication between children and adults often takes place through the medium of language and story-telling itself.

In this story, the imaginations of the two children, Hatty and Tom, are deepened and extended by their experiences of separations. Hatty suffers a dramatic and deep loss, through the death of her parents; Tom's is a more minor separation through illness and holiday. But Tom also feels rejected (even though he knows, when he compares himself with Hatty, that he has not really been abandoned), and bitterly misses his brother (who seems almost like a twin) with whom he had so wanted to play during the holiday. It's through experience of Hatty's loss, and exploration with her in play of what for both of them is a somewhat unfriendly and persecuting place, that Tom is able to make something of his separation and of the opportunities for new experiences which it brings about.

Extracted from 'Loneliness, Dreaming and Discovery: *Tom's Midnight Garden*', in *Narratives of Love and Loss: Studies in Modern Children's Fiction* (London and New York: Verso, 1987), pp. 27–39.

The question of what is alive in feeling, and what is dead, is a recurrent theme in the story. We learn through the story of the many catastrophes in Mrs Bartholomew's life – the death of her parents, then of her two sons in the Great War (this explains to us her interest not only in Tom, but also in his brother Peter), and finally, some years before, of her husband Barty – Mr Bartholomew. She is perceived by her neighbours as a 'shrunken old woman' – a dead sort of person. We see Tom as merely resentful and lifeless when he is with his uncle and aunt – though nothing really terrible has happened to him. He experiences their house as lacking in anything alive for a boy (except for his aunt's good food) when he arrives there. The midnight garden is first seen by moonlight, with its life-in-death associations, and the idea of a gravelike place is also conveyed by its yew trees. Trees are important to all the children – Hatty, Tom, and his brother Peter. While Peter is listlessly carrying on with the tree-house at home which he was to have spent the holiday with Tom in building, Hatty hurts herself falling out of a tree-house she has built with Tom. But this leads to development for her, as her cousin James shows concern for her injury and decides to help her, in face of his mother's indifference. Illness or the threat of illness are (as sometimes in life) catalysts of growth for the children, evoking especially intense devotion in others, and bringing recognition of bonds that otherwise are taken for granted. Tom is desperately anxious that he hasn't hurt Hatty through his dangerous tree-games. Hatty is in turn protective and sisterly towards Tom, as she grows older and no longer so involved in their play together. At a moment of crisis in the story, on the eve of Hatty's wedding when she is having to say goodbye to her childhood and its imaginings, the tree in the centre of the garden is struck by lightning, and she is heard by Tom to cry out. But this, like other moments of loss in the story, also makes possible its new beginnings. For 'then I knew, Tom, that the garden was changing all the time, because nothing stands still, except in our memory'.

One of the most beautiful images in the story is of the great frost in the Fens, around the turn of the century, and of Hatty as a young woman, with her childhood companion Tom, skating all the way to Ely. This is her last great experience of the freedom of childhood, an extension of the earlier wanderings of the two children into the meadows beyond the garden. (These have led her into trouble, as the geese follow the children back on to the lawn.) But because it is frozen, it is somehow safe, even for a young woman on her own, and the adventurousness and independence which she has learned through her solitude are a strength for her. When she returns from Ely, the ice is thawing and she is told it may be dangerous – the figures she now sees on the river banks appear more frightening as it grows dark.

It is then that she meets Barty, and the unfrozen world of sexual love begins, as Tom and her childhood fade from her mind. So the great freeze becomes a metaphor for latency, suggesting an infinite expansiveness and pre-pubertal space – also the space of childhood memory – while for the time being other aspects of the self are hidden and safe. As the ice melts, Tom is displaced in Hatty's mind by Barty, whom she is later to marry.

The theory of art developed by psychoanalysts in the object-relations tradition is helpful in understanding the beauty of this story. Symbol formation, in the work of both the Kleinians[1] and Winnicott,[2] is linked with the capacity to retain an internal memory of loved objects in their absence. Imagination and play provide a space in which primary preoccupations with images of parents and feelings towards them are held in mind and explored. Tom is able to explore the experience of loneliness through identification with Hatty's loss of her parents, and his hostility to his uncle and aunt through Hatty's experiences of her adoptive family. Hatty's much greater deprivation enables Tom to come to terms with his lesser experience of loneliness and separation. The heightened feelings Tom has about the midnight garden, and about his aunt and uncle's home when he has to leave it, recall the strong attachments which children can develop for a holiday home, which are so intense in part because of the initial anxiety and strain of coining to a strange place. Even Uncle Alan's didactic lectures on time and its scientific properties are a provocation to him, to think about it for himself, from his own experience. His recognition of Mrs Bartholomew at the end, as the Hatty he knew as a child, seems to be a coming to life of a dead person, the old lady, as someone with feelings, and with love for him. In his separation from his home, Tom has had difficulties keeping alive a real awareness of his mother and father, and in accepting his uncle and aunt as substitutes for them. At the end of the story, his aunt witnesses and thus in part shares in Tom's unfrozen capacity for affection, the rediscovery of his capacity for love, in this transformed and unusual way.

For Hatty too, play is a way of coping with loss. We may think of her ghostlike playmate, Tom, as an echo of her own preoccupation with her dead parents. Abel's fear of Tom, and the danger he seems to be to Hatty (his knife, his climbing on the garden wall and the tree) suggest Hatty's preoccupations with death, as well as Tom's potential destructiveness. For old Mrs Bartholomew, the reliving of her childhood experience of bereavement and recovery enables her to renew her capacity for love and feeling in the present. Tom's arrival in her house seems to bring her back in contact with her childhood. Tom reminds her also of her own sons, for 'whom she had done all her crying . . . so long ago'. Mrs Bartholomew is sustained by her memories of relationships with loved ones as child, as wife, and as mother.

While the identifications established in infancy may be primary for psycho-analysis, this picture of an old lady shows that 'object relations' are re-made throughout the life cycle.[3]

Tom's Midnight Garden in fact depicts several characters' experiences in keeping alive good feelings in a state of loneliness and loss, and the relation-ships between them through which these are brought alive. Being left is shown to stir up quite negative and resentful feelings, as well as a sense of emptiness and deadness, most clearly in Tom, but also in Mrs Bartholomew. We should probably see Tom's uncle's and aunt's limitations as in part the product of his own grudging attitude to his holiday with them – they are made by him to be worse than they are. Tom's over-eating substitutes physical for emotional hunger. His emotional needs break out at night, though his dreaming is pro-saically ascribed to his rich meals. Tom's games with Hatty are perceived by Abel to be dangerous, and this seems to be more than the difference between his boy's and her girl's pastimes. The bow and arrow which Tom teaches Hatty to shape with a knife breaks a pane of glass, and his tree-house causes her to hurt herself – Tom's destructiveness is real, and he has to face its poten-tial consequences. He is on the edge of puberty, and his relationship with a girl is a new and positive development for him. She arouses feelings of com-passion, for example when he learns of her bereavement, and when she is hurt in her fall. Through Hatty he gets back into contact with his softer and more dependent feelings. For Hatty, there is an opposite development – her adven-tures with Tom support her in the independence that she will need, and help her to break out of the restrictive and submissive role in which her aunt, and the conventions of the time, have cast her. The unruly geese – introduced into the garden by the 'pauper child', and contaminating the rigid household order in the way that *she* does in her aunt's view – represent the more robust and ordinary life of a family, managing as Abel and Susan later do to raise their children when Hatty's more privileged cousins get into difficulties. The geese are like an irruption of a more ordinary and democratic social order into the world of inherited property and status. (They also evoke the story of the ugly duckling, in Hatty's complicity with them.) There is a suggestion that Tom is troubled by his aunt and uncle being together as a couple, in his irritation at their preparations for bed, as they are listening out for him (as he is listening out for them), and in his wandering around the house at night. His presence in the house does in fact seem to divide them, quite frequently, and his per-ception of their relationship is denigrating: 'Uncle Alan . . . would be read-ing aloud from his favourite, clever weekly newspaper; Aunt Gwen would be devotedly listening, or asleep'. One might suggest that the author has intuited in Tom a deeply buried envy and jealousy in relation to his brother Peter, who is still at home with their parents.

While less is said about Mrs Bartholomew's state of mind, she too seems to be lost in hostility to the world. She is felt by the tenants of her house to be spoiling and sour; this is the only evidence of her daytime state of mind that we have. Her feelings for life are in dreams; the contrast between her memories and her actual existence is conveyed in the description of her at night: she was 'lying tranquilly in bed: her false teeth, in a glass of water by the bedside, grinned unpleasantly in the moonlight, but her indrawn mouth was curved in a smile of sweet, easy-dreaming sleep. She was dreaming of the scenes of her childhood.' She, like Tom, emerges from this deadness to the discovery of love buried or frozen within her. Being able to call out to someone with intense feeling – Tom crying out Hatty's name, and Mrs Bartholomew asking to see Tom – is what both can do at the end of the story, but not at the beginning. Tom and his brother bring alive her two lost sons, and she the internal mother he has lost and found.

The similarities in the situations of Tom and Hatty – each feeling lonely and abandoned in their different ways – allows the writer to contrast the time and place in which they live, and thus to provide an imaginative entry into the past for her readers. Comparison between the lives of the two children leaves little doubt that Tom's life is the easier one, for where he has to put up only with a temporary absence from home through his brother's measles, and a few weeks with an uncle and aunt who are not accustomed to children (we sense from her eagerness to look after Tom that having no children has been his aunt's grief and disappointment), Hatty's parents have died, and her aunt is harsh and unkind to her.

Nevertheless, the story projects into the past a more spacious and humanly connected environment which Tom can explore through his contact with Hatty. A contrast is defined between a unified, hierarchical, safe world, cultivated inside its garden boundary but close to nature and the river outside it, and a blank and uninteresting suburb of the present day. The river has become polluted, between the time of Hatty's childhood, and the present. A sense of greater community in past time is conveyed by the scenes on the ice, in which the banter among strangers seems gentle and friendly. Whereas the old household was, for all its inequality, a set of relationships, the present-day inhabitants of the flats into which the house had been converted seem scarcely to be acquainted with one another, and live in silent animosity towards their owner. The beauty and mystery of the garden, with its flowers, trees, secret places and long history in which tracings and carvings can be left, is contrasted with the mean little dustbin yard which is all that remains. Tom's lifeless journey in his uncle's car contrasts with the expedition on the ice, and the eventful return journey in Barty's gig.

Mrs Bartholomew's childhood is underpinned by the presence of religious beliefs, which are especially important to the God-fearing Abel and lead him to protect and care for Hatty when his employer is harsh to her. The garden has associations to a pre-pubertal (and for Tom pre-oedipal) Garden of Eden, except that to Abel it is Tom that appears as a spirit of evil, tempting Hatty into danger. There is a suggestion of Blake in the description of the Angel painted on the clock face, announcing the day of judgement. Altogether, religious associations pervade the old house, providing an expressive if a somewhat fearsome language for feelings. In contrast to this religious outlook is the dry mechanistic rationalism of Uncle Alan, who seems out of contact with feeling altogether. The grandfather clock, a male counterpart to Mrs Bartholomew, screwed immovably to the wall and still tended carefully by her, metaphorically unlocks these associations as it provokes arguments between Tom and Uncle Alan about scientific, regular time, and the imaginary 'time no longer' which Tom experiences in the midnight garden, and which he defends, with some intuitive sympathy from his aunt, against his uncle's cutting scepticism.

Greater hardship and harsh social attitudes are located in the past – Hatty is despised as a 'pauper child' whom her aunt wants to exclude from the family property; Hatty has no money for the train when she wishes to return from Ely. She has, after all, lost both her parents from bereavement, a rare occurrence in Tom's world. The author balances a feeling for the greater spaciousness and connectedness of the Edwardian social world with knowledge that it was also frequently more cruel and pain-filled for children than the present.

Love of place is a powerful theme in several of Philippa Pearce's books. We are told that the house of this story was based on the millhouse where she grew up, and where her father was born. (While the landscape of the fens is lovingly described in this story, the more complicated associations of Cambridge are filtered by its renaming as Castleford.) One can regard the feeling of this book for nature, for the past, and for the spirit of place, as conservative themes, though they have recently been revived in a 'green' radical politics which perhaps draws a particular strength from people living close to the countryside. It is a characteristic feature of English culture that positive feelings are so much more easily symbolized in a kind of historic, rural pastoral setting, than in representations of the modern world. Even so, it is the contemporary Tom who has the experience, and children like Tom for whom the book is written. The principal commitment of the author is not to the past as a preferred world, but to the need to remain connected to it, in memory and relationships.[4]

A number of evocative metaphors enable the narrative of *Tom's Midnight Garden* to communicate states of mind which could not be described for children in more literal ways. The midnight garden itself is a metaphor of imaginative, dream-like space, related to the space in between internal and external reality which is described by Donald Winnicott.[5] The story insists on the real existence of this world for Tom, through his passionate belief in it, and later in the confirmation that it exists in Mrs Bartholomew's mind too. Also metaphorical is the description of the great freeze and of Tom and Hatty's expedition on the ice. As Hatty, she jokes with the men on the bank about her imaginary companion, with whom she will be safe. The frozen river suggests the spaciousness and safety of pre-pubertal childhood, but also enables the writer to evoke the change about to occur in Hatty as the ice melts, and as Tom is displaced in her mind by Barty.

The visit to Ely Cathedral also has a metaphoric/symbolic meaning. The tower gives Tom and Hatty, now at their different points of development, a vast new perspective on the landscape and the world. They meet by the font to go up the tower, and spend the afternoon, visiting the Lady Chapel. The tower makes up, with the body of the cathedral, the bringing together of male and female at the onset of Hatty's adult life.[6] This story is given a poetic as well as narrative coherence by recurring themes. The trees in the garden, the clock, Mrs Bartholomew, the river in its different states, the nature of time, Ely Cathedral, are referred to throughout the story, which is unified for the reader by these recurring images and topics.

Such metaphors of stages of emotional development play a crucial part in the best fiction for children, especially in the genre of so-called fantasy. The greater tolerance of young readers for departures from realism, and for interpretations of 'realist' and 'non-realist' modes of expression, have allowed writers to incorporate some of the metaphoric virtues of 'modernist' literary methods, while remaining within the framework of conventional narrative. The restriction of descriptive scope made necessary by the limited worldly experience and indeed vocabulary of their readers also imposes on children's writers the imperative that they must communicate with them about serious matters of life metaphorically and poetically, or not at all. Such writers have also been able to count on the existence of a common readership which shares many essential life experiences, where adults rather feel cut off from one another by the fragmentation and the scale of urban society. In the period after the Second World War, they could also share in a culture which for the time being felt hopeful about and strongly committed to the possibilities of childhood. This combination of factors may be what has made possible this flowering of metaphoric fiction for children.

It must be evident to child readers as well as adults that the events of the narrative could not really occur, yet the story in a number of ways refuses to trivialize them as 'mere' dreams, and insists on their deeper truth. There is, for example, a beautiful moment in the story when Tom finds the skates that Hatty has left for him, both moments after she has left them, in the midnight garden time, and in Tom's real present, fifty or sixty years later. There is a note left with the skates: 'To whomever may find this. These skates are the property of Harriet Melbourne, but she leaves them in this place in fulfilment of a promise once made to a little boy'. The skates themselves are one of the few signs of Tom's encounters with Hatty which remain as visible traces in the daytime world.

The other crucial conjunction of the two worlds is Tom's recognition that old Mrs Bartholomew is Hatty, grown old, and their childlike embrace which so startles the onlookers, (though Aunt Gwen, always emotionally attentive to Tom, does notice the strange quality of their contact). Is this just magic for children, the wish-fulfilment of being 'really' able to enter the past, or is something more truthful being said?

We believe that the ambiguities of this story regarding what is and what is not to be taken as real, are expressions of the nature of fiction itself. Tom's adventures in this story can be taken as themselves a metaphor for the experience of reading and story-telling. The passionate commitment, almost at times the addiction, of the children to their play with one another depicts the compelling power of the imagination. This state of mind in Hatty worries Abel, who fears that it will lead her into danger, and both flatters and dumbfounds Gwen and Alan who don't understand why Tom is so desperate to prolong his stay. This reference within the story to the power of fiction is made explicit. Tom has been writing letters about his adventures to his brother Peter, and when he forgets to write one day Peter is filled with such pangs of loneliness that he comes to find Tom and Hatty on the cathedral tower. (Incidentally, it is at this point that we see through Peter's shocked eyes that Hatty is now a young woman, and are prepared for Tom and Hatty's separation.)

The last chapter of the book, where Mrs Bartholomew meets and talks with Tom after the night-time crisis when he cries out and wakes everyone in the house, is called 'A Tale for Tom Long'. This hint enables us, if we wish, to re-interpret the whole story as Mrs Bartholomew's tale for Tom. It is open to us to imagine it as made up from her childhood memories, and from her multiple identifications with Tom (as her childhood self, and as a reminder of her dead sons), but, not necessarily as the whole truth. Tom's absorption with Hatty can be imagined as an equivalent to, or a metaphor for his involvement in a story about Hatty, who lived in the garden of the house long ago. It is certainly only through listening to stories told by people with memories ('What was it like when you were little?', children ask their grandparents) that children can enter the past through their imaginations. Mrs Bartholomew and Tom are strangers to one another, but they are emotionally the grandchild (Mrs Bartholomew's sons were killed in war) and the grandmother that they each at that moment need.

From this point of view, pursuing this level of interpretation of the story as itself a metaphor for a story told to a child, the trace left by the skates also has another quality of meaning. For Mrs Bartholomew, the house reminds her continually of her past life. But for Tom, it is the fen-runner skates, unmistakably from the past, but sent through the years with a note for him (or at least, to a 'little boy' who might be him) which brings this connection with Hatty so vividly alive. Within the story of *Tom's Midnight Garden*, this is the key that makes it come so alive. But we can also imagine this as the imaginative point of departure from which 'A Tale for Tom Long' could be successfully told to a real child like Tom. One explanation of the outstanding qualities of *Tom's Midnight Garden* lies in the way that its author has brought her understanding of the nature and transformative process of fiction within the narrative of her story. It is this which makes this work of fantasy into such a moving description of emotional possibility.

Notes

1. See Hanna Segal, *A Psychoanalytical Approach to Aesthetics* (1952) in *The Work of Hanna Segal*, Free Associations Books and Maresfield Library 1986.
2. Donald Winnicott, *Playing and Reality*, Penguin 1980.
3. For a psychoanalytic consideration of old age, see Lily Pincus, *The Challenge of a Long Life*, Faber 1981, and *Death in the Family: The Importance of Mourning*, Faber 1981; also Hanna Segal, *Fear of Death: Notes on the Analysis of an Old Man*, op. cit.
4. A contrast can be drawn between this concern to maintain an imaginative link with the past, and with a more escapist nostalgia for an idealized past world such as Humphrey Carpenter ascribes to a number of Edwardian children's writers (Grahame, Milne, et al.) in his *Secret Gardens*, Allen and Unwin 1985.
5. See D.W. Winnicott, *Playing and Reality* op. cit., and his 'Transitional Objects and Transitional Phenomena' in *Through Paediatrics to Psycho-Analysis*, Hogarth Press 1978.
6. See Hanna Segal's essay 'Delusion and Artistic Creativity' (in H. Segal, op. cit.) on William Golding's *The Spire* for a discussion of an adult novel exploring a similar theme.

Midnight Gardens, Magic Wells
Maria Nikolajeva

Like the Neverland, the magical *enclosed* garden (a *locus communus* of pastoral) is a paradise, where there is always summer and fine weather, since it is evoked by Hatty's nostalgic memories. Most of the descriptions are iteratives:

> Every night now Tom slipped downstairs to the garden. At first he used to be afraid that it might not be there. –
>
> He saw the garden at many times of day, and at different seasons – its favourite season was summer, with perfect weather.

> 44

There is only one winter scene, which is also the last encounter between Hatty and Tom, thus suggesting departure and the inevitable movement toward growth, aging, and death. The garden symbolizes lost childhood, and like the Neverland, it offers the child a temporal retreat. Thus, as in all utopian fiction, we note a transformation of a spatial concept – garden – into a temporal state – childhood (cf Jones 1985, 213ff). In Mikhail Bakhtin's terms, we see here an illustration of the *idyllic chronotope*, an entity of space and time, secluded space – mythic time (see Bakhtin 1981). Compare the following passage to any earlier description of Paradise:

> ... a great lawn where flower-beds bloomed; a towering fir-tree, and thick, beetle-browed yews that humped their shapes down two sides of the lawn; on the third side, to the right, a greenhouse almost the size of a real house; from each corner of the lawn, a path that twisted away to some other depths of garden, with other trees.

> 19–20

Or Tom's inner vision of his endless happiness in the garden:

> He would run full tilt over the grass, leaping the flower-beds; he would peer through the glittering panes of the greenhouse – perhaps open the door and go in; he would visit each alcove and archway clipped in the yew-trees – he would climb the trees and make his way from one to another through thickly interlacing branches. When they came calling him, he would hide, silent and safe as a bird, among this richness of leaf and bough and tree-trunk.

> 20

Extracted from 'The Haunting of Time', in M. Nikolajeva, *From Mythic to Linear: Time in Children's Literature* (Lanham, MD and London: Scarecrow, 2000), pp. 103–9.

But if the spatial aspect of Paradise is clear and unequivocal, the temporal aspect is all the more complicated, built up by the subtle balance of chronos and kairos. The clock, a magical object, which has naturally been observed by all scholars, has an ambivalent function: in chronos, it takes Tom closer to his departure, in kairos, it is his password to the garden: 'It would tick on to bedtime, and in that way Time was Tom's friend; but, after that, it would tick on to Saturday, and in that way Time was Tom's enemy' (157). The double nature of Time is emphasized. In general, there is more preoccupation with the notion and nature of Time in *Tom's Midnight Garden* than in most so-called time-shift fantasies. In Chapter 21, Uncle Alan tries to explain modern scientific theories of time to Tom (modern, of course, for the 1950s, when the book was written). The much-discussed inscription on the face of the clock: 'Time No Longer' (Rev. 10:1-6) is a Christian notion, definitely perceiving time as linear, as having a beginning and an end. Neil Philip views the river as a symbol of linear time (Philip 1982, 23). However, the presence of both chronos and kairos in the novel is apparent:

> In the Kitsons' flat Time was not allowed to dodge about in the unreliable, confusing way it did in the garden – forward to a tree's falling, and then back to before the fall; and then still farther back again, to a little girl's first arrival; and then forward again. No, in the flat, Time was marching steadily onwards in the way it is supposed to go: from minute to minute, from hour to hour, from day to day.
>
> 98

Kairos is in this case equal to what may be called 'memory-time,' which is naturally nonlinear: everything that happens in the garden is evoked by Hatty's memories of her childhood.

> Yet perhaps Mrs Bartholomew was not solely responsible for the garden's being there . . . never before this summer had she dreamed of the garden so often, and never before this summer has she been able to remember so vividly what it has *felt* like to be the little Hatty – to be longing for someone to play with and for somewhere to play.
>
> 223; author's emphasis

So what are Hatty's memories evoked by? Tom's longing? His reluctance to grow up? A plausible explanation is that Hatty and Tom are cocreators, while the creative source itself is their innocent, prelapsarian, presexual (cf Philip 1985, 23) love.

The question of who is the ghost, which has occupied many a scholar, including myself (Nikolajeva 1988, 101ff), can be viewed in a new light here. Actually, the question is irrelevant if we consider it in terms of mythical time. In the garden, both protagonists step out of their chronos into kairos: Mrs. Bartholomew by returning to her childhood and becoming a little girl again, Tom by going into the past. They are both ghosts – or rather guests – in this paradise. When Tom says that Hatty is a ghost, she at first protests (because she thinks him a ghost), but her second reaction is much more interesting: she begins to weep saying: 'I'm not dead – oh, please, Tom, I'm not dead!' (107). Are we dealing with the aging Mrs. Bartholomew's fear of death, transferred into her memories of childhood?

In his essay on *Tom's Midnight Garden,* Raymond Jones considers the twofold consequences of the child entering Eden, restoration and entrapment. Of the two protagonists, Hatty is the one who is reluctant to grow up, most probably because she has not much to look forward to. She is a poor orphaned relative, and her prospects are limited. Tom overhears a discussion by James and his mother of what is to become of Hatty when she grows up. James suggests that they must encourage Hatty to go out, meet other people and make friends, to which his mother retorts: 'She doesn't want to grow up; she wants only her garden' (141). Since Hatty is never focalized, we cannot be sure of her true feelings, but supposedly her aunt expresses her reluctance. Significantly, it is James, a male, who wishes to see Hatty grow up and join the ordered, linear world.

In contrast to Hatty, Tom is initially well aware of his own growth, for instance, when he reacts vehemently to his new room, a passage quoted in many studies: '. . . there are bars across the bottom of the window! . . . This is a nursery! I'm not a baby!' (6). But as his visits to the garden continue, he feels more and more trapped in its enchantment (the connection between the garden and Hatty's female power is something I will leave for a Freudian to speculate on). The garden offers a nearly *deadly* temptation for Tom (cf Jones 1985, 214), to stay there forever, a temptation, I may add, that almost all time travellers in children's fantasy are exposed to and more or less successfully reject – for instance, Penelope in A *Traveller in Time,* Abigail in *Playing Beatie Bow,* or Rose in *The Root Cellar* (see Nikolajeva 1991; Nikolajeva 1993; Scott 1996). This is also the temptation Wendy is subject to in the Neverland and which she withstands. This is the temptation to which C.S. Lewis makes his characters succumb in *The Last Battle.* This is the temptation Winnie struggles with in *Tuck Everlasting.*

Tom's attitude toward the newly recovered Eden is highly ambivalent. At one point, he thinks that he is stuck in Hatty's time: he goes to sleep on the floor in her bedroom, and wakes up in his own, feeling happy and relieved about it. He does not seem to be tempted to stay. However, as the novel progresses, his dilemma becomes stronger: '. . . suddenly he found that he did not want to go home. He wanted above all to stay here – here where he could visit the garden' (60). Home in this case means order, linearity, growing up. The garden symbolizes childhood where, as Tom suddenly realizes, he would like to stay for ever. And even measured by chronos, he stays much longer than he is originally supposed to. However, his desire of the garden is not unproblematic: 'He wanted two different sets of things so badly: he wanted his mother and father and Peter and home – he really did want them, badly; and, on the other hand, he wanted the garden' (153). Observe how the meaning of home changes, just as it did in *Peter Pan*. Home is not part of the idyll here, but the obstacle, the prison. On the other hand, Tom's and Hatty's secret meetings in the garden do not imply big adventures, just nice, simple games, harmless pranks, in other words, a complete idyll, which is radically different from many time-shift stories, involving adventures, quest, and safe homecoming. In their Arcadia, the children build a tree-house – a symbolic home of their own.

It is when Tom realizes that primary time stands still while he is in the garden (quite unlike *Peter Pan*) that he feels the temptation:

> He could, after all, have both things – the garden and his family – because he could stay for ever in the garden, and yet for ever his family would be expecting him next Saturday afternoon.
>
> . . .
>
> 'I could stay in the garden for ever,' Tom told the kitchen clock, and laughed for joy, and then shivered a little, because 'for ever' sounded long and lonely.
>
> 180

But actually he cannot stay for ever, as each time he falls asleep in Hatty's time he wakes up in his own. On the last night, the garden is not there, and the loss makes Tom desperate. It is never said explicitly that Tom is in love with Hatty. She is just part of the garden, its 'princess' and – although he does not know it – its creator. When she leaves the garden, he cannot enter it any more either.

Another clue to the significance of Tom's dilemma is given in the inscription on a memorial tablet at Ely Cathedral: 'exchanged Time for Eternity' (190). As Raymond Jones points out (Jones 1985, 216), this indicates death; Tom's staying in the garden would be the same as dying.

Paradoxically, in the novel Hatty grows up while Tom does not, which is possible because of its peculiar temporal structure. Hatty's time goes faster than Tom's, which is illustrated by many time twists, as when Tom says, 'I shall see you tomorrow,' and Hatty remarks: 'You always say that, and then it's often months and months before you come again' (149–50). In Tom's time, he comes to the garden every night. Therefore the discovery of Hatty's change is such a shock. 'Hatty had been growing up, just like the other Melbournes, and Tom had never noticed it, partly because they had been together so much and partly because he was not observant of such things' (144). He is not observant because so far he has not been aware of his own growing up and the 'dangers' of it. Hatty's growing up brings to his attention this dilemma. He is jealous of her life outside the garden and without him, and when she says that he is always welcome, he 'noticed that she spoke to him as if he were a child and she were not' (144).

What many scholars have overlooked is Peter's role in Tom's returning home. Peter is summoned into kairos when Tom and Hatty are on top of the tower in Ely, and as Tom points out Hatty for him, Peter says 'indignantly – "that's not Hatty: that's a grown-up woman!"' (195) It is thus Peter, a brother – blood relative and male – who makes Tom aware of the necessity to leave the garden. And indeed, after having spoken to Mrs. Bartholomew, Tom longs to go home. He has escaped from the temptation of the garden. If Neil Philip reads *Tom's Midnight Garden* as the story of Eden and the Fall, the pattern is somewhat distorted: Eve is not a seducer, but a Savior.

What about Hatty then? Neil Philip insists that the book is not nostalgic (Philip 1982, 24), but I have strong doubts in this matter. On the night before her wedding, Hatty thinks 'of all I would be leaving behind me: my childhood and all the times I had spent in the garden – in the garden with you, Tom' (219). In the old Mrs. Bartholomew's account of the events we suddenly see the whole story from another perspective. It is not only (and maybe not primarily) the story of a young boy who is tempted to exchange time for eternity. It is the tragic story of an old woman who knows from experience that time is irreversible. So, a feminist critic might inquire, why is it *Tom's* midnight garden?

References

Bakhtin, Mikhail. *The Dialogic Imagination.* Austin: U of Texas P, 1981.

Jones, Raymond E. 'Philippa Pearce's *Tom's Midnight Garden:* Finding and Losing Eden.' In Nodelman, Perry, Ed. *Touchstones: Reflections of the Best in Children's Literature.* West Lafayette, IN: Children's Literature Association, 1985, vol. 1: 212–21.

Nikolajeva, Maria. *The Magic Code. The Use of Magical Patterns in Fantasy for Children.* Stockholm: Almqvist & Wiksell International, 1988. (Studies published by the Swedish Institute for Children's Books no. 31).

———. 'A Typological Approach to the Study of The Root Cellar.' *Canadian Children's Literature* 63 (1991): 53–60.

———. 'Fantasy: The Evolution of a Pattern.' In Bunbury, Rhonda, Ed. *Fantasy and Feminism in Children's Books.* Geelong, Australia: Deakin UP, 1993: 1–9.

Pearce, Philippa. *Tom's Midnight Garden.* Oxford: Oxford UP, 2008.

Philip, Neil. '"*Tom's Midnight Garden*" and the Vision of Eden.' *Signal* 37 (1982): 21–5.

———. 'Kenneth Grahame's *The Wind in the Willows:* A Companionable Vitality.' In Nodelman, Perry, Ed. *Touchstones: Reflections of the Best in Children's Literature.* West Lafayette, IN: Children's Literature Association, 1985, vol. 1: 96–105.

Scott, Carole. 'A Century of Dislocated Time: Time Travel, Magic and the Search for Self.' *Papers* 6 (1996) 2: 14–20.

Tom's Midnight Garden
Roni Natov

Philippa Pearce's *Tom's Midnight Garden*,[1] published forty-seven years after *The Secret Garden*, strongly bears its influence in terms of imagery and effect. Although Philippa Pearce's vision is not overwhelmingly Christian, it shares the sense of pastoral, the garden illuminated as a heightened reality in contrast with daily life and its limitations. Like Burnett, Pearce distrusts the British upper classes and believes in children's ability to reach deep emotional states, particularly in the green world. But *Tom's Midnight Garden* is a time-travel fantasy and the garden here is linked inextricably to the past, to a rural life, and not one that is especially glorified. The garden is lush and bountiful but cultivated and guarded. It includes all the aristocratic Melbournes and is the chosen site of the cruel as well as the more innocent children. What is exalted in Pearce's pastoral is the bond formed between two alienated children, Tom and Hatty, and the freedom they find in each other's company in the garden.

Tom's *Midnight Garden* begins in 'tears of anger.' Tom is 'in exile,' where he is sent by his parents to live with his aunt and uncle, two singularly dense though well-meaning adults, to protect him from his brother's measles. As his mother looking past him bids him good-bye, he is dropped out of a relatively idyllic childhood into a fallen state of anger and isolation. Not that his mother intends to cut him off; not that his relatives don't try to please him. His is the ordinary and all too common isolation of childhood; he is Everychild, tyrannized by adult 'reason,' as when he is forbidden to get out of bed or put the light on because, as Uncle Alan insists, children need 10 hours of sleep each night. When Tom pleads, ' "But, Uncle Alan, I don't sleep!" ' he shouts, ' "Will you be quiet Tom! . . . I'm trying to reason with you!" ' (*Midnight Garden*, 12). Aunt Gwen, similarly out of sync with her nephew and the world of children, has chosen a nursery with bars on the windows as his bedroom, complete with her former 'girls' schoolbooks.'

The familiar pain of childhood – how children's hopes are betrayed by the impenetrability and tediousness of adults – drives Tom to discover the magnificent 'midnight garden.' What Tom misses is the companionship of his brother Peter, and the simple, small garden where they can play freely. Aunt Gwen and Uncle Alan live in a flat, 'with no garden' – at least during the day. But at night, Tom discovers a secret garden at the back of the house that

Extracted from 'Childhood and the Green World' in R. Natov, *The Poetics of Childhood* (New York and London: Routledge, 2003), pp. 95–101.

existed in late-Victorian times. And it is there, in that pastoral space, that he reconstructs the lost harmony of his childhood. There he meets the extraordinary child, Hatty, who emerges as a child in Tom's life, we learn at the end, out of her intense longing as an old woman to relive her childhood memories. It is Tom's need for affirmation and for imaginative expression that propels him into the distilled childhood memories of old Mrs. Bartholomew's dreams. Here in this garden the ordinary and the extraordinary meet. The darker potentially threatening side of the typical, though nonetheless painful, heartaches of childhood is mirrored in the pastoral fantasy. Tom's feeling that his mother doesn't really see him, for example, is actualized in the garden where he is literally invisible to those who are like his rather obtuse family. Here Tom meets the orphan Hatty, who has been left in the care of her cruel aunt, who is reminiscent of the wicked stepmother of the fairy tale. This fantasy functions like the fairy tale, where the magic at the center reflects and comments on the mundane world, intensified and enhanced to allow a recognition necessary for healing and restoring a sense of harmony.

This is a story about the development of consciousness in childhood. The awareness of more complex and alternative states of mind comes about through Tom's desperate need for freedom. As he is confined to his bed for ten hours each night, sleep or no sleep, another realm of time opens up for him, one that allows him to live in two orders of reality – the mythic and the linear.[2] Tom can live out his daily life during 'regular' time, where 'Time was marching steadily onwards . . . from minute to minute, from hour to hour, from day to day' (*Midnight Garden*, 98). At night he lives in the poetic time of the garden, where Time moves 'forward to a tree's falling, and then back to before the fall; and then still farther back again . . . and then forward again' (*Midnight Garden*, 98), all without losing a single minute in the 'real' world. This aspect of time travel expresses the two states in which we psychologically reside: the conscious and the unconscious. The growing awareness of the tension between the two is reflected in the two alternative landscapes, the 'flat' and the garden, and is dramatized by a split into two Toms – one Tom who 'would never let the sleepy Tom go to sleep' (*Midnight Garden*, 16) – right before he discovers the garden. This more imaginative and potentially darker self grows out of a longing for the larger world he discovers: 'a great lawn where flower-beds bloomed; a towering fir-tree, and thick beetle-browed yews that humped their shapes . . . from each corner of the lawn, a path that twisted away to some other depths of garden, with other trees' (*Midnight Garden*, 19–20). Here '[w]hen [the thickly interlacing branches] came calling him, he would hide, silent and safe as a bird, among this richness of leaf and bough and tree-trunk' (*Midnight Garden*, 20).

In this garden, the invisibility from which his suffering originated becomes a gift. He can move about freely, unseen except for those closest to his sensibility. As a relatively innocent child in harmony with the green world, he is recognized by its creatures – cows, geese, birds – and by Hatty, the poor relation of the aristocratic Melbournes. As in *The Secret Garden*, here privilege and class are a corrupting influence on the human spirit; only Hatty, who has experienced early trauma and loss, is 'privileged' to see Tom. In this story, the pastoral is where consciousness expands for the child Tom; what begins in longing deepens and is transformed into empathy. About halfway through the novel, at a turning point marking the beginning of the most intense series of scenes that resolve only at the very end, Tom comes upon 'the littlest Hatty,' and witnesses her in her earliest state of loss.

> Turning the corner into the sundial path, he saw at the end of it a tiny little figure, all in black: a little girl, half Hatty's size, in a black dress, black stockings, black shoes. Even her hair was black, and had been tied with a black hair-ribbon . . . [S]he was sobbing into her hands.
>
> Tom had never seen a grief like this. He was going to tiptoe away, but there was something in the child's loneliness and littleness that made him change his mind . . . [H]e could not say this was none of his business . . .
>
> He never saw the little Hatty again. He saw the other, older Hatty as usual, on his next visit to the garden. Neither then nor ever after did he tease her with questions about her parents.
>
> *Midnight Garden*, 95–7

As a child, Tom is still porous, receptive, ignorant and innocent of tragedy. At first he is unable to recognize Hatty, but as his consciousness deepens, he comes to understand through sympathy all of Hatty's selves: Hatty when he first meets her, at a similar age – about nine or ten; Hatty at four in the above passage soon after she has lost her parents; Hatty as she grows into a young woman, and finally, Hatty as old Mrs. Bartholomew at the end. Hatty is able to come to Tom, fully and with all her experiences, only in her dreams where she is in touch with the child selves of her memories.

In addition, time travel serves as a metaphor for the way we need to travel, fluidly, reflexively between our own childhood selves, held together in our consciousness, or recalled from our unconscious through dreams and recognized by the conscious self upon waking. This occurs in a kind of mythic time, similar to Wordsworth's 'spots of time,' where poetic moments of our childhood function as landscapes we return to to reflect on our daily lives.

Developing consciousness, Pearce suggests, is the growing ability to recognize and to empathize with others. It means learning to respect 'otherness,' that there is more than one reality, that neither the self nor the other is, as Pearce metaphorically asserts, a 'ghost,' but rather that both are real. Tom and Hatty's only 'real quarrel' comes about as they each assert that they are 'real' and that the other is only a 'ghost,' until '[t]hey were glaring at each other' (*Midnight Garden*, 106), challenging each other's very existence. Tom shouts, ' "You're a ghost, and I've proved it! You're dead and gone and a ghost!" ... and then [he hears] the sound of Hatty's .... weep[ing] "I'm not dead – oh, please, Tom I'm not dead!" ' (*Midnight Garden*, 107). But once Tom has seen into Hatty's feelings, he can no longer remain detached in his stance. Pearce seems to be saying here that once we have seen the child-fear or most vulnerable part of another person, she becomes 'real' to us. We see past our own vision or at least tolerate the possibility that ours is a reality others might not share. But this requires a lifetime of practice, as Pearce seems to understand when she begins the chapter following Tom and Hatty's reconciliation: 'And yet, in spite of his assurance to Hatty, Tom continued secretly to consider the possibility of her being a ghost, for two reasons: first, that there seemed no other possibility; and second – and Tom ought to have seen that this was the worst kind of reason – that if Hatty weren't a ghost, then perhaps that meant he was. Tom shied away from that idea' (*Midnight Garden*, 108). Pearce seems to understand the self-protective thrust of defenses that generate such marginalizing. And, of course, she also portrays the potentially heightened awareness that can come from such marginalization. For example, Abel, the gardener, disenfranchised as part of the lower class, is also protector of the garden and of innocence. As such he comes to see Tom and accept him for what he is – an innocent child, rather than a creature of the devil, as he first believed.

Time travel becomes possible for Peter, Tom's older brother, only after he becomes increasingly involved with the world of Tom's letters, when his intense desire to see what Tom sees intersects with Tom's own desperate longing for a witness – without which children can not possibly rest firmly grounded in their own perceptions. As the older brother, Peter is not traditionally slated for the role of 'hero.' In the fairy tale world, the youngest and least worldly is the one who stumbles on the quest. But Peter's desire propels him onto the landscape of Tom's skating adventure with Hatty, although he does not see what Tom sees – or rather he sees Hatty as she is at that moment of intersection – a young woman. This shift from Tom's vision of Hatty as a younger child reveals Tom's desire to remain a child with the child Hatty, who has become, by the end Tom's midnight journey – the point at which Peter comes to see him – a figment of Tom's denial.

In one particularly poignant scene, Tom and Hatty skate together, both with the same pair of skates, the shared symbol of their time travel, foreshadowing the reconciliation scene at the end, which brings the two worlds together. Until that time, Tom wanders between the two, attempting to make sense of it all. Despite Uncle Alan's 'blazing, angelic certitude' (*Midnight Garden*, 168) that anything beyond his sense of the reasonable is nonsense, Tom reasons, ' "You might say that different people have different times, although of course, they're really all bits of the same big Time . . ." – he saw it all, suddenly and for the first time, from Hatty's point of view – "she might step forward into my Time, which would seem the Future to her, although to me it seems the Present. . . . Whichever way it is, she would be no more a ghost from the Past than I would be a ghost from the Future. We're neither of us ghosts; and the garden isn't either" ' (*Midnight Garden*, 170–1). From here, Tom decides to remain forever in the fluctuating, timeless garden, while his parents forever await his return 'next Saturday.' But for Hatty, Tom is progressively 'thinning out.' Earlier, Tom had become aware 'of something going on furtively and silently about him' in the beginning shifts in his travel between the two worlds. He would catch 'the hall in the act of emptying itself of furniture and rugs and pictures. They were not positively going, perhaps, but rather beginning to fail to be there' (*Midnight Garden*, 23). Now as Hatty grows older, Tom is 'beginning to fail to be there,' along with her own child self. While Tom is most desperate to get back to her, she only wants him to watch her skate. Her natural young adult worldliness is creeping in, as she moves from childhood into sexual desire for young Barty, which takes over her childhood imagination for so many years – until this late season of her life, where it is recaptured in her dreams.

Tom's Midnight Garden invokes two central metaphors – time and the garden. At the center is the grandfather clock, a source of inspiration for both worlds, at the heart of which, inside the clock, is the angel of the Book of Revelation, who stands with one foot on land and one on sea. Tom and Hatty read the biblical passage together: ' "And I saw another mighty angel come down from heaven, clothed with a cloud: and a rainbow was upon his head, and his face was as it were the sun, and his feet as pillars of fire: and he had in his hand a little book open: and he set his right foot upon the sea, and his left foot on the earth" ' (*Midnight Garden*, 163). As the last book of the Bible, it prophesies 'Time no longer,' an apocalyptic vision that makes 'Tom's head, when he had finished reading, whirl . . . with cloud and rainbow and fire and thunder and the majesty of it all – perhaps like the head of the unknown dial-painter of long ago' (*Midnight Garden*, 164) – connecting him with the imagination of the past. Imagination infused with feeling is the source, Pearce suggests, that can link cloud, rainbow, sun, fire, land, and sea. 'Time no longer' suggests a final unifying vision 'in the end,' one that can reconcile opposites and provide the sacred space for a reunion of elements that have become fractured – past from present, child from adult, male from female, inner from outer self – the parts from the whole.

In the last recognition scene, Hatty as old Mrs. Bartholomew says to Tom, ' "Oh, Tom . . . don't you understand? You called me: I'm Hatty" ' (*Midnight Garden*, 215). This moment is sure to bring tears, chills, or perhaps deep sighs to readers young and old. It expresses the ultimate wish, an embodiment or projection of desire for harmony, the impulse behind all pastoral, to restore unlike things to their place, to see them as part of the whole. It contains both expectation and surprise – what Tom was prepared for, an old woman, 'small and wrinkled, with white hair,' and what he was not 'prepared for . . . her eyes.' Their familiar blackness in an unfamiliar context creates in him a feeling similar to Freud's uncanny. Hatty, too, 'stretched out a hand and touched his arm with the tips of her fingers, pressing with them so that she might feel the fabric of his shirt and the flesh under the fabric and the bone beneath the flesh' (*Midnight Garden*, 215) – to reach the deepest and most enduring part, the bare bones, the real person.

Pearce ends by asserting the power of feeling that makes this connection possible. Tom 'had longed for someone to play with and for somewhere to play; and that great longing, beating about unhappily in the big house, must have made its entry into Mrs. Bartholomew's dreaming mind and brought back to her the little Hatty of long ago' (*Midnight Garden*, 223). In the end, we are left with Aunt Gwen trying to explain to Uncle Alan what she, as outsider, saw: ' "He ran up to her, and they hugged each other as if they had known each other for years and years . . . [and] he put his arms right round her and he hugged her good-bye as if she were a little girl" ' (*Midnight Garden*, 227). We who have been witness to the internal emotional life here recognize it without the 'as ifs.' We understand that they have known each other 'for years and years' and that she is, in fact, 'a little girl.' The freedom to make these connections function like alternative landscapes makes it possible for Tom to return to 'normal' life, to his family, and to the progressive world of time, to which he also needs to be restored.

Notes

1. Philippa Pearce, *Tom's Midnight Garden* (Oxford: Oxford University Press, [1958] 2008); hereafter cited in text as *Midnight Garden*.
2. See Maria Nikolajeva's study of time in children's literature, *From Mythic to Linear*, pp. 216–20 in this book.

8

Mildred Taylor, *Roll of Thunder, Hear My Cry* (1976)

Introduction
Janet Maybin

At a time when mainstream children's literature was largely white, both in terms of authors and fictional protagonists, Mildred Taylor's *Roll of Thunder, Hear My Cry* was unique as an award-winning best-seller written by an African American author and focalised through a 9-year-old African American girl. Autobiographical in origin, blending story, history and pedagogy, Taylor's book also contributed significantly to a developing tradition of African American children's literature, which blossomed in the 1980s and 1990s.

In the early twentieth century, black characters in mainstream American children's fiction were still largely presented as plantation stereotypes, either as ridiculous and comical figures, or as loyal and faithful servants to white children and their families. While there had been a few early children's books by African American writers published in the nineteenth century, for instance Paul Lawrence Dunbar's *Little Brown Baby* (1895), a more substantial African American children's literature began to emerge during the Harlem renaissance in the 1920s, a key publication being *The Brownie Book* magazine (1920–1), published by W.E.B. Du Bois and Augustus Dill, which aimed to provide positive, inspirational role models for black children through a mixture of fiction, poetry, history and photos and letters from young readers. Although short-lived, the magazine provided an important outlet for young African American writers, including the poet Langston Hughes, who went on to produce a number of poetry collections for children (e.g. *The Dream*

Keeper, 1932) and, in collaboration with Arna Bontemps, the classic *Popo and Fifina: Children of Haiti* (1932). Bontemps, who published a variety of novels, poetry, history and folk tales, was a key figure in the establishment of a distinctive African American children's literature.

Despite the work of important authors like Hughes and Bontemps, however, African American children's books remained largely outside the mainstream. There were virtually no African American writers in the juvenile divisions emerging in the 1940s and 1950s through the large American publishing houses and, despite the official desegregation of schools in 1954, a survey ten years later found that only 6.7% of the 5,206 children's books published between 1962 and 1964 in the United States included a black character, and under 1% depicted contemporary African Americans (Larrick 1965). In the period following the Civil Rights and Black Arts Movements in the 1960s and 1970s this situation began to change. A new generation of African American writers began to produce a range of realist fiction, including books depicting contemporary urban ghetto experience and others, like Taylor's, documenting African American history, roots and heritage – e.g. Julius Lester (illus. Tom Feelings), *To Be a Slave* (1968), Rosa Guy, *The Friends* (1973), Camille Yarbrough, *Cornrows* (1979). These authors' and artists' creation of positive images of African American people, for an African American audience, was essentially a literature of protest, written against the established tradition of the all-white world of children's books (MacCann 2001; Martin 2006).

Origins, composition, reception

In 1974, Taylor's writing career was launched when the manuscript for her first novel about the Logan family, *The Song of the Trees*, won a writing contest sponsored by the New York-based Council on Interracial Books for Children, an anti-racist organisation set up in 1965 to promote literature with more positive images of black children. Visiting her family on the way home from the award ceremony, Taylor heard the story of a black boy who broke into a store and was saved from the lynch mob. This provided the seed for her second novel about the Logan family, *Roll of Thunder, Hear My Cry*. Originally thinking that the theme was more suitable material for an adult novel, Taylor was persuaded by her editor Phyllis Fogelman at Dial Books to write another book for children (Crowe 1999). Published in 1976, *Roll of Thunder, Hear my Cry* won the American Library Association's Newbery Award in 1977. It was followed by a further seven books about the Logan family, including *Let the Circle be Unbroken* (1981) and *The Road to Memphis* (1990), both of which won the Coretta Scott King Award.

Taylor's books have promoted black heroes and heroines, celebrated black family life and reclaimed and foregrounded black history and heritage. Like a number of other contemporary African American children's books, *Roll of Thunder, Hear My Cry* features strong family ties and love as a primary source of support for the child protagonists, and highlights significant cross-generational relationships and feisty characters struggling against social injustice (Bishop 2007). Taylor was explicit about her pedagogic purposes in the books, arguing that if young readers 'can identify with the Logans, who are representative not only of my family but of many Black families who faced adversity and survived, and understand the principles by which they lived, then perhaps they can better understand and respect themselves and others' (Taylor 1977: 407–8). She saw herself as having a particular responsibility as a black writer, believing it impossible for white writers to understand and convey the warmth of black family life, or how black parents taught their children to survive. Her books are therefore unapologetically and polemically biographical and autobiographical: 'Through David Logan have come the words of my father, and through the Logan family the love of my own family . . . . contrary to what the media relate to us, all Black families are not fatherless or disintegrating. Certainly my family was not' (Taylor 1977: 403). Thus, her depictions of life for African American people in the 1930s in her fiction were based on conversations among the older family members she visited during annual trips with her sister and parents back to Mississippi. Her relatives' accounts and stories 'were like nothing I read in the history books or the books I devoured at the local library. There were no Black heroes or heroines in those books; . . . . There was obviously a terrible contradiction between what the books said and what I had learned from my family' (Taylor 1977: 404).

Taylor's pedagogic intention has been amply realised in that *Roll of Thunder, Hear My Cry* has frequently appeared on school syllabi for 11–14-year-olds in both North America and Britain. It has proved acceptable to educationists because, firstly, the autobiographical stance and historical setting allow both empathy and distance, so that racism and other issues of social justice can be safely aired within an educational setting. Secondly, Taylor's characterisation is complex and interrogative. While historical fiction about the US southern states in the 1930s could have presented a simplistic view of ethnicity to a reading audience forty years later when racism and segregation were seen as wrong, Taylor creates more complicated positions for her characters so that the reader has to judge them by their actions and not by their ethnic identities (Martin 1998). Martin argues that Taylor's novels are powerful because, rather than being straightforwardly didactic and providing a single authoritative resolution, they are interrogative, bringing different points of view into collision. This makes the novels particularly valuable within multicultural education, because they reveal grey areas behind simple stereotypes and create uncomfortable questions for readers, leading them to reflect on their own position and identity.

The essays

In line with the perceived political pedagogy of Taylor's books, the critical literature on her work has tended to focus on its realism, whether of its autobiographical elements, or of its representation of 1930s Mississippi and its treatment of family, history and social justice. The first essay included here, by Hamida Bosmajian, focuses mainly on Taylor's treatment of law and justice. She suggests that these are unusual themes in children's literature, and that Taylor's treatment achieves narrative depth and complexity particularly through the representation of boundary crossers and scapegoats. The importance of Cassie as an active, questioning role model for the child reader has been seen as central to the book's pedagogic force; in the second reading, Kelly McDowell argues that Taylor uses Cassie's socio-historical positioning, and her co-option alongside adults into the struggle against racism, to convey a more robust, effective and subversive kind of child agency than that depicted in classic children's fiction. The final essay, by Cicely Denean Cobb, examines how Taylor uses the crucial role of education in the Southern black family as a driving force in *Roll of Thunder, Hear My Cry* (and its sequels), highlighting the special significance of the informal education which Cassie, like Taylor, received from her father and the black community.

Together, these authors examine different aspects of Taylor's representation of a disenfranchised community through strong storytelling which incorporates teaching about African American history, experience and identity. This distinctive cultural aesthetic, they imply, is an intrinsic part of her literary achievement.

References

Bishop, R.S. 2007. *Free within Ourselves: The Development of African American Children's Literature.* Westport, CT, Greenwood Press.

Crowe, C. 1999. *Presenting Mildred D. Taylor.* New York, Twayne.

Larrick, N. 1965. 'The All-White World of Children's Books', *Saturday Review*, 48(37), 11 September.

MacCann, D. 2001. 'Racism and Antiracism: Forty Years of Theories and Debates', *The Lion and the Unicorn*, 25: 337–52.

Martin, M. 1998. 'Exploring the Works of Mildred Taylor: An Approach to Teaching the Logan Family Novels', *Teaching and Learning Literature*, January/February: 5–13.

Martin, M. 2006. 'African American Literature', in J. Zipes (ed.) *The Oxford Encyclopedia of Children's Literature*. Oxford, Oxford University Press.

Taylor, M.D. 1977. 'Newbery Award Acceptance', *The Horn Book Magazine*, August: 401–9.

Further reading

Crowe, C. 1999. *Presenting Mildred D. Taylor*. New York, Twayne.

Martin, M. 2006. 'African American Literature', in J. Zipes (ed.) *The Oxford Encyclopedia of Children's Literature*. Oxford, Oxford University Press.

A Search for Law and Justice in a Racist Society
Hamida Bosmajian

Mildred Taylor's rich chronicle about an African American family in rural Mississippi during the years 1933–41 is narrated by the main character, Cassie Logan. The story she tells is not only about the adventures of her childhood and adolescence, not only about the deep bonds she has with her family, but also about the injustices a white, racist, and lawless society inflicts on the Logans and their neighbors. Although they are citizens in a nation that is framed by one of the most important legal documents in Western civilization, the Constitution of the United States, black Americans find themselves in Taylor's chronicle constituted in an unjust system of local laws and customs. It is not surprising, therefore, that as a child the intelligent and inquisitive Cassie is already quite aware of the binary injustice/justice. The first term of the binary is privileged in her life experience; it is the second, justice, that she yearns for.

The young reader of Mildred Taylor's *Roll of Thunder, Hear My Cry* (1976), *Let the Circle Be Unbroken* (1981), and *The Road to Memphis* (1990) will most likely focus on the adventures and relationships of Cassie Logan in rural Mississippi during the Depression and the years leading up to America's entry into World War II. It becomes quite clear, however, that these years also reveal Cassie's ongoing education in and growing consciousness of the liberating power of just laws. Moreover, Taylor treats law and justice and their opposites in a manner that is quite sophisticated, even

Extracted from 'Mildred Taylor's Story of Cassie Logan: A Search for Law and Justice in a Racist Society', in *Children's Literature*, 24 (1996), pp. 141–60.

technical on occasion. We can even say that her three narratives are novels of education in the need for law and justice. Although Taylor's story offers the literary critic a full range of interpretive opportunities, I shall limit my discussion to the significance of the theme of law and justice in Cassie's development.

It is a theme that is unusual in children's literature. Most often the law, especially in fairy tales, is expressed through irrational or tyrannical rules imposed upon the hero by persons in authority. The hero's trial, then, consists often of impossible hardships and tasks to fulfill these rules. The mysteries of adult law and legal systems may also befuddle the child hero who, like Alice in Wonderland, finds herself or himself in an absurd world. We may well conclude that children's literature tends to depict law in a preconscious, even dreamlike sense. Taylor's chronicle, however, shows us characters who are conscious of the value of American law as a heritage of an age of reason. Although the titles *Roll of Thunder, Hear My Cry* and *Let the Circle Be Unbroken* are prayerful imperatives that reflect the religious heritage of African Americans – the first asking for vertical divine intervention, the second for the continued connectedness on the horizontal level of human experience – the novels do not invoke or appeal to divine law, but place the responsibility for justice on laws made by humans.

The relationship between law and literature is profound. The patterns of tragic narratives usually are generated by the violation of a law that must be righted; the patterns of comic narration begin most often with an unjust and irrational law that the comic hero transforms or transcends through liberation.

As far as the values of law and justice are concerned, Taylor's trilogy is pedagogical in its rhetorical ethos. Mildred Taylor, a writer in the psychologically and socially realistic mode, focuses on justice and law issues by recording the ordinary routines and events of human life, as with Cassie Logan, who grows from a pranksterish tomboy to an aspiring student of the law. In the Mississippi of her childhood and adolescence, custom and the unjust statutes of segregation have institutionalized racism, and those in power can vent their rage with impunity whenever they feel that 'colored folk' are 'forgetting their place.' The victims of this willful power must constantly be vigilant and self-controlled, even if they are infuriated by the injustices inflicted upon them. To protect herself and her family, young Cassie has to learn that she cannot vent her anger.

Mildred Taylor shows us Cassie's development not only in the context of growing up in a warm and nurturing family but also in the context of the middle-class values of life, liberty, and the pursuit of property (happiness).

It is the Logan's landownership, threatened though it is by the difficulty of meeting tax payments, that is essential to their dignity, their life, and the liberty they claim. Her family's self-respect is based largely on the fact that they farm their own land, even though Mrs. Logan also teaches and Mr. Logan works on the railroad. This status helps Cassie avoid becoming the child Martin Luther King describes in his 'Letter from Birmingham Jail': 'The depressing clouds of inferiority begin to form in her little mental sky, and we see her begin to distort her little personality by unconsciously developing a bitterness toward white people' (King 81). Cassie gets angry at anyone who wants to designate her as inferior; she would agree with King's argument that 'any law that uplifts the human personality is just. All segregation statutes are unjust because segregation distorts the soul and damages the personality' (82). Her childhood experiences and observations give her ample evidence to observe that effect.

Socially and politically, Mildred Taylor's chronicle is squarely within the context of the values of constitutionally guaranteed rights, no matter how these rights are violated in temporal local statutes. Such values give her story an affirmative narrative pattern that has the reader consistently root for Cassie Logan's struggle toward right and lawful actualization of herself and her community. Nevertheless, the narrative is filled with ambivalent counter-memories and subtexts. Taylor's storytelling skill manages to include all these ambivalences yet lets her young hero continue her struggle. *Roll of Thunder, Hear My Cry* depicts one year during the Great Depression (1933–34) and frames that year with the restrictive horizon of racist Mississippi. In examining Cassie's growth and education in awareness of justice and law, I shall limit the discussion to several key incidents.

The first example is the prank as a relatively harmless tactic of revenge against persistent abuse. *Roll of Thunder* begins with the Logan children's trek to school along the narrow road that 'wound like a lazy red serpent dividing the high forest bank of quiet old trees on the left from the cotton field . . . on the right' (4). The school bus would come roaring down the road spewing red dust over the children while 'laughing white faces pressed against the bus windows' (12). On a rainy day, 'the bus driver liked to entertain his passengers by sending us slipping along the road to the almost inaccessible forest banks . . . [and] we consequently found ourselves comic objects to cruel eyes that gave no thought to our misery' (46).

Cassie's younger brother, Clayton Chester, or 'Little Man,' is enraged by this humiliation and eager for revenge. The children decide to dig a ditch across the road that, filled with water, traps the school bus whose passengers now get soaked in return: 'Oh, how sweet was well maneuvered revenge!' exclaims the narrator in retrospect. Their prank is a playful retaliation, a momentary empowerment against daily mistreatment, but it could easily become a more serious matter, with disastrous consequences.

Revenge, argues Judge Posner, is the irresistible impulse to avenge wrongful injuries, but it is also the underpinning of the corrective justice of criminal punishment and the breakdown of law and order when legal channels have become blocked (Posner 25–6). Revenge, however, precludes the possibility of eventual cooperation (30). Taylor's characters feel repeatedly the upsurge of anger that could lead them to revenge, but only in *The Road to Memphis* does that anger lead to violence; usually Taylor depicts the black community as venting its anger only in a prank or an attitude. An organized attempt at community action, such as the boycott of the Strawberry store organized by the Logans and supported by Jamison, is bound to fail as whites react by terrorizing blacks. Blacks experience the constant threat of violence, for anxiety makes the oppressor permanently vigilant against the slightest signs of insubordination, signs that nearly always trigger an excessive response. Shortly after the bus prank, therefore, when 'night riders' terrorize the neighborhood, the Logan children connect it with their prank and Cassie is overwhelmed by the terror she will feel often during her childhood and adolescence: 'Once inside the house, I leaned against the latch while waves of sick terror swept over me. . . . I climbed into the softness of the bed. I lay very still for a while, not allowing myself to think. But soon, against my will, the vision of the ghostly headlights soaked into my mind and an uncontrollable trembling racked my body. And it remained until the dawn, when I fell into a restless sleep' (*Roll of Thunder* 74).

The night riders in this case have another object for their revenge: an adult black male. Taylor does keep within the conventions of literature for young readers by preserving Cassie from witnessing extreme acts of violence, but the threat of it permeates even the most intimate 'at home' moments. The Christmas chapter in *Roll of Thunder* (159–74) is one such example. Here the narrator begins by nostalgically evoking the smells, sounds, and sights of Christmas in an almost Dickensian manner. Stories are told by the older folks and, as the night deepens, Mr. Morrison, the helper and protector in the Logan household, talks about how his ancestors were 'bred' for strength during slavery and how his family was killed on a Christmas Day. Mrs. Logan tries to quiet him for the sake of the children, but her husband admonishes her: ' "These are things they need to hear, baby. It's their history" ' (163).

How can a young person in such an environment still learn to value the idea of law? The values of personhood and community are instilled through the deep bonding among the members of the Logan family and their ability to 'talk things out.' Mary Logan's personal courage against injustice and

David Logan's kind and disciplined nature provide the children with strong values. Moreover, David teaches his children separateness from whites as a means of survival. The family survives by finding strength in one another, for all attempts to reach out and change the injustices in the community fail, as the attempted boycott in *Roll of Thunder* demonstrates. Publicly, the importance of law is projected for Cassie through Wade Jamison.

Jamison, solicitous of the Logans' concerns and welfare is 'Old South' and old money. He represents an agent of social change who does not come from the disempowered grass roots of the oppressed but whose education, property, and personal sense of justice have touched his conscience and enabled him to publicly represent and advise the oppressed. Well aware that there are as yet few of his kind, his effectiveness is limited to expressions of attitude, for the context of his culture keeps him from turning the gestures into effectual acts. Typically, Cassie aligns him with the positive expression of patriarchal values: 'He was the only white man I had ever heard address Mama and Big Ma as "Missus," and I liked him for it. Besides that, in his way he was like Papa: Ask him a question and he would give it to you straight with none of this pussy-footing-around business. I like that' (*Roll of Thunder* 11). The Logans deal with him because of their property but also receive his support when they boycott an oppressive store owner. Most significantly, Jamison is a key figure when he tries to stop a lynching mob.

T.J. and a white boy named Jeremy Simms function as complex scapegoat figures in the narratives. Typically, the scapegoat, ranging from the criminal to the sacred, manifests itself directly or subtextually in contexts where injustice generates an anger and rage that are vented on an individual defined as 'the one.' Both T.J. and Jeremy try to befriend the Logan children, and both want to cross the boundaries that separate blacks from whites. Cassie feels ambivalence toward both, for she cannot really understand their motivations.

In Taylor's narrative, T.J.'s profound lack of self-esteem motivates both his ego inflation and his desperate need to be accepted. Such needs flaw his action morally: it is he who informs on Mary Logan and causes her to be dismissed from her teaching post. He takes up with R.W. and Melvin Simms, Jeremy's crude older brothers, who promise him a pearl-handled pistol if he helps them break into Barnett's store. T.J. does not realize that they are setting him up when they mask themselves with black stockings. When Barnett comes upon them, R.W. Simms kills him (272), but it is T.J., as a black, who will be tried for the murder. The incident is a variable of the stereotype René Girard identifies as 'the mark,' the victim who is 'invited to a feast that ends with his lynching. Why? He has done something he should not have done; his behavior is perceived as fatal. One of his gestures was misinterpreted' (Girard, *Scapegoat* 32–3). T.J. is marked both as black and as a boundary crosser.

Cassie recognizes T.J.'s tragic isolation from both whites and blacks: 'I had never seen him more desolately alone, and for a fleeting second I almost felt sorry for him' (*Roll of Thunder* 266). For whites, T.J. is a scapegoat of convenience who will be burdened with the blame for a criminal act, but his role as scapegoat for the black community is more complex. Cassie feels both anger and guilt toward him: anger because he has hurt her family and guilt because she cannot make him a friend in spite of his need. T.J. turns to the Simms brothers in part because he is unable to befriend the black children. T.J. is never liked, only tolerated by the Logan children, whose anger against him is very real after he informs on Mama. But T.J. also exemplifies the dangers of boundary crossing, a temptation especially acute for Stacey, Cassie's older brother, who is open to friendship with Jeremy. When the Simms brothers brutally beat T.J. after the break-in, he seeks out Stacey who, with his siblings, accompanies him home, for Stacey, surmises the narrator, 'perhaps felt that even a person as despicable as T.J. needed someone he could call "friend," or perhaps he sensed T.J.'s vulnerability better than T.J. did himself' (274). As the Logan children are about to return home, they see night riders driving towards the Averys'. The lynching mob violently forces the Averys out of their house, including T.J., who is 'dragged from the house on his knees. His face was bloody and when he tried to speak he cried with pain' (279). As the savage beating continues, Jamison drives up and says quietly: 'Y'all decide to hold court here tonight?' (280). Jamison is unable to disperse the mob, whose rage now also begins to threaten Mr. Morrison, the Logans' live-in protector, and David Logan himself: 'A welling affirmation arose from the men. "I got me three new ropes!" exclaimed Kaleb' (282). The children gasp in terror and Stacey sends Cassie to inform Papa.

At this point a roll of thunder, the reply to the plea of the title, announces a storm that enables David Logan to diffuse the situation by setting fire to his crop, claiming that lightning struck a fence post. Everybody gets involved extinguishing the fire. When the truth of the situation dawns on Cassie, she realizes that 'this was one of those known and unknown things, something never to be spoken, not even to each other' (303). Cassie intimates the awful consequences her father's act could have and internalizes that terror into her inmost silence. In Jamison's confrontation with the lynching mob, his appeal to the law has been ineffectual; instead, it is David Logan's lawless act of arson that disperses the lawless mob. Cassie, the witness-narrator, learns here both of the law's fragility and of the danger when lawlessness is used to deter lawlessness.

References

Girard, René. *The Scapegoat*. Trans. Yvonne Freccero. Baltimore: Johns Hopkins University Press, 1986.

King, Martin Luther. *Why We Can't Wait*. New York: Mentor/Penguin, 1964.

Posner, Richard. *Law and Literature. A Misunderstood Relation*. Cambridge: Harvard University Press, 1988.

Taylor, Mildred D. *Roll of Thunder, Hear My Cry*. 1976. Reprint. New York: Bantam, 1984.

———. *Let the Circle Be Unbroken*. 1981. Reprint. New York: Bantam, 1984.

———. *The Road to Memphis*. New York: Dial, 1990.

Child Agency in *Roll of Thunder, Hear My Cry*
Kelly McDowell

In *Little House on the Prairie*, Pa instructs Laura: 'Do as you are told and no harm will come to you' (Wilder, 1971, p. 146). This is an example of the overt didacticism in which most classic children's literature is engaged. Classic works function on a didactic trajectory, which serves to instill the proper values of childhood, created by adults, in the errant child characters and, in turn, in the intended child reader. The effect, whether intentional or not, is the establishment of a clear division between childhood and adulthood. Children occupy the object position, dependent on the direction of adult subjects.

That children's literature is most often written *for* children *by* adults is necessarily problematic. Rose (1993) posits: 'There is, in one sense, no body of literature which rests so openly on an acknowledged difference, a rupture almost, between writer and addressee. Children's fiction sets up the child as an outsider to its own process, and then aims, unashamedly, to take the child in' (p. 2). Thus, children's literature depends on a slippage between childhood and adulthood. Furthering this idea, Rose says

> Children's fiction sets up a world in which the adult comes first (author, maker, giver) and the child comes after (reader, product, receiver), but where neither of them enter the space in between. . . . It (is) not an issue here of what the child wants, but of what the adult desires – desires in the very act of construing the child as the object of its speech. Children's fiction draws in the child, it secures, places and frames the child.

2

Extracted from 'Roll of Thunder, Hear My Cry: A Culturally Specific, Subversive Concept of Child Agency', in *Children's Literature in Education* 33:3 (2002), pp. 213–25.

The adult writer writes *to* the child, to draw the child into the story, while writing *for* the child, to instruct the child how the adult world desires her to be. The effect is to cement the distinction between childhood and adulthood, to uphold the boundary between the two worlds. The unequal relation and imbalance of power reveals the hierarchical relationship between the adult writer and the child reader. Classic children's literature and fairy tales are, of course, the most overtly didactic of the genre. Often, child characters, as well as intended child readers, occupy the object position and are directed by adult subjects. In this relation, children are denied subjectivity and agency.

Of course, more recent children's literature offers more diverse representations of children who are allowed greater freedom and agency. This is not to say that these works are entirely undidactic; any children's novel almost always falls into didacticism in one way or another. The didacticism present in more contemporary works is in not so much of a 'how to' or instructional style; rather, the ideas presented function more as *tools* for children to use (or not) in the building of their own subjectivity. The ideas exist as choices rather than rules; with choices, children are allowed greater opportunity to act with autonomy.

In *Roll of Thunder, Hear My Cry,* Taylor takes the modern concept of child agency and employs it in relation to the very specific position of cultural fixity and immobility of African-American children in the Depression-era South. She extends and refines the concept with regard to the specific social/historical position of her characters. Enabling child agency becomes a necessary part of resistance. The result is a modified type of subversive child agency. In this article, I consider the various ways in which this specific type of agency is manifest in the novel. I demonstrate that the novel depicts the necessity of child agency as a form of resistance for oppressed cultures.

The role of historical understanding

One of the ways that this type of child agency is enabled in the novel is through a demystification of history. History, for the Logan children, is not what they read in books at school because, of course, the African-American history found in the books is fabricated by the dominant culture. The Logan children get their knowledge of history from their family, mostly through the oral tradition. As a result, the children are very connected to their history. It becomes a vital force in their lives. Because it is passed on to them by their elders, history has special significance and becomes an intimate and *lived experience.* Narrator Cassie makes numerous references to the family's history. Her knowledge is extensive and unusual for her age. In the first chapter, she recounts the story of the Logan land:

> Once our land had been Granger land . . . , but the Grangers had sold it during Reconstruction to a Yankee for tax money. In 1887, when the land was up for sell [*sic*] again, Grandpa had bought two hundred acres of it, and in 1918, after the first two hundred acres had been paid off, he had bought another two hundred. It was good rich land, much of it still virgin forest, and there was no debt on half of it. But there was a mortgage on the two hundred acres bought in 1918 and there were taxes on the full four hundred, and for the past three years there had not been enough money from the cotton to pay both and live too.
>
> That was why Papa had gone to work on the railroad. In 1930 the price of cotton dropped. And so, in the spring of 1931, Papa set out looking for work, going as far north as Memphis and as far south as the Delta country. He had gone west too, into Louisiana. It was there that he found work laying track for the railroad. He worked the remainder of the year away from us, not returning until the deep winter when the ground was cold and barren. The following spring after the planting was finished, he did the same. Now it was 1933, and Papa was again in Louisiana laying track.
>
> 4–5

Able to recall exact dates and details, Cassie exhibits a strong connection to her history. She knows it so well because of the immediacy it has for her. Her history has impacted her life in ways that she can clearly see. It is because of past events that her father is forced to leave the family. Thus, Cassie can feel history's effects quite poignantly.

For the Logan children, history is represented through specific events that directly intersect with factors of race and class. It becomes transformative; knowing their history allows the Logan children greater freedom and agency. We see this effect when grandmother, Big Ma, tells Cassie the story of her grandfather, Paul. She explains that Paul, born into slavery, managed to work to save the money to buy their land. Hearing about her grandfather's strength and self-reliance gives Cassie a sense of pride and allows her to realize that, although she is oppressed, she is not devoid of agency. If her grandfather, born a slave, could rise above his situation to own his own land, perhaps Cassie, too, could be an agent in her own future.

The history of slavery is demystified for the children when Papa allows them to hear Mr. Morrison's tales of his family. He explains that his parents came from 'breeded stock.' When Cassie asks what this means, he answers her, in honest, uncoded terms.

> 'Well, Cassie, during slavery there was some farms that mated folks like animals to produce more slaves. Breeding slaves brought a lot of money for them slave owners, 'specially after the government said they couldn't bring no more slaves

from Africa, and they produced all kinds of slaves to sell on the block. And folks with enough money . . . could buy 'zactly what they wanted. My folks was bred for strength like they folks they grandfolks 'fore 'em. Didn't matter none what they thought 'bout the idea. Didn't nobody care.'

'But my mama and daddy they loved each other and they loved us children, and that Christmas they fought them demons out of hell like avenging angels of the Lord.' He turned his back toward the fire and grew very quiet; then he raised his head and looked at us. 'They died that night. Them night men kilt 'em. Some folks tell me I can't remember what happened that Christmas – I warn't hardly six years old – but I remembers all right. I makes myself remember.'

164–5

Mr. Morrison displays the intimacy of his connection to history. Because of the immediate and enormous effect on his life, he remembers his past vividly. In fact, it is crucial for him to remain connected to it. *He makes himself remember.* One of the ways to do this is to share his story with the Logan children. It is also necessary for them to know about racism's past in order to understand the origins of the unfair treatment that they experience in their own lives. This is why David Logan says to Mary: ' "These are things they need to hear, baby. It's their history" ' (163).

Although Mary is concerned with protecting her children, she, herself, often engages in the effort to demystify history for the children. One of the most important ways that she does this is by teaching the history of slavery in her classroom. Through a valiant and subversive act, she teaches her students the brutal reality of history. The act eventually costs her her job when members of the school board are alerted to the content of her classes. While sitting in on her class, board member Harlan Granger says, pointing to a text book: ' "I don't see all them things you're teaching in here." ' Mary responds by saying: ' "That's because they're not in there." ' When he warns her not to deviate from the textbook, she resolutely states: ' "all that's in that book isn't true" ' (203). She is willing to risk losing her job to teach her students a history that is realistic and uncoded. She interrupts and opposes the clean, unproblematic history found in White textbooks. By teaching the specific effects of slavery, she reveals its horrors – despite racist efforts to maintain silence. Through its specific manifestation in their lives, history is demystified, unlike the mystified history found in their textbooks. It becomes a radical history, one that exposes the inconsistencies and ruptures of a culturally unequal society.

Unveiling racist power structures

The effort to teach the history of slavery demonstrates Mary's concern for unveiling racist power structures. She continually attempts to teach her own children the ways in which power works against them. She feels that her children will be empowered through this knowledge and will be able to act more intelligently with a greater awareness of their environment. We see this when she takes the children to see Mr. Berry, who has been burned nearly to death by the 'night men.' The burning has left the man horrifically deformed. Cassie tells the reader: 'The face had no nose, and the head no hair; the skin was scarred, burned, and the lips were wizened black, like charcoal' (107). Mr. Berry is unable to speak, unable to stand light on his damaged eyes, or even the feel of clothes against his charred skin. The Logan children stand by silently as their mother talks to the debilitated man. On the way home, she explains her reason for bringing the children to see him. In a resolute tone, she says:

> 'The Wallaces did that, children. They poured kerosene over Mr. Berry and his nephews and lit them afire. One of the nephews died, the other one is just like Mr. Berry. . . . Everyone knows they did it, and the Wallaces even laugh about it, but nothing was ever done. They're bad people, the Wallaces. That's why I don't want you to ever go to their store again – for any reason. You understand?'
>
> 108

The children nod, 'unable to speak' as they think of the disfigured man they have just seen. There is no effort here to shield them from any unpleasantness, no accommodation for their youth. For Mary, it is more important that they understand the possible repercussions of incautious action than it is to shelter them from unpleasantness. She unveils the power structure for her children, showing them exactly what power is capable of, who wields it, and who is victimized by it.

On leaving Mr. Berry, Mary begins to organize her boycott of the Wallaces' store. She talks to the neighbors, sharecropping families who live on the land belonging to Harlan Granger. She tells the neighbors that the Wallaces are allowing the children to drink and smoke at their store while they accrue charges for which their families will be held responsible. She attempts to organize the community to patronize shops that would treat them more justly in the neighboring town of Vicksburg. And she offers to make trips to Vicksburg for the neighbors. Mr. Jamison, the attorney who has befriended the family, offers to back the neighbors' credit so that they may shop at the store in Vicksburg. The Logan children watch their mother as she works as a political organizer. She teaches them that they too can be active agents. She emphasizes the necessity of caution, as she demonstrates by taking the children to see Mr. Berry, but she also stresses the importance of agency. By revealing the ways in which power works, she shows them how agency is possible.

Mary's boycott is a subversive act, much like her act of covering the issuance charts on the inside of the textbooks of her students. The charts display the condition of the book each time it is reissued and the race of the student to whom it is reissued. It allows the board of education to ensure that African-American children only get books that are in the poorest condition. Each time the students open their books, the charts glaringly remind them of their inferiority. Mary takes it upon herself to cover the charts so that the students are not forced to look at them everyday. In an almost seditious act, she exerts an agency to resist the racist practice. By doing so, she displays to her students, as well as to her own children, that agency is possible and, in fact, crucial and that there are always ways to resist domination.

David Logan also serves as an example to the children. He exerts agency when he sets fire to the Logan crops in order to prevent a lynching. When the 'night men' come for T.J., David knows that the only way to prevent them from taking him is to create a diversion. Knowing that the men will be called away by Harlan Granger to fight the fire, whose own land could eventually be destroyed by it, David enacts the only means he can to prevent T.J.'s lynching. Although he loses a quarter of his own crops, he manages to save T.J.'s life. David does not tell his children what he has done, but Cassie and her eldest brother, Stacey, know. Cassie describes the moment of her realization:

> Stacey looked around at me sharply, his face drawn, his eyes anxious, and without even a murmur from him I suddenly did know . . . *Papa had found a way*, as Mama asked, to make Mr. Granger stop the hanging: He had started the fire
>
> 302; emphasis mine

Agency can, indeed, be exerted but, because of their oppressive environment, they must be clever about exerting it. Their parents serve as examples to them of how they can triumph. Their victories may never be large or obvious, yet, with an awareness of how power works, they have the ability to exert some control over their lives. They learn this despite their racist society, which suggests that any sort of agency is impossible.

Often, we see the elders allow the children to make their own decisions. The children are given information, but the choice of how to use the information is often left up to them. We see an example of this when Uncle Hammer responds to Stacey giving his new coat to T.J. Although Hammer thinks Stacey has made a bad decision, he does not take it upon himself to get the coat back from T.J. nor does he force Stacey to ask for it back. He is concerned with making Stacey aware of the outcome of his decision and allows Stacey to live with its effects. Hammer does reprimand him, but he does so in order to make Stacey aware of his own part in his fate. During the scene, Hammer emphasizes the importance of making intelligent decisions:

> 'Now you hear me good on this – look at me when I talk to you, boy!' Immediately Stacey raised his head and looked at Uncle Hammer, 'If you ain't got the brains of a flea to see that this T.J. fellow made a fool of you, then you'll never get anywhere in this world. It's tough out there, boy, and as long as there are people, there's gonna be somebody trying to take what you got and trying to drag you down. *It's up to you whether you let them or not.*
>
> 156–7; emphasis mine

Hammer makes Stacey aware of the realities of their environment, but he leaves it up to Stacey to decide what to do with the information. Hammer, in fact, forces Stacey to stand by his decision to give the coat away. When T.J.'s father brings him to the Logan house to return the coat, Hammer makes Stacey tell him that it now belongs to T.J.. He demonstrates to Stacey the impact of his decisions and, thus, makes him aware that he is an agent in his own future.

Another moment when the Logan children are allowed to choose their fate occurs when Mr. Morrison finds them at the Wallaces' store after Mary has forbidden them to go. He tells the children that he will not tell their mother but will leave it up to them to do so. He also does not reprimand Stacey for fighting with T.J.. Instead, he validates Stacey's need to attempt to solve problems, even, at times, through the use of violence. But he lets the children know that they must make decisions intelligently. He says:

> 'Sometimes a person's gotta fight. . . . But that store ain't the place to be doing it. From what I hear, folks like them Wallaces got no respect at all for colored folks and they just think it's funny when we fight each other. Your mama knowed them Wallaces ain't good folks, that's why she don't want y'all down there, and y'all owe it to her and y'allselves to tell her. But I'm gonna leave it up to y'all to decide.'
>
> 95–6

When Stacey tells Mr. Morrison that he will tell his mother, the two of them share an intimate moment of understanding. Cassie describes the scene: '[Stacey's] eyes met Mr. Morrison's and the two of them smiled in subtle understanding, the distance between them fading' (96). Here we see the distinction between 'child' and 'adult' collapse. The 'child,' Stacey, acts in an 'adult' manner by taking responsibility for his actions. Mr. Morrison realizes this and acknowledges Stacey's autonomy. At this moment, the two exist on the same level, the boundary that separates the child and adult worlds is destabilized.

The most powerful example of unveiling racist power structures occurs after Cassie is pushed off of the sidewalk in Strawberry by Mr. Simms and made to apologize for being in the way of his daughter, Lillian Jean. Cassie is humiliated when Mr. Simms demands that she call Lillian Jean 'Miz.' When Cassie asks her mother why Mr. Simms pushes her, Mary explains, in clear, unveiled terms:

> 'Because he thinks Lillian Jean is better than you are, Cassie [. . .] I didn't say that Lillian Jean *is* better than you. I said Mr. Simms only *thinks* she is. In fact, he thinks that she's better than Stacey or Little Man or Christopher John—'
>
> 'Just 'cause she's his daughter?' I asked, beginning to think Mr. Simms was a bit touched in the head.
>
> 'No, baby, because she's white.'

139

Here we see the chance for Mary to shield her daughter from racism's harsh reality. She could play on Cassie's naivete and give her a coded answer, but she does not. She goes on to explain to Cassie the long history of racism that has led to the imbalance of power. She ends her description by telling Cassie that she may be forced to call Lillian Jean 'Miz,' but she will never be forced to respect her. She hints of a tactic for resistance and, thus, encourages her daughter's own subversive agency.

Mary says: ' "Baby, we have no choice of what color we're born or who our parents are or whether we're rich or poor. What we do have is some choice over what we make of our lives once we're here. . . . And I pray to God you'll make the best of yours" ' (142).

When David returns, Cassie seeks his advice about the situation. David says: ' "You know the Bible says you're s'pose to forgive these things. . . . S'pose to turn the other cheek. . . . But the way I see it, the Bible didn't mean for you to be no fool" ' (192). David goes on to explain to Cassie that there will be many things that she, like him, will be forced to do in order to survive. Then he says:

> 'But there are other things, Cassie, that if I'd let be, they'd eat away at me and destroy me in the end. And it's the same with you, baby. There are things you can't back down on, things you gotta take a stand on. But it's up to you to decide what them things are. You have to demand respect in this world, ain't nobody just gonna hand it to you. How you carry yourself, what you stand for – that's how you gain respect. But, little one, ain't nobody's respect worth more than your own. . . . Now, there ain't no sense in going around being mad. You clear your head so you can think sensibly. Then I want you to think real hard on whether or not Lillian Jean's worth taking a stand about, but keep in mind that

Lillian Jean probably won't be the last white person to treat you this way. . . . This here's an important decision, Cassie, very important – I want you to understand that – but I think you can handle it. Now, you listen to me, and you listen good. This thing, if you make the wrong decision and Charlie Simms gets involved, then I get involved and there'll be trouble.'

193–5

The scene is one of the most powerful displays of respect in the novel. David knows full well the extreme danger of the situation. He is aware that the wrong decision could put Cassie and the rest of the family in harm's way. Yet, he validates his daughter's feelings and her need for self-respect. He explains that there are always compromises to be made. One should always exercise caution when determining how to act. But, he lets Cassie know that he believes that some things are worth fighting for. He encourages her to take a stand against Lillian Jean but to be clever about it. In essence, he advises his daughter to be covert in orchestrating her revenge. He acknowledges her need for subjectivity and validates her anger and hurt pride. We see that he considers his daughter's self-worth to be extremely valuable and worth fighting for and allows her to make her own decision about exactly how to fight for it.

The historical timing of the novel

Taylor's desire is to be an agent in the further passing on of history, her personal history that, for her, is a shared, symbolic history, a history of African-American experience. She is engaged in the effort to supplement (and contradict) the history that for so many years since the abolition of slavery has been laid down in books by white writers.

The effort to reclaim history has been increasingly crucial for race theory. Taylor joins many who have worked to rewrite the history books to include more accurate and realistic information. Homi Bhabha stresses the importance of reclaiming history for minority cultures. In his essay, 'The Location of Culture' (1998), he discusses the concept of allowing memory to speak both the good and bad of history. For Bhabha, it is necessary to revive the past through an intense engagement with memory. He cites Toni Morrison's *Beloved* as such an attempt. The women in the novel engage in an effort to resurrect the history of slavery, its 'murderous rituals of possession and self-possession, in order to project a contemporary fable of a woman's history that is at the same time the narrative of an effective, historic memory of an emergent public sphere of men and women alike' (937). In *Beloved*, Scethe undergoes a process of reclaiming her personal history, which is an act of reclaiming slavery's painful past for African Americans. Bhabha feels that a people can only be freed from the burdens of history through this sort of intense engagement with the past.

This seems to be the project with which Taylor is engaged. She joins in the effort to reclaim and revive a specific, realistic African-American history. Much like the Logan elders, she demystifies history and unveils power structures for her readers. The effect of this intense engagement with the past is a new, radical history, one that has the potential to transform those who have been denied a connection to the past through the mystification and fabrication of history by the dominant culture.

The didacticism found in Taylor's fiction is meant to enable the minority culture to resist domination. Thus, the child characters are treated in a way that is very different from those of classic children's novels. Because of the necessity of resistance, they are given greater autonomy and treated as subjects, regardless of age. And, they work as active agents, just as their elders do. This destabilizes the distinction between childhood and adulthood upon which the didacticism of classical children's literature so firmly rests. It deconstructs the barrier between the two worlds. Whereas it is necessary to construct and maintain this barrier in classical children's literature, in Taylor's novel, born of specific social/historical forces, it becomes necessary to deconstruct it.

As a result of this process, children are encouraged to question authority. Rather than blindly accepting the conditions of their racist society, they are prompted to oppose the authority that is forced on them and view themselves as powerful agents of change. The racial specificity of Taylor's novel necessitates this type of child agency. Because minority children face a world that denies them power, both in childhood and adulthood, it is crucial for them to develop and exert their own subversive agency. As we see in the novel, this opens the possibility for becoming child *and* adult subjects, despite the attempts of the dominant culture.

References

Bhabha, Homi, 'The location of culture,' in *Literary Theory: An Anthology*, Julie Rivkin and Michael Ryan, eds. Malden, MA: Blackwell, 1998.

Rose, Jacqueline, *The Case of Peter Pan, or, The Impossibility of Children's Fiction.* Philadelphia: University of Pennsylvania Press, 1993.

Taylor, Mildred D., *Roll of Thunder, Hear My Cry.* London and New York: Puffin, [1976] 1995.

Wilder, Laura Ingalls, *Little House on the Prairie.* New York: Harper Collins, 1971.

The Role of Education in Mildred D. Taylor's *Roll of Thunder*
Cicely Denean Cobb

In *Song of the Trees*, Mildred D. Taylor first introduced the Logan family. Like Virginia Hamilton, Taylor relied on both social and psychological realism to depict how Blacks attempted to survive in the racist South, circa 1930. She explored such themes as racism, poverty, and family resilience. It is in *Roll of Thunder, Hear My Cry*, and *Let the Circle Be Unbroken* that Taylor highlighted a fourth theme – the Logan family's emphasis on formal and informal education. Encoding education as a primary concern in southern Black families, Taylor's fiction became the first children's literature family saga to address the role that education would take in twentieth-century African American culture. Furthermore, Taylor showed her readers Black adult attitudes about the formal lessons children learn at school and compared them with the informal ones they learned from their elders and neighbors. Taylor was the first African American children's writer to address the importance of this theme.

In his poignant autobiography, *The Narrative of the Life of Frederick Douglass*, the Black abolitionist notes his slaveowner's sentiments regarding Blacks and education: 'If you give a nigger an inch, they'll take an ell' (45). One hundred years later, the vast majority of southern Whites continued to adhere to the same doctrine. As historian James D. Anderson states in *The Education of Blacks in the South, 1860–1935*, it was difficult for a significant number of southern African American men to achieve an education. Their parents sharecropped; southern society expected that Black boys would also partake in the humiliating cycle (79). Black male adolescents' education revolved around picking cotton and other farm tasks. If some African American boys were able to seek a formal education, it was usually a limited one (55). White northern philanthropists became interested in educating the southern Negro and stated that their primary goal was to 'challenge racism,' but they fostered its growth by demanding that Black formal education adhere to the doctrines of the Hampton-Tuskegee model (55).[1] This so-called 'right' way of educating African Americans benefited Whites by providing them with a 'sound investment in social stability and

Extracted from ' "If You Give a Nigger an Inch, They Will Take an Ell": The Role of Education in Mildred D. Taylor's *Roll of Thunder*', in P. Henderson and J. May (2005), *Exploring Culturally Diverse Literature for Children and Adolescents: Learning to Listen in New Ways* (Boston: Pearson Education, 2005), pp. 196–204.

economic security' (79). Thus, a vast majority of these students were incapable of achieving well-paying jobs. Despite gaining education, Black males remained 'good field hands' (81). Mildred D. Taylor's series shows that Black males were educated for manual labor.

The Logan men were modeled after Taylor's paternal relatives. While living in Mississippi, Mr. Taylor endured psychological pain from social injustice.[2] Formal education was not an option for him; work would be his key to social and economic mobility. An emphasis was placed on his informal education. This knowledge was derived from the daily experiences of life as a southern Negro. Throughout the Logan series, Mildred D. Taylor suggests that southern Black men who were from her father's generation probably benefited more from informal education than from formal education. These Black men used a wealth of 'plain common sense' as they faced prejudice and attempted to survive in such a 'racist culture' (Crowe 8).

Within the saga, Taylor demonstrates the importance of education to the southern Black family, and she openly acknowledges the role that Black women played in education. Mary Logan emphasizes the need for her children to receive a formal education. Throughout the series, Mary Logan is linked to formal education, whereas David Logan is linked to family education.[3] Papa Logan teaches his family that they should be watchful of both present conditions and past episodes that have shaped their experiences. They must have a 'wary eye upon the present, but yet another turned toward the past' (Smith 246). Thus, Taylor is true to southern history in her depiction of females and education. In *What a Woman Ought to Be and to Do*, Stephanie J. Shaw argues that, during this era, the only options that were available to the vast majority of Black women were marriage and/or domestic work and teaching (5). Aware that marriage 'unequivocally limited women to the home,' a small percentage of African American women sent their daughters away from the South in order to receive a formal education (47).

In *Roll of Thunder, Hear My Cry* and *Let the Circle Be Unbroken*, Mildred D. Taylor demonstrates the influences that grandmothers and mothers have on their daughters. After reading these novels and Chris Crowe's analysis of Taylor's works, one realizes that Big Ma is modeled after Taylor's maternal grandmothers – the 'wise ones'; Mama is modeled after Taylor's mother, whom she describes as 'the quiet, lovely one, who urged perseverance' (qtd. in Crowe 26). Thus, Taylor fictionalizes her personal experiences in these novels. She shows how limitations prevented the elder Taylors from accomplishing their goals; they relied on Mildred Taylor to execute them through her education and writing. Taylor reveals how both Big Ma and Mama – two women who were denied the full chance to 'bloom' – rely on Cassie, their 'strong-willed, plain-spoken and full of energy' granddaughter/daughter, to reject her 'fallen dead' role in order to become the 'tree' that refuses to be moved (MacCann 95).

In a sense, Cassie becomes these women's – and Taylor's – mouthpiece. This is especially important when looking at Big Ma. Her own daughter died in infancy. Thus, she was unable to preach the 'great sermon' to her. Cassie is essential to her. Both of Cassie's matriarchs realize that without an education, Cassie will 'have few economic alternatives' (Shaw i). Cassie's two educations enable her to believe that 'regardless of the limitations that others might impose on her (due to her race, class, and sex), none of these conditions necessarily determined her ability and aspiration' (i). Cassie's education will allow her to pass a legacy on to her daughters – and she will show them 'what [they] ought to be and to do' (3). The roots of their training will allow Cassie to survive, even when she leaves the South.[4] Taylor's young heroine becomes educated and independent within the series, and she is able to define a new position for educated African American women.

A small minority of Black southern women hoped that their children would receive a formal education, especially those female workers who had daughters, in opposition to a statistically significant number of African American women who believed that their daughters, too, would embark on the endless cycle of Black female drudgery. Black mothers who advocated for female emancipation from America's 'controlling images for black women' (Collins 45–67) wished to see their daughters formally educated in either the North or the South. Furthermore, some southern African American women used their 'community work' as the means to foster the 'black women's activist tradition' (143).[5] In 1980, Bonnie Thornton Dill studied domestic workers and their children, and she noted that some southern Black domestics and field laborers viewed their work as enabling their daughters to strive for opportunities that appeared to be unobtainable. Taylor's fiction reflects this urge for formal education found among a small group of southern Black women.

Over the years, scholars have questioned Mildred D. Taylor's motive for writing the Logan family series. When considering the historical events that occurred around the time that *Roll of Thunder, Hear My Cry* was published – events such as busing and school integration that had a tremendous impact on African American children – as well as Taylor's personal childhood, it should be no surprise that Taylor saw the need to create positive images of African Americans who overcame racial adversity as they strived for equality. Taylor had faced a number of racial problems while growing up. At age 8 (the same age as Cassie Logan), Mildred D.

Taylor experienced her 'first lessons about racism' (Crowe 117). Crowe writes:

> As a young child, she always loved her family's regular trips to Mississippi, viewing the trip itself as a 20-hour picnic. Later, she realized that her mother packed food to take along in the car because after they left Ohio, they wouldn't be allowed to eat in 'White Only' restaurants. She realized that they drove straight through because they wouldn't be allowed to stay in 'White Only' hotels or motels along the way to Mississippi. She learned that the police stopped her father in the South not for speeding or any other traffic violation but for being a black man driving a nice new car. She saw the signs, 'White Only, Colored Not Allowed' over restroom doors and drinking fountains. On her trips to Mississippi she learned much about her family and her heritage, but she also learned about racial discrimination in the South.
>
> 117

Taylor experienced similar problems when her family took a trip to California. Because they were traveling to the West Coast, Taylor assumed that her family would endure fewer racial problems. She was 'partially right' (118). Although the Taylors 'saw no signs barring "Coloreds" from businesses,' they were not allowed to stay at certain hotels and restaurants. That trip taught the ten-year-old Mildred D. Taylor that for 'black Americans second-class citizenship was not restricted to the South' (118).

Mildred D. Taylor's juvenile fiction accurately records her experiences and memories and emphasizes that Black women were intent on gaining formal education while maintaining informal family education within their southern Black society. In *Roll of Thunder, Hear My Cry*, Mildred D. Taylor explores the lessons that she learned both at school and at home, allowing the Logan children, but especially Cassie, to receive similar treatment.

Cassie is a winsome protagonist who serves as Taylor's astute female narrator.[6] The novel details one year of the Logans' traumas living as a strong and loving African American family in rural Mississippi during the times studied by Anderson and Collins. She aptly shows that southern Black families understood the importance of informal and formal education. When placing Cassie in scenes with her male siblings, Taylor alludes to the differences in male and female perceptions of education. Taylor contrasts Little Man's obsession with his appearance with Cassie's practical attitude. When the children are running late to school, Cassie warns them about the repercussions of being late:

> 'You keep it up and make us late for school, Mama's gonna wear you out,' I threatened, pulling with exasperation at the high collar of the Sunday dress Mama had made me wear on the first day – as if that event were something special. It seemed to me that showing up at school at all on a bright August-like October morning

made for running the cool forest trails and wading barefoot in the forest pond was concession enough; Sunday clothing was asking too much. Christopher-John and Stacey were not too pleased about the clothing or school either. Only Little Man, just beginning his school career, found the prospects of both intriguing.

1–2

The student body is composed of children who are needed in the fields from early spring until the cotton is picked. Thus, Great Faith 'adjusts its terms accordingly beginning in October and dismissing in March' (15). Each academic year, the student enrollment diminishes.

Cassie's mother is an outsider in this community, and she is outspoken about Black education. Her daughter is also assertive, as is noted in the incident involving Miss Crocker and Little Man. During Cassie's altercation with Gracey Pearson and Alma Scott, one senses that the protagonist's sassiness has caused her to be reprimanded on more than one occasion. When Miss Crocker overhears the girls' argument, Taylor writes, the 'yellow and buckeyed fourth grade teacher glares down [at Cassie . . .] with a look that say Soooo, it's you, Cassie Logan' (18). Miss Crocker's other nonverbal gesture – the pursing of her lips – signals that she is exasperated at having Mary Logan's rebellious daughter as her student. Taylor shows regional differences between Cassie's mother and the other teachers when Cassie refuses to join in unison with her classmates and say, 'Yes'm, Miz Crocker' (20). A third incident confirms the teacher's disgust with Cassie's informal upbringing. Miss Crocker announces that each student will receive a textbook. The readers are from the White elementary school. Immediately, Cassie realizes that Little Man is going to be displeased with the condition of his primer:

> I glanced across at Little Man, his face lit in eager excitement. I knew that he could not see the soiled covers or the marred pages from where he sat, and even though his penchant for cleanliness was often annoying, I did not like to think of his disappointment when he saw the books as they really were. But there was nothing that I could do about it, so I opened my book to its center and began browsing through the spotted pages.
>
> 22

Unsurprisingly, Little Man informs the instructor that the book is 'dirty' (23). Taylor's more mature narrator comes to her brother's defense, establishing that Cassie is her siblings' deliverer. Within the confines of the school, Cassie is learning to speak out for what is right, and she is learning the consequences when she does or does not voice her concerns.

In terms of informal education, the Logan children are taught by their parents, Big Ma, and Mr. Morrison. The elders educate them about the ordeals that both their family and neighbors have endured. The various lessons that the children are taught range from the family's rich history to the hardships that are associated with being Negro (e.g., inequality from social institutions – 'the judicial system, health and law enforcement agencies'), and that Blacks should not befriend Whites (MacCann 94; Crowe 124).

Although the children have been educated about the consequences that occur when a Black person does not remain in his or her place, none of them has personally dealt with the blunt force of White brutality. While in Mr. Barnett's store, it is Cassie, not her brothers, who is reminded of her subordinate state:

> After waiting several minutes for his return, Stacey said, 'Come on, Cassie, let's get out of here.' He started toward the door and I followed. But as we passed one of the counters, I spied Mr. Barnett wrapping an order of pork chops for a white girl. Adults were one thing; I could almost understand that. They ruled things and there was nothing that could be done about them. But some kid who was no bigger than me was something else again. Certainly Mr. Barnett had simply forgotten about T.J.'s order. I decided to remind him and, without saying anything to Stacey, I turned around and marched over to Mr. Barnett.
>
> 121

Taylor's main character reacts as any child would if faced with a prejudicial incident. However, when Cassie attempts to inform the storeowner of his error, he reminds Cassie that she is nothing but someone's 'little nigger' (11). Despite the fact that her family has owned land in Spokane County for over fifty years, Cassie is merely a child whose mother needs to remind her of her place within southern society.

In essence, Mildred D. Taylor demonstrates how the vast majority of women in southern Black families had to rely on social and psychological networks in order to survive racial discrimination. In *Roll of Thunder, Hear My Cry*, Cassie's need to receive both a formal and informal education is stressed. Throughout her series, Mildred D. Taylor shows her youthful readers the trials and heartaches of southern prejudice. She places Black history at the forefront and shows how Cassie 'takes an ell' through her informal and formal education. In doing so, Taylor shows her readers how to 'be' like Cassie, and, most importantly, how to function effectively in American society.

Notes

1. This model placed an emphasis on industrial rather than classical education.
2. In his critical study of Mildred D. Taylor and her work, Chris Crowe states that Taylor's father fled Jackson, Mississippi, because of a racial incident that occurred at his job. When

Taylor was three weeks old, her father punched a White coworker. Thus, the decision for Wilbert Taylor to leave the South was 'essentially made for him.' The character, Uncle Hammer, is 'patterned after [Taylor's] two legendary great-uncles who had shown great courage growing up in Mississippi' (2).

3. Taylor credits her father for providing her with the informal stories and values (concerning their family) that are found in her novels. Taylor describes her father as a man who 'shared with his [family] the wisdom and insight of his own experiences' (qtd. in Crowe 30).

4. Trees are important symbols for Taylor. The title of her first novel is *Song of Trees*. For Taylor, trees are a symbol of resilience. Thus, it is not coincidental that Taylor coins the name 'Logan' for her characters.

5. Community work, in Collins's text, refers to participation in organizations such as church groups and quilting bees, imagery that has been used by southern Black female writers.

6. Cassie is drawn from Taylor's family stories. According to Chris Crowe, Taylor used her Aunt Sadie and her (Taylor's) sister Wilma as her model for Cassie (36).

References

Anderson, James A. *The Education of Blacks in the South, 1860–1935*. Chapel Hill, NC: University of North Carolina Press, 1988.

Collins, Patricia Hill. *Black Feminist Thought: Knowledge, Consciousness, and the Politics of Empowerment*. New York: Routledge, 1991.

Crowe, Chris. *Presenting Mildred D. Taylor*: New York: Twayne Publishers, 1999.

Dill, Bonnie Thornton and Maxine Bacca Zinn, ed. *Women of Color in U.S. Society*. Philadelphia: Temple University Press, 1994.

Douglass, Frederick. *The Narrative of the Life of Frederick Douglass*. Ed. William L. Andrews and William S. McFeely. New York: Norton, 1997.

MacCann, Donnarae. 'The Family Chronicles of Mildred D. Taylor and Mary Mebane.' *Journal of African Children's & Youth Literature* 3 (1991–1992): 93–104.

Shaw, Stephanie J. *What a Woman Ought to Be and to Do: Black Professional Women Workers During the Jim Crow Era*. Chicago: The University of Chicago Press, 1996.

Smith, Karen Patricia. 'A Chronicle of Family Honor: Balancing Rage and Triumph in the Novels of Mildred D. Taylor.' In *African-American Voices in Young Adult Literature: Tradition, Transition, Transformation*. Ed. Karen Patricia Smith Metuchen, NJ: Scarecrow Press, 2001: 246–76.

Taylor, Mildred D. *Let the Circle Be Unbroken*. New York: Dial, 1981.

———. *Roll of Thunder, Hear My Cry*. New York and London: Puffin [1976] 1995.

9

Philip Pullman, *Northern Lights* (1995)

Introduction
Heather Montgomery

Northern Lights is the first novel of Pullman's trilogy, *His Dark Materials*. First published in 1995 in the UK and in 1996 in North America, where it was retitled *The Golden Compass*, it was followed by *The Subtle Knife* in 1997 and in 2000 by *The Amber Spyglass*. *Northern Lights* has sold more than 12 million copies worldwide, and won numerous awards. In 2007 it was voted by the public as the best children's book of the last 70 years in the 'Carnegie of Carnegies' (although Pullman himself felt that the accolade should have gone to *Tom's Midnight Garden*). It tells the story of 12-year-old Lyra Belacqua and her epic journey north to find her missing friend Roger, and her imprisoned father, Lord Asriel. Enjoyed by adults and children alike, it is sometimes classified as a crossover novel, although its mixture of fantasy and realism, science and theology, and its use of intertexts defies easy categorisation. There has been a highly acclaimed stage adaptation of *His Dark Materials*, which premiered at the National Theatre in 2003, and a less successful film version which appeared in 2006.

Origins and composition

Pullman wrote his first book, entitled *The Haunted Storm*, in 1972. By the time *Northern Lights* came out he was a well-established writer for both adults and children, most famous for his Sally Lockhart quartet which begins with *The Ruby in the Smoke* (1985). Pullman draws his inspiration from a number of sources, most notably William Blake and John

Milton, from whose poem *Paradise Lost* he takes the title of his trilogy. Pullman has described how *Northern Lights* and his other writings come into being, and the way that these other authors influence and inspire him: 'Books and stories don't just emerge from nothing in a sort of mental Big Bang. They grow more like plants, from a seed that's nourished by a rich and fertile soil. All my books have come out of the background of my own reading and from the things I've seen, or heard, or done, or thought about' (Pullman, n.d., a).

Reception/critical terrain

A large body of critical literature has developed around Pullman's work and *Northern Lights* has been examined in terms of its theology, its intertextuality, and whether or not it can best be seen as fantasy or psychological realism. It is distinctive in that Pullman has himself engaged in lively dialogue with the critics.

Pullman himself has claimed that he does not write fantasy and deals only with 'real' human characters. He has said: 'If I write fantasy, it's only because by using the mechanisms of fantasy I can say something a little more vividly about, for example, the business of growing up' (Rustin and Rustin, 2003: 93). Taking his books as a reflection of psychological reality, Margaret and Michael Rustin have read *Northern Lights* as an examination of domestic family relationships and the psychic interplay between parents and children. They have analysed it in terms of what it says about fundamental questions of belonging, parent–child relationships, personality formation and Freudian understandings of sexuality. They point out how deeply damaged and dysfunctional Lyra's family is and analyse the book as her search for better and more loving adult role models, be they Iorek the bear, Lee Scoresby, Serafina Pekkala or the dons at Jordan College, Oxford:

> The ambivalence of parental adults towards growing children is a primary theme of *Northern Lights*. Lyra's parents demonstrate an interest in her which is deeply damaged by its narcissist elements: she exists in their minds very little as a person in her own right, but more as a creature serving their needs of one sort or another. The college, by contrast, has provided love and care determined in a rough and ready way by Lyra's needs, a setting in which she can grow up to be herself.
>
> Rustin and Rustin, 2003: 94–5

Pullman has come in for criticism from those who view his depictions of adult/child roles and relationships negatively. Kristine Moruzi, for instance, has claimed that 'Pullman fails to offer any genuinely new ideas of the world with respect to adult–child relationships and the roles that children play in society' (2005: 55–6). She sees Pullman's vision as essentially conservative, supporting a status quo in which children must bow to adult authority and where their role is to obey and follow destiny rather than change it: 'Pullman's insistence on the subordination of children becomes ... problematic because he fails to understand the reality of life for his child audience and resists a genuine re-conceptualization of contemporary society' (2005: 67). Others have been critical of the ways in which *His Dark Materials* trilogy deals with theological questions of creation and eschatology, faith and the role of God in human's lives, objecting to the portrayal of God in *The Amber Spyglass* as senile, exhausted and dying. Pullman's treatment of organised religion has been particularly controversial and he has accordingly been called 'the most dangerous author in Britain' (Hitchens, 2003), while the Catholic Church has condemned Pullman's writings as anti-Christian and accused him of promoting a vision of the world which leaves no room for hope. In this respect, he has been accused of being overtly didactic, although he denies this charge, claiming: 'I'm not in the message business; I'm in the "Once upon a time" business' (Pullman, n.d., b).

His denial of an explicit ideological and moral agenda is disingenuous, however. Not only, as Peter Hunt argues, is it 'impossible for a children's book (especially one being read by a child) not to be educational or influential in some way; it cannot help but reflect an ideology and, by extension, didacticism' (1994: 3), but Pullman himself has elsewhere been happy to state his position explicitly:

> The trouble is that all too often in human history, churches and priesthoods have set themselves up to rule people's lives in the name of some invisible god (and they're all invisible, because they don't exist) – and done terrible damage. In the name of their god, they have burned, hanged, tortured, maimed, robbed, violated, and enslaved millions of their fellow-creatures, and done so with the happy conviction that they were doing the will of God, and they would go to Heaven for it. That is the religion I hate, and I'm happy to be known as its enemy.
>
> Pullman, n.d., a.

Pullman has deliberately set himself up against writers such as C.S. Lewis, whose Christian allegories, *The Chronicles of Narnia*, he despises. He has described Lewis's books as 'rather hateful propaganda for prigs and bullies', going on to describe them as 'profoundly racist': 'they are misogynistic, he hates women and girls, he thinks they are no good at all, they are weak, they are useless, they are stupid. In fact he hates life basically, because at the end of them the greatest reward these children have is to be taken away... and killed in a railway accident' (Pullman, 2002). For all his anti-Christian vehemence, however, there are others who see him as less atheistic than he might wish to appear:

> Indifference is certainly a far greater enemy to Christianity than atheism. The atheist still cares about God, even if he wants him dead. There is a kind of piety in atheism. It is this piety that keeps soaking through into the fabric of Philip Pullman's fiction. Even in his rejection of religion, in his hatred of the church and his contempt for God, Pullman is still asking theological questions and finding comfort in theological answers.
>
> Rayment-Pickard, 2004: 88

The essays

The three essays selected here from an increasingly crowded field deal with different aspects of Pullman's work and are representative in their concerns of the themes that have received most critical attention. Anne-Marie Bird takes one of Pullman's key concepts, Dust, and traces its antecedents in both Milton and Blake before looking at how Pullman rejects absolute dichotomies between good and evil, spirit and body. Naomi Wood discusses the links between Pullman and C.S. Lewis. Finally, Clare Squires looks at one of the central aspects of Pullman's work, his use of intertextuality and the influences of other authors.

Intertextuality is a central concern in all of these essays and the ways in which Pullman uses other works to give his books a particular authenticity and to situate them in a particular tradition are important. By drawing heavily on Milton and Blake, Pullman situates himself as part of a long tradition of religious dissent, which is thrown into sharper relief by comparison with the conservatism and religious orthodoxy of C.S. Lewis. In this regard all three essays deal with the same issues of sources and Pullman's role in the wider canon. They move away from any simplistic understanding of the 'meanings' or 'messages' of *Northern Lights*, concentrating instead on the book as a literary creation.

References

Hitchens, P. 2003. 'Is This the Most Dangerous Author in Britain?' *The Mail on Sunday*, 25 June.

Hunt, P. 1994. *An Introduction to Children's Literature*. Oxford, Oxford University Press.

Moruzi, K. 2005. 'Missed Opportunities: The Subordination of Children in Philip Pullman's *His Dark Materials*', *Children's Literature in Education*, 36, 55–68.

Pullman, P. n.d. a. *About the Worlds*. http://www.philip-pullman.com/about_the_worlds.asp, accessed 27 November 2008.

Pullman, P. n.d. b. *About the Books*. http://www.philip-pullman.com/about_the_worlds.asp, accessed 27 November 2008.

Pullman, P. 2002. 'Interview with Philip Pullman,' recorded at *The Readers' and Writers' Roadshow*, Hay-on-Wye, broadcast on Radio 4, 11 July.

Rayment-Pickard, H. 2004. *The Devil's Account: Philip Pullman and Christianity*. London, Darton, Longman & Todd.

Rustin, M. and Rustin, M. 2003. 'Where is Home? An Essay on Philip Pullman's Northern Lights (Volume 1 of *His Dark Materials*)', *Journal of Child Psychotherapy*, 29, 93–105.

Further reading

Hunt, P. and Lenz, M. 2001. *Alternative Worlds in Fantasy Fiction*. London, Continuum.

Lenz, M. and Scott, C. 2005. *His Dark Materials Illuminated: Critical Essays on Philip Pullman's Trilogy*. Detroit, Wayne State University Press.

Squires, C. 2006. *Philip Pullman, Master Storyteller: A Guide to the Worlds of* His Dark Materials. London, Continuum.

Tucker, N. 2007. *Darkness Visible: Inside the World of Philip Pullman*. London, Wizard.

Dust as Metaphor in Philip Pullman
Anne-Marie Bird

Few myths have had such an immensely powerful and prevailing influence on the Western imagination, or have generated quite so many retellings, as the Judeo-Christian myth of the Fall. One reason for its endurance lies in the fact that it provides a series of answers to the most basic and profound questions such as how the universe was made, how humanity began, and why suffering and death entered the world. Another reason for its pervasive influence is that like other myths (and especially cosmogonic myths), it is built on a system of classification – the notion that creation is a matter of naming, a matter of making distinctions, and of articulating opposites – in an attempt to organise or make sense of the universe. Indeed, the Genesis narrative opens with the concept of separation: God 'divided the light from the darkness,' the heaven from the earth and the day from the night. This idea of division continues in chapters 2 and 3 of Genesis as humanity's transgression of God's law leads to further, more ideologically loaded binary opposites, namely, innocence-experience, good-evil and spirit-matter.

Finding elements of their inspiration in the biblical story of the Fall and John Milton's elaboration of this narrative in *Paradise Lost*, Philip Pullman's 'His Dark Materials' trilogy (*Northern Lights* – or, in North America, *The Golden Compass* – *The Subtle Knife*, and *The Amber Spyglass*)[1] makes use

---

Extracted from 'Without Contraries is no Progression': Dust as an All-inclusive, Multi-functional Metaphor in Philip Pullman's "His Dark Materials"', in *Children's Literature in Education* 32:2 (2001), pp. 111–23.

of this myth on several levels. On a simplistic level, the books can be read as straightforward adventure stories in that they involve difficult journeys in which the protagonists must confront numerous challenges in the search for some object, place, or person. On a deeper level, the texts are an exploration of the fundamental themes of the Fall: initiation and the passage from innocence to experience, the nature of good and evil, the consequences of knowledge, and the notion of free will or individual responsibility. From this perspective, the books are representative of the adolescent 'rites of passage' narrative in which the most important journey is not an external event but an inner one concerning the child's journey toward adulthood.

However, if we investigate Pullman's treatment of these themes, it becomes apparent that, like the God of Genesis, human beings are also concerned with the idea of division or separation. Drawing on motifs found within Gnostic mythology and the poetry of William Blake – particularly Blake's concept of 'Contraries' – Pullman attempts to synthesise the opposing principles that lie at the core of the myth while leaving the innocence-experience dichotomy firmly in place. The effect of this is to transpose what is, in traditional Christian readings, a paradigm of disobedience and divine punishment into a scheme of self-development. The key to this ontological scheme is 'Dust,' a conventional metaphor for human physicality inspired by God's judgment on humanity: 'for dust thou *art*, and unto dust shalt thou return' (Genesis, 3:19). Underpinning the concept of Dust is Milton's metaphor for the mass of unformed primal matter left over from the construction of the universe; in other words, the 'dark materials' of *Paradise Lost* (II, 1.916). In Pullman's narrative, however, Dust contains much more than the beginning and end of humanity's physical existence or the origins of the universe.

Organising Milton's dark materials: dust as a means of classification

The very term, *Dust*, is highly ambiguous. Its indistinctness lies in its intrinsic amorphousness. Consequently, it is an extremely adaptable concept, offering an almost infinite number of possibilities or meanings. To the God of Genesis, Dust contains mankind's origins and is literally the substance that marks his demise. Pullman, however, uses the word in order to connect the plethora of seemingly incompatible elements that make up the universe. The desire to connect everything with everything else manifests itself on every level of the texts. For example, the setting for the narrative – its 'uncountable billions of parallel worlds' (*NL*, p. 374), none hierarchically superior, but 'interpenetrating with this one' (*NL*, p. 187) – epitomises the attempt to link together, and therefore equalises everything in its most simplistic form.

Striving to unite all things is more complex, however, when it is attempted through one metaphor in which all concepts, physical and metaphysical, apparently exist in parallel. In the first book, Dust is described as 'a new kind of elementary particle' (*NL*, p. 368), yet it functions as a metaphor for 'original sin' (*NL*, p. 369) and is experienced by Lyra as 'dark intentions, like the forms of thoughts not yet born' (p. 389). In the second text, Dust operates in both a literal and a metaphorical sense. Described by the particle physicists in a twentieth century research laboratory as 'dark matter' (*SK*, p. 90), Dust appears to correspond to the scientific phenomenon known as cosmic dust: the small particles of matter that are distributed throughout space and which, according to current theories of cosmology, make up at least ninety percent of the mass of the universe. In short, Dust is the actual physical 'stuff' that holds the universe together.

There is an obvious correspondence here between Dust as 'dark matter' and the 'dark materials' of Milton's *Paradise Lost* (which Pullman quotes in the epigraph to *Northern Lights*):

> ... Into this wild abyss,
> The womb of nature and perhaps her grave,
> Of neither sea, nor shore, nor air, nor fire,
> But all these in their pregnant causes mixed
> Confusedly, and which thus must ever fight,
> Unless the almighty maker them ordain
> His dark materials to create more worlds,
> Into this wild abyss the wary fiend
> Stood on the brink of hell and looked a while,
> Pondering his voyage ...

II, ll. 910–19

In Milton's text, the idea that God can 'create more worlds' by ordering or rearranging the primal matter left over from the creation is clearly not meant to be interpreted in a literal or scientifically accurate sense. What it does suggest is that the dark materials are brimming with almost limitless potential that merely awaits the Maker's transmutation. Moreover, in Milton's work the metaphor of dark materials is extended with the suggestion that the material that comprises the bulk of the universe's mass is made up of sentient particles in a state of rebellion. This is where Milton's metaphor ends. In the second book of Pullman's trilogy, the rebellious atoms of *Paradise Lost* are organised and arranged further, evolving into a system of classification that involves the entire spectrum ranging from pure matter to pure spirit – 'Dust,' 'dark matter,' 'Shadows,' 'shadow-particles,' 'particles of consciousness' (pp. 90–2) and 'rebel angels' (p. 260) – ultimately becoming the 'inheritance' of all human beings in the final book (p. 497).

The slippage between one concept and another, from one end of the spectrum to the other, and between the metaphorical and the literal, transforms Dust from the familiar closed configuration bequeathed to humanity by God into an open structure. Indeed, by developing Milton's 'dark materials' into an extremely composite metaphor, Pullman is suggesting that every elementary particle of Dust contains the entire universe (which is, in turn, akin to the Blakean metaphor, 'To see a World in a Grain of Sand'). Thus, having established what Dust includes – the numerous terms involved – we must turn our attention to how it functions in the trilogy.

Mind–body duality: toward an integration

Religious dualism – the doctrine that the world comprises two basic, diametrically opposed principles – is generally associated with Gnosticism. For example, Gnostic myth and metaphor centre around the dualities of light and dark, spirit and matter, and good and evil: the fundamental belief being that the spirit is 'good' and matter is 'evil.' However, the distinction between good and evil, or spirit and matter, is not only a distinguishing Gnostic characteristic, but is just as notably a feature of traditional Christianity in which the irreconcilable nature of the opposites arises from their moral emphasis. There is no such simple theological dichotomy in Pullman's texts. Rather, his work strives to convince the reader of the interconnectedness of these particular conceptual opposites.

The integration of the spiritual and the material is demonstrated most effectively by Pullman's innovative depiction of the human soul. However, before specifically exploring this, it will be useful to attempt to define the soul. According to conventional Cartesian philosophy, the soul is the immaterial 'I' that confers individuality and is often considered to be synonymous with the mind. In mainstream Christian theology, the soul is further defined as that part of the human that partakes of divinity. Pullman's interpretation of the human soul includes all but one of these definitions and brings us to what is perhaps the most striking characteristic of the world of *Northern Lights*.

In this world, every human has a 'dæmon' which is both visible and audible – a kind of 'familiar' in animal form, usually of the opposite sex to its human counterpart (the physical realisation of the Jungian idea that we have an *anima*, or *animus* which is part of our soul). However, the significance of the external soul is that it explicitly foregrounds the notion of dualism – the belief that the human being consists of two opposing and independent 'substances' – while maintaining that the body and soul are completely interrelated. Thus, the texts emphasise that human and dæmon are one being, linked by an invisible, telepathic bond, as is illustrated when Lyra tells her dæmon, Pantalaimon: 'I didn't have anything in mind and well you know it' (*NL*, p. 9). Their complete integration is reiterated in Lyra's statement: 'Your dæmon en't *separate* from you. It's you' (*SK*, p. 26), thereby echoing the Socratic and Platonic belief that the soul is synonymous with the 'essential' person, or the 'true' self.

The trilogy's insistence on diversity in unity suggests that denying difference in order to unite opposing principles is not part of Pullman's agenda. In fact, it could be argued that denying difference is not only impossible, but that difference has an important function in the texts. This brings us back to Dust and the narrative's basis in the Fall myth. It also brings us to another important aspect of the external soul. In book 1, we are told that the dæmon possesses a metamorphic ability to alter its form to reflect and, at times, to avoid betraying the emotions of its human counterpart – an ability that lasts until puberty, when 'dæmons lost the power to change and assumed one shape, keeping it permanently' (*NL*, p. 49). The difference between the adult's dæmon and the child's is caused by Dust, which, 'during the years of puberty they [the children] begin to attract ... more strongly' (*NL*, p. 368). Dust, therefore, is believed to accumulate in ever-increasing quantities during adolescence, its function being to act as some kind of catalyst that initiates the child's journey toward adulthood. It is when Dust has finally 'settled' on the individual that the dæmon acquires a definitive form that most accurately reflects the essential nature of the person. The narrative links this phenomenon directly to the Fall of 'man' with the idea that the 'fixed' dæmon is 'physical proof that something happened when innocence changed into experience' (*NL*, p. 370).

The transition from innocence to experience can be interpreted in two ways. The negative view is represented in the trilogy by the powerful and punitive Church. As far as the Church is concerned, Dust must be 'the physical evidence for original sin' (*NL*, p. 369) – the disastrous moment when the gulf between innocence and experience was traversed with the result that Adam and Eve's 'eyes were opened' and they became aware of their nakedness; a condition that, in terms of traditional Christian interpretations, became connected with guilt, shame, and sin. To the Church then, Dust symbolises the awakening of sexual awareness, humanity's rejection of the heavenly for the earthly, and thus, a descent from spirit to matter.

In order to disturb the value-laden Christian hierarchy of spirit and matter, Pullman is concerned to demonstrate the interdependency of soul and body. To this end, the texts present a more literal realisation of the descent from spirit to matter, through the 'severed' child in the first book and the severed adults in the second. As far as Mrs. Coulter (an agent of the Church) and her organisation, the 'Oblation Board,' are concerned, it is imperative to prolong the child's state of innocence, and in their view, the most effective method of preventing Dust from settling on the child is to separate the body from the dæmon before the onset of puberty – a castration of sorts, referred to as '*intercision*' (*NL*, p. 213), and '*cutting*' (*NL*, p. 372). The result is a permanent end to any imminent sexual awakening. As Mrs. Coulter tells Lyra:

> 'All that happens is a little cut, and then everything's peaceful. For ever! You see, your dæmon's a wonderful friend and companion when you're young, but at the age we call puberty ... dæmons bring all sorts of troublesome thoughts and feelings, and that's what lets Dust in.'

> *NL*, pp. 282–3

This 'little cut' has the opposite effect to the castration complex described by Freud. In his theory, the threat of castration enables the child to grow up. The Church's intention is to halt this process – to prevent the Dust or 'troublesome thoughts' ever entering by literally cutting away the soul, thus rendering mind and body as 'separate entities' (*NL*, p. 273).

However, preventing the child's development toward adulthood is merely one effect of intercision. Another is related to the complex question of the human personality: the notion that it is the soul that makes us human, or 'truly alive.' This idea seems to be derived from Aristotle's statement that the soul is 'the first principle of living things,' or as Lyra tells Will: 'You have got a dæmon ... Inside you ... You wouldn't be human else. You'd be ... half-dead' (*SK*, p. 26). Thus, the psychic damage incurred following intercision could be described as the destruction of the human being's identity as a human, while the person remains alive only on some purely physical level. This is evident during Lyra's encounter with the severed child, as when confronted by metaphysical absence, Lyra suffers what Freud would describe as an uncanny experience, doubting 'whether an apparently animate being is really alive':

> Her first impulse was to turn and run, or to be sick. A human being with no dæmon was like someone without a face, or with their ribs laid open and their heart torn out.

> *NL*, p. 214

Dust as a dynamic, unsettling principle

The idea that the separation of body and soul constitutes a 'psychic death,' a descent from 'human being' to 'non-being,' is expanded by the suggestion that the severed individual not only lacks a soul but is deprived of Dust: 'the energy that links body and dæmon' (*NL*, p. 373). Dust, therefore, does not only initiate the child's development toward adulthood, but remains as an underlying energy vital to human existence in general, without which, 'it would all vanish. Thought, imagination, feeling, would all wither and blow away, leaving nothing but a brute automatism' (*AS*, p. 476). [T]he nurses at Bolvangar experimental station have also undergone intercision. Following the 'operation' the dæmons are returned to the nurses. However, the mere possession of a soul is not as important as the psychic bond – the Dust – that forms some energic point of contact between human and dæmon; when this link is no longer present, the status of the dæmon is reduced to that of 'a little trotting pet ... [which] seemed to be sleepwalking' (*NL*, pp. 282), while the nurses themselves are totally indifferent too, having 'a brisk, blank, sensible air' (*NL*, p. 238).

Given that intercision is final, the individuals who have undergone this operation can never possess full subjectivity; thus they cannot become 'dangerously independent' (*AS*, p. 63), but instead are slaves to the oppressive Church. Therefore, like Blake, who railed against orthodox religion ('... the priest lays his curse on the fairest joys'), the State, and authority in general ('... God & his Priest & King / Who make up a heaven of our misery'), Pullman's narrative denounces the Church and its Oblation Board, or 'Gobblers' (*NL*, p. 90) – a combination of Church and State – which denies the child the opportunity to develop toward sexual maturity. The adult automata, irrevocably alienated from their humanity, represent a further condemnation of the totalitarian Church whose major concern is not worship but a concerted effort to eradicate those elements that might threaten its absolute power, namely, individuality, liberty, and human consciousness. To take the Blakean analogy further, the concept of Dust as some kind of powerful energy that connects and activates both mind and body – an energy which the Church views as 'something bad, something wrong, something evil and wicked' (*NL*, p. 282) – is comparable to Blake's notion of 'Energy' as 'the only life' and therefore, 'Eternal Delight.' This is neatly summed up in Georges Bataille's interpretation of Blake's work: 'The Eternal Delight is at the same time the Eternal Awakening. It is perhaps the Hell which Heaven could never truly reject.'

Bataille's suggestion of the coexistence of Hell and Heaven in Blake's work corresponds to Pullman's multifarious conception of Dust. On the one hand, in order to undermine the rigid theological hierarchy of spirit and matter (or good and evil), Pullman emphasises that human and dæmon share a common boundary, which he calls Dust. The word *boundary* is significant here, since collapsing hierarchies do not break down distinctions.

The complex paradox of simultaneous unity and difference, evident in the depiction of the mind-body binary, and in Dust itself, is significant in that it emphasises that what makes two concepts polar opposites is what actually unites them and creates a powerful psychic force. The most useful way of describing this would be as a necessary interplay of opposites – what Blake refers to as 'Contraries' – the coexistence of good and evil that traditional Christianity refuses to acknowledge (perhaps due to an underlying fear that opposites will be confused if their interdependency is made explicit). As far as the Church – 'a body of men with a feverish obsession with sexuality' (*AS*, p. 343) – is concerned, the human body and the world it inhabits is 'material and sinful' (*NL*, p. 31), whereas the human soul is spiritual (a fragment of the divine) and as such must be protected from Dust. The division of body and soul, therefore, would appear to be highly desirable in that spirit and matter would be separated, the individual would revert to a prelapsarian or innocent condition, and would remain so eternally. However, separation results in an individual lacking in 'Contraries,' which in Pullman's terminology is *Dust*. Consequently, the conflict or struggle between opposites that is imperative for human development would be absent, as [for Blake]

> Without Contraries is no progression. Attraction and Repulsion, Reason and Energy, Love and Hate, are necessary to Human existence. From these contraries spring what the religious call Good & Evil. Good is the passive that obeys Reason. Evil is the active springing from Energy.

Conclusion

Thus, the development of Milton's dark materials into an all-inclusive metaphor in which physical particles and abstract metaphysical concepts are one and the same, enables Pullman to avoid making the *absolute* distinctions that characterise both Gnostic and Christian thought. This, in turn, constitutes an attempt to mend the dichotomies of religious division, which, rather than acknowledging the mutuality between opposing ends of being, create the sense of the exclusive and distinctly separate states of spirit and matter. By envisaging everything as connected with everything else, Pullman effectively upsets and transforms the antithesis between conventionally divided entities, rendering them as two halves of a more complex and integrated whole.

In this sense, Pullman appears to share Blake's acceptance and appreciation of the human being as a dynamic, inclusive being comprising body and soul, good and evil, the notion being that opposites are inadequate unless synthesised. The horrific depiction of mind-less matter in the narrative's literal enactment of mind-body dualism and the obvious disadvantages of being composed of spirit only, indicates that Pullman also shares Blake's conviction that the separation of the contraries limits 'Energy': that is, imagination, consciousness and, related to this, the capacity to enjoy physical, or earthly pleasures.

Therefore, in Pullman's universe, Dust is not a punishment or an hereditary moral disease – the idea that we have to be ashamed simply because we are alive – but is re-presented as the positive inheritance of all human beings. Dust, according to the trilogy, symbolises the necessary convergence of contraries; an event that is synonymous with the first independent action taken by Adam and Eve, which is subsequently extended into the first essential step toward maturity for the generations that follow them.

Note

1. *Northern Lights* will be referred to as *NL, The Subtle Knife* as *SK*, and *The Amber Spyglass* as *AS*.

References

Bataille, Georges, *Literature and Evil*, trans. Alastair Hamilton. London: Calder & Boyars, 1973.

Blake, William, *William Blake: Selected Poetry*, ed. W.H. Stevenson. Harmondsworth: Penguin, 1988.

Milton, John, *Paradise Lost*, ed. Christopher Ricks. Harmondsworth: Penguin, 1989.

Pullman, Philip, *Northern Lights*. London: Scholastic Ltd, 1995 (as *The Golden Compass*. New York: Knopf, 1996).

Pullman, Philip, *The Subtle Knife*. London: Scholastic Ltd, 1997; New York: Knopf, 1997.

Pullman, Philip, *The Amber Spyglass*. London: David Fickling Books, Scholastic Ltd, 2000; New York: Knopf, 2000.

Obedience, Disobedience, and Storytelling in C.S. Lewis and Philip Pullman
Naomi Wood

Literature for children, partly because of its traditionally didactic role, often focuses on obedience as a central issue. *Obedience* is a fraught term; it may be understood as a natural and instinctive response to a superior or as coercive violation of individual choice through persuasion and/or physical force. It is esteemed by kings, generals, priests, parents, and other authority figures

Extracted from 'Paradise Lost and Found: Obedience, Disobedience, and Storytelling in C.S. Lewis and Philip Pullman', *Children's Literature in Education* 32:4 (2001), pp. 237–59.

but may be contested by those most vulnerable to authority's dictates: subjects, rank-and-file, laity, and children. The most important instance of disobedience in Judeo-Christian scripture is Eve's decision to eat the fruit of the tree of knowledge in order to be like God; her disobedience initiates humanity's fall. Themes and symbols surrounding Eve's disobedience and its metaphoric reflection of humanity's moral status have been appropriated by two important children's fantasy series with doubled and paradoxical effects.

In C.S. Lewis' *Chronicles of Narnia* [*The Lion, the Witch, and the Wardrobe* and its successors] and Philip Pullman's trilogy *His Dark Materials* [Pullman, 1995, 1997, 2000], the authors re-create the story of humanity's Fall from grace through disobedience as found in Genesis and Milton's *Paradise Lost*. The conservative Lewis advocates obedience, and the progressive Pullman questions it. But both pose obedience as a problem for children as each defines, explicitly and implicitly, legitimate authority and morality in his fiction. Each author's narrative choice uses his view of cosmic order to persuade readers that obedience should be understood as central to coming of age. At stake is the proper role of human agency in the world. Who, ultimately, writes the narrative that gives our lives meaning? Can children become narrators of their own lives – or are they fated simply to occupy narratives already written for them? Obedience and disobedience are inextricably connected with narratives of origin, of development, and of maturation. Both Lewis and Pullman model and problematize the process of independent storytelling in order to arrive at truth: must we retell the same stories or can we invent new ways of getting at old – or inventing new – truths? Lewis' and Pullman's treatments of obedience and disobedience explore each writer's sense of the nature of authority, storytelling, and the creative process.

Pullman vs. Lewis

Pullman has gained notoriety for his public attacks on Lewis' *Chronicles of Narnia* and on Lewis' God. In 'The Dark Side of Narnia,' Pullman writes that the series is too tainted with 'misogyny...racism, [and] sado-masochistic relish for violence' (Pullman, 1988, p. 6) to have any redemptive qualities at all for today's child. Pullman declares that Lewis' narratives 'cheat' readers by employing dei ex machina to solve narrational problems while indiscriminately and inconsistently mixing plural mythic traditions to produce a pastiche of a world rather than a 'secondary creation' as Tolkien defined it (Tolkien, 1996, p. 273). Although Pullman demonstrably chafes at Lewis' influence in the field of children's fantasy, they have a great deal in common: both authors earned degrees in English Literature from Oxford University; both write 'high' fantasies that draw on the Classical, Norse, and English myths and romances of the Western tradition; both are entranced by the past and its difference from the present; both use their fiction to comment on and criticize our world; and both write of naïve protagonists who find themselves responsible for the destiny of a world. Both Lewis and Pullman are intimate with the literature of the Fall: Lewis published a monograph on *Paradise Lost* in 1942 (C.S. Lewis, Preface to *Paradise Lost*), and Pullman relates that he reread *Paradise Lost* and William Blake before undertaking his own re-vision of the story for today's young adults (Alix Sharkey, 1999, p. 13).[1] Both authors posit a prohibiting authority, a moral choice, protagonists in whose hands the fate of a world is placed. Both link issues of obedience and story-telling to the moral and social consequences of coming of age. Finally, Pullman's vehement opposition to Lewis, coupled with his seemingly deliberate rewriting of crucial moments and characters in Lewis' fiction, suggests a deep connection between the two: both series begin with children hiding in a ward-robe and being jettisoned from there into world-shaping adventures; both feature beautiful, deadly women wearing furs who tempt and betray children through sweets; both feature youthful heroines – Lucy and Lyra – who have special relationships with powerful, dangerous beasts – Aslan, Iorek.

However, crucial differences exist between the two authors in their appro-priation of the characters, events, and themes of *Paradise Lost*. Lewis, a Christian whose doctrine is informed by his saturation in the writings of Medieval Europe and the theology of St. Augustine, posits a divinely estab-lished order with a built-in hierarchy 'that consist[s], in descending order, of God, men, women, and animals' (Bottigheimer, 1996, p. 198).[2] Pullman, in the republican tradition of Blake and of Milton's political writing, depicts corrupt ecclesiastical and political authorities to whom allegiance would be evil. Generally speaking, Lewis is Augustinian on obedience and the Fall, while Pullman is closer to gnostic theology.[3] In his monograph on *Paradise Lost*, Lewis asserts that obedience to authority is decorous and appropriate, even beautiful; we consent to submit, recognizing authority's right to control knowledge and power. Eve's sin was her desire to become godlike in knowl-edge and thus to rival God. On the other side, Pullman appears to agree with those gnostics who, 'instead of blaming the human desire for knowledge as the root of all sin, ... did the opposite and sought redemption through gnosis. And whereas the orthodox often blamed Eve for the fall and pointed to women's submission as appropriate punishment, gnostics often depicted Eve – or the feminine spiritual power she represented – as the source of spir-itual awakening' (Pagels, 1988, p. 68). Pullman advocates repeatedly the dis-obedient pursuit of knowledge as the key to maturity, and his heroine Lyra is called 'Eve again' to reinforce her role as disobedient liberator of humanity through knowledge and the creation of new true stories.

Authority, authorship, and narration

The ultimate authority in both Lewis' and Pullman's works is God; each draws on Christian scripture, theology, and history for the portrait. Lewis upholds what he terms 'merely Christian' doctrine while creating a world in which Christianity as such does not exist. Pullman creates a Christianity without Christ, exhibiting deep skepticism about divine power as it is deployed through institutional religion. Lewis' God is a benevolent liberator, while Pullman's is a tyrannical usurper. This difference is crucial to understanding the role and significance of obedience in each series, in the ways each author pictures and characterizes his version of God, and in the way each narrates his tale. As 'creator-god' of their respective tales, Lewis and Pullman employ narrators that capture structurally the qualities of their ultimate authority figures – narrators that mirror and implicitly comment on their respective visions of authority.

In the *Chronicles of Narnia*,[4] Lewis depicts the second person of the Christian trinity, Christ, rather than attempting to embody the ineffable first person, who never appears in his narrative except as a name, 'the Emperor Beyond the Sea.' Appropriately for a country of talking beasts, Lewis chooses the King of the Beasts to represent Christ, alluding also to the biblical Lion of Judah. Although the Lion Aslan's purposes are often mysterious and his visits to Narnia so far apart that some Narnians begin to doubt his existence, he is a personal, incarnate deity who punishes and rewards unambiguously (wine, dance, and picnics for the faithful, thrashing and humiliation for miscreants). In the words of evangelical cliché, a 'personal relationship' with Aslan is possible. But this relationship is not always necessarily comfortable: ' "Course he isn't safe," ' Mr Beaver tells the nervous Pevensies who are anticipating their meeting. ' "But he's good. He's the King, I tell you" ' (LWW, p. 76). At the same time, some characters, most notably Lucy, develop relationships with Aslan that permit caresses, kisses, and even romps.

Responses to the Lion reveal facets of his character, but even more they reveal the personality of the responder: those who hate or dismiss the Lion are damned, those who lean toward him, even if they fear, are saved. In *The Lion, the Witch, and the Wardrobe*, treacherous Edmund's instinctive response to the Lion is self-indicting, just as his siblings' response indicates their receptivity to the Truth:

> At the name of Aslan each one of the children felt something jump in his inside. Edmund felt a sensation of mysterious horror. Peter felt suddenly brave and adventurous. Susan felt as if some delicious smell or some delightful strain of

music had just floated by her. And Lucy got the feeling you have when you wake up in the morning and realise that it is the beginning of the holidays or the beginning of summer.

LWW, pp. 64–5

Aslan merits all these reactions as they result from the implied relationship each child has with the Good, Truth and hence with God; thus, the three 'good' children each experience Aslan's name as a metaphor of the thing they most delight in, the good in them turning to the good in God and thus experiencing him as the thing most good in themselves. Those who respond negatively to Aslan turn their backs not only on the divine Other but also on the good in themselves. To Lewis, God's authority is a consequence of his essence. In the natural hierarchy of value, some creatures are superior and others inferior; God, as maker of everything, must be the most superior of all. We obey God because that is the way we appropriately respond to his superiority, which Lewis also defines as 'goodness.' Disobedience of God's commands demonstrates our 'perversity,' a word Lewis frequently employs to describe any behaviors that do not match his sense of the norm: the everyday traditional English life – allied with 'fried eggs and soap and sunlight and the rooks cawing at Cure Hardy' (Lewis, [1945] 1996, p. 299). In Lewis' novels, the good tends to align with heterosexuality, with sexual division of labor and society; with the great chain of being. Perversity, often shading into evil, is good pursued through faulty humanism: progressive, socialist, and feminist efforts to institute programmatic social change. In the *Narnia* series, to obey Aslan is simply to align oneself with good. Those who disobey not only get punished, but idiotically frustrate themselves.

Lewis' narrator, the friendly uncle-cum-deus ex machina, presents the problem of identifying legitimate authority as relatively simple and the rewards relatively clear. Knowledge of 'true' authority is inherent in the *Narnia* books: because characters are *made* knowing the right and only their perverted will prevents them from acting on it, there is no need, most of the time, for outright instruction or directions. People like Edmund in *The Lion, the Witch, and the Wardrobe* or Digory in *The Magician's Nephew*, who might plead that they were enchanted and did what was wrong under those influences, are not absolved: they *knew* and must repent (see *MN*, p. 135). This degree of control does offer a degree of security: under the narrator's guiding hand, only so much can go wrong in Narnia. Although the child protagonists may temporarily suffer discomfort, hunger, and fear, no doubt arises that the Narrator and his image, Aslan, are in control.

Pullman's figure of God is different, much more distant than Lewis', without a corporeal intermediary such as Aslan. Introduced as an actual being late in the second book of the series, *The Subtle Knife*, 'the Authority' is the oldest of the angels, but no creator; he lied to those who came after him.

In the first book of the series, *The Golden Compass*, we only know the Authority through the Church. Unlike Lewis, who does not describe any kind of institutional relation in *Narnia*, Pullman exploits the known offenses of institutional religion, Christianity in particular, to buttress his thesis about the poisonous effects of religion on humanity and the rest of nature. Lewis, aware of the same dismal history, perhaps, exchanges for the institutionalized church a vision of individual relationships with the divine.[5]

In Pullman's world, the Church is monolithic, powerful, and combines the most authoritarian, formidable, and evil aspects of Protestant Calvinism and Roman Catholicism.[6] Pullman's fictive Church, described in orthodox manner as the Body of God, is similar enough to the Christian Church to make some of Pullman's characterizations pointed: his Church, like many in our world, silences heretics through Inquisition, castrates young boys to retain their lovely voices at the cost of their sexuality ('so useful in Church music' [*GC*, p. 374]), and generally opposes desire for the things of the material world while amassing great wealth and power. Pullman's Church sponsors all scientific research (called 'experimental theology') and uses resulting technology in its rituals. It approves or disapproves of individual discoveries referencing Church doctrine. Of chief concern in the series are elementary particles called Dust, identified as Original Sin by Church scholars. In an effort to fight Dust (which collects around human beings beginning with puberty), the Church commissions the 'General Oblation Board' to study Dust and solve the problem of its attraction to adolescents and adults. Led by the evil Mrs. Coulter (a 'coulter' is an iron blade fixed at the front of a plow to make a vertical cut into the soil, evoking the guillotine devised by Mrs. Coulter's employees to sever children and their dæmons), the General Oblation Board kidnaps children to sever them from their 'dæmons' – animal-shaped souls – in an experimental process euphemistically called 'intercision.' Those who undergo this process either die or become zombies without any wills of their own.

Clearly, Pullman and Lewis have different notions of deity: Pullman sees God as a despoiler of the material universe; the cosmos itself acts independently from the Authority; since other gods and powers exist and since the Authority himself was formed out of Dust, as were other conscious beings. Dust coalesced in the same way, 'becoming aware of itself' and gravitating toward other conscious beings over tens of thousands of years. Pullman's God-authorized Church is an illegitimate arbiter of a creation it does not seek to understand except to exploit and stands for repression, exploitation, and the most negative aspects of authority. Lewis on the contrary describes

God as the maker and sustainer of creation, which can only run properly if allowed to follow *its* 'nature,' a paradoxical notion since we are both naturally good, with truth built as it were into our cells, as we saw in the examples of responses to Aslan, but also naturally perverse, expressing essentially fallen natures.

Pullman's narrator does not tell us what to think about moral decision making – at least not in the direct and regulated manner of Lewis' narrator. If Lewis' narrator is avuncular, Pullman's is more like a documentary with very little voice-over: he shows us vignettes that enable us to see more than individual characters see. In one interview, he compares himself to a cinematic camera (Sharkey, 1999, p. 13). This technique creates dissonance between characters' and readers' understanding of situations. This dissonant space invites readers – one might say it forces readers – into judgments about characters' insufficient, incomplete grasp of a given event. For example, this dissonance heightens the ironic contrasts between what Lyra knows and assumes about life and what we know; privileged in our knowledge, we lament Lyra's lack of it. In 'Lyra's Jordan,' the second chapter of *The Golden Compass*, the first section is told from Lyra's point of view; the rest of the chapter reveals in shifting, episodic ways the activities of a mysterious group, switching from past tense to the present and back to past so that we have a sense both of immediacy and our own inability to do anything to prevent what is happening/has happened. In the present tense, we learn about 'slow' Tony Makarios and his life as a street child, 'his clumsy tenderness' for his drunken mother, and how he lives on handouts and minor pilfering. With promises of luxury sweets – 'chocolat!' – a beautiful lady in furs whose dæmon is a golden monkey lures him to a cellar. Shifting ominously to the past tense again, we learn that she promised the large group of children she had collected in the cellar that they would be cared for as they journey to the North and their parents notified. But no one is notified: 'The lady stood on the jetty and waved till she could see their faces no more. Then she turned back inside, with the golden monkey nestled in her breast, and threw the little bundle of letters into the furnace before leaving the way she had come' (*GC*, p. 44). When this same woman is introduced to Lyra at the end of the chapter as Mrs. Coulter, we have knowledge Lyra does not, that Mrs. Coulter is most likely the cause of the recent disappearance of Lyra's best friend, Roger the kitchen boy. Lyra's subsequent enthrallment by Mrs. Coulter is more excruciating to witness because of our special knowledge. Our narrator is no comforting uncle, for it is uncomfortable, indeed, not to know who will prevail and suspect as well that we might encounter another past-tense episode in which the future has already been decided against the heroes.[7]

Lewis' and Pullman's narrative voices embody the divine authority they imagine, though they require different responses from the reader. Lewis' narrator invites the reader to become part of the club, while Pullman's narrator raises questions about what belonging to a club might involve. Lewis' narrator encourages conformity to the good (which is assumed to be naturally apparent to anyone who is 'normal' in Lewis' limited sense), while Pullman's narrator demonstrates the difficulty of determining the good course of action when knowledge is always partial and impressions may be manipulated or mistaken. Although both write in the high-fantasy genre, Lewis' allegiance to fairy-tale romance conventions demands the 'happily ever after' – even as his apocalyptic Christianity posits eternal bliss Elsewhere, a Telos to which he holds creation is tending. In contrast, Pullman insists that his work is 'stark realism' at least in psychological terms (Achuka, 1999, p. 4); referencing evolutionary theory and physics, Pullman grounds his fantasy in contemporary science. Rather than occupying the all-knowing, all-powerful position of Lewis' God/narrator, Pullman's narrator creates ironic discontinuity, highlighting harsh contradictions between ideology and practice, culture and instinct, means and ends. Pullman's narrator is godlike in knowledge perhaps, but not omnipotent; unresolvable conflict must remain unresolved and no deus ex machina can make 'happy ever after.'

The truth in storytelling

Both Pullman and Lewis tell stories about life and love and obedience, but the truths they distill differ because of the writers' different positions on the divine and authority. In Lewis' children's books, no child becomes a storyteller in her own right; children instead choose (or fail) to obey – to become part of the overarching grand narrative that the Emperor Beyond the Sea has written (Glover, 1989). Rather than emphasizing independent agency or free will, in other words, the narrative encourages conformity to a predetermined pattern ('what the plot of that story is'). As Lewis concludes his series,

> for us this is the end of all the stories, and we can most truly say that they all lived happily ever after. But for them it was only the beginning of the real story. All their life in this world and all their adventures in Narnia had only been the cover and the title page: now at last they were beginning Chapter One of the Great Story, which no one on earth has read: which goes on for ever: in which every chapter is better than the one before.
>
> *LB* p. 184

Lewis' commitment to 'the end', to the idea that time is linear and the grand narrative of history is tending toward an apocalypse after which the real story can begin, belies his narrator's evident enjoyment of the materiality of the world. Still, Lewis' idealist repudiation of the chaotic and imperfect nature of the material world leads him to posit a 'true,' more material world elsewhere, a world that can only be entered through obedience to the master narrative, not through independent creation of new stories.

Pullman argues that storymaking should not be an escape from this world but a way to reinvent it. If chance through evolution over millions of years has produced both Dust and consciousness, when matter begins to understand itself, a strange synthesis occurs. One of the things that begins to happen is storymaking, and through storymaking, new ways of creating the world.

Both Lewis and Pullman insist on the 'real' implications of their fantasy stories. Pullman exhorts his readers to take an activist role in creating the world that they want:

> 'We shouldn't live as if [the Kingdom of Heaven] mattered more than this life in this world, because where we are is always the most important place. We have to be all those difficult things like cheerful and kind and curious and patient, and we've got to study and think and work hard, all of us, in all our different worlds, and then we'll build … The Republic of Heaven,' said Lyra.
>
> Sharkey, 1999, p. 518

The way we regain paradise is to embrace our real world, to live in it, to recognize our symbiotic relationship with it, and to strive to learn and tell true stories to those who come after. While this paean to human creativity and resourcefulness is inspiring, it undercuts the basis of fantasy writing. Shouldn't we then read and write realism alone, based on the possibilities inherent in 'where we are'? What good does it do to escape to wonderful imaginary places filled with satisfactions we can only yearn for, never experience – dæmons, armoured bears, mulefa? And if we are to create a democracy, what business have we naturalizing hierarchies, imagining children of destiny? Doesn't the romance form inevitably glamorize the very ideology against which Lyra and her companions have been fighting?

These paradoxes depict the strength and autonomy of the form both Lewis and Pullman have chosen for their tales. Even the author-creators confess their dependence on their form; if they insist on the real and true aspects of their stories, they also must submit to the ways their stories intractably unsettle their stated goals. The powerful relationship between tale, teller, and listener creates dynamic rather than static meaning. Stories that inspire new stories, stories that provoke thought, stories that ask the big questions ... all these require the reader to pay attention, to think, and above all to imagine and create. If the Genesis story with all its ambiguity might be said to affirm one thing, it is that desire for true knowledge is a human constant and the pursuit of that desire leads to new worlds and new challenges, for good and ill. And we must tell stories to give those worlds and challenges meaning, which is the only way to grow up.

Notes

1. As a teenager, Lewis contemplated writing an opera, *Loki Unbound*, with a promethean Loki as his hero, struggling against the arrogant and tyrannical Odin; with his reconversion to Christianity; however, Lewis returned to a more orthodox view of the authority of God as creator (*They Stand Together*, 6 October 1914; 50–3). His struggle with the idea that God might be a cosmic sadist, however, continued even into his last published work; in *A Grief Observed* he discusses these ideas again.
2. See also Peter Brown: 'Augustine's exegesis validated the rule of men over women and the rule of the father over his children as part of God's original order' (Brown, 1988, p. 400). For a discussion of nineteenth-century adaptations of *Paradise Lost* for children, which involved attempts to contain the subversive qualities of the poem, see Julie Pfeiffer's essay in *Children's Literature* (1999).
3. For Lewis, see his own Preface to *Paradise Lost* and Elaine Pagels's chapter on 'Gnostic Improvisations on Genesis' in *Adam, Eve, and the Serpent* (pp. 57–77).
4. I am citing all titles in text in abbreviated form: LWW = *The Lion, the Witch, and the Wardrobe*; MN = *The Magician's Nephew*; LB = *The Last Battle*; GC = *The Golden Compass*; SK = *The Subtle Knife*; AS = *The Amber Spyglass*.
5. Lewis, inconsistently perhaps, differs from St. Augustine, who advocated the centrality of the institutional church for the Christian.
6. Pope John Calvin moved the headquarters of the Church to Geneva, though the papacy has since been superseded by a Magisterium (*GC*, p. 30). Pullman carefully makes all Christian institutions culpable.
7. *The Amber Spyglass* does succumb to didacticism and exposition far more than the two previous books do, perhaps because of the need to 'wrap things up.'

References

Achuka: Children's Books UK, 'Achuka Interview – Philip Pullman,' December 1998. http://www/achuka.uk.co/ppint.htm, accessed 3 August 1999.

Bottigheimer, Ruth, *The Bible for Children: From the Age of Gutenberg to the Present*. New Haven: Yale University Press, 1996.

Brown, Peter, *The Body and Society: Men, Women, and Sexual Renunciation in Early Christianity*: New York: Columbia University Press, 1988.

Glover, D.E., 'The magician's book. That's not your story,' *Studies in the Literary Imagination*, 1989, 22.2, 217–25.

Lewis, C.S., *A Grief Observed*. Afterword by Chad Walsh. New York: Bantam, [1961] 1976.

Lewis, C.S., *The Lion, the Witch, and the Wardrobe*. New York: Scholastic, [1950] 1988.

Lewis, C.S., *That Hideous Strength*. Scribner Paperback Fiction. New York: Simon & Schuster, [1945] 1996.

Lewis, C.S., Preface to *Paradise Lost*. Oxford: Oxford University Press, 1942.

Lewis, C.S., *They Stand Together: The Letters of C.S. Lewis to Arthur Greeves (1914–1963).* Walter Hooper, ed. London: Collins, 1979.

Pagels, Elaine, *Adam, Eve, and the Serpent.* New York: Random House, 1988.

Pfeiffer, Julie, ' "Dream not of other worlds": *Paradise Lost* and the child reader,' *Children's Literature,* 1999, 27, 1–21.

Pullman, Philip, 'The dark side of Narnia,' *The Guardian* 1 October 1988, 6–7.

Pullman, Philip, *The Golden Compass.* Borzoi Books. New York: Alfred A. Knopf, 1996. Published in the UK as *Northern Lights.* London: Scholastic Children's Books, 1995.

Pullman, Philip, *The Subtle Knife.* Borzoi Books. New York: Alfred A. Knopf, 1997. London: Scholastic Children's Books, 1997.

Pullman, Philip, *The Amber Spyglass.* Borzoi Books. New York: Alfred A. Knopf, 2000. London: Scholastic Children's Books, 2000.

Sharkey, Alix, 'Heaven, Hell, and the Hut at the Bottom of the Garden,' interview with Philip Pullman. *The Independent.* 6 December 1998. Features: 13. Lexis-Nexis Academic Universe. http:web.lexis-nexis.com/universe/, accessed 25 July 1999.

Tolkien, J.R.R., 'On fairy-stories,' in *Folk & Fairy Tales,* 2nd ed., Martin Hallett and Barbara Karasek, eds., pp. 263–294. Peterborough, Ont.: Broadview Press, 1996.

Intertextuality
Claire Squires

In the acknowledgements that end *The Amber Spyglass* [AS], and thus the entire *His Dark Materials* trilogy, Philip Pullman makes this statement about his writing process: 'I have stolen ideas from every book I have ever read. My principle in researching for a novel is 'Read like a butterfly, write like a bee', and if this story contains any honey, it is entirely because of the quality of the nectar I found in the work of better writers' (AS 549). He then goes on to enumerate specific literary 'debts' that he owes, or writers from whom he has stolen, to use his own terminology. He mentions three writers in particular: Heinrich von Kleist and his essay 'On the Marionette Theatre' (1810; sometimes translated as 'The Puppet Theatre'); John Milton, for *Paradise Lost*; and William Blake. This chapter considers Pullman the literary thief or, to use more literary terminology, Pullman the intertextualist. For in writing *His Dark Materials*, Pullman uses intertextuality as a method, as a form of literary engagement and as a way of expressing his own artistic ambition. Intertextuality underpins and enriches Pullman's writing and is also the means by which he articulates many of his arguments.

Extracted from 'Intertextuality', in C. Squires, *Philip Pullman, Master Storyteller: A Guide to the Worlds of his Dark Materials* (New York and London: Continuum, 2003), pp. 115–33.

Intertextuality can be simply defined as 'the relation between one text and another' (Pope 2002: 246). But what might this mean for *His Dark Materials* and its interpretation? In *The English Studies Book*, Rob Pope further breaks down his definition of intertextuality into explicit, implied and inferred forms. Explicit intertextuality consists of other texts which are 'overtly referred to' and sources which are 'demonstrably drawn on'. Implied intertextuality includes the 'passing allusions' and 'effects' inserted into the text by the author 'so as to be picked up by the alert and similarly informed reader'. Inferred intertextuality, on the other hand, refers to the texts that readers 'draw on to help their understanding of the text in hand' and may well not have been in the writer's mind at the time of writing (Pope 2002: 246).

His Dark Materials has been declared a 'triumph of intertextuality', and the sources from which Pullman has drawn are numerous and varied (Scott 2005: 96). In his review of *AS* in the *Washington Post*, Michael Dirda reeled off a whole list of intertextual references, which is worth quoting at some length because of its brisk iteration of source texts:

> Besides finding hints of *Paradise Lost* and Blake's poetry, the astute will pick up echoes of the following: Christ's harrowing of Hell, Jewish Kabbalah (the legend of the god-like angel Metatron), Gnostic doctrine (Dust, our sleeping souls needing to be awakened), the 'death of God' controversy, *Perelandra*, the Oz books (the Wheelers), Wagner's *Ring of the Nibelungs* (Siegfried's mending of the sword), Aeneas, Odysseus and Dante in the Underworld, the Grail legend and the wounded Fisher King, Peter Pan, Wordsworth's pantheistic 'Immortality Ode', the doctrine of the hidden God and speculation about the plurality of worlds, situational ethics (actions, not people, being good or bad), the cessation of miracles, 'Star Wars', colonialist evangelizing, the fetch of British folklore, the 17th-century doctrine of sympathies (for the Gallivespian communication device, the lodestone-resonator), the popular mythology of the Jesuits as ascetic masterminds of realpolitik, superhero comics and even Pullman's own early novel for adults, *Galatea*. Fans of science fiction and fantasy may also detect undertones of Ursula Le Guin's Earthsea books, Fritz Leiber's sword-and-sorcery tales of Fafhrd and the Gray Mouser, Jack Vance's elegant Dying Earth stories.
>
> Dirda 2000

This esoteric and eclectic list is only a start to the intertextual source spotting that a 'similarly informed' or 'astute' (as Dirda puts it) reader of the trilogy might undertake. Pullman's background as a student and subsequently a teacher of literature is worth remembering here. For Pullman, as a school teacher and latterly a university lecturer, the genres of folk story and fairy tale, as well as the wealth of past children's literature, are added to the canonical mix. The borrowing from, use of and engagement with other texts is a crucial part of the creative process of *His Dark Materials*, central to its methods and also its interpretation.

This chapter examines this literary borrowing, first in terms of Pullman's debts and derivations and then by considering how, through his intertextuality, Pullman both negotiates with genre and establishes points of difference with other writers. Through intertextuality, Pullman also places a very visible marker of his own literary ambition but simultaneously continues to engage the multiple audiences by whom his intertextuality is variably received.

Paradise Lost is the overarching intertext for *His Dark Materials;* the themes and narrative structure of Milton's epic poem directly inspired Pullman's trilogy. In Pullman's narrative are rebel angels, characters readily identifiable as Adam (Will) and Eve (Lyra), a tempter figure (Mary Malone) and a stirringly portrayed Satan, leader of the rebels (Asriel). The narrative of both texts is centrally concerned with the biblical story of the Fall, which each takes as a source and then reworks. Pullman also takes into his reworking William Blake's commentary on Milton's *Paradise Lost.*

Paradise Lost has long been the centre of critical debate, and Pullman's trilogy brings another voice to the argument in the form of a creative intervention. Following Blake's line on Milton, that the latter was 'of the Devil's party without knowing it', Pullman sets out in the trilogy to reverse the morality of the biblical Fall and to celebrate knowledge, consciousness and sexuality. Pullman has knowingly echoed Blake's infamous statement on Milton in an interview, declaring, ' "I am of the Devil's party and know it" ' (de Bertodano 2002). Such statements are clearly part of the provocative persona that Pullman has developed in his commentary to the media, undoubtedly attracting increased attention to his books, leading critics such as Hitchens notoriously to name Pullman 'the most dangerous author in Britain'. Yet Pullman's engagement with Milton, and with Blake's interpretation of Milton, is much more than a mere act of provocation. In *Paradise Lost*, Milton recasts the biblical story of the temptation of Eve and the Fall of humankind. Yet Milton develops the narrative beyond the frame provided by Genesis and portrays a fully imagined cosmos in which the fallen angels and Satan – Eve's tempter – are set against the autocratic power of God. The vast landscapes – or rather universe-scapes – of *Paradise Lost* are described in a grandiloquent language that profoundly impressed the young Pullman when he first studied the epic poem at school. The ongoing critical debate about *Paradise Lost* – whether it succeeds in its stated aim to 'justify the ways of God to men' or rather, as the introduction mentions, depicts God and Christianity as essentially cruel, free will as a trap for humankind and the human desire for knowledge as wrong – is a central theme in *His Dark Materials*. Yet Pullman's rewriting of the Bible and *Paradise Lost* is explicitly anti-God and pro-temptation, with the Fall as 'completely essential'; and his chosen position as 'of the Devil's party' an intentional ideology. He consciously inverts the morality of the Fall and in his exploration of the rich imaginative possibilities afforded by the idea of rebel angels, Hell, and the multiple worlds travelled through by Satan in *Paradise Lost* pays a provocative homage to Milton.

In his reading of *His Dark Materials'* intertextuality, however, Tony Watkins argues that Pullman's engagement with *Paradise Lost* is partial and based on the first four of the twelve books of the poem. These, claim Watkins, are the ones in which Satan and the rebel angels are portrayed positively, whereas later sections undercut his heroism (Watkins 2004: 67–8). Carole Scott, for whom Pullman's interaction with his source texts (including the Bible as well as *Paradise Lost* and Blake) is a 'triumph of intertextuality', explores the creation of Pullman's world view through his engagement with his source texts. She argues that Pullman adds to the argument the 'relatively recent conviction' of the death of God and a 'debased church' (Scott 2005: 96), thus continuing in the dissenting tradition of Blake but, perhaps unexpectedly, remaining closer to the Church than might be imagined.

> Albeit with imaginative reconstruction, Pullman continues to employ Christianity's humanistic ethics, traditions, and values; its biblical themes and narratives; its symbolism expressed in both the Bible and church rituals; and often its diction. Finally, we find a religious, even puritanical streak in his sense of every person's ultimate responsibility to humankind, even at the expense of their own happiness.
>
> Scott 2005: 96

Scott's argument confirms that Pullman's ideology places him less in conflict with the real-life Church than might be anticipated. Some of his theology directly rewrites the Christian narrative, but the morality that he expresses is not so clearly in contradiction with Christian ethics, as implied by the appreciative commentary of some religious figures upon *His Dark Materials*. Nonetheless, Pullman's rewriting of the story of the temptation, as told in the Bible and retold in *Paradise Lost*, demonstrates how intertextual method allows the author to stir theological and ideological debate, to enrich his own narrative and to place himself – at least for consideration – alongside writers central to the canon of English literature.

In addition to the internal references to Milton and the mention Pullman has made of the influence of *Paradise Lost* on his own work in interviews, he has also in years subsequent to the publication of *His Dark Materials* introduced an edition of the epic poem, in which he again acknowledges the poem's role in his own creative work (Pullman 2005). Considering that C.S. Lewis also published a lengthy preface to the poem in 1942, based on a series of lectures, it is evident that Pullman is staking his claim for interpretive pre-eminence over Milton's work, as well as promoting his own writing over that of Lewis (Lewis 1942).

Within his introduction to *Paradise Lost*, Pullman refers to the ongoing interpretive debate surrounding the poem, making his own position clear by naming William Blake 'the greatest of Milton's interpreters' (Pullman 2005: 8). Yet Blake's poetic vision is also acknowledged, particularly in *Songs of Innocence* (1789) and *Songs of Experience* (1794). Among these lyrics is to be discovered one of the possible sources of Lyra's name, as a girl 'Lyca' is both 'The Little Girl Lost' and 'The Little Girl Found'. Pullman is indebted to Blake – as he is to Milton's *Paradise Lost* – for the visual imagery and the landscapes of his work. These he has thoroughly plundered for intertextual use in *His Dark Materials*. Blake's strange, disturbing and visionary landscapes in *Songs*, and Milton's grand depiction of Satan surveying the worldscapes around him, make their way into Pullman's own creation of multiple worlds, and particularly into the depictions of Asriel forcing his way into the Aurora, Lyra's imprisonment by Mrs Coulter, the world of the dead and the cosmic battles towards the end of *The Amber Spyglass*.

Blake is influential upon *His Dark Materials* in a further, thematic way, which is signalled by the titles of his lyric sequence. Innocence and experience are central concepts in Pullman's trilogy, drawing on, as Carole Scott has it, 'Blake's perception of innocence, experience, and higher innocence as stages of maturity, both physical and spiritual' (Scott 2005: 103). In his depiction of Lyra and Will's growing consciousness and experience, Pullman makes such themes central to his own narrative and also links to the third of his major debts, the nineteenth-century German writer Heinrich von Kleist.

Kleist's 'On the Marionette Theatre' tells of the encounter between the narrator and a dancer. Their discourse on the puppet theatre and their anecdotes of a young man coming to consciousness of his own grace, and so losing it, nourish Pullman's thematics in the trilogy. Kleist's metaphors of the Fall distil in only a few thousand words the central concerns of Pullman's one-thousand, three-hundred-page trilogy. Kleist's story also supplies the inspiration for one of *His Dark Materials*' chief characters, Iorek, as the narrator of 'On the Marionette Theatre' is told of a strange encounter with a fighting bear.

There is a particular analogy between Kleist's metaphor of the young man who loses his grace through consciousness and Lyra's capacity to read the alethiometer. When she first starts to read it in *Northern Lights*, while with the gyptians, her approach is unconscious. Farder Coram enquires what she is asking it, and she is 'surprised to find that she's actually been asking a question without realizing it' (NL 144). The method that she subsequently develops to read it is completely different from that used by the scholars trained for decades in its use. Lyra enters into a 'calm state' and experiences 'a sensation of such grace and power that [she] … felt like a young bird learning to fly' (NL 151, 152). Her readings are rapid, and her interpretation of its meanings swift. For the adult readers of the alethiometer, readings are much slower. The adult alethiometer readers rely on numerous interpretive books to read it correctly, whereas Lyra, in her childlike state, needs nothing other than her own mind.

His Dark Materials also uses many of the tropes of metamorphosis and transformation that occur in folk and fairy-tale plots. The shape-shifting of the dæmons is the obvious example of this and is explored at greater length in the epilogue to Marina Warner's *Fantastic Metamorphoses: Other Worlds* (2002). One of the most comprehensive sets of characters Pullman has developed from folk stories and fairy tale, however, is that of the witches. Yet Pullman imbues the witches with his own original vision. The witches of Lyra's world have a distinctive existence through their capacity to separate from their dæmons. They may engage in sexual relationships with short-lived human men, but because of their longevity, their partners age and die many centuries before they do. Witches are neither good nor evil characters, but like humans can be both. The witch who kills Will's father, for example, does so not out of malevolence but because of a broken heart. The witches are also used to articulate some of Pullman's anti-religious ideology. Drawing on the real-world history of the persecution of the witches, instituted via the Catholic Inquisition in the Middle Ages and continued until the eighteenth century in England and Scotland, Pullman writes one scene in *The Subtle Knife* [SK] in which a witch is tortured, and another in which the witch Ruta Skadi relates what she has learnt from Asriel about the actions of the agents of the Authority, the ' "hideous cruelties" ' enacted on witches (SK 39–41, 283).

In this way, Pullman intertextually incorporates into *His Dark Materials* some of the real-world history of witches along with the vast body of folk stories and fairy tales that have witches as characters, and canonical texts including witches such as Shakespeare's *Macbeth* (1606). Into this intertextual mix he also throws anthropological knowledge. Parkin and Jones refer to the Sami people, or Lapps, of the far north of Europe, who believe in a 'goddess of the underworld called Yambe-Akka' (Parkin and Jones 2005: 255). Yambe-Akka is the name Pullman gives to the 'goddess who came to a witch when she was about to die', as indeed she comes to the tortured witch in *The Subtle Knife* (*SK* 41). To continue the wealth of intertextual reference in his creation of the witches, Pullman has drawn Serafina Pekkala's name from the Helsinki phone book (Wartofsky 2001; Ross 2002). Thus, around the frame of established literary and fairy-tale characters, Pullman makes several other ingenious intertextual additions in the creation of his witches. In effect, genres intermingle.

A further genre that *His Dark Materials* takes from and contributes to is that of children's literature generally, but it is to children's adventure stories that Pullman's writing has a particular allegiance. One of Pullman's favourite writers from his own childhood was Arthur Ransome, whose *Swallows and Amazons* series depicts a quality of childhood freedom and an emphasis on moral responsibility, which is consonant with that of *His Dark Materials*. In these novels, Ransome created 'an idyllic playground in which children had to behave responsibly toward each other and the environment in order to get the best out of their situation' (Eccleshare 2002: 40). As such, *His Dark Materials* is also clearly borrowing from the form of the *Bildungsroman* or novel of growing up. Although Pullman hints at the teen sexuality that is the central concern of his contemporaries such as Melvin Burgess, however, *His Dark Materials* is neither as explicit nor as social-realist as their writing and essentially follows a more traditional pattern. In its brave, resourceful and self-reliant child protagonists, the trilogy is almost nostalgic in its echoing of earlier writers of children's adventure stories. There are other familiar tropes of children's fiction that Pullman follows, such as the ubiquity of orphaned or near-orphaned protagonists.

Another area of both children's and adults' literature that *His Dark Materials* is aligned with is science fiction and fantasy. In the profusion of different worlds presented in the trilogy, and in particular the manner in which characters make transitions from one to another, Pullman's work clearly draws on literary precedents. Karen Patricia Smith, writing a critical essay on the fantasy models Pullman is adhering to and developing, refers to this aspect of the trilogy as 'Excursions into Invented Worlds' (Smith 2005). She records particular similarities to the work of Susan Cooper and C.S. Lewis in these moments of transition, and links them more generally to the 'Perilous Journeys', as she phrases it, undertaken by the characters. In the opening scenes of *Northern Lights*, there is an allusion to a transition trope as Lyra hides in the wardrobe in the Retiring Room, surrounded by academic gowns, some fur-lined. Even though this is not the point at which Lyra travels to another world (this does not happen until the end of *Northern Lights*), it is from here that she becomes irrevocably involved with

Asriel's world of high politics, and she sees his photogram of the city in the sky, after which she embarks on her world-crossing adventures. Moreover, to any reader of C.S. Lewis, this scene is highly reminiscent of the most famous of his 'excursion' scenes in *The Lion, the Witch and the Wardrobe* (1950), in which Lucy, one of the child protagonists, first finds an opening to the other world of Narnia through a wardrobe filled with furs. As in *The Chronicles of Narnia*, this opening scene in *His Dark Materials* leads to many pages of otherworld adventure. And yet Pullman, as earlier chapters of this book have demonstrated, occupies a stance contrary to C.S. Lewis and also has made remarks about his distaste for the fantasy of another Oxford writer with whom Lewis was linked and Pullman is frequently compared: J.R.R. Tolkien. Unlike his acknowledged and appreciative debts to Milton, Blake and Kleist, then, there is another vein of Pullman's intertextuality which is more argumentative and contrarian.

It is possible to see Pullman's engagement with C.S. Lewis and J.R.R. Tolkien, on Pullman's part at least, as a battle for supremacy. The similarities between these three writers are at least as great as their differences, and it therefore makes sense to consider how Pullman takes on his predecessors and how his arguments with them are simultaneously intertextual engagements with their writing.

The similarities between the writers are biographical, generic and textual. Lewis, Tolkien and Pullman are all writers who were, or are, based in Oxford. All three are also best known for a series of books that feature different worlds and fantastical characters, thus lending their work a generic definition as fantasy. These three series – *The Chronicles of Narnia*, *The Lord of the Rings* and *His Dark Materials* – share an appeal to both adults and children, and so cannot be neatly categorised as children's or adults' literature. Yet Pullman has arguments with both of these series and disputes his similarities to them.

Pullman is ideologically opposed to the Christian perspective allegorised in *The Chronicles of Narnia*. Yet *The Chronicles* are a clear source of intertextual material for *His Dark Materials*, and Pullman's commentary upon them in the media has only served to draw attention to this link. Burton Hatlen's essay on *His Dark Materials*' 'challenge' to both Lewis and Tolkien suggests that 'rather than simply rejecting Lewis as a model, Pullman has ... offered a kind of inverted homage to his predecessor, deliberately composing a kind of 'anti-Narnia', a secular humanist alternative to Lewis's Christian fantasy' (Hatlen 2005: 82). Given the 'pernicious' influence that Pullman feels Lewis to have, it would seem that the nature of the intertextual link between Pullman's work and Lewis's is, at least in part, an intentional riposte to *The Chronicles*. This is undoubtedly a case of implied intertextuality, though one that is heavily trailed in Pullman's commentary external to the text of *His Dark Materials* itself.

Pullman also has engaged with J.R.R. Tolkien's writing in the commentary he has made outside the trilogy itself. Such remarks have occurred in response to comments that his own writing, like that of Tolkien, belongs to the genre of fantasy. Tolkien is the acknowledged master of fantasy fiction. Pullman's trilogy is also arguably a work of fantasy, defined in *The Oxford Companion to English Literature* as a 'liberation from the constraints of what is known, coupled with a plausible and persuasive inner coherence' (Drabble 2000: 550). *His Dark Materials* certainly displays such characteristics: a knife that can cut between worlds; a vehicle that works by thought-power alone; humans accompanied by dæmons. In interview, however, Pullman has stated that '*Northern Lights* is not a fantasy. It's a work of stark realism' (Parsons and Nicholson 1999: 131). Pullman extended his argument on his website in the form of a FAQ (frequently asked question) section. The mention of elves and hobbits is undoubtedly a reference to Tolkien:

> *You once said that* His Dark Materials *is not a fantasy, but stark realism. What did you mean by that?*
>
> That comment got me into trouble with the fantasy people. What I mean by it was roughly this: that the story I was trying to write was about real people, not beings that don't exist like elves or hobbits. Lyra and Will and the other characters are meant to be human beings like us, and the story is about a universal human experience, namely growing up. The 'fantasy' parts of the story were there as a picture of aspects of human nature, not as something alien and strange.
>
> www.philip-pullman.com

Pullman's own interpretation of his work is contentious – the reality of the worlds encountered in *His Dark Materials* is very different from that of our world – but perhaps what Pullman is suggesting is the conflict between fantasy and psychological realism. Elsewhere he has dismissed Tolkien's writing for being ' "not interesting psychologically; there's nothing about people in it" ' (de Bertodano 2002). The claim of 'stark realism' for his work is Pullman's way of promoting his own skill in developing character motivation: although the worlds of *His Dark Materials* may be unknown to us, the psychological manner in which characters traverse them is instantly recognisable. Pullman goes on to explain on his website that dæmons are a quintessential example of this: seemingly fantastical but actually an expression of human personality. Thus, in the desire to express his own creative and moral ideology, Pullman summons his predecessors Lewis and Tolkien, it would seem at first, in order to dismiss them, but in actuality to engage with them creatively. As with Milton and Blake, these intertexts inform and broaden the worlds of *His Dark Materials* but are also used as means by which Pullman has enabled himself to articulate his political and creative version. Explicit and implied intertextuality, then, are used in appreciation, as inspiration and for argumentation.

References

de Bertodano, Helena. 2002. ' "I Am of the Devil's Party" '. *Sunday Telegraph*. 27 January.

Dirda, Michael. 2000. 'The Amber Spyglass'. *Washington Post*. 29 October.

Drabble, Margaret, ed. 2000. *The Oxford Companion to English Literature*. Oxford: Oxford University Press. 6th ed.

Eccleshare, Julia. 2002. *Beatrix Potter to Harry Potter: Portraits of Children's Writers*. London: National Portrait Gallery Publications.

Hatlen, Burton. 2005. 'Pullman's *His Dark Materials*, a Challenge to the Fantasies of J.R.R Tolkien and C.S. Lewis, with an Epilogue on Pullman's Neo-Romantic Reading of *Paradise Lost*'. In Millicent Lenz and Carole Scott, eds. His Dark Materials *Illuminated: Critical Essays on Philip Pullman's Trilogy*. Detroit: Wayne State University Press. 75–94.

Lewis, C.S. 1942. *A Preface to Paradise Lost*. London: Oxford University Press.

Parkin, Lance, and Mark Jones. 2005. *Dark Matters: An Unofficial and Unauthorised Guide to Philip Pullman's Internationally Bestselling His Dark Materials Trilogy*. London: Virgin Books.

Parsons, Wendy, and Catriona Nicholson. 1999. 'Talking to Philip Pullman: An Interview'. *The Lion and the Unicorn*. 23: 1. January. 116–34.

Pope, Rob. 2002. *The English Studies Book: An Introduction to Language, Literature and Culture*. London: Routledge. 2nd ed.

Pullman, Philip. 2005. Introduction to *Paradise Lost by* John Milton. Oxford: Oxford University Press.

Ross, Deborah. 2002. 'Soap and the Serious Writer'. *Independent*. 4 February.

Scott, Carole. 2005. 'Pullman's Enigmatic Ontology: Revamping Old Traditions in *His Dark Materials*'. In Millicent Lenz with Carole Scott, eds. His Dark Materials *Illuminated: Critical Essays on Philip Pullman's Trilogy*. Detroit: Wayne State University Press. 95–105.

Smith, Karen Patricia. 2005. 'Tradition, Transformation, and the Bold Emergence: Fantastic Legacy and Pullman's *His Dark Materials*'. In Millicent Lenz and Carole Scott, eds. His Dark Materials *Illuminated: Critical Essays on Philip Pullman's Trilogy*. Detroit: Wayne State University Press. 135–51.

Warner, Marina. 2002. *Fantastic Metamorphoses; Other Worlds: Ways of Telling the Self*. Oxford: Oxford University Press.

Wartofsky, Alona. 2001. 'The Last Word'. *Washington Post*. 19 February.

Watkins, Tony. 2004. *Dark Matter: A Thinking Fan's Guide to Philip Pullman*. Southampton: Damaris Publishing.

www.philip-pullman.com

10

J.K. Rowling, *Harry Potter and the Philosopher's Stone* (1997)

Introduction
Nicola J. Watson

Origins, composition and reception

On 1 July 1997, the publication of *Harry Potter and the Philosopher's Stone* by Bloomsbury, a smallish independent publisher, inaugurated what was to become an unprecedented publishing and media phenomenon. The genesis of the Harry Potter series has been extensively recounted; the kernel of the story is the rags-to-riches story of the author, a depressed single mother, living on state benefits, writing up the book in a series of cafés in Edinburgh with a sleeping baby beside her. Neither the author, J.K. Rowling, nor the publisher anticipated what was to come; the manuscript, after all, had been turned down by twelve publishers before Bloomsbury picked it up, and there was little to suggest that it had the makings of a global brand. The initial print-run was a mere 1000 copies, of which half went to libraries. Critically it was well, but not ecstatically, received, picking up the Nestlé Smarties book prize, the British Book Award for Children's Book of the Year, the Children's Book Award, and being shortlisted for the 1997 Carnegie and the Guardian Children's Award. In retrospect, *The Scotsman's* generous verdict that it had 'all the makings of a classic' seems muted; by 2001, having been contracted by Scholastic Press in the States in 1998 and retitled there as *Harry Potter and the Sorcerer's Stone*, it had sold five million copies. By January 2008, the book stood at number twelve on the best-selling book list of all time; the film briefly became the highest grossing film ever in the UK. Even more spectacularly, the book inaugurated a series of six further books about Harry Potter totalling 4,195 pages in all, the final volume, *Harry Potter and the Deathly Hallows*, appearing in 2007. Those books picked up a string of prestigious awards, broke all sales records, were translated into sixty-five languages, generated a film series which (unfinished at the date of writing) is already the highest grossing film series of all time, made Harry Potter into a global brand with an estimated £76 billion, and made Rowling herself a fortune, estimated by the *Sunday Times* in 2008 as amounting to some £560 million.

An entire generation of children and their parents across the world have grown up with Harry Potter from his first entry into secondary school to his leaving the sixth form; they have read it cover to cover, and then started again, queued at midnight outside bookshops for the next instalment, played Harry Potter in the playground, dressed up as him for World Book Day, eaten their packed lunches from Harry Potter lunch boxes, made Harry Potter jigsaws, played Harry Potter board and video games, collected the stickers, traded the cards, insisted on seeing the films and complained at what was left out, and waited with waning hope and piercing disappointment for their own letter to arrive from Hogwarts to rescue them from ordinariness. The real world has undergone its own material transformations to suit; there now is a platform 9 ¾ at King's Cross Station, with half a luggage trolley vanishing through it, Christ Church, Oxford, is no longer primarily the haunt of Carroll's Alice, but one of the ghosts of Hogwarts, and Lacock Abbey is visited by those hoping to enter Snape's Potions classroom. If nothing else, *Harry Potter and the Philosopher's Stone* transformed the turn of the century understanding of children's literature as low in status and unremunerative, and it destroyed the notion that children's literature was simply for children, for it was clear that adults were equally transfixed.

Critical terrain

Such unprecedented success with children and adults alike attracted an enormous amount of critical attention, much of it not from dedicated literary scholars. In general, the Harry Potter books have been considered less as individual books, or even as a series, but in terms of their phenomenality, which has roused considerable anxiety. Although from early on, educationists were generally enthusiastic, hailing it as a book that could lure boys into reading and away from their Playstations, much of the commentary has been thoroughly suspicious of the pleasures promised by Potter. The Christian right in the States attacked the book for, in their view, promoting witchcraft and sorcery, and the Marxist left has been equally critical, focusing on the book's supposedly conservative politics. Critics have been variously dubious about its class politics, its gender politics, and its race politics. As the essays excerpted below make abundantly clear, literary criticism proper has tended to be driven by topicality and coloured by these political critiques, in its consideration of the roots of the appeal of the books.

Less partisan academic criticism has concentrated on the ways in which Rowling drew upon and updated long-standing traditions in children's fiction. Scholars have noted Rowling's revival of the boarding-school story, deriving from Thomas Hughes's *Tom Brown's Schooldays* (1857), and reversioned for girls by authors including Enid Blyton in her Malory Towers series, with its stock cast of characters (the bully, the sneak, the swot, the wet, the best friend, the enemy, the friendly teacher, the vindictive master), and its stock events (the contrast between home and the initiation into a new school, problems with uniform and equipment, the business of making friends, getting into scrapes, being undeservedly unpopular, and saving the day for the house at the match). They have remarked on the updating of the school story with a fantasy-twist into a wizard school, repeating the strategies of Ursula K. Le Guin's *The Wizard of Earthsea* trilogy (1968 onwards) and Jill Murphy's *The Worst Witch* series (1974 onwards). They have also noted that the Harry Potter series rethinks, as Rowling herself has acknowledged, T.H. White's *The Sword in the Stone* (1938), an account of the education of young Wart by Merlin and his eventual discovery of his burdensome parentage and national destiny as King Arthur. Other generic influences scholars have pointed out include that of the fairy tale and of individual myths and legends, and of the adventure story which centres on a family or band of friends, deriving for Rowling, at any rate, from E. Nesbit's *The Story of the Treasure-Seekers* (1899). Rowling intertwines her materials into a form of Christian quest-romance, a quest for identity on the part of the orphaned Harry, and the simultaneous discovery that upon him depends the outcome of an epic struggle between good and evil in the world.

The essays

The essays below have been chosen to sample some of the most polemical criticism of the book. Jack Zipes, in an early piece, lays out the argument for considering *Harry Potter* as a global 'phenomenon' rather than as literature, and explains it (with distaste) as the consequence of Harry Potter's repetition of stock conventions (most especially, its repetition of the common structures of the fairy tale). Suman Gupta offers a later and more developed effort to explain the phenomenon in terms of its comforting but, in his view, thoroughly dangerous endorsement of anti-rationality. Andrew

Blake suggests a British context within which to think through the genesis and initial appeal of the series; here, Blake explores the notion that Harry Potter has been part of the turn-of-the-century rebranding of England as 'heritage' fantasy for national and international consumption, and considers Rowling's literary debts, innovations, and combinations in terms of building a 'retrolutionary' sense of the past in the present and the present in the past.

Further reading

Anatol, G.L. 2003. *Reading Harry Potter: Critical Essays.* London, Praeger.

Blake, A. 2002. *The Irresistible Rise of Harry Potter.* London, Verso.

Gupta, S. 2003. *Re-reading Harry Potter.* Basingstoke, Palgrave Macmillan.

Heilman, E.E. (ed.) 2003. *Harry Potter's World: Multidisciplinary Critical Perspectives.* New York, Routledge.

Whited, L.A. 2002. *The Ivory Tower and Harry Potter: Perspectives on a Literary Phenomenon.* Columbia and London, Missouri University Press.

The Phenomenon of Harry Potter, or Why All the Talk?
Jack Zipes

Although there are now four published books in the Harry Potter series, it is difficult to assess them as literature *per se*.[1] We must talk about a phenomenon, and it is a mind-blowing phenomenon because it reveals just how difficult it is to evaluate and analyze children's literature or works that purport to be literature for the young.[2]

Anyone working in the field of children's literature cannot avoid Harry Potter. I am not certain whether one can talk about a split between a minority of professional critics, who have misgivings about the quality of the Harry Potter books, and the great majority of readers, old and young, who are mesmerized by the young magician's adventures. But I am certain that the phenomenal aspect of the reception of the Harry Potter books has blurred the focus for anyone who wants to take literature for young people seriously and who may be concerned about standards and taste that adults create for youth culture in the West. How is it possible to evaluate a work

This is an edited version of the essay originally published as Chapter 9 in J. Zipes, *Sticks and Stones: The Troublesome Success of Children's Literature from Slovenly Peter to Harry Potter* (New York and London: Routledge, 2001), pp. 170–89.

of literature like a Harry Potter novel when it is so dependent on the market conditions of the culture industry? Given the changes in the production and reception of children's and youth literature in the last ten years, what criteria can one use to grasp the value of a best-seller, especially when the buyers and readers are to a large degree adults? What constitutes a good fairytale novel? How do the Harry Potter books compare to other fantasy works? Is it fair to question the value and quality of J.K. Rowling's books, which have allegedly helped readers of all ages to read again with joy, just because they are so successful?

I believe that it is exactly because the success of the Harry Potter novels is so great and reflects certain troubling sociocultural trends that we must try to evaluate the phenomenon. In fact, I would claim that the only way to do Rowling and her Harry Potter books justice is to try to pierce the phenomenon and to examine her works as critically as possible, not with the intention of degrading them or her efforts, but with the intention of exploring why such a conventional work of fantasy has been fetishized, so that all sorts of magic powers are attributed to the very act of reading these works. The phenomenon is indeed beyond her control. She herself did not even conceive of its possibility. Yet 'everyone' appears to be spellbound and drawn to read the Harry Potter books. Might the stories about quaint Harry transform one's own life?

What has actually happened is that the conditions under which literature for the young is produced and received have been transformed through institutional changes of education, shifts in family relations, the rise of corporate conglomerates controlling the mass media, and market demands. Phenomena such as the Harry Potter books are driven by commodity consumption that at the same time sets the parameters of reading and aesthetic taste. Today the experience of reading for the young is mediated through the mass media and marketing so that the pleasure and meaning of a book will often be prescripted or dictated by convention. What readers passionately devour and enjoy may be, like many a Disney film or Barbie doll, a phenomenal experience and have personal significance, but it is also an *induced* experience calculated to conform to a cultural convention of amusement and distraction. It is this highly important connection between the conventional and the phenomenal that I want to explore in my essay on the Harry Potter books in an effort to take children's literature seriously within the political context of current globalizing trends predicated on fostering sameness throughout the world.

There are two common meanings for the word phenomenon. It generally refers to some kind of *occurrence,* change, or fact that is directly perceived; quite often the event is striking. Or the term is used to describe an extraordinary *person*, someone with exceptional talent, a *phenom*, whiz kid, or super star. Whether an occurrence or person, there is something incredible about the phenomenon that draws our attention. We hesitate to believe in the event or person we perceive, for a transformation has unexpectedly taken place. One of the reasons we cannot believe our senses is because the phenomenon defies rational explanation. There seems to be no logical cause or clear explanation for the sudden appearance or the transformation. Yet it is there, visible and palpable. The ordinary becomes extraordinary, and we are so taken by the phenomenon that we admire, worship, and idolize it without grasping fully why we regard it with so much reverence and awe except to say that so many others regard it as a phenomenon and, therefore, it must be a phenomenon.

Reason no longer applies after a phenomenon has appeared, especially when there is a series of phenomena that contribute to the 'Harry Potter phenomenon' such as:

- The rise of the myth of J.K. Rowling, single mother on welfare, sitting in a café and writing the books while raising a daughter by herself. This myth is the old rags-to-riches story and in our day and age has been spread through the mass media. It is the fairy tale about the diligent, hardworking girl who is recognized as a princess and lives happily ever after.

- The rejection of the first novel, *Harry Potter and the Sorcerer's Stone* [American title], by several publishers before being accepted by Bloomsbury Publishing in London. Neither the editors at Bloomsbury nor those at Scholastic, Inc. in New York would have predicted that the Harry Potter books would attract so much popular attention and sell in the millions. The long shot finishes a phenomenal first.

- The astonishing appeal of Harry Potter, the hero of all the books, a slight, modest, but confident boy who wears broken glasses. Despite his potentially nerdlike qualities, he has supernatural gifts that enable him to perform heroic deeds and defeat cynical forces of evil much like the knights of Arthurian legend. But Harry is much more successful – a postmodern whiz kid.

- The strange controversy surrounding the Harry Potter books caused by conservatives, even though the works are clearly didactic and moralistic and preach against the evil use of magic. But they have drawn the ire of the American religious right, which seeks to ban these books from schools, libraries, and bookstores because Harry is a wizard. Perhaps if Harry were seen as a Christian knight (which he actually is), he might be pardoned for his magical sins. But his stories, considered sinful, have stirred a phenomenal debate in the States.

All these incidental phenomena can be understood as tendencies that form the 'dialectics of the phenomenal' operative in the case of the Harry Potter phenomenon. What appears as something phenomenal turns or is turned into its opposite through a process of homogenization: the phenomenal thing or occurrence must become a conventional commodity that can be grasped or consumed to fit our cultural expectations. Otherwise it is not a phenomenon. There are other contributing factors operating here.

J.K. Rowling has overcome hardships and appears to have remarkable endurance and an extraordinary imagination. A divorced mother, she has written four compelling novels and has turned her ordinary life into the extraordinary. Therefore her personal story, or the little we know of it through newspapers, magazine articles, and various Websites, captures our attention and our hearts because of the astonishing turnabout that has occurred in her life, which follows our conventional wish fulfillment of rags to riches.

Her books are phenomenal because, they, too, are ordinary and yet have become extraordinary. There is nothing exceptional about Rowling's writing in comparison with that of many other gifted writers of children's and young adult literature. I am thinking here of such fantasy writers as Lloyd Alexander, Natalie Babbitt, Diana Wynne Jones, Francesca Lia Block, Philip Pullman, Jane Yolen, Donna Jo Napoli and many others who are constantly experimenting in innovative ways – and not always successfully. What distinguishes the plots of Rowling's novels, however, are their conventionality, predictability, and happy ends despite the clever turns of phrases and surprising twists in the intricate plots. They are easy and delightful to read, carefully manicured and packaged, and they sell extraordinarily well precisely because they are so cute and ordinary.

Harry Potter as a fictitious character is ordinary on first appearance because he more closely resembles a bookworm than a hero. Yet, like Clark Kent, he has more to him than his appearance would indicate. He is one of the mythical chosen heroes, called upon by powers greater than himself to rescue his friends and the world from diabolical evil. He is David, Tom Thumb, Jack the Giant Killer, Aladdin, and Horatio Alger all in one, the little guy who proves he's bigger than life.

There is something wonderfully paradoxical about the phenomena surrounding the phenomenon of the Harry Potter books. For anything to become a phenomenon in Western society, it must become *conventional*; it must be recognized and categorized as unusual, extraordinary, remarkable, and outstanding. In other words, it must be popularly accepted, praised, or condemned, worthy of everyone's attention; it must conform to the standards of exception set by the mass media and promoted by the culture industry in general. To be phenomenal means that a person or commodity must conform to the tastes of hegemonic groups that determine what makes up a phenomenon. It is impossible to be phenomenal without conforming to conventionality. Whether you are a super athlete, actor, writer or commodity – and there is tremendous overlap in these categories – you must be displayed and display yourself according to socially accepted rules and expectations of 'phenomenality.' In American and British culture, the quality of what rises to the top is always appropriated, and if the phenomenon does somehow contain some qualities that are truly different, they are bound to be corroded and degraded, turning the phenomenon against itself and into a homogenized commodity that will reap huge profits until the next phenomenon appears on the horizon. Difference and otherness are obliterated in the process. What appears unique conceals the planned production of commonality and undermines the autonomy of judgment. A phenomenon can sway us from ourselves. We become dizzy and delirious.

In the case of the Harry Potter books, their phenomenality detracts from their conventionality, and yet their absolute conformance to popular audience expectations is what makes for their phenomenality. So far there are four novels: *Harry Potter and the Sorcerer's Stone* (1998), *Harry Potter and the Chamber of Secrets* (1999), *Harry Potter and the Prisoner of Azkaban* (1999), and *Harry Potter and the Goblet of Fire* (2000). Each one is well over 300 pages. Indeed, the last novel, a tour-de-force, that demands patience and perseverance on the part of valiant readers, amounts to 734 pages. These works have been followed by Harry Potter commodities. Rowling has intended from the beginning to write seven novels altogether, a magic number, but if you've read one, you've read them all: the plots are the same, and in my opinion, the story lines become tedious and grating after you have read the first. Here is the formula for each novel:

Part I. Prison Harry the imaginative hero, the chosen one, lives in the home of Vernon and Petunia Dursley because he is an orphan. They have a fat slob of a son named Dudley, who becomes more disgusting and unlikable with each novel. All three are referred to as Muggles because they are not wizards. In other words, they lack imagination and are materialist philistines. Their home is more like a prison than anything else, or to be more precise, it is the domain of banal reality. The Dursleys and their kind are devoid of imagination. Indeed, they are afraid of magic and the world of fantasy.

Part II. The Noble Calling Since Harry is special, a member of the elect, he receives a summons, calling, invitation, command, or reminder to attend Hogwarts, the school for wizards, at the end of each summer after he has reached the age of ten. To accomplish this task, Harry must break out of the Dursleys' home.

Part III. The Heroic Adventures   Harry travels in some magical fashion to Hogwarts, where he will be tested in various ways, but he is always pitted against his archenemy Voldemort, a sinister wizard, who killed Harry's parents and tried to kill the boy as well. Thanks to his mother's sacrifice, Harry survived Voldemort's first attempt to murder him, but the evil wizard is on a mad quest to finish the job. Hogwarts and the environment (including a Forbidden Forest and a town called Hogsmeade) constitute the mystical realm in which Harry with his noble sidekick, Ron Weasley, fight against the sadistic Draco Malfoy and his cruel pals Crabbe and Goyle. Their fights, which often take place on the playing field of quidditch (a bizarre spatial game that resembles computerized baseball, basketball, and hockey played on broomsticks) are only the backdrop for deadly battles with the forces of Voldemort. Cheering Harry on are two girls, Hermione Granger and Ginny Weasley, Ron's younger sister. Whatever happens – and the plots always involve a great deal of manly competition and some kind of mystery – you can be sure that Harry wins.

Part IV. The Reluctant Return Home   Exhausted, drained, but enlightened, Harry is always victorious by the time summer recess is about to begin. Unfortunately, Harry must always return to the banal surroundings of the Dursley home.

The plots of the first four novels thus far resemble the structure of a conventional fairy tale: a modest little protagonist, typically male, who does not at first realize how talented he is and who departs from his home on a mission or is banished until he fulfills three tasks. He generally enters a mysterious forest or unknown realm on his quest. Along his way he meets animals or friends who, in return, give him gifts that will help him. Sometimes he meets an old sage or wise woman, who will provide him with support and aid. At one point he encounters a tyrant, ogre, or competitor, whom he must overcome to succeed in his mission. Invariably, he defeats his opponent and either returns home or settles in a new domain with money, wife, and happy prospects.

Rowling's novels are, of course, much more complicated and complex than your classical fairy tale. They have clearly been influenced by mystery novels, adventure films, TV sitcoms, and fiction series, and they bear all the typical trademarks that these popular genres exhibit. Indeed, the last novel, *The Goblet of Fire,* even had scenes modeled on the European soccer championship matches replete with cheerleaders and hooligans. Perhaps it is because the novels are a hodgepodge of these popular entertainments that her novels are so appealing.

[Equally, Harry is a conventional character.] He is white, Anglo-Saxon, bright, athletic, and honest. The only mark of difference he bears is a slight lightning-shaped scar on his forehead. Otherwise, he is the classic

Boy Scout, a little mischievous like Tom Sawyer or one of the Hardy boys. He does not curse; he speaks standard English grammatically, as do all his friends; he is respectful to his elders; and he has perfect manners. He would definitely help a grandmother cross the street, perhaps even fly her across on his broomstick. He is a straight arrow, for he has a noble soul and will defend the righteous against the powers of evil. This means that Harry the scout must play the role of a modern-day TV sleuth in each novel. In novel one, he is given the task of discovering what the sorcerer's stone is, who invented it, and how to prevent Voldemort from obtaining it. Ron, as in all buddy/cop films, is always at his side. Typically, the girls are always left to gawk and gaze at Harry's stunning prowess.

But what are we to expect when women are generally accessories in most TV police shows, detective novels, and mysteries? In the Harry Potter books they fulfill stereotypical roles, but so do most of the characters. As Schoefer has demonstrated, Professor Dumbledore is Harry's spiritual father, the ultimate saintly wizard, who operates behind the scenes to guide and help Harry. Then we have the bumbling but good-hearted giant Hagrid, who provides comic relief; the strict assistant principal Minerva McGonagall; the rich snob Draco Malfoy, Harry's nemesis at the school; Professor Snape, the snide teacher who holds a grudge against Harry, but will undoubtedly unveil a positive side; Argus Filch, the nosy caretaker; Ron Weasley, the dependable, faithful friend; Ginny Weasley, who has a love interest in Harry; Sirius the protective godfather; and last but not least, Hermione Granger, the bookish and bright girl, who always comes up with the right answers and can be a pain in the neck because of the strange causes that she supports. There are others, but these one-dimensional characters are planted in each one of the novels to circle around Harry with his phallic wand and to function in a way that will highlight his extraordinary role as Boy Scout/detective. There is indeed nothing wrong in being a Boy Scout, and I suspect that this is why many adults, especially parents, like Harry: he is a perfect model for boys because he excels in almost everything he undertakes. But this is also his difficulty as a literary character: he is too flawless and almost a caricature of various protagonists from pop culture. Like young heroes today, Harry appeals to young readers (and adults) because Rowling has endowed him with supernatural powers of the sort we can see in *The Power Rangers*, *X-Men*, *Star Wars*, *Buffy the Vampire Slayer*, and numerous other TV shows and films. Harry 'acts out' his role with wand, invisible cape, and broomstick to determine his destiny, and though adults may help him, he is literally the one who has the power to use for the benefit of goodness.

One of the difficulties in reading fairy tales and fairy-tale novels is that you know from the beginning that evil will be overcome. A fairy tale is not a fairy tale that does not have a happy end. You know from beginning to end that Harry will triumph over evil, and this again may be one of the reasons that her novels have achieved so much popularity.

In a world in which we are uncertain of our roles and uncertain about our capacity to defeat evil, the Harry Potter novels arrive and inform us that if we all pull together and trust one another and follow the lead of the chosen one, evil will be overcome.

In fact, there are people 'chosen' for the task of leadership because they have the right magical skills and good genes. It doesn't matter that they happen to be all white, all British, all from good homes, and that the men and boys call the shots. What matters is a feeling of security that we gain after reading one or more of Rowling's novels. They are carefully crafted to make us delight in the good clean way that her protagonists set the world aright without questioning the real conflicts that the majority of children in the United Kingdom and North America face.

The Harry Potter books are part of the eternal return to the same and, at the same time, part of the success and process by which we homogenize our children. Making children all alike is, sadly, a phenomenon of our times.

Notes

1.   The series of seven is now complete. In her article, 'At Last, The Wizard Gets Back to School,' Janet Maslin comments: 'The frenzy that has greeted the fourth book in the series, *Harry Potter and the Goblet of Fire*, would seem to go beyond any reasonable response to fiction, no matter how genuinely delightful that fiction happens to be. Instead, the current wave of Harrymania brings the Potter series to a fever pitch better associated with movie hype, major sports events and hot new Christmas toys,' the *New York Times* (July 10, 2000): B1.
2.   In a short editorial, Roger Sutton, editor of *The Horn Book*, alludes to the phenomenon and the difficulty it causes in evaluating children's literature: 'I don't have any opinions about *Harry*; at least I *didn't* have any opinions until J.K. Rowling's series became a 'publishing phenomenon' (ghastly but apt phrase) and ... children's books became All About Harry. So I'm not feeling suckered – neither by the book nor by the publisher, but by the cosmic forces that have ordained that this likable but critically insignificant series become widely popular and therefore news, and therefore something I'm supposed to have an opinion about.' 'Potter's Field,' *The Horn Book* 75 (September/October 1999): 1.

The Unthinkingness of Harry Potter
Suman Gupta

The creation of the Magic world – i.e. the construction of an institutional structure for it, the detailing of the environment and people within it, the focusing on it through the Muggle world, the systematization of magical processes within it, the invention of a history and mythology behind it, etc. – is such that it is fundamentally antithetical to our world. This is so despite its being used (generally unsuccessfully or in an unsatisfactory manner) to ostensibly reflect and comment on concerns in our world. Indeed, it is *because* there is an attempt to use the Magic world to illuminate certain pre-occupations of our world, to strike markedly familiar chords of our world, that its antithetical nature becomes all the clearer. Briefly, in being con-structed around a notion of magic the Magic world is necessarily, and quite deliberately, presented as being essentially anti-rational. There are strong limits to the questioning that is possible and the explanations that are avail-able in the Magic world. In the Magic world things and qualities are simply manifest – they just are so – there is no need, no ability, no desire, no will to explain *why* they are so. The self-evidently manifest is simply accepted as the generally unambiguous and unequivocal truth. That is why things and events are magical in Magic world. It is also therefore essentially a ritu-alistic world: spells are learnt and used, their effectiveness and process is not explained and nor is there any evidence that it can be explained; the proclivities of sentient beings are predetermined (Voldemort is bad, Dumbledore is good, house-elves are slavish, Trolls are stupid, a Veela is a *femme fatale*, Slytherins are Slytherins and Gryffindors are Gryffindors), they are not significantly moulded by experience and education; learning is a matter of constantly acquiring greater and greater levels of information and memorizing facts, it has little to do with understanding the principles underlying different ranges of information and being able to synthesize or collate facts; humans either have magic or they don't, they are either Magic or Muggle, and there is no point questioning why this is so (it might have something to do with blood). The Magic world is one where questioning cannot be imagined except to discover facts, to uncover what has happened. Evidently therefore, our ordinary sense of mystery, and curiosity about the mysterious, does not exist in the Magic world; the only kind of curiosity that can exist (and one that drives Harry and some of his friends) is one

Extracted from 'The Beginning', in S. Gupta, *Re-reading Harry Potter* (Basingstoke and New York: Palgrave Macmillan, 2001), pp. 151–64.

that tries to uncover a sequence of events that have happened – to uncover the facts of the past that are relevant for whatever reason. That is no more mysterious than history is mysterious. *The only sense of mystery that can be brought to the Magic world has to be brought by the readers of the* Harry Potter *books of our world: the magical beings and happenings are mysterious to readers of our world because we are accustomed to trying to explain things, to understanding principles, to trying to rationalize, and the magical is definitively inexplicable.* It is because we are rational and can hope to explain phenomena and look for deep principles, that we recognize that which resists explanation and understand its mysteriousness. Understanding its mysteriousness is also a powerful motive to try to explain it. In our use of language, in our engagement with the world, in our institutional structures, in our technological abilities, in every aspect of our present lives and that of our past the binding thread has been the desire, ability, will to rationalize. The comfort of faith (along with which comes religious acceptance, or reconciliation with the miraculous or magical) is constantly complemented by the desire to understand and explain. The institutional forms of faith (religions) themselves provide ways of explaining the apparently inexplicable. And when those explanations refuse to satisfy, more rational explanations emerge from within faith and defying faith; so that theology may lead on to philosophy and philosophy to science, and they can also lead back to or across each other in a variety of different ways. Our world is constantly, and both universally and at the same time pluralistically, predicated on the possibility, desire, ability, will to rationalize. This is so even when it becomes evident that rationalism is limited or can be devastatingly wrong-headed. End of catechism.

The Magic world is not predicated on rationality. It is based on the unquestioning acceptance of what is manifest or can be or comes to be manifested; on the acceptance of the way things just magically are. The Magic world is definitively anti-rational.

It is not enough simply to delineate what the distinction between the magic of the Magic world and the unavoidable rationalism of our world is. As far as the *Harry Potter* books[1] play on that distinction there are two significant inter-linked effects (of significant social and political import) that need to be laid bare: the deliberate anti-rationalism of the books; and the idea of *chosen* people that is simultaneously conveyed in them.

One of the happy circumstances of Harry Potter's entry into the Magic world in *Stone* is that he seems to be famous there already without his quite knowing why. He enjoys a celebrity status without apparently having done anything to deserve it. It gradually emerges that his fame is due to the conviction among wizards that he was responsible for Voldemort's fall from power. Voldemort had apparently killed his parents and cast a spell to kill him too, a mere infant at the time, but unsuccessfully. Voldemort's spell had left a lightning mark on Harry's forehead but no other visible effect, and had at the same time rendered Voldemort himself powerless. It is possible that Voldemort's failure in this regard was due to the extraordinary love that Harry's mother bore him (*Stone* 216; *Chamber* 233); it must have been extraordinary love since the affection that other victims of Voldemort must have enjoyed hadn't protected them as effectively. At any rate, it is clear that the happy circumstance of Harry's celebrity status does confer on him certain advantages. He is the object of envy and interest among his school-mates, and has to do little to make friends and, for that matter, enemies. It gets him a most interesting and loyal friend in Hagrid from the beginning. All his teachers are aware of his special status and respond accordingly – Snape with malice, and most of the others with indulgence (especially the all-knowing Dumbledore). Harry is from the beginning a kind of chosen person in the Magic world, who has acquired fame, friends and enemies, a peculiarly attractive status and great expectations without having made any conscious effort to deserve them. No one has any doubts that his innate abilities would be equal to his reputation – except naturally Harry himself.

Fortunately for Harry, his innate abilities do turn out to be more than adequate to his reputation: he is not mistakenly thought of as a chosen person, he is one. He appears to have a natural ability to fly on a broomstick, which lands him one of the most enviable roles possible in Hogwarts: that of a Quidditch Seeker (the youngest ever). Now Quidditch is an odd game[2] that, though apparently a team sport, is heavily dependent on one player alone to decide victory or defeat – the Seeker. This is how it works. There is something like a football or rugby field with goalposts on either side, and seven players in each team. There are three kinds of balls in the game: a Quaffle, Bludgers and a Snitch. From each team there is a goal keeper, or Keeper. Three players in each team, called Chasers, try to score goals with the Quaffle; each Quaffle-goal is worth ten points. The Bludgers constantly try to knock out team members, and two members of each team, called Beaters, are devoted to keeping the Bludgers at bay by hitting them when-ever they appear to threaten anyone. That leaves the Snitch – a fleet, small, golden ball – that flies around randomly. The Seeker in each team has only one job: they have to catch the Snitch, which effectively ends the game *and* gives the successful Seeker's team an extra 150 points. Quidditch, in other words, seems to be designed to give an extraordinarily important role to the Seeker. The Seeker's efforts are worth precisely fifteen times the efforts of the Chasers. So exclusive is the Seeker's role that it does not intersect at all with that of the larger part of the team: the Chasers and Keepers play their own game and cannot influence the Seeker in any way. Only the Beaters have a role that influences the Seeker, and it is that of protecting him. It might seem like a team sport, but it is one in which team-effort has no particular role to play; it is a team sport in which the rest of the team is *below* one person, pretty much entirely dependent on one person, by the rules of the game. That Harry's innate abilities makes him a natural Seeker is about as much confirmation of being a chosen person in the order of Magic things as could have been needed. Harry's natural abilities as a Seeker appear to be true in that in his first few Quidditch games he overcomes odds that have nothing to do with the game itself (a hexed broomstick in *Stone*, a Bludger that particularly targets Harry in *Chamber*) to decide victory. He never loses through a fair game, and usually wins despite unfair disadvantages. And it all comes naturally.

The team game that is designed to depend largely on one person is used to bring out the chosen-ness of Harry. This quality of being chosen is then magnified, taken to heroic proportions, in the more deadly games (each involving rules, each involving adversaries, each involving victory or defeat) that Harry has to play with Voldemort in each of the novels. Harry keeps winning despite himself. More interestingly, in these serious life-or-death games Harry wins against rational odds – and in each of these victory is literally beyond reason (one can't win by being rational, rationality plays a role but never a winning role, winning ultimately depends on being chosen to win or on being the chosen person). That is where the more explicit anti-rationality of the *Harry Potter* books kick in.

Harry Potter's victories in the life-or-death games are won through two means: by the shakiness of the rules of the game (these can be broken or superseded according to convenience at any time), and by the help of friends who deal with those aspects of the games that can be rationally dealt with so that Harry can finally win. The rational aspects of the game are seldom those that Harry deals with himself, and rationality is always secondary to the final stage where Harry's natural abilities – his chosen-ness (in terms of gifts unknown to himself, and courage which he seems to be born with) – shine through. The endgame of *Stone* sets the tone for these contests. Harry, Ron and Hermione go through the trapdoor to face the man with two faces (one Voldemort's), and encounter a series of obstacles. Hermione works out how to get through the Devil's Snare plant because she had read about it (she had prepared herself for it and reasoned her way through a tough situation). Harry catches the key to the door by using those innate flying skills that made him a Seeker. Ron gets Harry and Hermione through the deadly chess-game at his own expense by working out the moves that would enable that to happen (he also reasoned his way through a tricky situation). Hermione solves the riddle that gets Harry into the final stage – Hermione's reaction on seeing the riddle speaks for itself:

> Hermione let out a great sigh and Harry, amazed, saw that she was smiling, the very last thing he felt like doing.
>
> '*Brilliant*,' said Hermione. 'This isn't magic – it's logic – a puzzle. A lot of the greatest wizards haven't got an ounce of logic, they'd be stuck in here for ever.'
> (*Stone* 207)

Hermione lets Harry go unprotestingly into the final stage because she now knows the truth of the Magic world: that Harry is the chosen person – 'Harry – you're a great wizard, you know' – and that that is more important than her 'Books! And cleverness!' (*Stone* 208). And there Harry, with some courage and not a little serendipity, wins against Voldemort. The pattern carries on in *Chamber*. Hermione makes the Polyjuice Potion and solves the problem of what's in the walls of Hogwarts, but all that doesn't matter ultimately. Ron and Harry finally go to the Chamber of Secrets, Ron is put out of action, Harry faces the past incarnation of Lord Voldemort alone, and asks for help and magically gets it from Dumbledore. The sorting hat with a sword and a phoenix named Fawkes turn up and sort things out for Harry. And the pattern carries on in *Prisoner* – reasonable counter-moves getting ever less useful, luck and courage and help from friends (it is Hermione who turns the clock back at Dumbledore's suggestion for a happy denouement) serving Harry as well as before.

The ultimate and, really, only weapon that Harry needs and that works in the Magic world is that Harry is Harry, chosen adversary of Voldemort from infancy. When the awe-inspiringly powerful Voldemort and the novice Harry (who could scarcely do elementary spells without Hermione's instructions) duel with each other, incredibly they appear to be evenly matched.

The inference seems to me to be inevitable: all the *Harry Potter* books centre on the fact that Harry is *chosen* to be Voldemort's adversary in advance and *chosen* to win; innate abilities account for this victory far more than any rational ability or anything that Harry can think his way through and work out; indeed Harry's chosen-ness is a function of his innateness; rationality is only useful along the way, but ultimately doesn't matter and shouldn't be taken too seriously; innate abilities are best exercised in an ignorant and *unthinking* fashion. Who chooses Harry? one may ask. It doesn't matter. There is no answer – whoever gives magical abilities and innate powers, could be the answer. What does matter is this: the *Harry Potter* books are an extended celebration of unthinking courage and luck; to make this celebration possible an unthinking hero is placed in a Magic world that is definitively unthinking to be the chosen victor; and all this is largely deliberately presented at the expense of seeking explanations and using rational principles – which inevitably, and despite numerous failures and shortcomings, underlie our engagement with our world.

The anti-rationality and the deeply ingrained centrality of chosenness in the *Harry Potter* books is the reason why the various apparently obvious and well-meaning gestures towards our world made therein either fail or reach unsatisfactory resolutions on closer inspection. The liberal and well-meaning and anti-fascist veneer in the presentation of magical races as analogous to human races, and wizard racism to human racism, is under-cut under closer scrutiny by an endorsement of a deeper form of racism in the Magic world – equivalent to the patronizing, imperial-mission variety of racism of our world. This deep racism in the Magic world is not a purely invidious construction; it is a condition of the manner in which the Magic world is conceived. The inequality of races is close in spirit to the rule of innate abilities that can't be explained and the centrality of chosen-ness that is *a priori*. Anti-racist and anti-discriminatory ideologies in our world depend on rational arguments that are based on a fundamental equality of humans for social and political purposes. This equality has nothing to do with innate qualities and natural abilities; this equality devolves from any sane attempt to employ rational principles with social and political effect. Since everything significant in the *Harry Potter* books is innate, inborn, essen-tial, simply manifest, definitively inexplicable in terms of rational principles and processes, the wizard racial traits and house-elf servitude and wizard hetero-sexual desire have to be so too. And naturally then they have only tangential, unsatisfactory, contradictory and, often, ominous implications in our world. But all this is nevertheless attractive, nevertheless apparently suggestive in our world, because the possible – the failing – analogues are carefully deployed, nowhere more effectively than in the use of advertisements and advertising tech-niques, or in cinematic renderings. In our world we are accustomed to being lured by the magic of advertisements; in the *Harry Potter* books advertisement magic becomes real and draws us into what is effectively a massive advertise-ment for magic, for the magicality in advertising, itself. The *Harry Potter* films in our world are pre-determinedly satisfactory concretizations of agreements that are the *raison d'être* of the virtual reality market itself.

The effect of these carefully posed juxtapositions and separations between the Magic world and our world is that we tend to accept magic in its own terms, i.e. unthinkingly – with little analysis and a great deal of acceptance, being light-heartedly lured by the manifest rather than being seriously con-cerned with the not-too-immediately-obvious implications. It is possible that in the process some of those distinctly unsatisfactory, contradictory, even omi-nous social and political connotations of the *Harry Potter* books would unthinkingly convey themselves along with the superficial and comforting liberal morally correct gestures and the pleasure of being lured into an unthinking world. Or perhaps it is precisely all those qualities – the superficial unthinking qualities as well as those insidiously underlying them – that actually agree with what a very large readership in our world (those who have made the *Harry Potter* phenomenon a phenomenon) already inclines towards. Perhaps the current social and political condition of our world is gradually inclining us away from the rationality that is (often inadequately but nevertheless inescapably) constituted within it, towards a desire for the unthinking *with* some of the implications that follow. Perhaps, in other words, the *Harry Potter* phenomenon is such because these books offer exactly what we unthinkingly desire *within* our world and *because* of the current condition of our world and *despite* the constitution of our world. These are desires born in our world; these are not created by the *Harry Potter* books, merely realized in them in a certain (attractive, readable, undemanding) form. More and more people in more and more contexts unthinkingly read the *Harry Potter* books, absorb their film versions and the advertisement images and computer and video games and other consumer products that derive from them, because they are inclined by our world to do so. The question is: are the *Harry Potter* books really *read – read*, that is, as being thinkingly understood?

Notes

1. The following editions of the *Harry Potter* series are used for this essay: J.K. Rowling, *Harry Potter and the Philosopher's Stone* (London: Bloomsbury, 1997); J.K. Rowling, *Harry Potter and the Chamber of Secrets* (London: Bloomsbury, 1998).
2. In this context also see 'What if Quidditch, the Enchanted Sport of Wizards and Witches Featured in the Harry Potter Books, Were Regulated by the NCAA?', *Sports Illustrated*, 21 August 2000, p. 33.

Harry Potter and the Reinvention of the Past
Andrew Blake

Why Harry Potter? Why now? The answer has nothing to do with the author's life before fame and fortune, or whether or not the books are 'original' or 'good' or follow any particular spiritual or moral code. It is, in short, because Joanne Rowling's creation hits the spot by addressing many of the anxieties in our changing political and cultural world, and if we are

Extracted from 'Harry Potter and the Reinvention of the Past', in A. Blake, *The Irresistible Rise of Harry Potter* (London and New York, Verso, 2002), pp. 4–26.

going to understand why Harry Potter has become a global hero we have to see him in his times – namely, 1997 and after. We need to track the movement of the books, tapes, films and merchandise against a set of reference points – including the ways in which we think about the past, education, childhood and adulthood, work and creativity in the cultural industries, the consumer, and the reader. And, yes, magic.

In 1997 a new government came to power in Britain. Its supporters sang that things could only get better. But how? And anyway, what was so bad? One problem was identified in an influential pamphlet published by then-trendy think tank Demos in 1997. Mark Leonard's *Britain*™ argued that Britain – especially England – was stuck up its own past. Parliament's Lords preserved the feudal system, and the monarchy preserved itself as a Victorian matriarchy despite the modernising attempts of the young women who had married into it. Those tourists who came to the UK – a declining number – wanted cream teas and Tudor houses. Leonard claimed that despite the predominance of this 'heritage culture', Britain could and should escape from its past and rebrand itself as the hub of the new communications and service industries which were the future for exports and employment. But if this was to happen England, once the imagined centre of an empire and of a united kingdom, must reimagine itself as part of this hi-tech future. Or the globalising world would leave England behind.

As Benedict Anderson has claimed, the 'imagined community' is crucial to modern nationhood. An England imagined only through its past can hardly be said to exist in the present. Politically, however, there is a problem which no change in representation can address. History seems to be all that England has – especially since the legal and political status of the constituent parts of the United Kingdom of Great Britain and Northern Ireland has changed markedly since 1998. At this point the peoples of Wales and Scotland voted for limited political autonomy, with their own elected assemblies, and the peace process in Northern Ireland resulted in the return of devolved government, with the potential for closer ties to the Republic of Ireland. There is no similar legislative autonomy for England. The geographical area 'England' is virtually alone in the world in having a passionately supported national football team, but no national government. Its MPs share their parliament with Scots, Northern Irish and Welsh representatives, but there is no reciprocal arrangement. Politically, England does not exist. The imagined centre of the UK has begun to lose its periphery, without gaining a legal identity of its own; this makes it very difficult for an 'imagined community' to form successfully around the notion of England or Englishness.

At precisely this moment an Englishness that deals with both the local past and a more inclusive present appeared, and in subsequent years it has become a global commodity through one of England's most consistent cultural exports: fiction. Harry Potter has indeed rebranded Britain – but surely his low-tech magical world, with its Victorian London shopping alley and a Highlands boarding school, belongs to the heritage past, not to Mark Leonard's future-looking scheme? The literary agent who accepted Rowling's manuscript, Christopher Little, has underlined the problem: 'It was a very difficult book to sell. Quite a large number of publishers turned it down. It was too long, it dealt with going away to school, something that was regarded as being not politically correct.'[1] Before Harry Potter, the 1990s children's book tried to deal very directly with the 'real' – and an uncomfortable real at that: stories and novels dealt with issues such as housing-estate poverty, teenage pregnancy, and drug abuse. Whatever its sociological accuracy, this politically correct mode of literary production was out of kilter with the 1990s times; Harry Potter, on the other hand, was right on the button.

We first meet Harry at his aunt and uncle's suburban home, number 4, Privet Drive, Little Whinging, Surrey. This claustrophobic (and distinctly unmagical) address was captured perfectly in the *Philosopher's Stone* movie's opening – small, boxy houses, brand-new but trying to look like country cottages, each with a company car in the driveway: a very English way of living. Harry's irresistible rise starts from here; and assessing it means we first have to ask the question that bothered Mark Leonard: why do the English live like this, using the past in order to make the present bearable? It's a form of insulation against modernity. The pace of technological change and the constant bombardment of information, the humiliation involved in trying to use any transport system, the difficulties of learning or earning, and of maintaining relationships with families and friends, means that we perforce *exist* in modern life, but most of us want to live somewhere else; and many of us choose to inhabit 'tradition'. We ache for a past that we have constructed ourselves – we buy old, or old-style houses (such as those in Privet Drive). We copy the old, rather than turn to the new. England is the land of the mock-Tudor suburb and the restored Victorian house. But we are happy with central heating and air conditioning in those old-seeming houses. Either the old is remodelled so that it can contain the new, or the new is represented as traditional.

The English, to paraphrase Patrick Wright, live in an old country, and their culture reflects this fact. Popular and classical music, art and architecture, film and television are all informed by the past, which often seems more vital and meaningful than the present. In order to address the seeming impossibility of constructing a non-retrospective future, politicians and cultural imagineers have acted in a 'retrolutionary' way – presenting aspects of the future through terms set by the past, in order to make it seem palatable. The Harry Potter books do this very well, but they didn't invent the recipe; even in 1995, before the publishing deal was complete, before a book had been sold, retrolution was in the air.

The very past itself – our sense of 'history' – had been remodelled during the 1980s. The boom years of the 1980s indicated that almost any aspect or the past – including historic houses, Victorian gardening techniques, even opera – could be packaged as luxury consumer items for people with new wealth. With this in mind a younger generation of historians (and museum workers and archaeologists) tried to reinvent the past for present-day consumer culture, and to sell it.

Historians started to produce biographies of the well-born or influential, or studies of scientific discoveries. Museums offered not exhibitions, but simulated experiences of the past. Schools offered simulations of past experience rather than curricula centred on interpretation; pupils would dress up as medieval peasants rather than learn about the causes of the Wars of the Roses. Their adult equivalents, the Sealed Knot and other societies, spent their weekends replicating historic battles in literally painstaking detail, without entering into arguments about who was wrong or right, or debating Marxist, feminist, liberal or conservative explanations as to why the wars they were mimicking had happened in the first place.

The broadcast media responded to the new mood. As history finally got its own (cable/satellite) television channel, the detailed television series that had characterised history on the UK's terrestrial channels, such as the twenty-six-episode *The World at War*, were supplemented by briefer and more sensational programmes on crime, or biographies of the famous. Archaeology, meanwhile, was made into a televised spectator sport. In *Time Team*, a group of professional archaeologists, encouraged and abetted by an enthusiastic, knowledgeable (and New Labour supporting), professional comedian, dug against the clock. The past was also available on the high street. A chain of shops, Past Times, offered copies of historical artefacts such as eighteenth-century maps or Victorian lamp stands, alongside classic novels and videos of televised costume dramas. History had become 'heritage'.

In its symbolic architecture, too, England found it difficult to move with the times. The national library, rebuilt after twenty years of Treasury-led delays and budget cuts, at least offered some kind of integrity of design. 2000 was the year of the Millennium Dome; what could have been a triumphant showpiece was a disaster. The concept seemed audacious and positive: a vessel 320 metres in diameter, suspended in midair by a series of twelve 100-metre steel masts, dominating a festival site of 130 acres of land, was meant to signify the emergence of Britain from its manufacturing past – the ground it stands on was poisoned by a century's gas production and storage, and the antiseptic cleanness of the new building signifies the post-industrial commercial world of the information age. It incorporated contemporary technologies – but unlike its 1851 Great Exhibition forebear the Crystal Palace, the Dome relied on the past for its design image. The technical audacity was represented in a backward-looking structure, a fantasy based on the science fiction comics of the 1950s and the futurist designs that characterised a previous exhibition, the 1951 Festival of Britain. The Dome's futurism was caught in the past.

Popular music was also meeting its past. In the mid-1990s, bands such as Pulp, Blur and Oasis were labelled 'Brit-pop' by a press eager to find local popular-culture heroes. They were, and were seen as, deliberately English rather than Anglo-American (the 'Brit' was always a misnomer), and their music echoed 1960s pop. Britpop's bands and fans, whatever their ages, wallowed in nostalgia for the days when the Kinks wrote about Waterloo sunsets, the sixties were swinging and all was right with the world. Brit-pop was located in the same culture of nostalgia and the rediscovery of a national past as other aspects of the leisure industry. Music too became 'heritage culture'.

Meanwhile 1990s films such as *Four Weddings and A Funeral, The Full Monty* and *Bridget Jones's Diary* established a register of Englishness that is as powerful as any offered by architecture or music, and here again the nation seemed to be looking back. The hedonistic and vacuous upper middle class of *Four Weddings* and *Bridget Jones*, and the unemployed working-class men of *The Full Monty*, represent an England that is grotesquely caught by its past, politically ignorant and inept, and unable to do much more than laugh, along with the audience, at its own situation.

Of course this cultural nostalgia was only part of the story. In music, for example, a number of less Anglo-centric forms also emerged in the 1990s, chiefly because of the musical contact produced from the immigration of Commonwealth people into British cities which began in the 1950s.

All this is also part of the re-engagement with history, but here the imperial past and the multicultural present take an imagined Englishness in different directions. They offer a potential, at least, for a cultural definition of a nation that is ethnically inclusive, globally connected, and aware of the present.

Harry Potter is part of this political and cultural world. Harry is English; indeed he is a Home Counties suburban child. But he lives in the present, even when he is translated to the parallel but old-seeming world of the Hogwarts School of Witchcraft and Wizardry. Unlike Oasis, he doesn't merely look back. Hogwarts represents the multicultural contemporary England that has produced Roni Size and Najma Akhtar. And though there is a class system in operation at Hogwarts, it doesn't dictate the plot as you would expect from a Victorian novel or even a 1920s public school story. The community is not given; it is made, by the abilities and activities of all its members – by the incompetent Neville Longbottom as much as by heroic Harry. Harry Potter isn't just part of [a] museum culture; he is a *retrolutionary*, a symbolic figure of the past-in-future England which is in desperate need of such symbols.

Harry Potter is a deliberately retrolutionary creation. The stories explore the old, and a little under the surface deal with the new: past literary forms and present concerns exist side by side. The novels combine various ways of telling a very similar story in which a young person living in obscurity is transformed. The traditional folk tale, for instance: Harry is very like Cinderella, who works for cruel stepsisters until an older woman, her fairy godmother, rescues her and takes her, through magic, into a world where she will find romance and escape from the cruelty of her daily environment. Another prototype for Harry can be found in the medieval legend of the young King Arthur, working as the body-servant of a nondescript young knight, Sir Kay, until he is guided by Merlin, an older and wiser man who has magical powers, into his inheritance of power and majesty. T.H. White's twentieth-century version of this story, *The Once and Future King*, is among Harry's many sources.

The Arthurian tales are also among the sources for more recent sword-and-sorcery fantasies such as J.R.R. Tolkien's epic novel *The Lord of the Rings*, their comic-book equivalents – *Superman*, for example – and their science-fiction equivalents, such as the *Star Wars* movies or *The Matrix*. The shared outline story has been very influential in Hollywood thanks to the influence of the comparative mythologist Joseph Campbell, whose 1949 study *The Hero with a Thousand Faces* proposed that all cultures share a single pattern of a heroic journey. Our Hero, usually an orphan, is plucked from obscurity, told of his destiny by someone older and wiser than he, grows in confidence, and goes on a quest to defeat the powers of darkness. These stories, like those of Cinderella and Arthur, share a point of origin: the Hero/ine is uncertain about who her/his parents are or were, and equally uncertain about who she or he really is. They seek their own true identities, including the truth of their lineage, as well as the defeat of evil.

Sitting between the lonely orphan and the quest, in all the Harry Potter books, are the public school story and the friends' adventure story. Some of the school stories – the classic is Thomas Hughes's *Tom Brown's Schooldays* – are versions of the story of manifest destiny. Our Hero survives (step)parental domination and underachievement at home, then in his early experiences at school also survives bullying and isolation from schoolmates. Finally – with the support of the older and wiser headmaster – he becomes the general hero of the day by helping to win a cricket match. Harry has friends who give important help in achieving his quests; his stories also owe something to the Famous Five model. The prolific Enid Blyton wrote dozens of relatively sanitised adventure stories in which a group of middle-class children such as the Famous Five or the Secret Seven (plus a pet, and sometimes plus a friendly but non-parental adult – such as Kiki the parrot and Bill the adult, who feature in the 'Adventure' series) defeat one or more wicked adults. Blyton also wrote the 'Malory Towers' and 'St Clare's' sequences, which feature friends growing up together at boarding school – that is, in the absence of parents. Other school-based sources include Frank Richards's Billy Bunter stories – which contain more comedy than Blyton's – and Anthony Buckeridge's Jennings novels (which are currently being republished, thanks to Harry's success).

The many and various sources are repackaged for contemporary readers. All the Harry Potter stories have something to say about the ways in which we currently think about childhood, adulthood and the family; about the relationship between education and work; and about questions of good and evil, personal and collective responsibility. [T]he outside surfaces may look familiar, but underneath, a lot of what drives the stories is contemporary.

Harry Potter and the Philosopher's Stone is very like many other inventive stories for children that mix legend, magic and the modern world. The retrolution is in the detail. Harry travels to his new school on the Hogwarts Express, a steam train which leaves from platform nine and three quarters at King's Cross station in London before heading for a destination somewhere in the Scottish Highlands. Sitting in the train and knowingly leaving the suburban existence of his first ten years, we experience Harry, and Harry experiences himself, in a different part of what Salman Rushdie calls the 'sea of stories'.[2] He becomes part of the public school story – but he experiences it as a contemporary boy. Some aspects of the Hogwarts set-up could have been written any time after the mid-nineteenth century, but it also has contemporary features. Harry is introduced to some of the greats of the wizarding world – and thus to his own newly discovered identity – through buying chocolate frogs which are packaged with collectors' cards identifying various famous wizards and witches.

Looking through the cards, Harry also receives a clue which will eventually help him to unravel the book's mystery. Similar chocolates and cards are currently available in a store near you. This very self-aware mixture of past styles, current awareness, and the use of significant detail prefiguring the rest of the narrative is typical of the Potter formula.

In the spring of 1997, at the very moment of Harry Potter's literary birth, British politics was also moving in a retrolutionary direction. New Labour was elected to power in Britain.

Notes

1.   Christopher Little, interviewed on 'J.K. Rowling: Harry Potter and Me', *Omnibus*, BBC1, 28 December 2001.
2.   Salman Rushdie, *Haroun and the Sea of Stories*, Vintage 1990.

Part 2

Contemporary Trends

11

Fiction for Adolescents: Melvin Burgess, *Junk* (1996)

Introduction
Ann Hewings and Nicola J. Watson

Melvin Burgess's *Junk* (published as *Smack* in the USA the same year) is included here as probably the most prominent instance of recent so-called social realist young adult (YA) fiction. Although fiction for adolescents was very much a feature of the late 1960s and 1970s, and books such as Alan Garner's *The Owl Service* (1967) or John Rowe Townsend's *Goodnight, Prof, Love* (1970) dealt with adolescent love and sex for a teen audience, the boundaries between adult and children's books have at the millennium seemed more permeable than they have been in the past. Fiction directed at the burgeoning YA market has started to foreground controversial issues such as sex and drugs in an aggressively realistic and streetwise style, with a view to being shocking and therefore attractive to a teen market.

Burgess has some claims to being the instigator of modern teen fiction, and has attracted and courted a marketable notoriety as such. As he has remarked:

> There are so few books published that are truly for young adults. If you are aged sixteen or seventeen and you want to read fiction that talks about your life – your recreation, your sex life, your feelings and emotions – you're either stuck with stuff about twenty-somethings, or you're reading soft stuff that seems to be written for younger readers, or you're reading some polite, carefully edited stuff that doesn't dare talk about reality.

He attributes the impact of *Junk to* its willingness to 'talk about reality' and to its being drawn 'from life':

> *Junk* is set in Bristol, where I lived myself for eight years in the late seventies and eighties . . . I think that one of the main reasons for the book's success is the fact that is painted very much from life. The culture of inner city Bristol, the lifestyles of many of the characters, was something I lived myself. Tar and Gemma, Lily and Rob, come across as real people because they are based on real people, and their story rings true because it *is* true. All the events in the second half of the book are real. They didn't always happen to those particular characters in that particular way, but they did happen. I had nothing to invent.
>
> Burgess, 2009

Certainly *Junk* has been Burgess's most successful novel to date, winning both the Carnegie Medal and the Guardian Children's Fiction Award in 1997, translated into 28 languages, and becoming a transatlantic bestseller. It was one of the best-known children's books of the decade, in part because it caused very considerable controversy. *Junk's* explicit and uncompromising subject matter – violence in the home, heroin addiction, prostitution and teenage pregnancy – was controversial in itself, as was his subject matter in the book which followed, *Doing It,* which dealt explicitly and extensively with underage sex. But Burgess's subject matter became doubly disturbing because of his use of multiple unreliable first-person narrative voices which obscured the clear moral line traditionally taken on such subject matter when treated for the young. Burgess's fiction requires some sophistication from his teenage readership; the highly moral tendency of the piece is only realised if they recognise the disconnect between the characters' self-justifications and the outcomes of their actions.

The essays

In his essay, Burgess attributes the apparent lack of reading by teenagers to, in part, the lack of books that interest them or touch on the concerns of their lives, and claims that *Junk* was designed to meet this gap in the market. While Burgess thus stresses the importance of 'authenticity' and realism in writing for young people, John Stephens's essay challenges *Junk's* claims to unmediated realism. Through detailed analysis of the text, Stephens describes how Burgess's fictive world is built up, argues that its apparent espousal of indeterminacy and relativism through the competing first-person narratives of its protagonists is 'more apparent than actual', and considers how the fiction is anchored in the moral and didactic.

References

Burgess, M. 2009. Official website, www.melvinburgess.net accessed 4 March 2009.

Sympathy for the Devil
Melvin Burgess

When my first book, *The Cry of the Wolf*, was published in 1989, I was told I was writing for teenagers. I was surprised; as far as I was concerned, *Wolf* was a children's book, but who was I to argue? The next few I wrote were also marketed as teenage books, but as I began to go on school visits it became clear that all was not as it seemed. If I was writing for teenagers, why was I being paraded in front of 11–12-year olds? Librarians and teachers confirmed that few people over the age of 13 ever read teenage books. People such as Robert Westall, Anne Fine, Bob Swindells, Gillian Cross and myself were really writing for pre-teens despite what it said on the back cover.

So – where was the fiction for real teenagers? The received wisdom was that teenagers didn't read, or else they read adult stuff and by and large, this was true. Still today there's a great deal of soul-searching about boys in particular not reading. But is it because books are only for old and uncool people, like opera or bingo? Or could it be that the books that might interest people of that age are simply not being written?

This was a period when writing for young readers was changing. Modern themes – I say modern even though these areas had been issues for decades – such as sexuality, drugs culture, family break-down were being more honestly portrayed, and people were discovering that young people were far more sophisticated than the material previously written for them would suggest. Publishers dealt with this trend by calling books with a content some parents might object to, 'teenage fiction'. All this was working very nicely, thank you very much. Eleven and twelve year olds were pleased to be told they were reading teenage fiction; publishers were able to fob off complaints about pre-teens reading it by saying that it was aimed at teenagers; educationalists were able to use these more serious books in the classrooms; and the Christian far right who look after the nation's morals, were able to flap around convinced that the tide of filth was being staunched for our children's sake at least.

Some time in about 1994, my publisher suggested I write a book dealing with drugs. I liked the idea. For one thing, it was something I knew about. I come from one of the first generations where drugs were widely used recreationally; if I hadn't done it myself, I'd certainly known someone else who had.

This is an edited version of the article originally published in *Children's Literature in Education*, 35:4 (2004), pp. 289–300.

I read the few other books that had dealt with this area, and I was not impressed. There was a great reluctance to deal with the realities, the way drugs are used, why they are used, the kind of decisions that people make, practically, socially and ethically. Drugs and drug culture were portrayed as a kind of dark force that turned ordinary well-meaning people into evil shadows, like the Nazgul, who could occasionally be brought back to decency by innocents, who usually only escape corruption themselves by the skin of their teeth. In other words, it wasn't social realism; it was fantasy in disguise.

I'd already built up a reputation for honest writing, dealing with issues directly, and I wanted this book to show those same virtues. Above all, I wanted it to be authentic. Authenticity had a number of attractions – partly because it is by its nature honest, but also because this book was going to have a rough ride, and I didn't want to be accused of making anything up. That's why the novel, *Junk*, is set in a real place, involving characters based on a real group of people, with real music, real fashions, real everything, including as far as possible, real events. There are a wide range of different people shown – people having a good time on drugs, all the fun of young people enjoying themselves, as well as the darker side – addiction, casualties, despair. Predictably, it was both those areas that were singled out for criticism – the good times, because moronic teenagers were obviously going to copy-cat and end up as junky whores, and the bad times because the poor sweet things were too fragile to cope with the realities of addiction.

Junk was an experiment; we all thought it stood a good chance of languishing on the shelves – Puffin did some research which suggested that even those librarians who liked the book would be reluctant to stock it. In fact, it sold like hot cakes, greeted with glee by young people, teachers and drug workers alike, and snarls of rage by the moral right and, of course, the press. After winning the Carnegie Medal in 1997, it was front-page news. The *Daily Mail* was outraged, the BBC *Today* programme started exhuming moralist pressure groups that had been interred sometime in about 1963. The broadsheets did a great deal of soul-searching and growling on about the loss of innocence, children growing up too quickly, and the dangers of sensationalists such as myself exploiting childish curiosity.

I have to say it was fun. I enjoyed the publicity and the attention, which authors usually feel they don't get enough of, and I enjoyed arguing my corner. I had written the book for a reason and I felt it was something to be proud of. Not only that, it seemed to me that most of my opponents had little to support their case but professional outrage. My book might not support their particular moral position, but it had its ethical side; the people in it were making real ethical judgements and the reader was invited to do the same. Were people really surprised that teenagers wanted to read this sort of thing? After all, drugs are in the news daily, and it's a rare school where everyone doesn't know someone who smokes cannabis by age fifteen.

I learned a number of important lessons from that book. For starters, it exploded the myth about teenagers not reading – they read this one in droves. Admittedly it still wasn't being read by anyone much over 15 – perhaps even 14 in those days; something which is changing in that teenagers have become aware that material is being written for them that they might actually like – but it had hiked the age range for teenage fiction up a year or two at least. It convinced me that it was the material that was faulty – not the readership.

The second myth it exploded was that of the moral majority. From reading the papers and listening to the radio, you would have thought that whether young people were safe reading a book like this was a burning issue in schools and families up and down the country. Well, it isn't. People know perfectly well that a great many young people will experiment with drugs, that most of them will come through it okay; that parents have to learn to let go before their kids leave home rather than later on, and be prepared to watch them take risks and make mistakes. Those who truly believe that we can ring-fence our children against the adult world lost the plot a long time ago, even with children far younger than those who might read *Junk*. The real question is, why is this such an issue in the press when the public in general have moved on? The answer is simple: it makes a good story. It doesn't move the debate forward, it's not informative in any way, it helps no one, despite protests from journalists. It provokes a good rant or a ding-dong in the studio, is all. Really, the only sensible response to this sort of stuff is to treat it as entertainment – it makes good publicity, that's its only real virtue. Of course there is a contemporary debate about this kind of issue, and some of it – not much but some – takes place in newspapers and on the radio. More of that later.

Since *Junk* was published in 1996, I have had not one letter or e-mail of complaint about it.

The gulf between the official and unofficial views of teenage morality, which I think says a great deal about the traumatic way we view adolescence, is never clearer than with the issue of youth censorship. Adult films, for 18+, are regularly seen in cinemas by girls of 13 and 14, slipping in with the aid of a stick of lippy and a bit of slap. The boys soon follow and even if they can't be bothered, they probably saw their first 18 film at the age of six with the rest of the family. This has been true, literally, for over half a century. The same goes for computer games for 18+. The nine o'clock watershed on TV is breached regularly by every primary schoolchild, and material with an 'adult' content is splashed enthusiastically all over radio, internet and TV without a scruple.

Even if your parents disapprove, restrictions are easily circumvented. We all know this goes on and yet when something is produced with any adult content directly for young people, throats are clutched, the guilt begins, the groaning starts. Why is our legislation on this matter so hopelessly out of date? Young people of course have no vote, no pressure groups, no voice, no say, whereas every moralist with a unilateral agenda for good and bad makes very sure that they do. Does it matter? Often, not at all. The nation *en masse* simply allow their young people to fall through the gaps and do what they like. But it does have some bad effects. If you are 15 or 16 and you want to read about people with sex lives, those people will have to be in their twenties or late teens at the earliest – no one writes for you. The whole entry into adult life is substantially unsupported by literature; which is so much bollox as far as I'm concerned.

So let's admit for starters – most of the controversy about my work is a paper tiger. People recognise the realities of everyday life, are concerned but not scared by the fact that there are few secrets from children these days, and recognise young people's ability to contextualise fiction on their own, without adults pointing out which conclusions are right and which are wrong. In fact, in a world more embedded in fictions than ever, in the form not just of books but gaming, politics, film, TV, adverts, even education, kids are probably more able than their parents to appreciate the different ways stories are used.

The final lesson of *Junk* was this: that we massively underestimate our young people. We're so used to watching them struggle with Shakespeare and grunting at us when we ask them what sort of a day they had at school, we forget that in terms of their own culture they are extremely sophisticated and able to deal with concepts, particularly fictional concepts, with ease. Of course they struggle with Shakespeare – you have to spend years of study to pick up the references. Of course they struggle with Hardy and Dickens – the same thing is true. But if we take the trouble to speak directly to them on their terms of reference instead of ours, they stop waddling clumsily and become intellectually easy and graceful, just like they're supposed to be. We've been putting up hurdles when we should have been listening.

Of course this isn't so easy for us oldsters, given that we aren't any more *au fait* with their cultural references than they are with ours. But contemporary fiction is a common language. Kids have been practising it for years. It's a question of trust, and of making books interesting – surprise surprise!

Since Junk I've had a lot of fun and satisfaction identifying those areas that have been neglected for teenagers, and trying to write books to fill them. The first of these after *Junk* was *Bloodtide* – an attempt to publish a book, as I said at the time, 'with no educational value of any sort whatsoever'. We've paid too much attention to that lucrative school market, which has driven book sales to young people for years. Schools, like all institutions, are far more wary than individuals. The result has been an emphasis on the relationship between the book and the child in education, rather than the simple and genuine relationship between the reader and the text. The classroom brings a different kind of reading to the fore – sometimes critical, sometimes educational ('What do you think Gemma should have done, Katy?') – all good stuff; but it leaves behind the primary thing – that you the reader are in control, you set the agenda, that this book is yours, and tells you things that you perhaps never thought about, but that you recognise; that it's about *you* in some indefinable way.

Once you have decided that young people can contextualise narrative in their own right, make a moral judgement on it in their own right, recognise the difference between story and real life in their own right and understand that it relates to their own lives in many more ways than simple example or advice, you can let go of any attempt to lecture them, help them or, worst of all, educate them, and simply tell your story. The feelings and ideas that arise out of it are there for the reader to exploit as and if they will. The context they already have.

As far as the future of fiction for young adults is concerned, things do look rosier than they did a decade ago. Publishers are investing a great deal in cross-over fiction – books that have a market with adults as well as children, and teenage fiction certainly comes within this range. There are more writers showing interest in this area – people such as Malorie Blackman, Paul Magrs, Julia Bell, Kevin Brooks, Bali Rai, Patrick Cave and Matt Wyman, but there are still too few, and many of them are still writing for younger teens. Literature for the older teenage age group is still a fragile thing. Teenagers still have no voice; they only have their spending power, which ain't all that much. Many schools are still running scared of the bullies and although there are centres of real excellence here and there, in general they cannot be relied upon to appeal directly to the readership. Cross-over is undoubtedly the future. The best hope we have to create a genuine literature for young adults is to write books both they and we want to read – edgy, dangerous, forceful, thought provoking, funny – all sorts. But definitely not educational. They get enough of that at school.

People will stop writing issue-led books, I think. I've done them myself more as brooms to sweep away the mess before you get down to the real thing, and although I am best known for my two attempts at social realism, *Junk* and *Doing It*, they aren't typical of my work. Sex, drugs and rock and roll will much more likely be incorporated in stories rather than dealt with head on. With any luck, books for teenagers will become more common-place, more embedded in literature in general and, like movies and films, part of our normal cultural life.

References

Burgess, Melvin, *The Cry of the Wolf.* London: Andersen, 1989.
Burgess, Melvin, *Junk.* London: Andersen, 1996.

'And it's so real': Versions of Reality in Melvin Burgess's *Junk*
John Stephens

Aimed at upper teenage and young adult readers, Melvin Burgess's *Junk* became highly controversial because of its version of realism, especially after it won both the Carnegie Award and the Guardian Fiction Prize. A critical response to the novel might thus ask, first, how 'real' it is, beyond the relativism of perspective suggested by the way point of view shifts from chapter to chapter, and second, whether the failure to produce a unified narrative vantage point by the close (see Rudd, 1999) entails that readers are refused any kind of ethical vantage point. Two of the principal characters, Gemma and Tar, who between them narrate two-thirds of *Junk*, at different times commend things for being *real*: for example, when Gemma first meets Lily (the person primarily responsible for introducing her to heroin) she enthuses, 'She was more real than anyone I'd ever met' (125), and toward the novel's close Tar describes the experience of a heroin injection as 'so real' (323). In such cases, readers will be likely to question the application of the adjective *real*, and will understand that such judgements are not nec-essarily grounded in an objective or verifiable property but are an attempt to elevate a subjective response to a universal value. In other words, they point to self-deception.

Junk reflects a social realist tradition that had emerged in children's lit-erature in the 1970s. This literature developed a focus on social issues and strove to depict the realities of the everyday life experiences of society's urban underclasses. It has structural elements in common with documentary genres, especially its widespread use of first-person narration, which mirrors the documentary strategy of filming subjects telling their own stories. The strategy conveys an assurance of authenticity and enables access to stories that lack aesthetic appeal or happy endings, but which draw critical attention to the social environment that produces underclasses or forms of exclusion from mainstream society. In *Junk*, alienation, boredom, drugs and the craving for sensation combine to create situations in which the characters do terrible things to themselves or others or take terrible risks which they scarcely acknowledge to be risks.

In thinking about *Junk*, then, we need to think about the nature of reality in realist fiction. Are we considering a transcription of reality, or a complex literary strategy for representing a version of reality? Negative criticism of *Junk* hinged on suggestions that it depicted a distasteful version of reality, and Burgess's own comments on the novel, offered as an oblique defence of his work, themselves slipped into the easy assumption that consensus reality is to be defined by *content*, and measured by the degree to which it reflects everyday lived experience:

> The second part of the book is based loosely on people I knew at the time. I think that one of the main reasons for the book's success is the fact that it is painted very much from life. The culture of inner-city Bristol, the lifestyles of many of the characters, was something I lived myself. Tar and Gemma, Lily and Rob, come across as real people because they are based on real people, and their story rings true because it *is* true.
>
>   http://web.onetel.net.uk/~melvinburgess/Junk.index.htm

While this assertion of authenticity can be readily understood, it elides the extent to which realism is a conventional form. One of the major discoursal features of *Junk*, the multiple narrative voices, simultaneously creates the illusion of documentary reality, in offering readers access to the thought stream of so many characters, and demands of readers that they accept a major convention: the various narrators directly or implicitly address a common narratee (who may be a reader), but who is this person? Where is s/he situated? How may such a narratee be addressed by eleven speakers over a period of several years? The alternation of narrators is also carefully orchestrated, so that either Gemma or Tar narrates every second chapter, with only chapters 24–25 and 27–28 deviating from this pattern. Four characters narrate two chapters each (Skolly, Richard, Vonny, Rob), and four others have one chapter each (Lily, Sally, Emily Brogan and Tar's father). Further, quite violent breaches of notional reality occur, such as the chapter narrated by Lily (Chapter 14). This chapter is a sustained direct address to an indefinite *you*, and sets out Lily's philosophy of life ('The only thing that isn't free is you' [156]; 'You're wonderful and everything that you do is wonderful because it's you doing it. You're that strong' [159]). The greatest weakness of the characters in the novel is their solipsism, and Lily is the most solipsistic of all. Her chapter-long monologue is in actuality not Lily addressing the novel's common narratee, but a set-piece disclosure of her self-justificatory, fragile and febrile mental state. Its grounding premise, that paid employment is both unnecessary and destructive, is only super-ficially logical, since its corollary that individuals simply follow their own path and take or steal whatever they need ignores the reality that the princi-pal source of production of the things she steals is human labour. As such, it is a travesty of what Trites identified as the work of the young adult novel. Only this chapter is narrated by Lily, but it is a pivotal statement of the ethos to which Tar and Gemma commit themselves in the chapters on either side. It is also an important chapter in relation to the argument that mean-ing in *Junk* is indeterminate and the multiple narrative voices deny read-ers a stable interpretative position (see, for example, Rudd, 1999: 121), for Lily constitutes a point of reference against which meaning and moral sense can be ascertained. There are numerous points at which readers will rec-ognize this – an often quoted example is Tar's recollection of Lily inject-ing into the veins between her breasts while feeding her baby: ' "Nice fat veins when your breasts are big and milky," she said. And no one said a word. That's junk. You think, if you don't say the truth, the truth somehow doesn't exist' (252). When Gemma finds that she is pregnant, it is a clear perception about Lily that proves the turning point in her life: 'I thought to myself, I've followed you everywhere you've gone. I've followed you every-where but I'm not following you here' (290). The patterned repetitions and contrasts in Gemma's utterance ('followed . . . followed . . . not following'; 'everywhere . . . everywhere . . . [not] here') constitute a rhetorical and lit-erary formulation of her conclusion that endows it with a resonance that reaches well beyond Gemma's own moment of decision.

Although realism is a mode of writing that aims to depict a recognisable social and physical world – that is, it aims to represent or reflect 'the world as we know it' – it does not, of course, reproduce events and experiences that take place in the actual world but is rather a *representation* of events and experiences similar to those which take place in the actual world. Hence another way to understand the structure of *Junk* is to observe that the strategy of multiple narrators allows the novel to be organised system-atically and to reveal an underlying pattern of cause and effect that is more structured than in actual life. Both the characters and their interactions are fictional, and have been selected and organised for their contrasting or com-plementary attributes.

The formulation, 'the world as we know it', undermines the idea that art can simply reflect reality from the outset: how do we or anyone else 'know' the world? The idea that 'the world as we know it' is the same as the world as other people know it assumes that the cultural institutions, social behaviours, intellectual practices whereby meanings are ascribed to objects in the world are essentially the same from one society or culture to the next, which clearly they are not. It assumes that knowledge – and the various practices whereby the world can be known – is also essentially the same. Thus, in general terms, concepts of 'realism' vary according to social, cultural and historical context. In so far as the term realism can be applied to a specific text, it might be said that a realist text reflects an image of the reality of the society in which it is produced at a particular time and place – that is, it reflects the world as members of a specific society know it. On the other hand, a novel such as *Junk* can create a strong reality effect by suggesting that particular social groups inhabit realities that differ from what society more generally perceives as normal, everyday reality, or from a previous generation's preferred conception of what society is like. *Junk* is thus grittier and more confrontational than the young adult realist fiction of twenty years earlier.

Another problem with the notion that realism reflects 'the world as we know it' is the notion of 'reflection' itself. The idea that art reflects the world assumes two things. It assumes that language can simply reflect the actual world; and that reality both exists and has meaning in a simple and easily apprehendable way independent of the language that we use to describe and comprehend it. On the contrary, meaning is not inherent in an object, but is an aspect of social practices and cultural traditions: it is socially constructed, and it is thus subject to change over time and within different social contexts. For this reason, meaning often seems to be unstable or relative while interpretation of social situations is apt to be shaped by attitudes and understandings that prevail within society at any particular time. The process is clear in the following example from *Junk*, in which Gemma comments on her first encounter with a punk band: '[That band] must have been famous or become famous soon after because they were just so *obscene* and rude and wonderful' (101; original emphasis). Gemma's opinion is based on a cause-and-effect structure ('this happens *because of* that'), a structure which underpins realist narrative, both at the level of the sentence and the level of events and outcomes. Her particular logic of cause and effect, however, illustrates how relative and restricted her world-view is, because based on a relative value system and a dissociation of words from their customary meanings. The connection of *famous* with *wonderful* brings together terms compatible within a familiar parameter of meaning, which associates fame with achievement; but the connection of *famous* with *obscene and rude* involves a clash of meanings; there is then a further clash between *obscene and rude* and *wonderful*. The linguistic clashes can be resolved once it is seen that the most common notion of achievement is not operative here, but is redefined by a context in which *obscene and rude* are equated with *wonderful*, and *famous* designates what mainstream society might rather term *infamous* or *notorious*. The instability of meaning that pivots first on the meaning of *famous* and then on the unexpected causal logic overturns customary values and associations. We can then argue that, on the one hand, the characters of *Junk* inhabit a world of relative values, which is also evident on the macro level, and on the other hand, the way language functions in this example constructs those values as always deviant from customary social morality – and hence reader alignment is implicitly with those social values rather than with the values of the characters.

As this example shows, there is never a perfect fit between language and the world. Language is a sign system which we use to describe, to mediate and to assign meaning to the world (that is, to the physical observable world as well as to social and cultural reality), and there is not a fixed relationship between the words we hear, speak or read, the ideas we form in our minds, and the objects in the world. In short, the relations between signs and things are mediated by the concepts or meanings that we ascribe to things. This is not an argument that the object-in-the-world does not exist outside language, but that reality itself is not inherently meaningful. We use language and narrative to represent, mediate and comprehend our experience of the world. In doing so we also ascribe meaning to reality and to our experience of it. Our knowledge of the world is formed by means of the language which we use to describe and to articulate our experience of it; and, needless to say, this language is something which is learned. Meaning is always subject to social conventions about how specific words and phrases are used and understood within a linguistic community. It is determined by and within the signifying practices of a community, that is, the ideologies and belief systems of that community. Thus in learning language, we also learn ideologies. It is here that what Roberta Seelinger Trites has identified as the work of the young adult novel becomes crucially relevant: 'protagonists must learn about the social forces that have made them what they are. They learn to negotiate the levels of power that exist in the myriad social institutions within which they must function, including family, school, the church, government' (Trites, 2000: 3). The young adult novels Trites here describes are grounded in a liberal humanist paradigm of maturation and understanding which is widespread in children's and young adult literature: it assumes that although human beings may not have complete freedom, young people can make choices as to the kinds of selves they become, transforming the self by intersubjective engagement with other individuals and with the political and social dimensions of human life in society. Personal development thus grows out of the development of social responsibility, moral values and ethical insights. *Junk* engages directly with this relationship between ideology and young adults, but by mapping its characters' withdrawal from intersubjective relationships with other people and society in general portrays an anti-humanist position that questions the efficacy of the liberal humanist concepts implicit in Trites's formulation.

It is arguable that the indeterminacy and relativism of *Junk* are more apparent than actual. To assess their extent and reach we need to pay close attention to the text, starting with the multiple narrator structure. This strategy is not unusual for the period, as a vogue for multiple points of view in children's literature had developed during the 1980s (Robyn McCallum's *Ideologies of Identity in Adolescent Fiction* (1999) identifies about sixty examples by the mid-1990s). Burgess's originality (at the time) in employing the strategy lies in how he has linked it with the major theme of young adult literature, subjective maturation and development. As Andrea Schwenke Wyile points out (1999: 186), narrators in first-person young adult literature are 'not always cognizant of this development'. Burgess complicates perspective by shifts in the temporal location of narration, so that relation between the time of narration and the time at which events occurred is undetermined, but none of the characters is situated at a point sufficiently distant in time from the events to enable considered reflection. Reader expectations that the end of the novel will deliver a unified narrative vantage point and a sense of closure are effectively mocked over the final three chapters, narrated in turn by Gemma, Tar's father, and Tar. These chapters present story details in chronological order, and so suggest a tying-up of threads, but because each narrator is a less trustworthy informant than the one preceding, any assertions of the self-development characteristic of young adult literature become increasingly unreliable. Development is thus present mostly as an unrealised possibility. There is a suggestion that Gemma has at least stabilised her life, but her narration ends – is effectively truncated – while she is still living with Tar, with the break-up told about in the overtly intrusive chapter narrated by Tar's father which takes events a couple of years into the future. The final chapter, narrated by Tar, gestures towards self-awareness when Tar asserts, 'I know myself a lot better now' (325), but there is then abundant evidence in the chapter that Tar frequently deceives both others and himself, and is a long way from a cure for his addiction. The novel's close thus encapsulates the strategy for destabilising meaning in *Junk*.

The absence of a clear perspective from the close does not entail that readers are refused any kind of ethical vantage point, however. No narrative exists without an orientation towards the social world which readers must engage with and interpret. *Junk* is set in a world of moral uncertainty and dehumanisation, where heroin addiction stands for the abandonment of agency, of responsibility for the self or others, and of moral choice. One of the starkest representations of this condition is the sequence of incidents recounted by Tar in Chapter 18 – unrelated as story elements, the sequence has a powerful thematic impact that hinges on Tar's nihilistic question, 'If you don't mind not reaching twenty there's no argument against heroin, is there?' (199). Framed by present-tense narration, the chapter is set at some time when Tar and Gemma lived with Lily and Rob. The present tense asserts an immediacy of perception, although the narrative then moves back in time to narrate first a visit from Richard, inviting Tar to travel abroad with him, and then Tar and Rob finding the bodies of Alan and Helen and searching their flat for the heroin stash that had killed them. Finally, the chapter returns to the present tense to describe a typical phone call made by Tar to his mother. The challenge to readers is to see the connections, especially to consider Tar's attitude towards the bodies and towards his mother, and to grasp the significance of the shifts in tense. In the chapter's opening paragraphs Tar describes a complex and multifarious society, and affirms his separation from them. The opening thus thematises social cohesion and alienation, and the rest of the chapter plays out the forms of Tar's alienation. The centrepiece is Tar's contemplation of the dead bodies, which encapsulates the meaninglessness of these lives and deaths. Once again he observes, 'It was all so realistic,' and presumably readers will differentiate between Tar's sense of reality and their own, and understand how the tense shifting enacts Tar's lack of any form of grounded perception.

A key element in making such differentiations is the function of metonymy in realist texts. Metonymy is a device by which an attribute of something stands in for the whole (by means of an overlap of literal and figurative function). It is easily recognised in descriptions of clothing, as in '[Vonny] was done out in a Mohican and a ring in her nose while I was still in fluffy jumpers' (96): the contrasting dress codes stand for contrasting lifestyles. The discourse of realism is extensively metonymic because of a tendency for objects, details, situations, and so on, to have a literal function – they are an aspect of the realistic surface of the text – and a figurative function: they stand in for larger more abstract concepts and hence represent a larger social world than that immediately depicted. In other words, the discourse of realism means what it seems to mean and it also forms part of a larger signifying structure. Metonymic effects in *Junk*, while pervasive, don't always have a strong signifying force, however, because the novel's style tends more towards overstatement than understatement and metonymic significances are thus often overtly explicated within the text itself (as in Gemma's concern with dress codes), which has the effect of foregrounding how a character ascribes meaning to reality and his or her experience of it. Metonymy has a central function in the novel, nevertheless, because it contributes a thickness of significance without requiring conscious acts of interpretation by readers, and because it reinforces parallels across the novel's multiple perspectives. The following remarks from Richard's narration in Chapter 25 illustrate these aspects of the discourse:

> That's where I met Sandra. She was living in the same house as my friends and we started to have an *affaire du coeur*. Unfortunately I'm not very good at that sort of thing. Then she got a place in college at Reading. Reading! I must have been mad! I went and interviewed at a bike shop there and they offered me the job.
>
> That's life. I came back thinking I'd earn enough money to get off to India fairly quickly. Instead I ended up with Sandra in a flat in Woodley. The worst of it was, Sandra liked it.
>
> I keep falling in love but it always makes me unhappy, I've no idea why.
>
> Tar was his usual shifty self. I mean, that's usual for him since he got on to smack. He'd lost that open look he used to have about him quite early on, after about six months of leaving the squat, I'd say. It was funny. I actually hadn't liked him for years. I loved him when he first turned up. He had this way of trying to hide everything but it all came shining through anyway.
>
> (270–1)

This kind of contrast between a character's apparently sharp observation of other characters and an almost complete absence of self-knowledge is the most obvious characterisation strategy in *Junk*. No character is free of it, and while the strategy is highly effective in depicting a highly dysfunctional society whose members are universally incapable of intersubjective relationships, its pervasiveness does contribute to a feeling of sameness about the characters. The first of these extracts suggests that readers will readily see why Richard's relationships fail and why he is a dislikable character: he is self-centred to the point of solipsism, and his emotional evasiveness is evident in his evasive language ('*affaire du coeur*'; 'that sort of thing'). His attitude is also evident in his metonymies – 'Reading'; 'a flat in Woodley'; 'off to India' – and the language which instantiates the metonymic effect, 'I ended up with Sandra'; 'The worst of it was'. In other words, the places named are not simply part of the story but have a larger symbolic resonance expressing Richard's inability to inhabit everyday ordinariness. He shares this inability with the novel's junkies. An important point about metonymy is that it functions below a reader's conscious perception because it taps into social belief and practice. Thus while readers may need to work quite hard to explain metonymic effect, it communicates readily and requires very little unpacking during the act of reading.

The metonymies that frame Richard's description of Tar are even less evident. The contrast between *shiftiness* and *openness* draws on a common social judgement that prefers the latter, and which is adduced by Richard's affirmation that he had loved Tar when he had displayed openness. The metonymy is not left to do its own work, however, and the novel's tendency to overstatement is evident in the embedded explanation: 'usual for him since he got on to smack'. The link between shiftiness and drug addiction runs throughout the second half of the book, but is an acquired character trait particularly associated with Tar, and highlighted in both Gemma's and Tar's own narrations. The contrast between Richard and Tar on pages 270–1 actually establishes a parallel between them and has a clear characterising function (each character is shifty and dislikable); it also establishes the thematic grounding for the rest of the chapter in concepts of manipulativeness and communication failure. The scarcely registered metonymies in each extract further construct the illusion that the fictive world is an extension of the real world, that is, a 'slice of life', because the social structures and systems of behaviour represented in the fictive text are to be read as an extension of those structures and systems in the real world. At the same time, the extracts exemplify the crucial function metonymy has within the realistic mode: metonymies constantly shape the discourse so that it points from story to significance. Realism has a strong need to suggest that its structure moves inevitably towards meaningful closure and in doing so it seeks to engage its readers in an active response. Metonymy serves these needs by revealing a depth of significance lying behind seemingly ordinary things, and – importantly for our purposes here – links that significance with moral or ethical insights that sustain social forms and human relationships.

The appearance that the multiple narrative perspectives of *Junk* are random is finally an illusion, as is the novel's apparent anti-humanist stance. The relationships between chapters are artfully constructed to produce an effect of thematic comparison and contrast, and a reader's subconscious interpretation of metonymies in terms of ethical, social frames furnishes a context for understanding the novel's close. The reality of *Junk* is not that of the random flow of lives living out a particular form of everydayness, but a reality understood as self-deception and loss.

References

McCallum, R. 1999. *Ideologies of Identity in Adolescent Fiction*. London and New York, Routledge.

Rudd, D. 1999. 'A Young Person's Guide to the Fictions of *Junk*', *Children's Literature in Education,* 30(2), 119–26.

Schwenke Wyile, A. 1999. 'Expanding the View of First-Person Narration', *Children's Literature in Education*, 30(3), 185–202.

Trites, R.S. 2000. *Disturbing the Universe: Power and Repression in Adolescent Literature*. Iowa City, University of Iowa Press.

12

Radical Agendas: Beverley Naidoo, *The Other Side of Truth* (2000)

Introduction
Ann Hewings and Nicola J. Watson

Beverley Naidoo's *The Other Side of Truth*, published in 2000, is included here as an exemplum of social realist fiction with a political agenda. A white South African exile to England, Naidoo had already had a past as an anti-apartheid activist before beginning her career as a writer for children in 1985 when she published *Journey to Jo'burg*. Promptly banned in South Africa, where it only became available in 1991, this book inaugurated a string of novels for children by Naidoo set in South Africa and critical of the apartheid regime. *The Other Side of Truth*, written post-apartheid, was a new departure, set substantially in England. The novel takes on the task of depicting 'children who struggle against injustice and other difficulties' in the persons of two Nigerian refugee children who arrive in Britain seeking safety after the political assassination of their mother and the enforced disappearance of their journalist father (Naidoo, 2009). It won a string of awards, including the Carnegie Medal, and confirmed Naidoo in a writing and speaking career that has been defined by an effort to draw children into political engagement. Her novels aim 'to reveal the impact of the wider society and its politics on the lives of young characters' (Naidoo, 2001), and are calculated to move the child-reader beyond concerns centred on their own immediate lives and choices to consider the workings of society at large.

Political oppression, war, displacement, migration and forging a new life as a refugee are the topical concerns of *The Other Side of Truth*. The innocence of the migrant child protagonists is juxtaposed with the bullying meted out to them by their peers in a British school and with the harshness of a bureaucratic state focused on controlling immigration to the point of committing gross injustice. Before being rescued into a happy ending, the children are successively let down by welfare and social systems, adults, and other children in a story that challenges child-readers to empathise with outsiders and to question the fairness and humanity of the society in which they live. For all her conscious topicality, Naidoo's willingness to tackle sensitive political issues and her political agenda places her as a writer within a long tradition of moral-political fiction produced for children. It is perhaps ironic that such fiction might well trace its roots back to the very different politics of Victorian and Edwardian books meant to train boys for heroic imperial endeavours.

The essays

The first essay included here is written by the author herself and offers an autobiographical insight into both her motivations and the writing process. She traces the genesis of the novel from her own roots as the granddaughter of migrants and her experiences of exile in the UK, but also points to the depth of her supporting research and fieldwork in Britain and Nigeria. She concludes by discussing the potential power of children's fiction to influence the reader's political viewpoint. Jana Giles's essay places *The Other Side of Truth* in relation to the postcolonial politics of Nigeria whilst also foregrounding its ambition to be a 'critical' text. She argues that Naidoo incites her child readership to an act of critical literacy, which she characterises in terms of a disruption of assumptions and beliefs as well as a confrontation of issues of power and choice. At heart, she concludes, Naidoo's fiction challenges young people in societies such as Britain and the USA to reconsider their own received histories, both personally and nationally.

References

Naidoo, B. 2001. *Carnegie Medal acceptance speech*. www.booksforkeeps.co.uk/issues/130/56, accessed 27 May 2008.
Naidoo, B. 2009. Official website. www.beverleynaidoo.com, accessed 4 March 2009.

A Writer's Journey: Retracing
The Other Side of Truth
Beverley Naidoo

Reconstructing why and how I wrote *The Other Side of Truth* is a tricky business. A novel takes root in the imagination and grows there. The most vital part of the creative process remains mysterious and out of view, even to myself. For instance, I might go to bed tussling with a problem of plot and character and wake up in the morning with an idea that could provide a solution. Have I dreamed it? The most I retain of my dream are fleeting images that seem completely unconnected and defy the logic associated with the word 'solution'. Yet something has happened, like an arrow suddenly appearing before me in an unmapped forest, suggesting the way to go.

This declared, I intend in this essay to reflect on some of the more conscious decisions and details in creating and shaping the work that became *The Other Side of Truth*. To aid my memory – the story that I tell myself – I shall use old notebooks, files of research materials and a photograph album made at the time. It's well over a decade since I began the work in January 1997 and I approach the present task in the spirit of author as detective. I intend to take a fresh look at why and how I wrote the novel and what were or might have been some of my influences. I shall end by considering: 'Do you write for instruction or delight?' and share a response from a schoolboy that clearly questions this dichotomy. But first, to set the context, I need to tell you a little about my own background. In this narrative you may detect a strand here or there that reminds you of something within the novel.

Migrations

My four grandparents were economic migrants to South Africa from Britain. My mother's ancestry was Russian and Jewish and my father's Cornish and Church of England. My forebears had set off from Europe in the nineteenth and early twentieth centuries with the implicit knowledge that, whatever their fears and the challenges, colonial life offered excellent prospects to white-skinned Europeans with an eye for enterprise. The door was wide open and the vast continent of Africa signalled untold riches. In South Africa the prospects were especially good with the discovery of gold and diamonds, indeed worth fighting a war over – one European tribe against another, British and Boer. I hint at that wider debt of Europe to Africa because of so much historical amnesia about what happened both before and after a group of white men, representing the powers of Europe, gathered around a table in Berlin in

1884. In front of them lay a map of Africa that, with their rulers and pens, they proceeded to carve up amongst themselves.

I was born during the Second World War and grew up in Johannesburg accepting apartheid and the world as presented to me in my whites-only school and community. When my older brother came home from university questioning our deeply racialised existence, I initially dismissed his challenges. When I entered university myself in 1961, most organisations that opposed apartheid had been banned. Nelson Mandela and other activists had gone underground. The University of the Witwatersrand had been ordered to close its doors to black students. Somehow, a few black students had managed to get special permission to complete courses. A friend introduced me to a small group of black and white students who met on the lawn outside the library to debate intensely what was happening in the country. Gradually I shed my blinkers.

It was not a time for sitting on the fence. Choices had to be made. My brother, now a journalist, was arrested and warned for handing out leaflets. That didn't deter him from becoming more deeply involved. In July 1964, a month after Nelson Mandela and his comrades were sentenced to life imprisonment, the security police swooped to smash what remained of the resistance. Eight weeks of detention without trial and solitary confinement made me understand more fully how the country felt like a vast prison for most of its people. I, a small fish, was released while my brother and others were put on trial.

Exile, reading and writing

When I left South Africa the following year, to study further at the University of York, I had to deal with a deep sense of disconnection. I was physically in England but my head was in South Africa, constantly imagining my brother and others locked away in prison. One of the few people who understood where I was coming from – and my dislocation – was a Nigerian academic, David Okẹ, studying for his PhD in Linguistics. His wife Bisi, a medical student, later joined him to do her houseman year in a British hospital. It was the beginning of an enduring family friendship. We had endless conversations about South Africa and shared our idealism. David would joke how, if he ever went into politics, he would push for Nigeria to help liberate South Africa.

I immersed myself in literature from the African continent, some of it banned back home. Apartheid aimed to segregate us physically, intellectually and emotionally. But here were African writers inviting me to cross boundaries into their very diverse, particular worlds, inviting me to enter and engage with them. Their works had a profound impact on me as a reader.

Autobiographical accounts of childhood by Ezekiel (now Es'kia) Mphahlele in *Down Second Avenue* and Peter Abrahams in *Tell Freedom* hit me in the gut as a white South African who had grown up so oblivious of the everyday brutality experienced by black South African children. Once imagined, through print, how could I ever forget the terrible injustice of the uncle beating the little boy Lee at the behest of the white farmer in *Tell Freedom* because the child hadn't said 'Baas'? Abrahams wrote so simply, directly, vividly. The dialogue brought his people into my room, into my head. I marvelled at the apparent simplicity of such dramatic storytelling that could engage young and old. At the first opportunity, as a newly qualified teacher in London, I read extracts to my class of teenagers, many of them Caribbean-born, and felt how they too were gripped by the imagined reality. One tough boy cried. I too had cried on my first reading. Despite our very different life histories, including harshly racialised and different experiences as white and black immigrants to Britain, we shared together the power of literature that derives from life experience. As a teacher, literature became for me a small but invaluable bridge with my students.

Another writer whose work deeply engaged me was the South African writer Nadine Gordimer, now a Nobel Laureate. Her literary skill, complex and layered, was grounded in a commitment to witness and transform into fiction ordinary incidents that revealed her individual characters in umbilical connection to the fabric of society. While South African writers offered me a window onto the world I had left, writers like Chinua Achebe, Amos Tutuola, Ngugi wa Thiong'o and many others opened windows onto the vast continent to the north. For a child brought up on stories in which black people were portrayed only as savages, comic buffoons or faithful servants, each book was a new journey. As for children in Britain, my school history books had left me profoundly ignorant and misinformed. My non-fiction library on Africa expanded alongside that of fiction. They were intimately connected.

One non-fiction book made a particular, potentially life-changing impact. It was called *Thinking With You*, a collection of highly critical, often satirical articles and lectures by Dr Tai Solarin, a Nigerian educationist, social critic and commentator who published regularly in the Nigerian press. Passionate about education, he and his wife had founded Nigeria's first and sole secular humanist school, Mayflower School. The Mayflower philosophy was committed to self-reliance, excellence and anti-elitism. Tai Solarin stood fiercely against corruption in the newly independent Nigeria. His outspoken critique and human rights activism were to land him in jail a number of times in the ensuing years. After meeting a young Englishwoman who had taught art in his school, I wrote to him during my PGCE year. He responded by immediately offering me a teaching post! But I never reached Mayflower.

While earning money for my fare, I met my husband-to-be, another South African exile. South Africa's contemptible 'Immorality Act' outlawing marriage between black and white – like the 'anti-miscegenation' laws in various states in the USA – was yet a further reason that ensured exile. After marrying, we remained in England and I began teaching in London.

By the time the young people of Soweto rose up in 1976 against apartheid and a schooling designed for servitude, I was the mother of two children. Our children inherited parents who belonged to two worlds – the one in which we lived and the other about which we frequently spoke. We were members of the Anti-Apartheid Movement. Our children grew up knowing about marches and protests. When I began writing for young people, it was inevitable that the setting would be South Africa. My first novel *Journey to Jo'burg* was an imaginative journey for me, exploring the psychological reality for two black children whose childhood lives had been totally different from mine. I imagined telling the story to my own children who were 6 and 10 at the time. I think that I was also writing the kind of book that I wished I could have read as a child. A deep anger remained about the censorship and misrepresentations in my colonial childhood and that, frankly, were still largely current in children's books in Britain in the 1970s. Significantly, *Journey to Jo'burg* was first published in an education series for teenagers but rapidly found its way into primary schools and a trade edition for younger readers. An American edition and translations soon revealed international interest.

The banning of the book in South Africa was simply a spur to more writing. Not that I needed a spur. As I wrote more novels and stories set in South Africa, I developed the habit of detailed research and then, with that grounding, I relished the freedom of creating my own plot and characters with the imaginative crossing of boundaries and barriers that fiction enables. I was still teaching part-time and it was a while before I began to believe in myself as a 'real writer'. I began to understand that stories were a way of making sense for myself first of all and then, hopefully, for others. Receiving letters from teenagers and younger children, as well as adults, in response to the same book made me realise that the process I adopted was allowing me to write with layers of meaning that could speak to a wide range of readers internationally.

Turning my antennae to Britain

At the time of South Africa's first democratic elections, when Nelson Mandela became president in 1994, I was still involved with writing *No Turning Back*, a novel about a street child in Johannesburg who inherits the legacy of apartheid with a fractured home and society. But when that was behind me, I felt it time to turn my antennae to the country that had given our family a home when South Africa had denied us one. I knew that on the streets of London I would find themes that explore our potential for humanity and inhumanity as readily as on the streets of Johannesburg. I also instinctively knew that my central characters would be refugees and that I should like to make them Nigerian. The evidence is in my notebook. On the first page, dated 6 February 1997, I made notes from *Refugee Children in the Classroom* by Jill Rutter, who was then Education Officer at the Refugee Council in London. By 10 February 1997 I had a set of questions for a meeting with her that day. Top of the list, I wrote: 'Options from Nigeria?'

Why Nigeria? There was the awful irony of Nigeria experiencing its most brutal dictatorship, under General Sani Abacha, at the point when South Africa had achieved the near miracle of its first democratic elections. In the preceding years we had seen Nigeria slide from one coup to the next. At one stage, my university friend who had hoped to help liberate South Africa had entered Nigerian politics. Professor Ọkẹ had become Senator Ọkẹ. But his integrity got in the way. There had been an assassination attack. Thankfully it had gone awry and the gunmen didn't find him. Their intended victim survived to return to academic life. His tales revealed how painfully difficult it is for people of honour to survive when corruption becomes a way of life. It was the condition about which Tai Solarin had been so passionately warning in the little book on my shelf.

My writer's notebook

Reviewing my writer's notebook, I am surprised to see that already on page 6 I had jotted down a diagram that shows possible characters, happenings and themes as well as a possible structure. I projected a girl of 12, a boy of 11 and a mother who arrive at Heathrow airport as asylum seekers. They don't know what is happening to their father in their home country. I have also noted 'INFO THROUGH LETTERS, PHONE CALLS, NEWS ITEMS' in relation to their father. 'PAST/DAYDREAMS FLASH-BACKS PHOTOS NIGHTMARES' are noted as a way of communicating their background, including 'Memories of stable family, grandparents, cousins etc'. Perhaps the writer Ken Saro-Wiwa was already in my mind because I have also written 'ENVIRONMENTAL ISSUE?' linked to 'political crisis and trauma'. Saro-Wiwa had vociferously challenged what he saw as the unholy alliance of multinational oil companies and the military dictatorship in despoiling the Niger delta. Despite his international reputation as a writer and human rights activist, General Abacha had him falsely charged in a military court and executed on 11 November 1995. The newspaper files in the Refugee Council contained reports of other writers who had also challenged the regime and suffered bans. That was how it had been for outspoken writers in South Africa. I don't know when exactly I began to think of a writer father for my novel but the choice opened up possibilities for both character and themes.

It must have been after meeting Jill Rutter that I decided that my two fictional children would arrive alone. I also instinctively knew that I wanted to see this story from the viewpoint of the girl who is more mature than her younger brother. Seeing events through the eyes of a young person always encourages a freshness of vision. It forces me to research from a particular viewpoint, to be extremely observant and to make leaps of imagination. The child's perspective often throws up sharp contradictions between what the child expects and what happens. What child getting ready for school, preparing her schoolbag, expects to hear their mother screaming, followed by gunshots?

My notebook over the next few months shows visits to various refugee projects, including one inside Heathrow Airport behind doors that are out of bounds to most passengers. Frequently one interviewee would suggest other people or places to visit. Research is like being on a detective trail, except that the crime or crisis is waiting to be created within the fiction. While I gather information and understanding, I am always on the lookout for clues that can be of use.

There are pages of notes jotted down while I trailed classes in a couple of London secondary schools. In one of these, I was introduced to a group of refugee students at lunchtime. My questions suddenly sparked a heated discussion about how to deal with racism. There was a strong view that it was pointless reporting it to teachers and that the only way was to fight. In another school, I ran my own workshops, beginning with the question: 'What do you need most when you come to school here?' 'Get a friend', I was told. In my conversation with Sheila Melzak, head of the child and adolescent psychotherapy team at the Medical Foundation for the Care of Victims of Torture, she gave one example after another of traumatised children. Her cameos were deeply disturbing. She invited me to return and do some storytelling at one of her group sessions. The eyes of one boy in particular remained with me long afterwards. When I recall those eyes now, I think of Femi.

My second notebook contains an amateur sketch of rows of barred windows behind a high metal fence topped with swirling razor wire. Not exactly what you expect at the end of a leafy Oxfordshire lane on a fine June day, nor from the name Campsfield House. The visitors' room looked bright and newly furnished: an unexceptional waiting room once you forgot the clanging external door and the cameras. When Ola (not his real name) appeared, he looked younger than my son. He was still a student but had been working as a journalist for a former politician opposed to military rule in Nigeria. One day in May he had arrived at the office to see his employer being carted away by soldiers. Friends advised him that it was unsafe to remain in the country. They obtained a false passport and airline ticket for him and, with only a small bag of clothes, he had managed to get out of Murtala Muhammed Airport. Unfortunately no one explained that he should claim political asylum the moment he landed on British soil. Instead he tried to enter on the passport. Immigration officers let him dig a hole full of lies. When they finally told him that they knew the passport was false, they were not interested in his story about fear of persecution. He was now a proven liar.

I didn't always use my notebook, especially if I didn't want to draw attention to myself, like when I joined the long queue forced to wait outside the gigantic Immigration and Nationality Department in Croydon, Lunar House. Instead I let the experience seep in. It stirred childhood memories of the dismal queue outside the Pass Office in Johannesburg, a place of great humiliation for black people. Once inside Lunar House's Screening Unit, I simply sat and watched the ebb and flow of people being called by number to a kiosk window. I couldn't hear the conversations but could observe the body language of officer and applicant, while feeling the suppressed tension in this bleak room in which life decisions were being determined. I went to great lengths to check my understanding of the asylum process from the perspectives of various refugee workers, a lawyer and an immigration officer. It was vital to me not to be accused of fabrication.

While I was readily able to research my London setting, when I made the original decision to create a Nigerian family, I had not visited Nigeria. Through various Nigerian friends, I had a strong sense of a close-knit middle-class family, at ease in both Yoruba and English, where the parents not only place enormous value on education but on personal qualities of integrity and truth telling. I was aware that in order to bring my characters' memories of home to life, I needed something more than my reading about Nigeria. The chance came when I was invited by the British Council to run a writing workshop in Ghana. I booked my return via Lagos. In the space of two days, David and Bisi Ọkẹ took me to Ife, Ibadan, and back to Lagos. It was a wonderful weekend, meeting younger family members (now three generations) but also of heightened imagination as I absorbed the sights and sounds that would be imprinted on my characters' minds. I also came back with a reel of photos inside my camera, fortunately not detected by the soldier whom I snapped setting up his unofficial roadblock to collect unofficial 'dash'. This was January 1998 and General Abacha still very much alive in his military boots.

Writing: probing the imagination

I hope that I have conveyed how my wide-ranging research was also a period of gestation for thinking about characters and action. Plotting is a discipline for me, making me question where the novel is going. Projected plots and synopses are never cast in stone but more like sounding boards. As I begin writing the narrative, I feel myself more deeply into my characters and new aspects emerge. Below is the opening of my first synopsis for *The Other Side of Truth*, written only a few months into my research:

> 12 year old Sade and her 10 year old brother Femi witness their mother being shot in broad daylight as she throws herself in front of their father when gunmen pull up in a car outside their house in a suburb of Lagos. Their father, Folarin Solaja, is a political journalist who has been openly critical of the military government. It is the time he regularly sets off for work. Their father carries Mama, who is bleeding profusely, into the house. When he lays her on the sofa, they know she is dead. Neighbours rush in to help and call a doctor. When the phone rings shortly afterwards, Sade answers. A man's voice tells her to give Folarin a message: '*If we get the family first, what does it matter?*' When Uncle Tunde arrives, their father insists that he arrange for the children to be got out of the country immediately, 'by any means' . . .
>
> [*This introductory scene to be told sparsely and shown in the form of images imprinted on Sade's mind, e.g. in first-person present tense and possibly italicised: their mother falling, children racing towards father cradling their mother, snatches of conversation, etc.*]

When I came to write the first chapter, instead of Sade directly witnessing the shooting, she hears the sounds. As I imagined myself into the situation more fully, that seemed more powerful. We can be profoundly affected by what we don't directly see because imagination takes over. In a similar vein, in this early synopsis I had Papa immediately wanting to get the children out of the country. However, when I came to writing, Papa's emotions became far more complex as he tussles with Uncle Tunde and with himself.

I am intrigued also to see the note that I made above to myself about how the opening scene should be told: '*sparsely and shown in the form of images imprinted on Sade's mind*'. Memory was to become an important theme in the novel as Sade experiences the loss of mother, family and home. The images in Sade's head play an important part in creating her interior life. She also holds on to voices. Recalling Mama's favourite proverbs helps Sade survive. The threads of how she remembers her parents' words are already woven in to her consciousness from the first chapter. When Papa is quiet in the face of Uncle Tunde's exhortations, Sade recalls what he might have said in other circumstances: 'The truth is the truth. How can I write what's untrue?'

I can't recall this weaving of memory being a conscious decision. As I moved beyond plotting into writing, I began to find out more about Sade. But it was only some time after the novel was published that I realised how much Sade's mental processes echoed my own disconnection during my own early years of exile.

Writing a novel is such a many-layered process. If we create characters in whom we believe and in whom others can believe, can we ever get to know them fully? Perhaps that is what leaves a novelist sometimes feeling there is unfinished business at the end of a novel. That was my feeling at the end of *The Other Side of Truth*. Despite enormous relief at Papa's release from detention, this is no fairytale ending. I knew that the family's problems were far from over. I was also very aware that Sade's love of words had helped her but Femi's emotions were locked inside him and potentially explosive.

On the day I travelled up to London to receive the Smarties Silver Award for my novel, I saw a young Nigerian boy's face on the front of everyone's newspaper in the underground train. He looked so like my Femi – and the image in Sade's head of her previously happy little brother before he had been catapulted into London. The news was shocking. The schoolboy Damilola Taylor had been murdered on his way home from Peckham Library. Although it was to be some years before there were convictions, his suspected murder by a gang of young people in November 2000 compelled me to explore Femi's vulnerability further. I needed to dig deeper into the conflict of values between the 'might is right' world on the streets and Papa's values. The result was my sequel *Web of Lies*. I also changed my dedication in *The Other Side of Truth* to include a commemoration of Damilola and my publishers initiated an on-going donation of 10p from every book sold to the Refugee Council. It was an example of life acting upon literature.

Instruction or delight?

I am frequently asked, 'Have you a message in what you write?' My reply is that writing fiction is quite different from declaiming from a soapbox or through a microphone. I do not write to deliver a 'message'. Yet I believe passionately in the importance of literature that engages with life and our moral human universe. I believe absolutely in what Nadine Gordimer has called 'witness literature' (2002) and in Mario Vargas Llosa's defence of 'committed literature': 'I believe that literature must address itself to the problems of its time . . . without ceasing to be entertaining, literature should immerse itself in the life of the streets, in the unravelling of history, as it did in the best of times' (Vargas Llosa, 1997).

Twenty years ago I carried out doctoral research into the impact of a year's course of literature on a class of young white teenagers. The books were chosen to engage them to journey, at least in their imaginations, beyond their own experiences. My findings were sobering. Despite plenty of evidence of empathy with fictional characters who experienced racism – whether in Nazi Germany, American South, apartheid South Africa or 1980s Britain – as well as evidence of stereotypes being challenged, there was little evidence of students moving beyond the fiction into critical thinking about their own society. During the research, I came to appreciate more fully the importance of the context of the classroom and wider culture in which books are read and entitled my ensuing book *Through Whose Eyes? Exploring Racism: Reader, Text and Context.*

Nevertheless, I returned to writing fiction. I am also heartened when, in some of the many letters I receive from whole classes of young people, I sense a genuine desire to communicate a personal response beyond the exercise of writing to an author. One of my favourite examples came from an 11-year-old schoolboy who wrote:

> Dear Beverley Naidoo
>
> Thank you for writing The Other Side of Truth. We read it in class every day and we thought it was incredible. Sometimes when I got home I looked at my globe for Nigeria and its capital city Lagos . . . Femi was my favourite character because he was moody and a bit like me when I am at home . . . I shouldn't tell you this but our teacher had to stop reading to hold in tears.
>
> James, letter, 11 December 2001

I guessed that this must be a teacher who believed in the power of literature and who was open enough to show honest emotion. When I was later able to visit the school, which I found on a bleak estate in Glasgow, the teacher and his children had transformed their classroom into an Amazonian jungle. They were reading Eva Ibbotson's *Journey to the River Sea*! Here was literature being read as a window into a wider world. I was right to have been struck by the image of a Glasgow boy carrying home a new narrative in his head and searching for Lagos on his globe. In shifting between fiction and reality, and crossing boundaries in his imagination, he was mirroring what I frequently do as a writer. I cannot tell what long-lasting impact his empathy with Femi might have but I hope that it might add to an awareness of our common humanity. When, to my vast surprise, *The Other Side of Truth* was awarded the Carnegie Medal, what pleased me most was that

British librarians, in acknowledging the book, were acknowledging the existence of a submerged world of refugees in our midst. In acknowledging my particular writer's map as a route into that world, they also honoured a journey profoundly shaped by its African origins.

Bibliography

Abrahams, P. 1954. *Tell Freedom.* London, Faber & Faber.

Gordimer, N. 2002. 'Testament of the Word', London, *Guardian Review,* 15 June.

Ibbotson, E. 2002. *Journey to the River Sea.* London, Macmillan.

Mphahlele, E. 1962. *Down Second Avenue.* Berlin, Seven Seas Books.

Naidoo, B. 1985. *Journey to Jo'burg: A South African Story.* Harlow, Longman.

Naidoo, B. 1992. *Through Whose Eyes? Exploring Racism: Reader, Text and Context.* Stoke-on-Trent, Trentham Books.

Naidoo, B. 1995. *No Turning Back.* London, Penguin.

Naidoo, B. 2000. *The Other Side of Truth.* London, Penguin.

Naidoo, B. 2004. *Web of Lies.* London, Penguin.

Rutter, J. 1994. *Refugee Children in the Classroom.* Stoke-on-Trent, Trentham Books.

Solarin, T. 1965. *Thinking With You.* Lagos, Longman Group.

Vargas Llosa, M. 1997. 'A Literary Engagement'. London, *Prospect.* May 1997.

What is *The Other Side of Truth*?
Jana Giles

This chapter considers Beverley Naidoo's *The Other Side of Truth* (2000) in the context of contemporary historical and social conditions in Nigeria and Africa generally, as well as Britain and more globally. It begins with a discussion of some of the issues surrounding children's literature, introduces some historical background for the novel, and then moves on to a consideration of the novel itself.

Introduction: children's literature and critical literacy

Beverley Naidoo's work can be viewed as a commentary on the historical and social contexts that she has experienced in Africa and Britain, and in *The Other Side of Truth* she invites readers to view the world from these different contexts. Naidoo's fiction features child protagonists in situations which challenge received views and asks for a critical engagement with stories from the past and the present. The book juxtaposes two children from post-colonial Nigeria with young people in contemporary Britain. The main protagonists struggle with physical and psychological hardship as well as ethical dilemmas which question the notion of truth and its value, learnt from their family.

Children's literature often raises concerns (for adults) over whether children will be able to understand – and tolerate – stories of the victimised, or whether they 'need to be protected from knowing the brutal facts of history' (Hall 2003: 167). Tensions exist around children's literature which deals with politically or emotionally difficult issues, because many of those involved in the business of children's books are also concerned to preserve what they regard as characteristics of childhood: innocence, lack of experience, and an optimistic attitude to the future. It could be argued that texts which explore topics such as racism, substance abuse, bullying, divorce, death and disability in realistic ways require their readers to acquire kinds of knowledge that impinge on innocence and make optimism seem naïve and misplaced (Pinsent 2005: 191).

Of course, for those children who are experiencing oppression and victimisation, the question of the appropriateness of knowing the brutal facts of history is moot: they do not have the luxury of reading about it as outsiders; they are living it. And it is this experience which Naidoo wishes to bring alive for readers whose lives are more privileged, and who may live in those parts of the world where the policies of the powerful have a global impact.

Attitudes towards children's literature such as those described by Pinsent have changed in recent years, reflecting the general changes in attitude towards marginalised and oppressed groups that arose in the 1960s and 1970s. Simultaneously there emerged a greater awareness that taking a position on the question of appropriateness was, itself, an ideological one. Previously, children's literature in Britain tended to be written from the perspective of the imperial coloniser, or of the middle class; thus, even if social justice was being advocated, it often took on a patronising tone or assumed a readership that shared the protagonist's experiences and world-view (Pinsent 2005). In literature as well as historical study, there had been a marked tendency for writers from the British Empire to 'display, explicitly or implicitly, completely different attitudes towards those exerting dominion over subjugated peoples from those they reveal towards the members of the subject peoples themselves' (Pinsent 2005: 174).

With the advent of postcolonial studies, New Historicist and cultural materialist approaches to reading literature and history, however, there has been an increased foregrounding of marginalized people as the central characters (Pinsent 2005: 177). These approaches share the view that all texts are historical documents and all historical documents are texts: that only in combination can literature and history help us understand past and present. They emphasise how European traditions have been regarded as normative, marginalising the cultures of indigenous peoples and minorities. Within these newer approaches Naidoo's work is concerned to illuminate the experience of the formerly colonised. As a white South African, she might have shared the views of the hegemonic group, but instead has consciously allied herself with the black underclass. In her acceptance speech for the Carnegie Medal, Naidoo states that her writing deliberately engages with the problem of 'historical amnesia' over the uncomfortable matter of European colonialism. She believes writers 'have a particular responsibility not to engage in amnesia' and to acknowledge that 'all individuals are umbilically connected to a wider world. There is such a thing as society and it matters' (Naidoo 2001: 4). Regarding her first novel, *Journey to Jo'burg* (1985), Naidoo explains she was concerned about the misinformation about South Africa in books for young people, finding that very few books of the time discussed the 1976 children's rebellion against their inferior education in Soweto, or how apartheid politics had killed hundreds of young people and jailed many others (Naidoo 2008: 1–2). While most of her works focus on South Africa, in *The Other Side of Truth*, she writes about Nigerian refugees and members of the greater African diaspora, emphasizing global interconnectedness.

Within education in the UK today, Naidoo finds that a racialised frame remains among some: 'librarians still tell me of young white people who look at book covers with black people and think that the story will have nothing to do with them. . . . . There is a tremendous need in this society for literature that enables young people to cross boundaries . . . that enables them to explore issues of 'race', class and gender' (Naidoo 2001: 5). What authors like Naidoo attempt to stimulate, then, is the act of 'critical literacy' among their readership, that is, reading with a critical eye towards historical, social and political contexts, as well as examining issues of representation and power, self and other, and agency (Bean and Harper 2006: 96–7). Critical literacy encourages the view that literature may disrupt assumptions and beliefs that are otherwise taken for granted without reflection.

Historical backgrounds

Naidoo, South Africa and apartheid

To understand Naidoo's work it helps to consider the background in which she was brought up. Despite being born into a white, middle-class family in South Africa, she joined the anti-apartheid movement as a student and was imprisoned for eight weeks in solitary confinement. She went into exile in Britain, only returning to South Africa in 1991. Her first book, *Journey to Jo'burg* (1981) was banned in South Africa until 1991, but became an international success, deepening thousands of readers' knowledge of the daily realities of life under apartheid. In the sequel, *Chain of Fire* (1989), the child protagonists are now living in Bophelong, a 'black spot' run by a chief whose family has owned the land for 75 years. But the chief submits to government pressure, and the community has to endure the murder of their organisers, and being forced into a resettlement camp, a place of iron huts and starvation. Naidoo's focus on the plight of children in authoritarian or war-torn regimes continues in her other books about South Africa, *No Turning Back* (1995) a novel about a runaway boy in Johannesburg, the short-story collection *Out of Bounds* (2001), and a collection of contemporary testimonies from child refugees from the world over, *Making It Home* (2004). She has also published a sequel to *The Other Side of Truth, Web of Lies* (2004).

The historical roots that gave rise to the contexts in her books lie in the colonisation of the Southern Africa region by the Dutch in the seventeenth and eighteenth centuries, and the British in the nineteenth. The African people of the region have been profoundly affected by two centuries of domination; some communities were decimated, while others were conquered but retained some independence under European governance. In the late 1800s, diamonds and gold were discovered, and a European monopoly market was built upon the work of black migrant mine laborers housed under brutal conditions. By the early twentieth century, about three-quarters of the land in what is now South Africa was owned by whites, with many blacks working as tenants.

The 1930s saw the rise of apartheid, the aim of which was to protect white supremacy, achieved by stark definitions of race, exclusive white control of political institutions, segregation of institutions and territories, control of black movement to urban areas, and tight racial division in the labour market (Beinart 2001: 148). A series of laws proceeded to entrench apartheid. Black Africans were disallowed from buying land and participating in the market farming system. Pass laws controlling movement were instituted and interracial marriages outlawed. Many blacks were displaced to rural slums which offered merely the rhetoric of independence. 'Black spots,' farms owned by African people for decades, became susceptible to appropriation by white farmers. The policy of forced removals was a major mechanism for political repression and economic exploitation. At least 4 million people were forced to move, a policy which became a focal point for local resistance and international condemnation (Unterhalter 1987: 26). By the 1980s, many South Africans were refugees in their own land, and children and families were frequently separated indefinitely, as Naidoo details in *Journey to Jo'burg*.

Systematic resistance was difficult: prior to colonialism there existed no single African political system, and widespread illiteracy made it hard to organise across ethnic lines. But protests broke out frequently, and the African National Congress (ANC) emerged as the most effective resistance group. White minority opposition, such as that in which Naidoo participated, also existed, but the government outlawed most political activity in 1967, and reacted to protests by arresting around 10,000 people, including Nelson Mandela. Ruthless methods of suppression included torture, intimidation, imprisonment without trial, and police assassination, but persecution only incited further resistance. Finally, in 1990 Prime Minister F.W. de Klerk released Mandela and lifted the ban on political movements. South Africa elected Mandela president in 1994 in its first fully democratic elections. The Truth and Reconciliation Commission was established to elicit evidence about the political oppression and violations of human rights of the apartheid era. Although it was seen as a compromise for the sake of stability and to enable a wounded nation to move forward, nevertheless, the white population has dropped from 20 per cent in 1950 to 11 per cent in 1996 (Beinart 2001: 336–7). The country has since struggled to cope with the transition to democracy, and with problems of conflicts between tribal leadership and central government, poverty, crime, violence against women, the AIDS epidemic, and increased immigration from other parts of Africa.

Widening the context: Nigeria and Somalia

The Other Side of Truth is set in the late 1990s, and moves beyond South Africa to a more global contemporary context which involves the experience of Nigerian children as political refugees in Britain, bringing the colonial experience back to the metropole. It is set initially in Nigeria just after the execution of activist Ken Saro-Wiwa in 1995. Saro-Wiwa was the leader of the Movement for the Survival of the Ogoni People (MOSOP) which sought justice, a share of Nigeria's enormous oil revenues, and remediation of environmental damage caused by oil extraction. In 1993, MOSOP organised huge protests, drawing international attention to the military dictatorship of General Abacha. Subsequently, Saro-Wiwa and eight other leaders were arrested by the military government and executed on fabricated charges. *The Other Side of Truth* also draws on the troubled history of Somalia. Prior to European colonisation, Somalia did not exist as a nation-state but was inhabited by various ethnic groups, also maintaining an ongoing conflict with the neighboring Ethiopians. In the post-colonial era, the head of state, General Barre, sought to increase Somali nationalism, intending to unite Somali lands and peoples that had been divided under colonialism. When diplomatic efforts to reclaim areas of Kenya and Ethiopia failed, Barre engaged in failed wars (1977–8), ultimately leading to the Somali Civil War (1988–2006). By 2006, there were at least 240,000 Somalian refugees in Kenya, with 300–400 arriving every day (*Medical News Today*, 2006).

Folarin, Sade's father in the novel, is a journalist attempting to expose the wrongful death of Saro-Wiwa and other human rights violations by the Nigerian government, while the story of Mariam and her family is indicative of those who left Somalia for Kenyan refugee camps during the early years of the Civil War. By drawing on these histories of the aftermath of colonialism across different nations, Naidoo endeavours to create books for children which both engage readers in the lives of the characters and promote a critical appreciation of their social, cultural and historical contexts. For Naidoo, the genre of fiction is one of the best methods of sharing experience: 'What I hope . . . is that readers will become so imaginatively engaged with their characters and their dilemmas that they will begin to ask questions not only about "What will happen next?" but "Why is this happening?" . . . . Close readers may pick up signals within the story that suggest there is a bigger picture and begin to ask bigger questions' (Naidoo 2008: 2–3). For Naidoo, then, literature and education should engage both our heads and our hearts to enable critical literacy. The question of audience is thus important: who will read the text, and what kinds of assumptions might they bring with them?

What is 'the other side of truth'?

The book's title indicates its major theme, asking the reader to examine critically what 'truth' may mean. One way in which to interpret 'the other side of truth' is in terms of how we view the world differently depending on our context: Western audiences may be unaccustomed to reading a book from the perspective of African child refugees; Sade and Femi discover that their view of themselves as middle-class children is challenged when they escape political oppression in Nigeria only to confront racism and misunderstanding in Britain. Another way is to see 'the other side of truth' as expressing the novel's central moral conflict; Sade struggles with her parents' dictum to tell the truth when her father's journalistic truth-telling led, inadvertently, to her mother's death.

One of the earliest hints that Naidoo wants her readers to both identify with and be challenged by the text is the opening line: 'Sade is slipping her English book into her schoolbag when Mama screams. Two sharp cracks splinter the air' (1). We learn that Mama has been killed in a drive-by shooting, political retaliation for her husband's work as a journalist. Naidoo thus engages her Western readers with the familiarity of the 'English book' and the 'schoolbag' while simultaneously defamiliarising their experience. The 'English book' is not as safe and detached as one might expect, just as *The Other Side of Truth* may be written in English and take place largely in Britain, yet presents a set of experiences potentially disturbing to those who have been oblivious to the experience of refugees.

Some readers may also wonder what an African girl is doing reading an English book: this is a political and historical reference to English education arising from Britain's colonial rule of Nigeria from 1901 to 1960, as well as the dominance of English in the global media. Any expectations that readers might have that all Africans are impoverished are also dispelled by the English book, which signals the fact that Sade and her family are members of Nigeria's professional middle class. Also, stereotypes are both confirmed and challenged when the children confront people in the UK who repeatedly ask them if they speak English, which they do very well (93, 110), in addition to Yoruba and pidgin. These African children are trilingual, unlike their British counterparts, and in many ways better educated and disciplined.

Finally, Naidoo performs a classic act of good writing in juxtaposing the peaceful ease of reading a book with the sharp cracks of gunshot: in two sentences the action moves from what appears to be a bourgeois tale of a school-age child, to one in which that child's world is ripped apart by violence. In his *Poetics*, Aristotle wrote that successful writing begins *in medias res*, or in the middle of the action, because that immediately engages one's emotions and further curiosity. The harrowing events unfolding may incite empathy for a child who experiences her mother dying before her eyes. Thus, before readers might set up an 'us versus them' framework for reading they find themselves caring about what happens to Sade.

Ideas themselves take on different meanings – different 'truths' – depending on one's context and knowledge. At the airport Sade encounters an African American man wearing African dress who praises air travel for having created a global village: his life's ambition had been to travel to Nigeria and discover his roots (30). But while Sade had dreamt of flying, she had not anticipated that it would be as a refugee (33). Her present reality as political exile stands in sharp contrast to his romantic search for a lost past.

The children's experience of the UK contradicts the messages they have absorbed from the BBC World Service about British ideas of justice and fairness. When the children ask for help after Mrs Bankole abandons them at Victoria Station, they are treated like beggars (50). From the bus they see a 'postcard' London, but it seems dreamlike compared to the reality they face on the streets where they are first robbed and then accused of being robbers (58–64). Unlike in Nigeria, however, where the police set up roadside blocks to collect bribes (21), being turned in to the British police sends them on to better people. Yet the dishevelled office of Mr Nathan, the refugee lawyer (87), and the long queues at the Immigration Office (89), indicate the underfunded services for refugees and immigrants. Sade finds it strange that her father is imprisoned near Oxford, recalling that Folarin kept a copy of the *Oxford English Dictionary* on his desk at home (151); the idea of Oxford as a center of humanistic learning seems incompatible with the experience of Oxford as a center of detention. These situations subvert assumptions that Europe and the West are uniformly affluent and fair, and that all Africans are impoverished and corrupt.

Naidoo's representation of the school experience is not flattering to British children, but the kinds of students who torment Sade and Femi might be some of the audience for whom she is writing. Sade and Femi encounter bullies who are white children, but not essentially different from the military police in Nigeria in their attitudes towards those who are different (120–4). She remembers that her father says you have to stand up to bullies: 'Otherwise they get inside your head. That's how they succeed in controlling us' (118). Internalised oppression can happen anywhere, and may come from letting the bullies take over our internal dialogue. Ironically, the African refugees are better students than the poor, racist, and competitive children they encounter in Britain. Sade observes that since they don't teach much in her school about Africa, most of the students think it is one country and one language, rather than many countries and hundreds of languages, while in Nigeria their teacher made them learn all the European countries and languages (162).

Sade's parents have raised her to be truthful. Her mother tells her, 'Truth keeps the hand cleaner than soap' (74), and Folarin's journalism career is centred around his view that the bully gets away with it because others let him (22). Folarin puts himself and his family in danger by publishing photos of students killed in a political demonstration (64–5) and writing articles protesting that Saro-Wiwa and his fellow leaders would not be given a fair trial (78–9). Mama says that he should take care because the Nigerian government isn't interested in what the rest of the world thinks; Folarin says that he has to face himself in the mirror and show his children that bad men succeed when we look the other way. But only a few days later Mama is shot, and now Sade is confused: doing the right thing can lead to awful consequences (78).

The potential dangers of truth-telling are highlighted in other ways. Sade and Femi lie constantly to the British authorities to protect their father. Sade gives in to the school bullies and steals a lighter from the store owned by the family of her friend, Mariam, because she is coerced by threats that

Femi will be hurt. But when Sade learns that Mariam is also a political refugee, she tries to make amends. Mariam's uncle says there is no point in fighting bullies, but Sade thinks her father would never accept that, so 'How did people know what was the right thing to do?' (196)

Finally, although emigrating abroad had seemed like the solution, this is also not so simple. In London their Uncle Dele disappears because he had been involved with Nigerians for Democracy but began receiving death threats after Saro-Wiwa was executed; he had gone into hiding because one of his political contacts must have been a spy (190). And Folarin's deportation from Britain to probable death in Nigeria is averted not by his truth telling but by Sade's efforts to publicise his situation in the media.

Truth and the media

Writing, news and the media play an important role in *The Other Side of Truth*. Folarin's journalistic activity and the dangers it brings represent the challenges many face in speaking out under difficult conditions. Speech and writing become acts, not only abstractions, because they lead to actual consequences, such as exposing human rights violations and encouraging political activism, or being persecuted for doing so. As in several of her other works, Naidoo has her protagonists become or work with political activists, conveying the feeling that hope remains if some are willing to act, even if this comes at great personal sacrifice.

The news media in Britain offer opportunities for national and international exposure and dialogue that are not guaranteed in Nigeria. Since the press is censored in in Nigeria, the family first heard about Saro-Wiwa's execution on the BBC World Service. Sade's efforts to make her family's situation known to the *Seven O'clock News* brings attention to Folarin's plight and mobilises his release despite resistance from immigration authorities. Her mastery of the English language gives her the skills needed to navigate London alone and communicate with the news broadcaster. As a result of her own efforts, *Making News* wants to make a programme on refugees with her class (161–2), and in the end even the school bullies wish her well. Folarin quotes to her from a letter sent by an American university, 'Our students need to hear you. We need more people like you who are prepared to tell those hidden stories. We might not have assassination squads here but there are many other ways of making journalists keep quiet' (212). Readers are reminded that freedom of expression does not guarantee that one will be heard.

An answer to the problem of truth-telling is suggested in the folktale of the Tortoise which Folarin writes to his children in a letter from prison.

Tortoise is captured by Leopard, who plans to eat him but grants a reprieve during which Tortoise scratches the earth deeply so that everyone would know an animal struggled for life there. Folarin writes: 'If we keep quiet about injustice, then injustice wins. We must dare to tell. Across the oceans of time, words are mightier than the sword' (193). The message seems to be that we must strive to tell our stories non-violently so that the 'other side of truth' can be known. Critical literacy requires that we hear everyone's stories in order to understand and evaluate multiple truths.

Yet this may come at a great price. At the end of the novel, Sade writes a letter home to her grandmother who has lost her daughter and grandchildren and is now all alone. Early in the novel, Sade sees a friend of her grandmother's, an old woman who now has to sell oranges as a street vendor because she has lost all her children (20). Was it worth Mama's death, Grandma's poverty, and their own new status as migrants to tell the world the truth about Nigeria?

References

Bean, T.W. and Harper, H.J. 2006. 'Exploring Notions of Freedom in and through Young Adult Literature', *Journal of Adolescent and Adult Literacy* 50(2), 6–104.

Beinart, W. 2001. *Twentieth-Century South Africa*. New Edition. Oxford, Oxford University Press.

Hall, C. 2003. 'Children's Literature'. In M.J. Kehily and J. Swann, *Children's Cultural Worlds*. Chichester, John Wiley.

Medical News Today. 'Rising Tide Of Somali Refugees Strains Food Stocks in Kenya's Camps.' 30 September; http://www.medicalnewstoday.com/articles/52831.php

Naidoo, B. [1985] 1999. *Journey to Jo'burg*. New York, Harper Collins.

Naidoo, B. [1985] 2001. *Out of Bounds: Seven Stories of Conflict and Hope*. New York, HarperCollins.

Naidoo, B. [1989] 1993. *Chain of Fire*. New York, Harper Trophy.

Naidoo, B. [1995] 1999. *No Turning Back*. New York, Harper Trophy.

Naidoo, B. 2000. *The Other Side of Truth*. London, Penguin.

Naidoo, B. 2001. 'Acceptance Speech, Carnegie Medal', *Books For Keeps* 130, 4–5.

Naidoo, B. 2004. 'Introduction', in *Making It Home*. London and New York, Puffin.

Naidoo, B. 'An Interview with Beverley Naidoo.' By Madelyn Travis. http://www.writeaway.org.uk/component/option,com_mtree/task,viewlink/link_id,3014/Itemid,99999999/24February 2008. Accessed 26.11.2008.

Pinsent, P. 2005. 'Postmodernism, New Historicism and Migration: New Historical Novels' , in K. Reynolds (ed.) *Modern Children's Literature: An Introduction*. Basingstoke, Palgrave Macmillan, pp. 173–90.

Unterhalter, E. 1987. *Forced Removal: The Division, Segregation and Control of the People of South Africa*. London, International Defence and Aid Fund for Southern Africa.

13

Past Worlds: Jamila Gavin, *Coram Boy* (2000)

Introduction
Ann Hewings and Nicola J. Watson

At first glance, the hard-edged contemporary topicality of *The Other Side of Truth* would seen to have very little in common with Jamila Gavin's *Coram Boy*, published in the same year, except that both won prestigious awards. *Coram Boy* is included here as an exemplum of the recent renaissance in children's historical fiction, a genre that stretches back deep into the nineteenth century's love of Sir Walter Scott and which boasts still classic titles such as Captain Frederick Marryat's *The Children of the New Forest* (1847) and Rosemary Sutcliffe's *The Eagle of the Ninth* (1954). Historical fiction arguably waned in popularity for a time over the 1980s and early 1990s, but the millennium saw it 'in a vibrant state' (Bramwell, 2005: 109), perhaps as a response to the perennial need to bring history alive for school-children. The historical settings of six out of the seven titles shortlisted for the Carnegie Medal in 2008 underscore this trend. It would be a mistake, however, to assume that because fiction is historical it does not address contemporary issues; race, empire and colonisation are the subject matter and context of Jamila Gavin's fiction.

Born in India of an Indian father and English mother and now settled in Britain, Gavin began her career as a children's writer in 1979 with her first volume of stories for children. Her work has spanned many modes and genres: short stories, retellings of Hindu tales, teen novels set in India, ghost stories set in England, science fantasy. She has in fact only written two historical novels – *Coram Boy*, and *The Bloodstone* (2003), set in seventeenth-century

India and Venice. What all Gavin's otherwise apparently eclectic work has in common is 'a need to reflect the multicultural world in which my children and I lived' (Gavin, 2009). Her protagonists typically traverse different worlds, connecting apparently distinct spheres, whether between the living and the dead, the European and the Indian, the earth-bound and parallel reality accessed through wormholes in space. When such connections are made, it often entails the suturing of family generations, as in *The Bloodstone*, in which a young boy travels to find and release his father held hostage in Afghanistan.

Coram Boy opens in 1741 in the cathedral city of Gloucester and moves its young protagonists across the agrarian landscape of the Cotswolds into the rapidly expanding colonial capital city, London. Centred upon the intertwined fates of two orphans who come together at the Coram Hospital for Deserted Children, Toby, saved from an African slave-ship and Aaron, the abducted and abandoned heir to a great estate, the novel focuses on rediscovering the hidden histories of children in the eighteenth century, and especially the hidden histories of invisible children – the illegitimate, the foundlings, the black, the poor, the enslaved. As such, this is not merely an exercise in re-creating eighteenth-century England for the young reader, but has an ethical and political dimension in its discussion of oppression and injustice. Dealing with the fates of children black and white, male and female, in a London driven by the business of making money from its colonies, the novel tackles the vexed history of empire and its legacies at one remove, while endeavouring to recuperate loss and oppression through the mechanism of romance. It had a pronounced success, winning the Whitbread Children's Book Award in 2000, being adapted for the stage, and achieving two successful runs at the National Theatre in 2005–6 and 2006–7, before transferring to Broadway in New York.

The essays

In the first essay included here, Gavin discusses her choice of a historical setting and the imaginative freedom that moving away from the contemporary gives her, noting that historical fiction enables her to explore issues that might be more challenging or unsettling for children if dealt with in an explicitly contemporary context. Christopher Ringrose's essay provides a wider literary and theoretical context within which to place *Coram Boy* as a historical fiction. Reading *Coram Boy* together with recent historical novels for children by Paul Bajoria, Kevin Crossley-Holland and Alan Garner, he defends the subgenre from attacks of formal naïveté and political conservatism, describing its mechanisms for producing historical authenticity, and suggesting that its key innovative role is to establish a sense of the past for new generations whose awareness, through school, of the stories of history is declining. Historical fiction, according to Ringrose, is politically 'live' in that it helps children experience 'structures of feeling' relevant to the past, empathise with real or fictional historical characters, and absorb a sense of lives lived before they were born.

References

Bramwell, P. 2005. 'Feminism and History: Historical Fiction – Not Just a Thing of the Past', in K. Reynolds (ed.) *Modern Children's Literature: An Introduction.* Basingstoke, Palgrave Macmillan.

Gavin, J. 2009. Official website, www.jamilagavin.co.uk, accessed 4 March 2009.

New Historical Fiction for Children
Christopher Ringrose

At the start of the twenty-first century, historical fiction written for children is a thriving, vibrant genre, attracting new practitioners such as Paul Bajoria and Kate Pennington, as well as established and celebrated authors like Jamila Gavin and Kevin Crossley-Holland. It also maintains its educational mission, represented directly by attractive but more functional novellas such as those in A&C Black's *Flashback* series (Clarke, 1996).

In the British tradition, we can distinguish at least two types of children's fiction about history. In the first, a number of important female writers counselled the spiritual and imaginative duty of reattaching the young to a living sense of the past, which was in danger of being lost. Adrienne E. Gavin has shown how, in the 'time-slip' novels of Lucy M. Boston and Philippa Pearce, children gain some kind of magical access to history. In books such as Boston's *Green Knowe* series, or Pearce's *Tom's Midnight Garden*, modern child protagonists experience the past directly, often through rites of passage into a different dimension of a particular setting or house:

> In these houses the key with which the child character unlocks the door to the past is the imagination or memories of an older woman or women. These older women characters act as conduits to the past, and enable readers and the child protagonist to enter the past through the female imagination.
>
> Gavin, 2003: 163

The second type of historical writing for children extends the tradition of 'realist historical fiction'. Here the narrative is set completely in the past. There is less need for encounters with ghosts or time shifts, gateways and transitions, since the reader encounters past events directly. Recent examples include Jamila Gavin's *Coram Boy* (2000), Kevin Crossley-Holland's *Gatty's Tale* (2006), Kate Pennington's *Charley Feather* (2005) and Paul Bajoria's *The Printer's Devil* (2004).

On the face of it, such realist historical fiction for children offers a rich artistic experience. It provides readers with contact with the past, nourishes their sense of their place in time, teaches them about historical difference, and re-creates past lives. However, modern critics and theorists have sought to challenge what they see as naïve assumptions about fiction's ability to recreate 'authentic' past experience. Deborah Stevenson, for example, has argued that while recent historiography and adult fiction have questioned the very nature of historical representation, children's fiction has lagged behind and still 'offers certainty' when it should be drawing attention to what is unknowable and 'untellable' about the past (2003: 28). Stevenson points to a divergence over the last 25 years between children's historical fiction and critically acclaimed adult historical fiction. She approves of changes in the historiography of children's textbooks, whereby books such as Steven Jaffe's *Two Hundred Years of Reinventing American History* (1996) and Lori Lee Wilson's *The Salem Witch Trials* (1997) examine the *process* of history-making and its provisional nature. However she argues that 'The genre [of historical fiction for children] seems unmoved by the newer currents in history. Effects of postmodernism are difficult to detect in juvenile historical fiction; the texts remain cohesive and constructed' (Stevenson, 2003: 26–7).

Stevenson's concerns about the artistic conservatism of realist historical fiction echo those of the celebrated contemporary theorist Linda Hutcheon. In 1989, Hutcheon coined the influential term 'historiographic metafiction' to designate a new kind of anti-realist novel which asks radical questions about the status of historical narrative and 'problematizes almost everything the historical novel once took for granted' (Hutcheon, 1989: 69). While some critics, like Fredric Jameson, had questioned the value of 'pastiche', or the imitation of the form and style of earlier texts, as a way of writing about the past, Hutcheon endorsed it as creative and a mode of writing with politically radical potential.

This debate about the credentials of historical fiction raises at least three questions for those studying historical novels written for children: whether realist fiction is inevitably naïve in its attempt to offer a 'window into the past'; how far its writers consciously or unconsciously copy or pastiche past writing in their work; and the extent to which the 'unknowable' nature of the past needs to be signalled to young readers.

I believe that the genre of realist historical fiction, as practised by writers like Alan Garner, Kevin Crossley-Holland and Jamila Gavin, can be defended against charges of naïveté and conservatism. In fact, the division of the genre into (a) self-conscious and experimental fiction which makes us reconsider our ways of knowing the past and (b) realist fiction which deals complacently with such issues, is a false one. First, children's writers have developed subtle ways, including varieties of what the Russian Formalist critic Viktor Shklovsky called 'defamiliarization', to invoke past subjectivities. Second, the historical novel retains its role as a transmitter of historical information, even though it may use pastiche and various kinds of stylistic innovation to establish a sense of the past and past ways of experiencing the world. The novelist's procedure in establishing such a world-view is speculative, of course, but then so are all our ways of inhabiting the past through artistic means. A fruitful account of the difficulties and rewards involved in the re-creation of historical experience is provided by Raymond Williams in his study of British culture *The Long Revolution.* Writing about the problem of grasping a sense of how people thought, felt and experienced in the past, he devised the term 'structure of feeling':

> It is only in our own time and place that we can expect to know, in any substantial way, the general organization. . . . The most difficult thing to get hold of, in studying any past period, is this felt sense of the quality of life at a particular place and time: a sense of the ways in which the particular activities combined into a way of thinking and living. . . . The term I would suggest to describe it is *structure of feeling*: it is as firm and definite as 'structure' suggests, yet it operates in the most delicate and least tangible parts of our activity.
>
> Williams, 1961: 47–8

One way to think about how a *structure of feeling* might be evoked in children's historical fiction, and linked to its ideological stance, is through brief consideration of some examples of the genre.

> A bottle of cold tea; bread and a half onion. That was Father's baggin. Mary emptied her apron of stones from the field and wrapped the baggin in a cloth.
>
> Garner, 1976: 11

This is the opening of Alan Garner's *The Stone Book,* the tale which initiated his Q*uartet* of historical fictions about his ancestors and their lives in Cheshire from 1864 to 1941. In the verb-free first sentence, three objects lie slightly forbiddingly on display, guarding the entrance to the book. They are at the same time resoundingly ordinary – a commonplace meal – and unfamiliar, with the defamiliarising freshness of poetry, as conceived by Shklovsky, for whom 'the technique of art is to make objects "unfamiliar", to make forms difficult, to increase the difficulty and length of perception because the process of perception is an aesthetic end in itself and must be prolonged' (Shklovsky, 1965: 12).

In its determination to honour the world of work and the largely unwritten history of working men and women, the first sentence of *The Stone Book* also has a history, or at least a historical moment of its own. First published in 1976, it takes its place alongside other texts of the time which sought to honour, and increase the visibility of, the British working class, such as Charles Parker's 1960 Radio Ballad *Singing the Fishing*, E.P. Thompson's 1966 historical study of *The Making of the English Working Class*, or Jeremy Seabrook's 1974 account of changes in working-class Northampton, *The Everlasting Feast*. Like all the historical novels discussed here, *The Stone Book* is itself a historical text, with a dual relation to our need to 'invent the past' (Lawson Lucas, 2003: xiv). We will see this pattern of reading the past through the present repeated in the work of Paul Bajoria and Jamila Gavin. The historical novel has another object, however, which is to recreate a different mode of subjectivity, as a way of evoking a different world.

This kind of defamiliarisation is a feature of the opening page of *Gatty's Tale*, Kevin Crossley-Holland's story of a young girl's participation in a pilgrimage from the Welsh Marches to Jerusalem in 1203:

> 'Light of light! Oh, flight! Oh, flight! ' trilled the early birds. In one corner of the cow-stall, the heap of dirty sacking shifted. Something buried beneath it made a sound that began as a gentle murmur and ended as a grouse.
>
> Then the cock crowed and that loosed the tongues of his disciples. Half the neighers and brayers and bleaters and grunters in the manor of Caldicot welcomed the day's dawning, chill and misty as it was.
>
> Crossley-Holland, 2006: 1

The passage suggests how the poetic function of language is allied to the historical imagination. The startling opening is different in register from much narrative fiction. It is packed with allusions and contrasts, and with a sense of a structure of feeling different from our own – not so much in the experience of sleeping in the straw in the cowshed, but in the mode of thought. It begins almost like a creation myth, as though this were the first day of the world and simultaneously the first day of the book, with the birdsong echoing the Nicene Creed ('God of God, Light of Light'), the cock crowing and the 'brayers and bleaters and grunters' taking up the refrain. These names themselves skilfully evoke a medieval bestiary or alliterative verse.

Historical fiction has always needed to use a degree of mimicry, and its use of pastiche might be construed as a strength (in Linda Hutcheon's view) or a weakness (in Fredric Jameson's). Paul Bajoria's 2004 novel *The Printer's Devil* is interesting in terms of the debate over the use of pastiche in representing the past. In his charming, lively account of the adventures of Mog, the printer's devil of the title, in the docklands of Victorian London, Bajoria makes deft allusions to the work of Dickens, deploying familiar ingredients: the orphan hero; the child's first-person narration; the maze of streets; the series of surrogate mothers and fathers; the mystery plot with its enigmatic figures; the sense of everything being slightly more vivid, distorted and larger than life.

The gravitational pull of Dickens is so strong that Bajoria has to work within that rich structure of feeling. In this respect the writer of historical fiction set after 1800 has a different context from the one dealing with earlier periods. The actual appearance of child protagonists in literature dates back only as far as the Romantic period, so Crossley-Holland's thirteenth-century heroine Gatty has to be created out of his sense of that culture, rather than out of a pastiche of earlier child-protagonists and their sensibilities. Paul Bajoria, however, makes a virtue of the rich textuality that comes down to us from the Victorian period.

Jamila Gavin's *Coram Boy*, published in 2000, brings into focus many of the debates that characterise children's historical fiction in general. Though it might at first seem more traditional in form and structure than *The Stone Book, Gatty's Tale* or *The Printer's Devil*, it can be approached through similar critical issues relating to the genre: pastiche, 'historical knowledge', metafiction, the question of historical 'authenticity', the extent to which historical fiction addresses the ideological concerns of the years in which it was written, and the question of how 'structures of feeling' can be conveyed in literature.

Coram Boy dramatises many elements of Hanoverian England and Georgian mercantile culture. Children's fiction is well placed to revive interest in the extraordinary story of the Coram Foundling Hospital opened in London in 1741, since the founding of that institution is in important respects a 'children's story'. Though *Coram Boy* does refer to the 'cruel lotteries' (Glickman, 2006: 314) that determined admission to the Hospital, and the internal scandals that beset it, it provides relatively little detail about the day-to-day living conditions and moral regime of that unique environment. Those interested in the extraordinary story of the Hospital's founder, Thomas Coram, and his practical, moral mission can find more detail in Gillian Wagner's biography (2004). Jamila Gavin's imaginative move is to make the musical dimension of the Foundling Hospital central to the plot and the novel's sense of human fulfillment, through Alexander and Aaron's talent for singing, and the way it reunites them. We know from historical records that the celebrated concert of Handel's music given in the Hospital Chapel on 25 May 1749 contained a performance of *The Peace Anthem* with a solo by someone designated in the records only as 'The Boy' (Burrows, 1977: 271). *Coram Boy* elaborates on that textual fragment and develops it into a historical romance, by using the familiar romance motif of lost children.

In its story of the lost illegitimate child, Aaron, given up for adoption or worse, his friendship with the African 'orphan' Toby, and his return to the country estate and his parents after dangerous adventures and series of unabashed coincidences, *Coram Boy* uses pastiche as much as Paul Bajoria's *The Printer's Devil* does. It was one of Hayden White's insights in his celebrated book *Metahistory* (1973) that historians structure their work through 'emplotments', that is, by using a literary form of plot structure based on genre. White analysed the work of nineteenth-century historians and found that they tended to opt for romance, tragedy, comedy or satire. It is easy to see why historical fiction written for children tends to base its 'emplotment' around the traditional genre of romance. Romance emphasises the way that catastrophe, disruption and loss (particularly parents' separation from children) can be redeemed through quest, coincidence and reconciliation, so that the narrative may end in harmony. (When such an ending is denied, as in Anne Fine's recent historical fiction *The Road of Bones*, about a child caught up in a world of totalitarianism and gulags, the result can be quite disturbing to readers and reviewers.) Henry Fielding's 1749 novel *Tom Jones*, in which Tom turns out after many adventures, coincidences and wanderings to have been an illegitimate scion of the Allworthy family, has a romance plot similar to that of *Coram Boy*.

Coram Boy raises many issues about historical fiction, however, over and beyond its links to literary history and history as pastiche. Like a number of other historical fictions for children (by Alan Garner and Anne Fine, for example) it is ideologically sophisticated in politicising childhood, showing how children were far from immune from systematic injustices of the past – and by implication, the present. Undeniably, too, *Coram Boy* does give us information about the past. A reader of the book would find out much about eighteenth-century England, including the fate of children taken on by the Parish and the workhouse, and the high mortality rates involved; the existence of abusive employers of children; the existence of the slave trade; Handel's patronage of the Coram Foundling Hospital; and the use of African children as servants and pages in fashionable London homes.

The way in which such information is conveyed in *Coram Boy* is characteristic of the approach of children's historical fiction. The opening pages use the point of view of Meshak, the simpleton son of Otis, the 'Coram man' who undertakes to convey illegitimate or burdensome children from the countryside to the newly founded, innovative London Foundling Hospital (founded in March 1741, shortly before the action begins). However, the narrative also has to provide circumstantial information about the West Country in 1741, to supply the reader with details unfamiliar to them but not to Meshak. For example, there is a catalogue of objects that figure daily in Meshak's world, but need to be enumerated for us:

> pots and pans, knife sharpeners, meat hooks, scissors, graters, mincers, goblets, griddles, knives and axes, as well as kick-knacks like combs and beads, bobbins and cottons, balls of string, trinkets and baubles. He spread out a large piece of sail cloth in a clearing by the side of the road and laid everything out . . .
>
> Gavin, 2000: 16

This is a kind of footnoting and scene-setting through which the narrator helps the young reader enter a past world. Jamila Gavin's presentation of information is discreet, at times signaled only by shifts in tone. At other times she will insert a scene such as that involving the committee meeting to discuss the parish orphanage at Ashbrook, which plausibly allows Lady Ashbrook to think through her preoccupations (which happen to be those of the book as a whole) and guide the reader at the same time:

> But it was the plight of little children which exercised her the most: children who had been abandoned, exploited, maimed, orphaned and abused. She knew the committee would argue all over again about making improvements at the orphanage.
>
> Gavin, 2000: 77

In comparison, Kevin Crossley-Holland does not feel bound by real or imagined period authenticity in writing his dialogue.

For the contemporary literary critic, such inconsistencies are part of the art of writing historical fiction. John Fowles remarks in 'Notes on an Unfinished Novel' that when he was writing dialogue for his 'Victorian' novel *The French Lieutenant's Woman*, he found that taking his models from the dialogue in Victorian fiction would not work; it just sounded too 'modern' to contemporary ears, and did not give the illusion of Victorian-ness required. He had to go back a further fifty years in English fiction to find phrases and modes of address that provided this effect (Fowles, [1969] 1977: 139). Finding a convincing but vigorous idiom can be difficult. 'You are a one, Gatty', says Snout in *Gatty's Tale* after he finds she has spent the night locked into the Church of the Holy Sepulchre at Jerusalem (Crossley-Holland, 2006: 316).

In *Coram Boy*, Isobel's dislike of Otis is initially expressed carefully in the idiom of the period, when she says that 'There was such a lack of respect in his bearing.' However, she follows this up by saying that Otis and Meshak – 'those awful fellows' – had been seen '*hanging around* the house on the day of the ball' (Gavin, 2000: 129).

Do inconsistencies and anachronisms matter, or is the pursuit of historical authenticity a chimera, when it is the access to the period's structure of feeling which is more important? Certainly no historical fiction will be successful unless it can link current concerns to historical scenarios, whilst maintaining that sense of 'strangeness' which is a valuable element of the genre. Jamila Gavin brings to *Coram Boy* a modern interest in difference, race and justice that characterizes much of her fiction. She approaches the Age of Reason through the 'pathetic squeals' of abandoned brats (Gavin, 2000: 12) in the sacks of the Coram Man, and through Otis's later graduation to white slavery, drawing upon her contemporary readers' fascination with and revulsion from the abuse of children. The introduction of the African child Toby, simultaneously separated from his mother and rescued from the slave trade, threads an awareness of the existence of the that trade on to the stories of cruel treatment of native-born children within an apparently prosperous mercantile nation, and poses questions about the nature of true civilisation and prosperity. In making Toby's friendship with Aaron significant to the plot, Jamila Gavin does in fictional terms what recent historical and literary studies of the eighteenth century, such as David Dabydeen's *The Black Presence in English Literature*, have done: she draws attention to the importance of race and cross-cultural contact for eighteenth-century culture.

The Stone Book and *The Printer's Devil* insist on awareness of family trees as a key element in children's historical awareness. In *Coram Boy*, family is as important as ethnicity; not only is Alexander self-exiled from Ashbrook because of his desire for agency and for a career of his own, but the third of the trio of abandoned children from Part Two, Meshak, extends the range of the family theme into the unglamorous and less sentimentalised aspects of childhood and parenthood. Notably, Meshak also finds a version of family in the Coram Hospital, where he comes as close as he can to fatherhood in caring for Aaron. It is Meshak, too, who pathetically appeals to his own 'bad father', Otis, in one of the book's climactic scenes, to take care of him and his surrogate child Aaron, whom he has abducted.

It is not a coincidence that all the novels discussed above deal with gender, class and race in ways that place their approach squarely in the period after second wave feminism, the Welfare State and post-war immigration into the UK. Each of them features spirited young people who make their own way in the world with fortitude and imagination: questing, journeying and playing a full role in the affairs of a world of adults illustrating how twentieth-century children's literature has gradually come to accommodate and represent marginalised and minority groups in a 'process of democratisation' (Collins and Graham 2001: 21). As a part of that process, Gavin's Aaron and Toby, Garner's Mary, Crossley-Holland's Gatty and Bajoria's Mog are designed to assume contemporary ideological responsibilities and, in that, they may seem to inscribe contemporary aspirations upon the past.

I would argue, however, that the foregrounding of modern ideological concerns is one of the ways in which these books convey the complexities which confront us all when we use our historical imagination. Since many young readers are astute about the conventions of media and textual representation, such modern concerns seem set to continue, as exemplified in the 2008 Carnegie Medal-winning book, Philip Reeve's *Here Lies Arthur*, with its iconoclastic and revisionist view of the 'great' king and his spin-doctor Merlin.

Not all historical fictions need to overtly advertise their status as 'historiographic metafiction', and those which use realism are not necessarily naïve. Often they draw upon modern historical research whilst assessing the nature of past 'structures of feeling' and dealing with questions of historical difference. It is their ideological dimension, their use of pastiche and their poetic and speculative recreation of the sameness-yet-strangeness of the past, that make their 'journey backwards' compelling.

References

Bajoria, P. 2004. *The Printer's Devil*. London, Simon & Schuster.

Boston, L.M. 1975. *The Children of Green Knowe*. London, Puffin.

Burrows, D. 1977. 'Handel and the Foundling Hospital', *Music and Letters*. 58 (3): 269–84.

Clarke, N. 1996. *The Doctor's Daughter*. London, A&C Black.

Collins, F.M. and Graham, J. 2001. 'The Twentieth Century – Giving Everybody a History', in F.M. Collins and J. Graham (eds) *Historical Fiction for Children: Capturing the Past*. London, David Fulton, pp. 10–22.

Crossley-Holland, K. 2006. *Gatty's Tale*. London, Orion Children's Books.

Dabydeen, D. 1985. *The Black Presence in English Literature*. Manchester, Manchester University Press.

Fielding, H. 2005. *The History of Tom Jones*. London, Penguin Classics.

Fine, A. 2006. *The Road of Bones*. London, Corgi.

Fowles, J. 1977. 'Notes on an Unfinished Novel', in M. Bradbury (ed.) *The Novel Today: Contemporary Writers on Modern Fiction*. London, Fontana, pp. 136–50.

Garner, A. 1976. *The Stone Book*. London, Collins.

Gavin, J. 2000. *Coram Boy*. London, Egmont.

Gavin, A. E. 2003. 'The Past Reimagined: History and Literary Recreation in British Children's Novels after World War Two', in A.L. Lucas (ed.) *The Presence of the Past in Children's Literature*. Westport, CT and London, Praeger, pp. 159–65.

Glickman, G. Review of Gillian Wagner, *Thomas Coram, Gent, 1668–1751*. *English Historical Review* 121 (February): 490–1.

Hutcheon, L. 1989. 'The Pastime of Past Time: Fiction, History, Historiographic Metafiction', in M. Perloff (ed.) *Postmodern Genres*. Norman and London, University of Oklahoma Press, pp. 54–74.

Jaffe, S.H. 1996. *Who Were the Founding Fathers? Two Hundred Years of Reinventing American History*. New York, Henry Holt.

Jameson, F. 1992. 'Postmodernism and Consumer Society', in P. Brooker (ed.) *Modernism/Postmodernism*. London, Longman, pp. 164–79.

Lawson Lucas, A. 2003. 'The Past in the Present of Children's Literature', in A.L. Lucas (ed.) *The Presence of the Past in Children's Literature*. Westport, CT and London, Praeger, pp. xiii–xxi.

Parker, C. and McColl, E. [1960] 2005. *Singing the Fishing*. Topic Records.

Pearce, P. 1998. *Tom's Midnight Garden*. Oxford, Oxford Children's Modern Classics.

Pennington, K. 2005. *Charley Feather*. London, Hodder.

Reeve, P. 2007. *Here Lies Arthur*. London, Scholastic.

Seabrook, J. 1974. *The Everlasting Feast*. London, Allen Lane.

Shklovsky, V. 1965. 'Art as Technique', in L.T. Lemon and M.J. Reis (trans. and intro.) *Russian Formalist Criticism: Four Essays*. Lincoln, University of Nebraska Press, pp. 3–24.

Stevenson, D. 2003. 'Historical Friction: Shifting Ideas of Objective Reality in History and Fiction', in A.L. Lucas (ed.) *The Presence of the Past in Children's Literature*. Westport, CT and London, Praeger, pp. 22–30.

Thompson, E.P. 1966. *The Making of the English Working Class*. New York, Vintage.

Wagner, G. 2004. *Thomas Coram, Gent., 1668–1750*. Woodbridge, Boydell Press.

White, H. 1973. *Metahistory: The Historical Imagination in Nineteenth-Century Europe*. Baltimore, MD and London, Johns Hopkins University Press.

Williams, R. 1961. *The Long Revolution*. London, Chatto & Windus.

Wilson, L.L. 1997. *The Salem Witch Trials*. New York, Lerner.

Coram Boy as History
Jamila Gavin

History is exciting and fun; full of extraordinary stories, and an astounding mixture of tragedy, comedy, aspiration and failure; stories about us; which is why writers, both for adults and children, will go back again and again into the past. There is always an appetite for history as entertainment, whether it's Terry Deary's *Horrid Histories* for children, or the historical novels of Philippa Gregory. Sixteen-year-old schoolgirl Marjorie Bowen's imagination was so fired by fourteenth-century Milan that she plunged into a novel about intrigue, politics, romance and death. *The Viper of Milan*, published in 1906, remains an icon of passionate and inspired storytelling which brings alive fourteenth-century Milan. You can hear her relishing the names and places, and identifying, as perhaps only a schoolgirl can, with the loves and losses of her characters.

Every now and then, there is an extra surge of interest in the historical novel – but that's how fashion goes with any genre – and it is usually
because a particularly well-written book has been such a success, that others
step in hoping the formula may work for them too. But fashion and for-
mulas aside, a well-researched, yet exciting historical novel can generate
an interest far beyond any straightforward historical account of particular
events, and can give a real flavour of a period, interesting a wider readership. *The Alexander Trilogy* of Mary Renault took me, as a teenager,
straight into the world of Alexander the Great and the Persian Empire,
and it was only later as an adult, rereading those books, having myself
researched the Persian Empires, did I realise how sound her history was.

These days, writers of history have been hugely influenced by the narrative of television – whether with Simon Schama or Dr Who – and have been
making history more appealing to a mass audience than ever before. Arguably, most children are made more aware of history because of fiction and
television than from the classroom. However, if the glamorisation of history
is not supported by a scholarly discipline, then what may be lacking is the
developing ability to challenge and analyse the version presented or even
understand that it *is* history, rather than fictional events which took place
in some random past. History is appearing in so many guises, being written not just as non-fiction, or the historical novel, but crossing borders into
travel books, biography and even cookery, often taking on the format of the
novel. But then, of all subjects, history is far more lateral than vertical, able
to creep into all sorts of areas and, when you think about it, is the very hard
core on which our storytelling stands.

But there is more than just the enticement and romance of another period.
Going back in time often enables a writer to explore events, issues, relationships or situations, which sometimes can be easier to deal with when
removed from a contemporary context. Fantasy and science fiction can
perform this role too. It can provide a larger stage on which to tell a story,
though the great contemporary novel is often already taking its place in an
historical context even before the ink is dry. Shakespeare is a good example
of someone who could be subversive and exploratory, and who could express
his ideas through a mixture of fantasy and history, by setting his plays in past
history, distant lands, foreign cities, magical woods, and islands. This freed
his poetic imagination, and enabled him to be explosive and controversial
without risking contemporary criticism or loss of patronage.

I suppose one needs also to define 'history'. History is an overview of
the past, usually, as has been pointed out, written by the winners, not the
losers. But in our world, which seems able to change in the blink of an eye,
the past and present overlap alarmingly and, with a powerful media, is no

longer just written for us from one or two powerful points of view – nor fed to us through books alone. We expect history now, not just to be dates and events which define a country's political public persona and status, but to include social history – histories which explain ethnicity, gender and identity; histories which can be brought to us from everywhere and by anyone; the underbelly of history. We have a greater realisation that everyone is history in the making.

My *Surya Trilogy* was partly material from my own life; things I knew from my childhood in India, and not just my place in history, but also my parents' history of a previous generation; remembering their stories, their take on events as they unfolded, dating back to two world wars, the colonial struggles for independence, and the gradual fragmenting of the British Empire. I quote my foreword to the books:

> When I am asked if the *Surya Trilogy* is autobiographical, the answer is yes and no: yes, in that I couldn't have written it had I not been born in India into the period leading up to the Second World War, Independence and Partition; yes, that as a child, I lived both in a palace in the Punjab, and a drab flat in a war-damaged London street; yes, that sea voyages, schools and friends were all part of my rich Anglo-Indian existence, but no, in any accurate sense to do with the plot or events as described in the books. Everything I experienced simply became material with which I could overlay a complete fantasy. As a child can turn a table into a house, or two chairs into a train, I turned my life into a fiction in which any resemblance to characters living or dead is purely coincidental – as they say in the movies.

However, for children reading those books today, my life is already history, as one child beautifully put it, 'born in the days of black and white' – based on the images she saw in old photographs. But books of the past which, when written, were contemporary, are historical for us – such as those by Tolstoy, Dickens, Jane Austen or Victor Hugo – and such novels can be such important evidence when read alongside present-day studies of their periods, and surely enhance the academic teaching of history, and vice versa.

First and foremost, a writer of fiction is telling a story, so sometimes, intentionally or unintentionally, accuracy may not be as thorough as it would be in non-fiction. Fiction is usually trying to explore different truths rather than merely facts and figures: emotional truths, social truths, the effects of power and domination, or sex and rivalry, families, friends and enemies, race and gender. Sometimes, one truth gives way to try and tell another truth. Fiction writers are often not historians or academics and I'm sure many, like me, write on a wing and a prayer, inspired by a story unfolding in their brains which happens to be set in the past. But occasionally, if facts interfere with the truth of the story, there is the kindly explanation called 'poetic licence'! I have never checked out Marjorie Bowen's facts, nor do I feel compelled to!

I have always hated the word 'lies'. I dislike writers of fiction saying they are telling lies. We are surely writing a truth, of our own, while acknowledging that there are many truths. I prefer to think we are trying to be truthful, but occasionally stretching a truth or distorting a fact which, in my view, may be less important than the truth which one is trying to get across. In *Coram Boy*, I stretch credibility when I have my young aristocratic eighteenth-century boy, Alexander, go to the cathedral school in Gloucester because he has a beautiful singing voice and loves music, but this would have been a virtual impossibility in his time – even up to the twentieth century. Musicians until the late nineteenth and twentieth century were 'trade', – even if highly regarded, if not revered. When Haydn lived on the Esterhazy estate in the Austrian Empire, he used the servants' entrances, and always went into the concert hall by the back stairs. Mozart famously quarrelled violently with the Archbishop of Salzburg, outraged by his treatment as one of the lower orders. So an aristocrat like Alexander would not have been allowed to go to school and mix with the lower orders, and make friends with Thomas, a carpenter's son. However, by creating this scenario in the cathedral for Alexander, and trying to justify it by him having an uncle who was a canon, meant that I could write about class and status; ponder over what 'freedom' really means, and question whether Alexander, the aristocrat, was freer than Thomas, the carpenter's son.

I got it wrong when I had the Coram Hospital give Aaron and Toby the tokens which came with them when they were brought to the Foundling Hospital. There is no such record that this happened, though there was the intention. But when I somewhat belatedly discovered this fact, I didn't want to change that scene in the book as it illustrated a far more important emotion; children longing to know their identity, and connect with their mothers. But one has to recognise when accuracy matters – especially if you insert real people within your fiction as I did with *Coram Boy*, where Handel, Charles Burney and Captain Coram make an appearance or are referred to. Even if one is compromising one truth for another, the most important thing is to be alert to inaccuracies which can damage the internal credibility of the story. This can so easily happen; the wrong name, or one wrong fact in the wrong place, can question the whole viability of a book. Even when you are writing fantasy – creating your own worlds and rules – you have also to create credibility, and having done so, stick to its inner logic.

Coram Boy started with a passing reference made in conversation about the use and abuse of children in contemporary Romania, and went on to a discussion about child labour in India or the Far East. It was as though such things always happened elsewhere. So when a friend remarked, 'but the highways and byways of England are littered with the bones of little children', I was shocked and asked what he meant. I was used to hearing – indeed seeing – child labour in India, and talk of female infanticide, and though I knew of the shocking treatment of British children through the novels of Dickens, or from Charles Kingsley's *The Water Babies*, I thought of children in this country suffering more from indifference and neglect, rather than deliberate, wide-scale murder. 'The Coram Man' was of the eighteenth century, my friend thought rather vaguely; men – tinkers and drovers – who roamed the towns and villages picking up unwanted and abandoned children and babies, either to sell off into the army or navy, or the newly burgeoning mills at the start of the Industrial Revolution, or to simply dispose of. But why was he called 'the Coram Man?' I asked, to which my friend had no answer.

I have never started a book just because I wanted to write about a particular period in history. A story always came first – or a trigger leading to a story. This extraordinarily brief but powerful nugget of information was a trigger. Almost immediately, a story began to grow in my mind. Kipling's six honest men came beating at my door: Who, When, Where, Why, What and How? Although I was working on other projects, I found myself reading up on the eighteenth century, looking at eighteenth-century pictures with more intensity – being drawn particularly to Hogarth. The more I thought about the times, the more I instinctively began to understand that such an activity could well have been going on. Until how recently could illegitimacy destroy the reputation of a young woman from the highest to the lowest in society, and was seen as a scourge on the family? And hadn't I personally witnessed, in India, the difficulty of poor families feeding numerous, unwanted children? Indeed, I soon realised that I could make comparisons between present-day India and eighteenth-century London, and this gave me a real sense of what it must have been like. It didn't take much thinking time to understand how such a trade could come about. However, the subject was dark and shocking. Could this be a children's book? I wasn't sure, and I didn't start work on it immediately, even though a story was growing and growing, and characters, almost fully formed, were leaping on to my imaginative stage. Every time I found myself walking through the leafy woods of Gloucestershire, where I live, stumbling across half-hidden and forgotten drover's roads, or walking parts of the great trading routes which criss-cross England: the Fosse Way, the Ridgeway, or the Cotswold Way, I felt the presence of the Coram Man.

My decision to start writing *Coram Boy* came one day while walking near Hebden Bridge. Here there are steep wooded valleys, and the remnants of ancient mills, whose chimneys reach above the tree canopy like periscopes. I had walked through the woods down to the stream and, one day, met a local also taking a walk. I commented on the abandoned mills, and he told me, with a sigh, how those mills had employed children, whose lives were impoverished, short and cheap. When they died, the cost of a funeral was far beyond the ability of families to pay, and so their bodies were often just roughly buried in the woods. Local people claimed to hear their ghostly cries, he told me, and they called those woods, 'the crying woods'. I was immediately inspired to write a few paragraphs, which later became the epilogue. I realised that I wanted to write this story, and that it would indeed be a children's book. After all, I had always argued, children should be able to read stories about any situations which affected children. It's what had made me want to find a way of writing about the horrors of Partition in India in *The Wheel of Surya*.

The first thing I did was track down the name 'Coram'. I had never heard it before. I needed to know why such a man, trading in children, would be called a 'Coram Man'. I went to the London telephone directory and found a number of Corams – not many – and began to telephone them. This brought me to the Coram Foundation in Brunswick Square, which had been founded in the eighteenth century by a Sir Thomas Coram for the maintenance and education of unwanted and foundling children. I felt an incredible excitement, which increased when I was put onto their archivist, Rhian Harris.

After hearing her account of the Coram Hospital, of how and why it was founded by Sir Thomas Coram (so it was a person's name after all!), I then asked the crucial question which, in a way, was going to determine whether the story growing in my head had any validity. 'Did the hospital employ men known as "Coram Men"?'

'No', was her direct answer, but before my heart had a chance to fall, she continued, 'not officially.' This was exactly what I wanted to hear. Not officially. It gave me the freedom to invent a Coram Man; a tinker, moving across England from town to town and village to village, trading in unwanted children, and being prepared to dispose of inconvenient babies, using the respectable name of the Coram Hospital to persuade young women to trust him. I say, 'invent' a Coram Man. I was certain such men existed, and that if I researched hard enough, I would find proof. But I trusted my hunch. I was terrified of too much research undermining my imagination. Research had to be there, but kept in check; earnest, but not used too earnestly! Better to feel sucked imaginatively into the period, as I'm sure Marjorie Bowen was.

I began to write my story. The embryos of the characters, already there from the very beginning, started to develop and grow and find their voices, but I was going to the history books regularly to check facts, and get the feel of the period. Now I was finding the name Coram everywhere: the Foundation's own book, *Coram's Children* by Ruth McClure, was invaluable, as was Jenny Uglow's biography of Hogarth, and Roy Porter's book on eighteenth-century England. But it was never a case of reading these books cover to cover. Suddenly, the wealth of eighteenth-century life and culture was overpowering; there was so much one could write about, so much one might be tempted to put in. I had to concentrate on my story, my characters, and see them through their journey to the end – writing by intuition and guesswork, and then following up by research to make sure I hadn't written anything too wrong.

But it was not just history books which reinforced my hunch about this particular dilemma to do with unwanted children. History is often hidden away, embedded in folk tales, fairy tales and nursery rhymes. As a child, I have skipped to traditional rhymes which may have contained truths and insights into the past – 'My mother said, I never should, play with the gypsies in the wood', or, 'Here comes an old lady from babyland, with three small children in her hand, one can cook, the other can bake, the other can make a pretty round cake. . . .' ending with the plea, 'Please, ma'am, will you take one in?' The Grimm brothers, whose stories I had devoured as a child, retold old folk stories and legends containing the most appalling horrors – not just for titillation – but because of ancient truths about the behaviour of families in a superstitious and hostile world, and, because, crucially, there were moral lessons to be drawn. One story which fascinated me greatly was that of Hansel and Gretel, especially because, in it, the parents themselves had abandoned their own children – to me, as a child, an utterly appalling thought; something which returned to my mind when writing *Coram Boy*.

Despite my having stretched credibility in allowing my young character, Alexander, to go to the cathedral school, nonetheless, I knew it was important to understand social class and status. It adds a vital tension between characters. Besides, it is something which has always interested me having grown up with the Hindu caste system. Otis Gardiner, the 'Coram Man' and his son, Meshak, are working-class, but Otis is ambitious; determined to achieve status and wealth, and reinvent himself as a 'gentleman' in looks if not deeds. I was also able to suggest the corruptibility that exists in any power structure, from small parish councils, to government departments, desperate hovels, to the aristocratic drawing rooms of England and, even within the Coram Hospital itself, where records show they were always battling with misdeeds and corruption.

Thomas was a working-class boy, who could only go up in the world because of his skills, and the education he acquired at the choir school. Mrs Lynch, the housekeeper, may have started life as a working-class parlour maid, but through her intelligence and capability, rose up to the position of housekeeper. Mrs Milcote and her daughter, Melissa, were high born, but poor relations, and dependent on the Ashbrooks. Mrs Milcote knew it was vital for her daughter to marry well, within her class and status, and encouraged her relationship with Alexander. So it is a poignant irony that, when Melissa gives birth illegitimately to Alexander's baby, her mother gives it to the Coram Man. I was conscious of how vulnerable all classes can be – but especially dependent women. The slightest shift of the building blocks can send an edifice tumbling. But one shouldn't confuse intimacy with familiarity. Tabitha, as Melissa's personal maid, is extremely intimate with her young mistress, but that is not the same as being familiar – and when Melissa feels Tabitha has overstepped the mark by suggesting she is pregnant, Melissa slaps her.

I was interested in the relationship between Mrs Lynch, a clever, scheming woman, and Mrs Milcote, so weak and vulnerable. Mrs Lynch despised Mrs Milcote, superior to her in class, but less powerful. She knew what her secret ambitions were for her daughter, and so gained power over her. In the stage version, Mrs Lynch makes a speech in which she accuses the Ashbrooks of hypocrisy when her role in disposing of Melissa's baby is revealed. This is another case of 'poetic licence', taken this time by the playwright Helen Edmundson. I can hardly think of any circumstances when such a speech could be made in that period, or that she could even conceive of what is more a twentieth- or twenty-first-century argument – when she sneeringly says that just the ring on Lady Ashbrook's finger could pay for a dozen orphanages. But how effective it was before a modern audience, familiar with the raging debates about how money is best spent in our own society – even echoing some people's opinions that to give too much welfare to single mothers only encourages immorality.

Although it was clear that *Coram Boy* would be for the older child, I had no particular readership in mind when I decided to write the book, just a burning desire to tell this story, and to write it in whatever way it needed to be written. I often find that I store a number of stories in my head which have a natural readership for a particular age, so that if I'm asked for, say, a story for 9–11-year-olds, I can usually select one. I was asked to write the history of the Taj Mahal as an historical backdrop to a piece of fiction for top juniors. The fiction was *Danger by Moonlight* which transmuted into the bigger book, *The Blood Stone*, for an older readership. Perhaps frustratingly, nowhere in the book is the period stated, although it is set in the mid-seventeenth century. For some reason, perhaps misguidedly, my editor and I agreed that the clue to the period lay with the fact that it ended with the building of the Taj Mahal. This might not have screamed 'seventeenth century' to the average reader, but defined it as a novel set in the past, as did my descriptions of life in Venice. But perhaps we were wrong.

At the very beginning of my career, with my early books for young children such as *The Magic Orange Tree*, there was a deliberate targeting of the younger readership. I was inspired to write because of the distress I felt about racism in Britain, and my feeling that there were not enough books which portrayed multicultural Britain. Whatever age I am writing for, I feel very strongly that the reader should be able to identify with characters; see their mirror image; be able to say 'that could be me'. I also realised that the more ethnic communities knew of their own histories and culture, the more they would understand why they were in Britain in particular, and the more confidence they would find in themselves, and not feel so dispossessed of their own heritage. I am very sad that the attempt to acknowledge people's culture, history and religion has brought the term 'multiculturalism' into disrepute. Certainly, my aim, as an avowed multiculturalist, was never to create divisions but, on the contrary, to heal and show a shared history, while celebrating difference.

I believe that the overriding power of Kipling's *Kim* is his love and sympathy for Indians, his hatred of hypocrisy and cruelty, and his understanding of India's multiculturalism. This, for me, far outweighs his politics, and his imperialist belief in British supremacy. Anyone wanting to understand the British Empire should read Kipling – especially his short stories. Fiction can help us so vividly to put history into perspective, and better evaluate consequences – and see that, in the end, it's all about being human – whatever the period. This is certainly what Kipling did. Salman Rushdie's *Midnight's Children* is another case in point.

History as a subject should never be overly categorised nor viewed vertically. It embraces almost everything we do and think and, in my view, should always have remained at the heart of the National Curriculum. Not only is it a discipline, teaching one to disseminate information, criticise, analyse and discuss, but it is a third and fourth eye of experience. It bids the imagination to understand. It is a natural handmaiden of literature, and a springboard in any direction, into almost every other subject. It is at the heart of the Humanities and our understanding of ourselves.

References

Bowen, M. 1906. *The Viper of Milan.* New York, McClure, Phillips & Co.

Deary, T. 1993. *Horrid Histories.* Southam, Warks, Scholastic Hippo.

Gavin, J. 2000. *The Magic Orange Tree.* London, Mammoth.

Gavin, J. 2001. *The Surya Trilogy.* London, Mammoth.

Gavin, J. 2002. *Danger by Moonlight.* London, Egmont Books.

Gavin, J. 2003. *The Blood Stone.* London, Egmont Books.

Kingsley, C. 1863. *The Water Babies.* London, Macmillan.

Kipling, R. 1901. *Kim.* London, Macmillan.

Kipling, R. 1902. *Just So Stories.* London, Macmillan.

McClure, R. 1981. *Coram's Children.* New Haven, CT, Yale University Press.

Porter, R. 1998. *A History of England: England in the Eighteenth Century.* London, Folio Society.

Renault, M. 1984. *The Alexander Trilogy.* Harmondsworth, Penguin.

Rushdie, S. 1981. *Midnight's Children.* London, Cape.

Uglow, J. 1997. *Hogarth: A Life and a World.* London, Faber & Faber.

14

Future Worlds: Philip Reeve, *Mortal Engines* (2001)

Introduction
Ann Hewings and Nicola J. Watson

Mortal Engines finds a place here as an example of modern science-fantasy fiction for children. Science-fantasy fiction for children is not new: boys' magazines from the 1890s onwards ran such material, inspired and inflected by the work of Jules Verne, author of *2000 Leagues under the Sea* and that of H.G. Wells, who published *The Time Machine* in 1895. These stories variably combined fantasy exploration, futuristic epic wars, and fantasised machines. By the second half of the twentieth century, a number of notable writers were experimenting with science fiction for children, including Robert Heinlein, John Christopher, Peter Dickinson, William Mayne and John Rowe Townsend. Perhaps John Christopher's *The Guardians* (1970) is the most obvious precursor to Philip Reeve's work as an exercise in invoking a dystopian Britain of the future, 'a country divided into two races, the proletarian Conurbs and the patrician County, all under the control of an oligarchy' (Carpenter and Prichard, 1984). But whereas dystopias of the 1970s tended to envisage a world reverting to primitivism, Reeve's exercise in dystopia imagines eco-catastrophe and resultant global warfare, a world destroyed by the greed of capitalism and blighted by the urban.

Reeve achieved his first substantial success as a children's writer with *Mortal Engines*, published in 2001, the first of a quartet of novels which concluded with the publication of *The Darkling Plain* in 2006. They feature twinned protagonists, Tom Natsworthy and Hester Shaw, who live in a lawless post-apocalyptic world inhabited by roving cities which predate upon each other in a blasted landscape. *Mortal Engines* is notable for its elegiac casting of historians as unlikely heroes against engineers and scientists who, as a body, represent the mistakes of both the past and the present; and it is also notable for its unusually dark sensibility, killing off a high percentage of those characters who would in children's fiction conventionally survive into a happy ending. Like both *The Other Side of Truth* and *Coram Boy*, *Mortal Engines* thus has a strongly foregrounded political agenda; and like them, too, it places faith in the resilience and uncorruptedness of children.

The essays

Both essays included here consider the difficulties of writing dystopian fiction for children. Kay Sambell considers the history of children's science fiction and dystopian fiction with special reference to *Mortal Engines*. She argues that Reeve establishes new possibilities for children's science fiction by endorsing a new form of comic child-heroism which at once critiques adult incompetence and allows for the hope of survival and regeneration. Janis Dawson also focuses on Reeve's presentation of political, moral, and ethical questions, evaluating the extent to which the novel's formal experimentation and postmodernist play with pastiche and parody are controlled by the older form of the *Bildungsroman* with its investment in maturation, which ultimately softens the bleakness of Reeve's critique.

References

Carpenter H. and Prichard, M. 1984. 'Science Fiction', in *The Oxford Companion to Children's Literature*. Oxford, Oxford University Press.

Carnivalizing the Future: *Mortal Engines*
Kay Sambell

Dominant trends in recent science fiction for the young

Since the 1960s futuristic science fiction for young readers has been dominated by authorial fears about the violent, inhumane social and political

Extracted from 'Carnivalizing the Future : A New Approach to Theorizing Childhood and Adulthood in Science Fiction for Young Readers', in *The Lion and the Unicorn* 28:3 (2004), pp. 247–67.

worlds young people seem likely to inherit. Postapocalyptic, admonitory scenarios are rife, depicting horrifying visions of hostile societies that are shockingly indifferent to injustice, oppression, persecution and the suffering of the masses. The future is typically represented as a terrifying nightmare that child readers must strive to avoid at all costs. Often these stories expose and critique totalitarianism. The authors pull no punches in depicting brutally enforced inequality, horrifying violence and the systematic dismantling of individual rights in their future worlds.

This substantial body of writing is based on the dominant genre model of the classic dystopias, *1984* and *Brave New World*. As in these didactic adult novels, the dystopian form for children is used to make serious and daunting comment on where we are really going as a society and, worse, what we will be like when we get there. Its primary purpose is to puncture old myths and dreams, by proving, in the form of a literary experiment, what human aspirations and ideals are *really* likely to mean for the future of mankind. Above all, children's dystopias seek to violently explode blind confidence in the myth that science and technology will bring about human 'progress'. They achieve this by working through the application of science in worst-case scenarios, demonstrating that it can be used to bring about oppressive, inhuman and intolerable regimes, rather than 'civilized' ones.

On the most obvious level, then, the dystopia didactically foregrounds social and political questions by depicting societies whose structures are horrifyingly plausible exaggerations of our own (Scholes 70). Dystopian authors predominantly teach by negative example, 'making the familiar strange' (Rose 8) in order to shock and frighten readers into recognition of the dire need to question official culture and to expose the corruption of the present adult world that could plausibly lead to such bleak and intolerable futures. The dystopia foregrounds future suffering, then, to force readers to think carefully about where supposed 'ideals' may really lead, underlining the point that these hugely undesirable societies can and will come about, unless we learn to question the authority of those in power, however benign they may appear to be. Grim irony is the main weapon in the dystopian author's armory and the future must be seen as incontrovertibly bleak for its admonitory function to be effective.

At deeper imaginative levels, though, children's dystopian texts 'issue a warning about destructive tendencies in human behaviour' (Stephens, 'Post Disaster' 126). They reveal a prevalent crisis in confidence in the human species itself, fuelled by the evidence of world events since 1945, which have led to a powerfully pessimistic conviction that hope is unreal and 'fundamentally irrational . . . in our fallen world' (Ketterer 99). This dark interpretation renders the concept of heroism, zeal and cultural confidence as dangerously problematic. As Dudley Jones and Tony Watkins state:

> We live, after all, in a post-heroic age: heroes are for debunking and deconstructing. The gendered associations of the terms 'hero' and 'heroism' – macho posturing, manliness, celebrations of physical bravery (often in a context of imperial conquest), and a consequent devaluing of what are often seen as feminine qualities – have been analysed and condemned. (1)

The dystopia; life represented as a tragic, bloody spectacle

The concept of heroism, fatally combined as it is with this dark reading of human nature as predatory and aggressive, is played out ironically and tragically in the dystopia in order to caution readers about its terrible consequences. *1984*, for instance, classically imagines a world which is horrifyingly seen to be dominated by the 'masculine' aggression of the tyrannical Party, whose heroic quest for power has allowed it to conquer, invade and use physical and mental might to dominate and rule by force. Orwell thus represents future life as a 'tragic, bloody spectacle' (Meeker 33), in which the would-be 'hero,' Winston Smith, the tragic inheritor of such a system, is inevitably bound to fail. The author unswervingly uses irony to show that this is not simply a case of the 'weak' Winston being unable to withstand the brute force of the powerful Party. Winston brings about his *own* tragic demise, because he is unable to see life in any other way than as a 'heroic' battle for power. He, like the reader, must learn that to view life in terms of heroic aspiration and 'higher' ideals is a false hope, and ultimately self-destructive.

In the dystopian future it is too late for hope, and Winston's abject defeat is used to underline how self-destructive and unsustainable the 'heroic' interpretation of Darwinism really is. Orwell warns that if the 'survival of the fittest' is taken to mean that the most aggressive, ruthless and powerful will 'win,' and society is structured according to this principle, the outcome will be inexorably undesirable.

Combining honesty with hope: the challenge of adapting the dystopian form for the young

In children's science fiction, the crisis accounts of human society and human nature that I have outlined are further compounded by a perceived crisis in the nature of childhood, or, more accurately, in the confidence that adults still know best how to ethically inform and guide children's future lives.

As Mary Galbraith highlights, 'the dominant schematic metaphor of much postmodern writing seems to be to puncture all balloons of transgenerational zeal and referential confidence, since such zeal and confidence led to or allowed the unspeakable' events of the Holocaust (Galbraith 190). The bulk of futuristic fiction produced for young readers has forcefully exploded the 'myth of the innocent, protected child' (Jenkins 2) by presenting dark future worlds that radically critique adult ethical legitimacy. These worlds spell the death of childhood as a secure, cherished state, deliberately calling constructions of 'childness' and 'adultness' into serious question. In most children's science fiction to date this sense of perceived crisis surrounding the adult world has been rendered in extraordinarily negative terms, often with child characters pitted against a powerful adult regime.

The metaphorical death of childhood is often depicted literally in the children's dystopia as child characters are often cast in the role of helpless victim. In many novels innocent child victims (although rarely the main child protagonist) actually die in order to highlight the negligence and corruption of the adult-created world they have inherited. In many children's dystopias we see the differences between the figure of the tyrant controller and the powerless main protagonist represented as a sharp distinction between corrupt adulthood and innocent childhood.

I have argued that most children's science fiction writers display a desire to 'tell it as it is' and use future fictional time to cast a heavily critical eye on the adult world. This tendency poses significant challenges for authors who wish to adapt the form to become suitable fare for young readers. Although most children's authors have, to date, based their futuristic alternative worlds upon Orwell's classic dystopian model, few have risked doing so without compromise. The educational and ethical responsibilities typically associated with the act of addressing a non-peer audience, based, paradoxically, upon the notion of the adult informing, guiding, and protecting the child, present significant authorial dilemmas. They often cause authors to heavily control their narratives in ways that fail to repose trust in implied young readers to think for themselves, based on authorial fears for child readers. What, for example, if children infer that such ruined worlds are hopelessly inevitable, rather than preventable? How can the imaginative world truthfully present the dark truth of the forces against which one cautions, while simultaneously guiding, the reader towards hope, often viewed as essential for young readers? In other words, how can authors 'find an honest hope to share with a reader' (Bond 41)? Furthermore, how can authors find ways of talking, supporting, and negotiating with children via an emancipatory narrative model, rather than instructing and molding them, in a socializing approach?

Futuristic fiction to date has presented varying contested images of the child protagonist as a result of these implicit authorial concerns. In short, most children's authors appear to feel the need to adapt the classic 'adult' dystopia, usually by compromising the dire warning and supplying hope within the text itself, rather than leaving it implicit or barring it completely. Furthermore, Romantic conceptions of childhood lead the children's author to represent childhood as an antidote to corrupt adulthood, as well as seeing childhood as being at the mercy of it. The child as an emblem of hope for the future, capable of transforming and transcending adult mores, and the image of the child as helpless victim are often held in acute tension in dystopian writing for young readers. Writers often seek to portray the 'child-as-utopian' within their novel, in an attempt to signal hope for a better world.

By pointedly dealing with the theme of future suffering, horror and despair, however, many of these didactic texts incline, at least at deeper imaginative levels, towards what Julia Kristeva has identified as 'abject' literature (cited in Stephens, *Language* 148). In the bleakly ironic landscape of the dystopian form, dominated as it is by fear, aggression and a 'heroic' view of life as a battle or contest, child-utopians are predominantly imaginatively cast as innocent and vulnerable victims. Like Winston, they are hopelessly at the mercy of those in power. Their innocence means they are likely to be viewed as easy prey, tragically illequipped to survive in the aggressively masculine world of the imagined future. Their survival thus risks seeming like an implausible escape: a jarring and clichéd device to present a hopeful alternative that undermines or counteracts the narrative logic of the preceding story. Some children's authors hold their nerve, however, and trace through the abject 'failure' of the main child protagonist. Sometimes, like Winston, their child characters come to represent a hopelessly debased or dangerously polluted form of humanity themselves.

In short, unprecedented levels of pessimism for a young readership typically characterize this significant body of children's literature. The overwhelming emphasis on tragedy and the abject to evoke shock, horror, pity, and terror, pose immense tactical dilemmas for children's writers. It is exciting, then, to find a recent novel by Philip Reeve that adopts an innovative and radical means of presenting these issues for a young audience.

Mortal Engines: carnivalizing the future

Mortal Engines is a postapocalyptic novel, set in the far future in the aftermath of a worldwide war. In order to survive, most of the decaying cities have literally torn themselves up by the roots to form itinerant Traction Cities that can roam around the wasteland preying upon each other. The story follows the fortunes of London, whose built environment has been remodeled in a series of layers that correspond with the rigid social hierarchy now in force. In common with most dystopias, London's social stratification is based upon exploitation, inequality and overprivilege.

Yet despite the stock motifs and themes it shares with other children's science fiction, *Mortal Engines* adopts an entirely different narrative approach to questioning the heroic myth, in a way that leaves hopeful possibility within the textual world intact. Reeve's futuristic novel importantly eschews the stark admonitory stance adopted by most writers. The story focuses upon three child protagonists, Tom, Katherine, and Hester, all of whom represent a different way of viewing and interacting with the future society they inhabit. Each assumes a different role as a result, and this allows Reeve to playfully trace through the consequences of each outlook. In so doing, he turns received ideas upon their head, achieving a playful form of humorous subversion by creating 'roles for child characters which interrogate the normal subject positions created for children within socially dominant ideological frames . . . by using the strategies of "carnivalesque" texts, which function to interrogate official culture in ways comparable to the traits of carnival identified in the work of Mikhail Bakhtin' (Stephens, *Language* 120, 121). *Mortal Engines* sets out to dismantle socially received ideas and replace them with their opposite, privileging childhood over adulthood, playfulness over sobriety, everyday life over grand aspirations, the here and now over the long-term future. It achieves this inversion mainly through humor and gentle mockery, rather than relying exclusively upon violence and horror to provoke and warn the readers.

Debunking adulthood: ideological precepts of municipal Darwinism

The first way that Reeve achieves playful debunking is through parody of adult authority and the intellectual ways in which the future world's power brokers conceptualize life by drawing upon supposedly scientific, rational arguments. Europe in the far-future, a thousand years after the 'Sixty-Minute War,' has developed its social and technical model based upon the idea that life is dominated by the hunter-predator, which, in order to survive, must win by becoming stronger and faster than its competitors. The concept of 'Municipal Darwinism' has led the adult engineering elite to develop the 'Traction Cities,' which are ridiculously ungainly and 'lumbering' mechanical parodies of the living predators they try to emulate. The novel opens by showing London in a childish game of hide-and-seek: 'skulking' in hiding from those bigger cities 'who had begun to look hungrily' at it or blundering 'in hot pursuit' of a mining town, which 'saw the danger and turned tail' (3). The playfulness of the language, which is deliberately hackneyed and theatrical, calls attention to the comic, juvenile absurdity of Municipal Darwinism. The novel thus displays the self-conscious textuality of the interrogative text from the outset, emphasizing the role-playing that is being performed by the Traction Cities, and calling the official culture into immediate question.

London's adult elite is immaturely self-deluded in its view of the city as a ruthless predator. The principle of scavenging and making do with others' detritus, not hunting and aggression, is really what keeps London 'alive.' 'The Gut,' the 'sprawl of factories and yards' in which workers scavenge what they can from whatever London finds or catches, is the real powerhouse of the City. The 'salvage gangs' working in the 'Digestion Yards' are the only people to produce anything of practical worth.

London's mayor, Magnus Crome, however, deludes himself into thinking he can bring about London's 'progress' by arming her in order to make her 'strong' and competitive. He plans to resurrect ancient technology that he can unleash upon the settlements that have chosen not to adopt the policy of Municipal Darwinism. Crome seeks to rebuild 'Medusa,' foolishly blind to the fact that the weapon of mass destruction will probably evaporate the settlements beyond the Shield-Wall that marks the edge of the 'Hunting Grounds,' rather than provide him with sitting ducks that London can consume.

Crome's 'elite' band of scientists and engineers are actually shown to be foolish, deluded, and childish. Again, this serves to debunk adult authority and interrogate the 'heroic' view of the world epitomized by their official culture. This is done by playfully inverting the socially accepted roles of adulthood and childhood. London's grotesque body is carnivalized yet further, revealing the 'reality' beneath the idealized veneer of Municipal Darwinism. Crome's Chief Engineer, Nimmo, takes the young protagonist, Katherine, on a tour of London's 'Turd Tanks,' where he tries to explain the concept of Municipal Darwinism, in doing so he demonstrates a scurrilous fascination with human excretory functions, in a manner that opposes normal expectations of adulthood. It is Katherine who primly appears more adult in her sensibilities, prudishly using euphemism: '"You mean . . . poo?"' (122). Here the self-censorship of Katherine's language is a means of measuring the child character's level of civilization and socialization – in a way that comically inverts adulthood and childhood as constructed within the novel. The adult Nimmo is allowed to be more indulgent, outrageous, and revolting than the younger Katherine, who is more respectful, not only in terms of her prudery and the self-control exercised over her language, but also her respect for the hapless individuals (petty criminals) who are made to wade in the Turd Tanks, salvaging material. In this episode adulthood is pointedly dismantled as a superior, knowing state. Adults in *Mortal Engines* do not become the source of moral maturity, self-regulation, wisdom, or knowledge. Far from it, the young play this 'adult' role, radically requalifying constructions of 'childness' and 'adultness' when measured against the concepts of restraint, ethics, and civilization, Reeve uses humor, then, to gently undermine and redefine commonly held theories about the essential differences between childhood and adulthood, which in turn pave the way for a radical reinvention of the potential roles that may be performed by his child.

Nimmo's childish fascination with excreta reveals that he lacks the capacity for discrimination. Furthermore, his scientific logic-chopping, which ideologically weds him to the myth of Progress and the masculine heroism of Municipal Darwinism, blinds him to the reality that life cannot be controlled and artificially created by science, regardless of discrimination and moral awareness. He continues, in what sounds like a parody of contemporary advertising, in his explanation of the Turd Tanks, comically assured that science and rationality can, with time, be developed to fulfill any human aspiration:

> ' "Waste not, want not," is the Engineer's motto, Miss. Properly processed human ordure makes very useful fuel for our city's engines. And we are experimenting with ways of turning it into a tasty and nutritious snack. We feed our prisoners on nothing else. Unfortunately they keep dying. But that is just a temporary setback, I'm sure.'
>
> 122

The reader, not Nimmo, registers the tasteless joke, situating the reader in opposition to adult society's official structures of authority as represented in the text. The engineer is not a cruel man, but simply one who plays a role that he perceives to be necessary, unthinkingly unaware of its moral dimensions. Nimmo is, quite simply, a fool and the deserving butt of Reeve's joke.

Reeve's tactic relies on constructing adulthood as a period of helplessness, ignorance, and incompetence. Adult childishness emanates from the fact that not one of them has understood the first principle of freedom: that the rights of others bound freedom of action. They, not the young, are stuck in the solipsism of early childhood. Viewed as a carnivalesque text, *Mortal Engines* thus breaches these boundaries, exploring where they, in a moral rather than purportedly amoral ('natural') system, should lie. In this way the text requires the reader to consider the ideological bases for determining where these boundaries should be drawn.

Roles and role-playing in *Mortal Engines:* parodying the adventure story

Adult status, political authority and ideological principles are all radically transgressed by Reeve parodying the traditional heroic adventure story. *Mortal Engines* self-consciously parodies the literary embodiments of misguided ways of thinking and seeing the world. Crome is a parody of the stock character of the adventure story – the evil, sinister villain – but the power-crazed tyrant is really a bungling, incompetent child, who is 'as mad as a spoon!' (271).

Reeve casts all his characters in exaggerated roles. His fictional world is peopled throughout with farfetched, pantomime characters that undermine the illusion of fictionality. In the way that London grotesquely apes a living creature, these human characters ape the laws of nature in Municipal Darwinism, showing their parody of the natural world for what it is: an absurd and incompetent farce. Reeve's dramatis personae include, for example: the pirate, Peavey, replete with monkey and complaining, murderous crew; the swashbuckling adventurous superhero, Valentine, adored and revered by the London mob; the hideously disfigured assassin, Hester, bent on avenging the murder of her parents: the mysterious Oriental aviatrix, Anna Fang, and the 'squat, white-coated barrel of a woman,' Evadne Twix, who 'may look like someone's dotty auntie' but is an 'utterly ruthless,' mad scientist, aligned with the sinister, rationalist priests of the engineering elite.

Reeve repeatedly draws attention to the ludicrous and theatrical nature of his text. In his description of the ultimate battle for London waged between the Engineers and Historians, for instance, he points out that the Historians 'looked like a chorus of brigands in an amateur pantomime.' The battle smacks of childish slapstick comedy and overexaggeration. This playfully undermines the literary form of the heroic adventure story, highlighting the ludicrous view of life as a quest for power and ambition.

At root, though, Reeve uses the stories of his three child protagonists to interrogate, parody and debunk a tragic, heroic view of life, by representing the literary embodiment of each individual character's idealized outlook. While the females, Katherine and Hester, single-mindedly pursue sublime ideals and play out tragic roles, Tom eventually finds the concepts of heroism and adventure that his society has equipped him with to be utterly redundant. In contrast to his female counterparts, Tom plays out an essentially comic role. The part of comic fool, via which Tom ultimately learns to consciously turn his back on high-minded heroism, actually equips him for survival in the world that Reeve has consummately created.

Debunking the heroic, tragic mode

Reeve comically inverts the male and female roles being played out, thus questioning the roles of 'masculine' and 'feminine' as social assumptions. Katherine and Hester each act out a heroic quest. Both single-mindedly pursue 'higher' principles and ideals. They, unlike Tom, deliberately choose a tragic, sublime journey throughout the novel. Hester knows that her parents were brutally killed by the apparently ideal swashbuckling adventurer-hero of London, Thaddeus Valentine, when he attempted to steal Medusa from them so that he could gain fame, wealth and glory (rather than acting upon the 'higher' idealized principle of helping Crome recreate London's heroic prowess). Hester dedicates her life to avenging the murder. Throughout the novel she aspires single-mindedly to kill Valentine, only hoping to stay alive long enough to achieve her ambition. As such, she redefines the role of the heroine in dangerously masculine, destructive, and tragically self-destructive ways. Her motive for revenge is further driven because Valentine maimed rather than killed her, as a toddler, which has, she thinks, denied her the possibility of playing a more feminine role.

Katherine, Valentine's daughter, by contrast, seems cast to act out the idealized role of a heroine in a traditional adventure story. When we first see her she is represented as the 'perfect' woman of Tom's dreams, witty, clever, rich, and one he can, as a Third Class Historian, never hope to win. Katherine gradually learns the truth about her father. On finding that his heroism, wealth, and social status mask his self-seeking, self-aggrandizing crime, she, like Hester, decides to strive to put things right. She casts herself in the role of the moral hero, who will fight, use violence, and stop at nothing to prevent Medusa being unleashed. In trying to bomb Medusa, Katherine accepts life as a battle, a tragic bloody spectacle. She works for an ideal 'higher' moral principle, for human futurity.

By contrast, Tom is cast in a completely different role. He takes 'time-out' from the carnivalized city, when he impulsively lunges forward to prevent Hester from theatrically assassinating his hero, Valentine. He has always dreamed of being a hero in an adventure: 'After all those dull years spent dreaming of adventures, suddenly he was having one! He had saved Mr. Valentine's life! He was a hero!' (24).

But the reality is far from what Tom had imagined, and his fanciful aspirations are comically deflated. Valentine repays Tom's heroic gesture by shoving him out of the city, down the waste chute! He is thus brought down to earth, literally and metaphorically.

As soon as Tom experiences the reality of adventure, he regrets it. Initially he imagined himself winning Katherine, an idealized perfect image of kindness and beauty. He soon transfers this romantic allegiance to Hester, casting himself in his mind as the heroic rescuer of a 'murderous beautiful assassin' as he pursues her through the Gut. But the woman he catches is far from ideal in a traditional sense: '. . . she was hideous. A terrible scar ran down her face . . . making it look like a portrait that had been furiously crossed out. Her mouth was wrenched sideways in a permanent sneer, her nose was a smashed stump and her single eye stared out of the wreckage . . .' (26).

Nor does Hester's female behavior live up to Tom's idealized view of womankind: far from swooning into his arms and seeing him as the new center of her universe, she merely exclaims: '"You're alive then . . . I thought you'd died." She sounded as if she didn't care either way' (29).

Tom's journey through the book takes him from social incompetence, when he blindly accepts his socialization and the childish stories he has inherited about heroism, adventure, and girls, to competence and an awareness of the reality beneath the veneer of the ideal, silly fictions he has been fed. He finds, for instance, that the role of male 'hero' is neither glamorous nor easy. He is neither brave, aggressive, nor heroic, and rather prone to panic, as when he faces a robotic Stalker:

> 'It's impossible!' Tom whimpered. 'They were all destroyed centuries ago!' But the Stalker stood there, horribly real. Tom tried to back away, but he couldn't move. Something was trickling down his legs, as hot as spilled tea, and he realized that he had wet himself.
>
> 89

Reeve uses Tom's comic disillusionment as a different means of interrogating the received wisdom of official culture. Whereas Katherine's demystification was hard won, intelligent, and noble, Tom's is utterly haphazard and coincidental. His journey takes him through the various scavenger communities that effectively populate the dump-culture outside London. Tom has no master plan, and blunders through life, simply trying to keep out of trouble. Gradually he learns to set aside his preconceived ideas of chivalry, honor, and higher ideals and learns to live for the here and now. Outside, it is every man for himself, and he must learn to make the accommodations that allow him to modify his behavior to agree with environmental conditions, rather than dreaming of changing it as the novel's adult politicians do.

Ultimately, however, it is Tom, the comic hero, rather than those adopting tragic roles, who helps bring about the end of Crome's plans, albeit by sheer mistake. Tom, having followed Hester throughout, in the hope that she will lead him back home, finally decides not to enter an increasingly violent London after all. He waits, hovering in the wings in an airship above London, while Hester descends, to bravely pursue the role of a male adventurer, intent on killing Valentine Meanwhile, Katherine simultaneously reaches the stage on which the future is being dramatically played out, armed with a bomb to destroy Medusa and thwart Crome's sinister plan. But as the two tragic heroines finally converge, both heroically facing their fears, Katherine's heroic certainty and zeal waver, because her father is standing right by Medusa. She is tragically unable to set aside her view of him as father, rather than murderer, which prevents her from throwing the bomb which will preserve the life of millions beyond the Shield-Wall. As a result, Valentine is there for Hester to attack, and he draws his sword to fight to the death. 'Suddenly she [Katherine] understood why the goddess had brought her here, and she knew she must make amends for Father's crime.' Bravely rushing forward to prevent him slaughtering Hester, 'suddenly it was she who was in his path, and his sword slid easily through her and she felt the hilt jar hard against her ribs' (283).

This high, overexaggerated melodrama has an air of pantomime, as meanwhile the engineers, 'clustering round their machine in a frantic scrum,' comically lose control of Medusa, while London burns around them. Katherine starts to 'hiccup' as her life slips away. At last she sees life as it really is in Reeve's future world. Looking down at the sword that has killed her, she 'watched it slither out of her. It looked ridiculous, like a practical joke' (283).

The 'higher' idealism has been inverted to the level of the 'practical joke.' Katherine's death parodies the tragic literary form, actively embodying what John Stephens claims to be one of the functions of carnival, which '. . . is, through the dialectic of high and low, to affirm the temporal and material against the higher claims of the eternal and transcendent' (*Language* 124).

Tom, the comic fool who lives the 'low' life of the here and now, not Katherine, who adopted the sublime and pursuit of lofty ideals, ultimately has survival power in Reeve's alternative world. Tom turns his back on London, his home, and heroism. Hester, released from vengeance by finally pitying Valentine's devastating loss of his child, suggests she and Tom strike out for the settlements. Trying to raise his spirits, she tells him,

'They'll probably think you're a hero.'
  But Tom shook his head . . . He didn't know what he was, but he knew he was no hero.
  'All right,' said Hester, understanding . . . 'You aren't a hero, and I'm not beautiful, and we probably won't live happily ever after.' . . . 'But we're alive, and together, and we're going to be all right.'

293

The role of the scavenger in locating a survival ethic

According to John Stephens, 'Carnivalesque children's literature . . . can well mask a didactic and educational purpose' (*Language* 125). He continues, 'By making the familiar strange and by overturning some conventional aspects of narrative . . . modes, these books are able to see the world differently, less seriously, and to question and sometimes subvert a variety of its ideologies and structures of authority' (*Language* 156).

Via Tom, Reeve has overturned the conventional hero myth, and enabled life to be seen from a different perspective. Tom's playing a comic role makes him capable of representing a form of 'literary ecology' that embodies a new type of scavenging hero who is humble, absurd, and importantly imperfect. The ecologist Joseph Meeker suggests that the science of ecology proves that evolution really favors such adaptive, accommodating behaviors. Tom discovers that life is not a battle, but a game that has no 'higher' goal or purpose. In fact, it's a terrible mess. The only important thing, however, is to keep the game going, to participate, because it is not a competitive game that one can win. When he learns this, Tom is freed from the bands of self-destruction that fetter the tragic actors.

In this way Reeve establishes a scavenger ethos that comically challenges the heroic hunter view of life. The child-as-scavenger can, like common 'pest' species such as rats, effectively populate the dump-cultures of far-future fantasies. In Reeve's carnivalized future Tom learns that '. . . the world is chaotic and meaningless, and perhaps it can't be saved, but it can be understood and endured by reaching out' (155). In this way Reeve skillfully and innovatively uses the comic rather than tragic mode to rewrite and assert a plausible, life-affirming view of human nature and human society.

Reeve's work thus establishes new possibilities for children's science fiction by finding ways of telling stories about the future that importantly transcend the artistic challenges that have bedeviled the literature produced to date. By carnivalizing the future, Reeve is able to present new angles of perception of the meanings of child-adult relationships, while still challenging young readers to critically consider the social foundations of our own world. Replacing the sense of vehement attack and denunciation that underpins much children's science fiction with an openly playful, subversive, and comic approach, *Mortal Engines* seems likely to encourage the reader to avoid responding with despair or distress, while simultaneously facing some hard truths. Given the strong desire to protect young readers, Reeve's strategies encourage readers to play with ideas in an imaginative environment that is affirming and supportive rather than hostile and threatening. If one seeks to empower young readers to become active agents of future change, as I believe most children's science fiction authors do, perhaps Reeve's narrative tactics have much to offer in forging a new style of didacticism within this important and growing body of children's literature. Experimental, genuinely mind-expanding, and liberating-books like *Mortal Engines* are rare and should be highly prized.

References

Bond, Gwenda. 'Honesty and Hope: Presenting Human Rights Issues to Teenagers through Fiction.' *Children's Literature in Education* 25:1 (1994): 41–52.

Galbraith, Mary. 'Hear My Cry: A Manifesto for an Emancipatory Childhood Studies Approach to Children's Literature.' *The Lion and the Unicorn* 25.2 (Apr. 2001): 187–205.

Jenkins, Henry, ed. *The Children's Culture Reader*, New York: New York UP, 1998.

Jones, Dudley, and Tony Watkins, eds. *A Necessary Fantasy? The Heroic Figure in Children's Popular Culture*. London: Garland, 2000.

Ketterer, David. *New Worlds for Old*. Bloomington: Indiana UP, 1974.

Meeker, Joseph. *The Comedy of Survival: Studies in Literary Ecology*. New York: Scribner, 1972.

Orwell, George [Eric Blair] *1984*. 1949. Harmondsworth, U.K.: Penguin, 1984.

Reeve, Philip. *Mortal Engines*. London: Scholastic, 2001.

Rose, Mark. *Science Fiction: A Collection of Critical Essays*. Englewood Cliffs, NJ: Prentice-Hall, 1975.

Scholes, Robert. *Structural Fabulation: An Essay on Fiction of the Future*. London and Notre Dame, IN: U of Notre Dame P, 1975.

Stephens, John. 'Post Disaster Fiction: The Problematics of a Genre.' *Papers* 3, No. 3 (1992): 126–30.

———. *Language and Ideology in Children's Fiction*. Essex: Longman, 1992.

Traction Cities, Postmodernisms, and Coming of Age: *Mortal Engines*
Janis Dawson

Introduction

Philip Reeve's *Mortal Engines* [ME], a fast-paced young adult novel of adventure, espionage, and futuristic mobile predator cities, was an immediate success when it appeared in 2001. In addition to enthusiastic reviews, *Mortal Engines* (2001/2004) garnered an impressive array of prestigious British and American awards.

Extracted from ' "Beneath their cheerful bunny faces, his slippers had steel toe caps": Traction Cities, Postmodernisms, and Coming of Age in Philip Reeve's *Mortal Engines* and *Predator's Gold*', in *Children's Literature in Education* 38 (2007), pp. 141–52.

Reeve's penchant for parody and pastiche, his fondness for wordplay and puns, and his obvious delight in absurd and grotesque characters and situations (for example, the 'charming' turd snacks served up at London's last gala [*ME* p. 261]; the 'soft farting noises' made by mud as it 'gulps down' Chrysler Peavey, a would-be posh pirate [*ME*, p. 164]) owe much to his background as a professional illustrator for Kjartan Poskitt's humorous puzzle books for children. Reviewer praise for Reeve's 'cinematic eye' (Burkam, 2004, p. 596), attributable to the author's experience as an amateur film maker, is a particularly apt description of Reeve's ability to vividly convey not only the Great Hunting Ground where the great traction cities trawl for prey, the sweeping vistas of the mountains of Shan Guo, but also the camera-like images of different sections of the tiered cities. But as Reeve himself describes his work, 'All sorts of things can spark off an idea. I read a lot of history and travel books, but often something I see by chance on the telly can set my brain working' ('Author Profile').

But turd snacks, absurd characters, and sweeping vistas are only part of Reeve's story. 'The ideas are big,' Mendlesohn writes, referring to the way in which Reeve's 'huge, travelling traction cities [. . .] prey on smaller towns, destroying and cannibalizing them for their parts' (p. 307). 'What are the rights and wrongs of Municipal Darwinism? Is this a way of discussing capitalism?' she wonders. Perhaps it is. Readers with an interest in history and current events will readily associate Reeve's sympathetic young protagonist, Tom Natsworthy, with politicians, economists, and well-intentioned individuals in the present era who shut their eyes to the dark side of a system that is driven by competition, consumption, and the savage exploitation of human beings and natural resources. Tom's insistence on the fairness of a system that is fundamentally unjust is a major theme in Reeve's novels. Significantly, the structure of the great tiered cities mirrors the hierarchical organization of their societies: the upper tiers are reserved for the wealthy and privileged, while the lower tiers house the working classes, prisoners, and slaves.

In addition to the big ideas associated with Municipal Darwinism, Reeve also raises moral and ethical questions about environmental issues and the responsible (or irresponsible) use of technology. The narrative is haunted by images of landscapes scarred by the wheels of mobile cities, and there are ominously few references to thriving plant and animal life. Reeve has confirmed that the idea of traction cities and Municipal Darwinism was inspired by 'urban sprawl and the way our own cities are eating up the surrounding towns and countryside' ('Author Interview'). Technological marvels and abominations abound in his novels – his recycled human and animal corpses (Stalkers) are among the latter – but he gives particular attention to the dangers of biological warfare (virus bombs and plagues) and weapons of mass destruction. In the latter part of *Mortal Engines*, London's Chief Engineer (described as 'mad as a spoon') predicts his city will develop the technology to expand into outer space: 'A million years from now our city will still be traveling, no longer hunting towns to eat, but whole new worlds!' (*ME*, p. 271). As events unfold, however, the Engineer's prediction is never fulfilled, for in the final pages of the novel, London is destroyed in a fiery holocaust that, in its vivid details, suggests contemporary accounts of the destruction of Hiroshima and Nagasaki at the end of World War II.

More often than not, however, the big ideas seem to compete with the form of the novels for the reader's attention. Reeve's novels are not unlike riddles that invite – even demand – unraveling or resolution. Why, for example, is the protagonists' airship, the *Jenny Haniver*, named after a general term for fake creatures or 'monsters' constructed from the carcasses and body parts of different animals? Reeve's novels are an eclectic, sometimes bizarre, blend of genres and forms punctuated with scores of parodic references to classic texts, histories, popular literature, film, and advertising blurbs. They are, in effect, literary Jenny Hanivers, and as such, they reflect many of the characteristics of the postmodern novel.

At the same time, however, the extent to which Reeve's novels follow the pattern of conventional YA *bildungsroman*/adventure narratives raises questions about their status as postmodern works. Despite their cleverness and originality, the novels are not really experimental, 'writerly' or metafictional texts which place considerable demands on young adult readers (see Moss, 1992). Like most YA SF, Reeve's novels 'tend towards the *bildungsroman.*' As YA novels, they draw extensively on many of the literary tropes of young adult literature. Foremost among these tropes is the search for identity and sense of self. Although Reeve gives his greatest attention to the growth and development of his female characters, all of the young protagonists in *Mortal Engines* are engaged in an identity quest. For some characters, that quest is particularly difficult and dangerous. For example, Katherine Valentine, the pampered daughter of London's most celebrated and respected archaeologist and historian, must forge a new sense of self after learning that her beloved father is a dangerous secret agent who has murdered a scientist in order to acquire long-lost information about MEDUSA, an Old-Tech weapon of mass destruction. For Hester Shaw, the daughter of the murdered scientist and a sister Katherine has never known, the search for identity involves not only coming to terms with her loss and all-consuming rage but also learning that despite her terrible disfigurement at the hands of her father, she is both likable and loveable. According to the conventions of young adult novels, Reeve's characters establish their sense of self through resisting authority and challenging the standards of their society: Katherine attempts to make amends for her father's crimes by forming an alliance with a working-class apprentice engineer who helps her devise a plan to sabotage the deployment of MEDUSA; Hester, a fierce outlaw, is determined to assassinate Valentine.

According to postmodernist theory, the search for identity and sense of self are Enlightenment constructions. Yet Reeve's novels depart from the conventional YA narrative in a number of significant ways. Although some of the author's characters are more central to the narrative than others, no protagonist's voice or perspective is privileged throughout the narrative, nor is any protagonist represented as simply heroic. Moreover, the reader is involved in the construction of the protagonists through the author's method of representing his characters through the shifting, often ironic or capricious perspective of the narrator. Particularly important is the fact that, unlike many traditional YA narratives which might be termed didactic, 'readerly,' or 'closed,' Reeve's novels invite plurality of meaning through the blending of genres and the emphasis on intertextuality. But does Reeve use postmodern techniques as window-dressing simply to give his novels a smart contemporary appearance?

Postmodernisms and bunny slippers with steel toe caps

Reeve's young adult science fiction novels are a compelling blend of genres: adventure, romance, mystery, the gothic, and the *bildungsroman.* They are not unique in this respect; the blending of genres, or the deconstruction of genres, also characterizes postmodernism. Reeve skillfully mixes generic metaphors in his novels: crossbows with gas pistols, grappling hooks and boarding ladders with atomic bombs, and swashbuckling sword play atop fortress walls with fierce battles in airships. He has created a rich gallery of colourful and fascinating, often absurd, heroes, villains, pirates, secret agents, warrior women, and cold-blooded murderers. Some of his particularly memorable characters include (in addition to the young protagonists themselves): the charming and romantic red-toothed Anna Fang, an accomplished aviatrix, swordswoman, secret agent, and architect of the *Jenny Haniver*; Chrysler Peavey, the would-be posh pirate who 'employs' Tom to teach him 'ettyket' (a literary echo of Barrie's 'good form' conscious Captain Hook, perhaps, or Stevenson's gentlemanly Long John Silver, 'no common man' who 'had good schooling in his young days' [Stevenson, 1883/1998, p. 54]); and Pennyroyal, the Alternative Historian. Nor is there any shortage of daring escapes, skirmishes, explosions, blood, gore, corpses, secret missions, cliff hanger endings, or technological marvels and gadgetry. The gothic is well represented in the labyrinth-like passageways of the gut and engine areas of the great cities.

Reeve's skillful blending of both literary and cinematic genres is the source of much of the tension, humour, and playfulness that characterize his novels. But Reeve does more than merely exploit generic forms; *Mortal Engines* is a clever pastiche of multiple works. Through direct reference and casual allusion, Reeve introduces a strikingly wide range of texts (including film adaptations and non print forms), each with its own multiple associations, creating, in Umberto Eco's words, '[a] dialogue between the text and all other previously written texts' (1983, p. 45). In addition to the more obvious examples, Reeve's novels also include allusions to Greek and Scandinavian mythology; *Beowulf*; narratives of navigation and exploration; and film production. Other texts include product names and advertisements: Chrysler, Cortina, Twix candy bars, and C[h]rome.

Pastiche, whether used for humorous, parodic, or serious purposes in a novel, is a way in which an author opens a text to multiple interpretations. Reeve expands his texts through allusion, layering, and juxtaposition, thereby setting up almost unlimited opportunities for alternative, sometimes conflicting or contradictory perspectives on characters and situations. Reeve's characters repeatedly challenge the notion that 'what you see is what you get.' Characters present interesting, often ironic contradictions: Bevis Pod, the gentle, tender-hearted apprentice engineer can coolly manufacture a satchel-sized bomb from cleaning supplies; Anna Fang, also known as Wind-Flower, has 'the gentle smile of an angel in an old picture' (193) and a ruthlessness that equals that of her chief enemy, Valentine; and Valentine himself, a man capable of cold blooded murder, is deeply devoted to his daughter Katherine.

Reeve's characters assume additional dimensions through their association with other literary models. Grike (Shrike in the UK edition) becomes more than a programmed killing machine through his literary kinship with Grendel and Frankenstein's monster. Despite their bloody deeds, Frankenstein's monster, Grendel, and Grike are pitiful creatures, condemned to roam through desolate spaces. They are sublime outcasts, cut off from the pleasures of companionship and love. The image of Grike stalking Hester through the Rustwater marshes recalls Grendel's lonely trek through the fens seeking the feasting warriors of Hrothgar's hall. Grike is driven by something other than the order to kill: '*His heart's desire! Soon he will find her again, and the loneliness of his everlasting life will be over*' (p. 117). Despite Hester's claim that Grike has no feelings or memories (she knows otherwise) – 'They cleaned all his feelings and memories away when they made a Stalker of him' (p. 97) – it is clear that Grike has the ability to feel love, loneliness, and loss. He is willing to sacrifice himself in order to possess her forever: 'When she is dead, he will carry her gently through the drowned sunlight and the forests of kelp [. . .].

He will take her into London in his arms like a father carrying his sleeping child' (p. 161). Disturbing and macabre though Grike's desire is, the scene is not without pathos.

The Grike–Hester relationship raises important questions about what it means to be human. This question has particular appeal for young adults because it is associated with personal development and the quest for identity (problematic for a postmodernist reading of the novels). If humanity is associated with the emotions – the ability to feel empathy, love, loneliness, loss – what distinguishes Grike from ruthless characters like Crome or Valentine – cold-blooded men who kill to advance their own interests with no regard for the lives of countless others? Who is the monster (or the machine) – Grike, who roams the marshes as a bounty hunter and saves the life of an orphaned child, or Crome, who plans to destroy entire civilizations with MEDUSA? Or Hester, who has suffered such crippling emotional damage? Even though Grike's death is extravagantly melodramatic, it is strangely moving and not easily dismissed because of the important questions his character raises.

> Grike carefully sheathed his claws so that she could take his hand. Unexpected memories fluttered through his disintegrating mind, and he suddenly knew who he had been before they dragged him onto the Resurrection Slab to make a Stalker of him. He wanted to tell Hester, and he lifted his great iron head toward her, but before he could force the words out, his death was upon him, and it was no easier this time than the last.
>
> 179

For Tom, Grike's killer, there is no question about Grike's humanity: '*All right, so he was dead already, technically, but he was still a person. He had hopes and plans and dreams, and I put a stop to them all*' (p. 195). Sensitive Tom feels the 'guilt and shame' of a murderer.

The case of Grike also raises moral and ethical issues about certain forms of scientific experimentation. Grike was resurrected by Dr. Twix who 'look[s] like someone's dotty auntie and decorate[s] her laboratory with pictures of flowers and puppies' (pp. 53–4). She may be 'utterly ruthless' when it comes to her work, but she bows, twitters, and dances after Crome when he visits the laboratory where she dismantles, dissects, and studies Stalkers. 'Have you come to visit my babies?' she simpers when the Mayor asks to see Grike (p. 54). Dr. Twix is one of Reeve's absurdities, and as such, contributes to the humour. Even so, the fact that Grike's latest resurrector is an absurd character with a candy bar name poses an interesting question. How does she (or does she) affect the seriousness of the issues or 'the big ideas' associated with Grike? Is she simply an absurd character or does she herself represent something more serious and unsettling? Under the circumstances, her fondness for puppies is hardly reassuring; it is well known that Hitler was particularly fond of dogs. She is, of course, another manifestation of Reeve's recurring theme that 'things are not what they seem,' but she also draws attention to the postmodernist emphasis on listening to the voices of the gaps, the margins, and the contradictory or the absurd. As Len Hatfield [personal communication] observes, 'It's our assumption about the dominance of logic, together with our reliance on convention and tradition that incline us to expect evil not to be, as well, silly. That the sociopathic monster is cuddly might just be the big idea.' Twix is dangerous indeed, and her involvement with Stalker technology is an expression of Reeve's concern with the irresponsible use of technology.

Historians fare better than scientists or engineers in Reeve's novels. Tom is a decent, kind-hearted character, and fusty, musty, dusty, and eccentric though his colleagues at the London Museum may be, they are respectable, well-meaning men and women who take a brave stand against the engineers for the preservation of culture, learning, and humanity. By contrast, Reeve's scientists and engineers are characteristically cold-blooded, ruthless, not quite sane, and deficient in social conscience. Katherine observes that even 'gentle Bevis' is 'someone who can kill quite coldly, as if the Engineer in him really does have no regard for human life' (p. 256). It is significant that Grike, resurrected through technology, is killed by an historian. Reeve's method is characteristic of the postmodernist approach, which combines opposites, embraces the paradoxa, and retains the contradictions.

Fundamental to postmodernist discussions has been the discrediting of metanarratives, or 'great narratives' that underpin Western civilization such as Christianity, Marxism, capitalism, democracy, national destiny, and the myth of human progress and human perfectibility. In Reeve's futuristic world of traction cities, the metanarratives that are questioned include the belief in scientific and technological progress and Municipal Darwinism. Reeve's novels also challenge the illusion that fairness, justice, honour, and truth itself are real, fixed entities that can be known and described. While it is evident that some of Reeve's characters know otherwise or are too cynical and hardened to care much about such things (Hester, for example), many, acting out of a desperate need for security, no matter how illusory, retain some form of idealism.

Although Reeve actively challenges metanarratives and other illusions through characters and situations, his narratives also support the idea that ideals are worth fighting for, and that to do otherwise is to live without direction, purpose, or dignity. For example, the romantic Anna Fang battles to break the tyranny of Municipal Darwinism and to preserve the green spaces of the earth. Viewed from this perspective, it may be that Tom represents not naiveté but rather a kind of essential human goodness. This would explain Hester's attraction to Tom as well as her desire to protect him not only from villains but also her own darker self.

Conclusion

Mortal Engines is a literary collage underpinned by familiar narrative forms. Although the novel itself is not postmodern – this is precluded by Reeve's focus on the protagonists' personal development – the author has used post-modernisms to construct an entertaining and compelling young adult series that not only introduces 'big ideas,' but also combines fast-paced adventure with the *bildungsroman* in a wonderfully imagined futuristic world.

References

Author Interview: Philip Reeve. (7 August 2005). <http://www.scholastic.co.uk/zone/authors_reeve_interview.htm>.

Author Profile: Philip Reeve. (29 December 2004). <http://www.education.powys.gov.uk/english/literacy_special/reeve.php>.

Burkam, A.L. (2004). Rev. of *Predator's Gold. Horn Book Magazine, 80(5)* (September–October 2004), 596. 21 December 2004, <http://www.web3.opnet.com/citation.asp?tb-1&_ug-sid+F7AC6DF7%2...>.

Eco, U. (1983). *Postscript to The Name of the Rose.* New York: Harcourt Brace Jovanovich.

Moss, G. (1992). Metafiction, illustration, and the poetics of children's literature. In P. Hunt (Ed.), *Literature for Children: Contemporary Criticism.* London: Routledge, pp. 44–66.

Mendlesohn, E. (2004). Is there any such thing as children's science fiction?: A position piece. *The Lion and the Unicorn 28,* 284–313.

Reeve, P. (2001). *Mortal Engines.* London: Scholastic.

Stevenson, R.L. (1883). *Treasure Island.* Oxford: Oxford University Press, 1998.

Further reading for Part 2

Reynolds, K. 2007. *Radical Children's Literature: Future Visions and Aesthetic Transformations in Juvenile Fiction*. Basingstoke, Palgrave Macmillan.

Stephens, J. 2005. 'Analysing Texts: Linguistics and Stylistics', in P. Hunt (ed.) *Understanding Children's Literature*, 2nd edn. London, Routledge.

Trites, R.S. 2000. *Disturbing the Universe: Power and Repression in Adolescent Literature*. Iowa City, University of Iowa Press.

Watkins, T. 2005. 'Space, History and Culture: The Setting of Children's Literature', in P. Hunt (ed.) *Understanding Children's Literature*, 2nd edn. London, Routledge.

Index

Note: Definite and indefinite articles are ignored in the alphabetical sequence, but are not inverted. For example, *The Bad Boys' Paper* is filed under 'B'. Page numbers in italic refer to illustrations.